Lang/Schuch/Staringer

●

ECJ – Recent Developments in Direct Taxation

Schriftenreihe zum Internationalen Steuerrecht
Herausgegeben von Univ.-Prof. Dr. Michael Lang

Band 41

ECJ
Recent Developments in Direct Taxation

herausgegeben von

Michael Lang
Josef Schuch
Claus Staringer

IFA Austrian Branch
WIEN KULTUR
Linde

Gedruckt mit Unterstützung des Bundesministeriums für Bildung, Wissenschaft und Kultur in Wien.

This book is a coproduction of Linde Verlag Wien and Kluwer Law International.

Supported by the Wolfgang Gassner Research Fund for International Tax Law, the Austrian Branch of the International Fiscal Association (IFA), and die City of Vienna.

ISBN 3-7073-0878-2 (Linde)
ISBN 90-411-25094 (KLI)

1210 Wien, Scheydgasse 24, Tel.: +43/1/24 630
www.lindeverlag.at

Druck: Hans Jentzsch & Co. GmbH., 1210 Wien, Scheydgasse 31

Preface

The European Court of Justice is a driving force in the field of direct tax harmonisation. Therefore, cases pending at the ECJ are very carefully analysed both by academics and practitioners.

On 13-15 October 2005, we organised a conference to discuss the cases pending in connection with the fundamental freedoms with respect to direct taxation and the possible consequences of future ECJ decisions. About 160 leading experts on European tax law accepted our invitation. The results of this conference are published in this book.

Without the support of the Wolfgang Gassner Research Fund for International Tax Law, the Austrian Branch of the International Fiscal Association (IFA), and the City of Vienna, neither the conference nor the entire project itself would have been feasible.

We are very grateful to the authors who not only gave us impressive presentations of the pending cases but who also committed themselves to an extremely ambitious schedule. This allowed us to complete the book within days and to present the outcome to the scientific community shortly after the conference.

The publisher Linde agreed to include the following publication in his catalogue. We would like to express our sincere thanks for the co-operation and swift realisation of this publication project.

Above all, we would like to thank Mrs Brigitte Dudli for the smooth organisation of the conference and Ms Daniela Hohenwarter who supported us in deciding on the structure of the conference. During the process of publishing, we were greatly supported by Ms Sabine Heidenbauer to whom we would like to say thank you, as well.

Michael Lang   Josef Schuch   Claus Staringer

Contents

Preface 5

Contents 7

Claus Staringer
Pending Cases Filed by Austrian Courts: The Holböck Case 9

Jacques Malherbe/Melchior Wathelet
Pending Cases Filed by Belgian Courts: The Kerckhaert-Morres Case
Pending Cases involving Belgium: The Belgian Coordination Centres Cases, Commission v Belgium, Commission v Belgium
Pending Cases Filed by French Courts: The Denkavit Case 29

Niels Winther-Sørensen
Pending Cases involving Denmark: Commission v Denmark 73

Marjaana Helminen
Pending Cases Filed by Finnish Courts: The Turpeinen Case and the Esab Case 87

Jürgen Lüdicke
Pending Cases Filed by German Courts I: The Meilicke, CLT-UFA, Keller Holding, Lasertec, Rewe Zentralfinanz, Ritter-Coulais, Kolumbus Container Services, and Stauffer Cases 113

Alexander Rust
Pending Cases Filed by German Courts II: The Scorpio, Centro Equestre, Conijn, Schwarz, and Meindl Cases
Pending Cases involving Germany: Commission v Germany 175

Pasquale Pistone
Pending Cases Filed by Italian Courts: The Banca Popolare di Cremona Case 203

Eric Kemmeren
Pending Cases Filed by Dutch Courts I: The Van Dijk and Bujura Cases 219

Dennis Weber

Pending Cases Filed by Dutch Courts II: The Van Hilten-van der Heijden Case
Pending Cases before Dutch Courts: "Bosal Holding" with third countries 261

Francisco Alfredo García Prats
Pending Cases involving Spain: Commission v Spain 277

Bertil Wiman
Pending Cases Filed by Swedish Courts: The Skatteverket v A, Skatteverket v A and B, and Bouanich Cases 297

Philip Baker
Pending Cases Filed by UK Courts I: The Cadbury Schweppes Case, the CFC and Dividend GLO, and the Vodafone 2 Case 311

Malcolm Gammie
Pending Cases Filed by UK Courts II: The ACT, FII, and Thin Cap Group Litigations, and the Marks & Spencer Case 323

Annex: List of Authors 349

Pending Cases Filed by Austrian Courts: The Holböck Case

*Claus Staringer**

1 The Facts

2 The Question

2.1 Request for preliminary ruling

2.2 Explanations to the request Given by the Austrian Supreme Tax Court

3 Austrian Tax Law

3.1 Austrian Income Tax Act 1988

3.2 Austrian Income Tax Act 1988 (as Applicable for the years at issue)

3.3 The „final taxation“ regime

4 The Free Movement of Capital and Payments

4.1 The rules of the Treaty

4.2 Does the free movement of capital and payments apply to third-country dividends?

4.2.1 Is a dividend protected?

4.2.2 Timing issues for dividends

4.2.3 Free movement of capital and payments vs. right of establishment

4.3 Is the free movement of capital and payments violated in the Holböck Case?

4.3.1 The Lenz case

4.3.2 Are third-country dividends comparable with intra-Community dividends?

4.4 Is the discrimination justified?

4.4.1 No justification in the Lenz case

4.4.2 Loss of Member States' tax revenues?

---

* The author would like to thank Ms Sabine Heidenbauer for her assistance in completing the footnotes to this article and Ms Daniela Hohenwarter for the discussion on numerous issues of the article.

4.4.3 Member State's lack of information?
4.4.4 The cohesion argument
4.4.5 The proportionality test
4.5 The stand-still clause
4.5.1 Article 57 para 1 of the Treaty
4.5.2 The grandfathering date
4.5.3 Grandfathering for „direkt investments"
5 Conclusions

The Holböck Case (C-157/05)

1 The Facts

Mr Holböck is an Austrian resident individual. He holds two thirds (i.e. 66.67 %) of the shares in a Swiss resident corporation. Austrian tax authorities have claimed that Mr Holböck has received dividends from this Swiss corporation in the years from 1992 through 1996.

Under Austrian tax law, such Swiss sourced dividends are subject to Austrian Income Tax at the full Austrian tax rate (marginal tax rate up to 50 %). In the case at hand, for the years 1995 and 1996, which were at issue in the proceedings, Mr Holböck was charged with an income tax for such dividends in the overall amount of approximately € 5.5 million. In the light of the rather substantial tax amount, Austrian tax authorities expected the collection of Mr Holböck's income tax to be endangered and ordered a pledge over Mr Holböck's assets to secure the tax claim.

In the proceedings, Mr Holböck challenged the tax authorities' order for pledge on grounds of the freedom of capital and payments in Article 56 of the Treaty. He argued that the levying of income tax at full rates (or the order for pledge to secure the tax claim) has violated the freed movement of capital and payments. This was based on the argument that Austrian law taxes dividends received by domestic individual shareholders at only half the average income tax rate if distributed by an Austrian resident company, while such dividend is taxed at full marginal income tax rates if distributed by a company that is resident in a foreign country (EU Member State or third country).

The case was heard by the Austrian Supreme Tax Court (Verwaltungsgerichtshof) who referred the case to the European Court of Justice.[1]

2 The Question

2.1 Request for preliminary ruling

The Austrian Supreme Tax Court referred the following question to the ECJ for preliminary ruling:

> Does it infringe the rules on the freedom of capital and payments (Arts 56 ff of the Treaty), if Austrian tax law foresees a rule on

[1] VwGH 28 January 2005, 2004/15/0105.

December 31, 1993 (such rule being also in existence after Austria's accession to the EU as of January 1, 1995), which taxes dividends from domestic shareholdings at half the average income tax rate of the shareholder, while dividends distributed by a corporation resident in a third country (in the case: Switzerland), in which the taxpayer holds an interest of two thirds, are taxed at ordinary (full) income tax rates?

2.2 Explanations to the request Given by the Austrian Supreme Tax Court

In explaining its request for preliminary ruling, the Court stated that it had doubts as to the effects of applying Articles 56 and 57 of the Treaty in the Holböck case. The Court held that it may constitute a restriction of the freedom to invest capital in third countries, if the dividends of companies resident in third countries remitted to Austria are taxed higher as dividends distributed by Austrian resident companies. For example, Austrian residents could be prevented by such a rule from investing their capital in third countries through the establishment or the acquisition of companies in such third countries.

In this context, the Court explicitly referred to the Lenz case, which was decided by the ECJ in 2004, where the ECJ already had dealt with the Austrian tax system for treatment of domestic and foreign dividends in the hands of Austrian resident individual shareholders.[2] In the Lenz case, the ECJ ruled that it violates the freedom of capital and payments if a foreign dividend is not eligible for being taxed at half the average income tax rate of the shareholder provided for by Austrian law (while a domestic dividend is).[3]

In its request for preliminary ruling in the Holböck case, the Austrian Supreme Tax Court, however, pointed out that the ECJ, in the Lenz case, only dealt with dividends distributed by companies resident in another

[2] ECJ 15 July 2004, C-315/02 *Lenz* [2004] ECR I-7063.

[3] See, for example, Kofler, Lenz: Österreich darf ausländische Kapitalerträge nicht diskriminieren, *ÖStZ* 2004, p 343; Polivanova-Rosenauer, ECJ Rules on Austrian Discrimination of Foreign-Source Investment Income, *ET* 2004, p 416; Toifl, Besteuerung ausländischer Dividendeneinkünfte und Kapitalverkehrsfreiheit, *SWI* 2002, pp 458 et seq; Tumpel, Zweifel des Verwaltungsgerichtshofes an der Vereinbarkeit der Dividendenbesteuerung in Österreich mit der Kapitalverkehrsfreiheit, *SWI* 2002, pp 454 et seq; and also Aigner/Kofler, Austria Clarifies Third-Country Impact of ECJ's Lenz Decision, *Tax Notes Int'l* 2004, p 477.

Member State. Therefore, the similar issue of the taxation of dividends coming from third-country companies is (at least for the Court) still open. In the view of the Austrian Supreme Tax Court, it is not sufficiently clear that the principles developed by the ECJ in the Lenz case could be equally applied to a third-country dividend case like the Holböck case.

Therefore, the Court referred the case to the ECJ, specifically pointing out the following potential issues:

- In the Manninen case, the ECJ indicated that there might be a cohesion between the taxation of companies, on the one hand, and the taxation of dividends in the hands of the shareholders, on the other hand. Within this background, it is not clear for the Court whether it is of relevance for the cohesion principle if the distributing third-country company is taxed significantly lower than it would be taxed if being resident in a Member State.
- The Court mentioned the „stand-still clause“ in Article 57 of the Treaty. According to this clause, Member States may stick to their restrictions of the freedom of capital and payments that have already been in existence as of 31 December 1993.
- Article 57 para 1 of the Treaty allows for restriction of the transfer of capital „in relation to direct investments“. So far, the content of the term „direct investment“ appears not to be sufficiently clear. For instance, it may be assumed that there is a „direct investment“ if the shareholder achieves, through the size of the interest, a controlling position in the foreign company. In the given case, Mr Holböck's shareholding was clearly more than 50 %.

3 Austrian Tax Law

The Austrian legal background relevant for the Holböck case can be summarised as follows:

3.1 Austrian Income Tax Act 1988

According to the Austrian Income Tax Act 1988 (effective from 1989), dividends in the hands of Austrian resident individual investors are taxed at half the average income tax rate of the shareholder, provided the dividends are „Income from dividends“ (offene Ausschüttungen) in the meaning of Sec 37 para 4 of the Income Tax Act (see Sec 37 para 1 of the Income Tax Act).

Further, under the definition in Sec 37 para 4 of the Income Tax Act, income from shareholdings is defined, inter alia, as dividends (offene Ausschüttungen) from domestic companies.

As a result, domestic dividends are taxed at a lower rate (half the average rate) than foreign dividends are (which are taxed at full rates).

3.2 Austrian Income Tax Act 1988 (as applicable for the years at issue)

For the years 1995 and 1996, the above-mentioned provisions of the Austrian Income Tax Act were not identical to the initial version of the Austrian Income Tax 1988, but slightly different:

According to Sec 37 para 1, the reduced income tax rate (half the average tax rate of the tax payer) was available for income from "shareholdings" (Beteiligungen) (para 4). Sec 37 para 4 defines income from shareholdings, inter alia, as "revenues from shareholdings" (Beteiligungserträge), which are further defined as profit shares of any kind resulting from a shareholding in a domestic company.

Although the wording of the relevant rules has slightly changed, it appears that they are nevertheless in substance the same as in the initial Austrian Income Tax Act 1988. Specifically, the different treatment for domestic and foreign dividends is still in place for the years 1995 and 1996.

3.3 The "final taxation" regime

In addition, from 1993 on, Austrian tax law has provided for „final taxation" (Endbesteuerung) of dividends received by domestic individual shareholders. Under this „final taxation" regime, a withholding tax imposed on the dividend by the distributing company (in the amount of 25 %) is considered to be final for the receiving taxpayer, who is therefore not obliged to report the received dividend as income in his annual tax return. Only in case the taxpayer's half average income tax rate is lower than 25 % (the withholding tax rate for dividends in Austria), he may opt to include the dividend in his annual tax return, thereby subjecting the dividend to regular dividend taxation (at half the average income tax rate) and crediting the withholding tax against his income tax.

This „final taxation" regime is only available for domestic dividends (and not for foreign dividends) as the „final taxation" effect is only triggered by the deduction of an Austrian dividend withholding tax.

However, when requesting for preliminary ruling in the Holböck case the Austrian Supreme Tax Court did not refer to this „final taxation“ regime's exclusivity to Austrian sourced dividends.

4 The Free Movement of Capital and Payments

4.1 The rules of the Treaty

Article 56 of the Treaty reads as follows:

1. Within the framework of the provisions set out in this chapter, all restrictions on the movement of capital between Member States and between Member States and third countries shall be prohibited.
2. Within the framework of the provisions set out in this chapter, all restrictions on payments between Member States and between Member States and third countries shall be prohibited.

Article 57 of Treaty reads as follows:

1. The provisions of Article 56 shall be without prejudice to the application to third countries of any restrictions which exist on 31 December 1993 under national or Community law adopted in respect of the movement of capital to or from third countries involving direct investment – including in real estate – establishment, the provision of financial services or the admission of securities to capital markets.
2. Whilst endeavouring to achieve the objective of free movement of capital between Member States and third countries to the greatest extent possible and without prejudice to the other chapters of this Treaty, the Council may, acting by a qualified majority on a proposal from the Commission, adopt measures on the movement of capital to or from third countries involving direct investment – including investment in real estate – establishment, the provision of financial services or the admission of securities to capital markets. Unanimity shall be required for measures under this paragraph which constitute a step back in Community law as regards the liberalisation of the movement of capital to or from third countries.

4.2 Does the free movement of capital and payments apply to third-country dividends?

4.2.1 Is a dividend protected?

In the Holböck case, the issue is obviously whether the free movement of capital and payments applies not only to cross-border dividends distributed by a company resident in another Member State (to a shareholder resident in a Member State), but also to third-country dividends that are distributed from a company resident in a third country to a resident of a Member State.

Before going into the third-country aspects of the case, it might be worth clarifying whether and how a dividend payment is to be seen as protected by the freedom of capital and payments. This might be doubted insofar as the dividend could arguably be seen to be, by its nature, not an investment of capital, but rather the return on such investment.

However, the ECJ has held in its case law (beginning with the Verkoojen case[4]) that the freedom of capital and payments covers not only the investment of share capital in a company by its shareholder (as a „direct investment“ within the meaning of the Capital Transfer Directive[5], which is seen to be of relevance for the scope of the freedom of capital and payments[6]), but also the return resulting from such investment. Precisely, the ECJ has stated that the receipt of dividends necessarily presupposes a „direct investment“.[7] Therefore, the ECJ has taken the view that the dividend itself is also covered for purposes of applying the freedom of capital and payments. Moreover, in the Verkoojen case (where the dividend was paid by a publicly listed company) the ECJ has held that, for purposes of the freedom capital and payments, the receipt of dividends may also be linked to an „acquisition by residents of foreign securities dealt in on a stock exchange“ which is also covered by the freedom.[8]

As a result, the ECJ has made it rather clear that a dividend payment (and not only the initial investment of capital in shares) should also be protected by the freedom of capital and payments. As the scope of the freedom of capital and payments is clearly designed to cover not only intra-Community transactions but also transactions with third countries, it seems that, at least at first sight, the Holböck dividend is actually covered by the freedom.

4 ECJ 6 June 2000, C-35/98 *Verkooijen* [2000] ECR I-4071.

5 Council Directive 88/361/EEC of 24 June 1988 for the implementation of Article 67 of the Treaty; OJ L 178, 8 July 1988, p 5.

6 Eg, ECJ 14 December 1995, C-163/94, 165/94, and 250/94 *Sanz de Lera* [1995] ECR I-4821, para 34; 16 March 1999, C-222/97 *Trummer and Mayer* [1999] ECR I-1661, para 21; 4 June 2002, C-483/99 *Commission v France* (Golden Shares) [2002] ECR I-4781, para 36; 7 September 2004, C-319/02 *Manninen* [2004] ECR I-7477, paras 27 et seq.

7 6 June 2000, C-35/98 *Verkooijen* [2000] ECR I-4071, para 28.

8 6 June 2000, C-35/98 *Verkooijen* [2000] ECR I-4071, para 29.

4.2.2 Timing issues for dividends

However, there may a timing issue for the protection of dividends by the freedom of capital and payments which could play a role in the Holböck case:

It seems to be unclear whether a dividend received after the implementation of the freedom of capital and payments in the Treaty (i.e. after 1 January 1994) should also be protected by the freedom if the initial investment in shares was made before 31 December 1993, i.e. before such freedom was part of the Treaty. This issue is of particular practical relevance for all countries that have later acceded to the EU.

For instance, in the Holböck case, Mr Holböck has apparently acquired its shareholding in the Swiss resident company some years before Austria's accession to the EU (i.e. before 1 January 1995), but he received dividends from this shareholding after Austria's becoming a Member State in 1995 and 1996. Implicitly, the Austrian Supreme Tax Court assumes that, for applying the freedom of capital and payments, it is sufficient that the dividend be received within the period of membership of Austria to the EU. Under such view, it would be irrelevant whether the initial investment in shares has been made at a time when Austria was not yet a Member State. The underlying assumption of this view is that the receipt of dividends is not only a result of the previous investment in shares (and for this reason protected by the freedom) but in fact protected independently from the initial investment in shares. In fact, this seems to be supported by the opinion of Advocate General Kokott in the Bouanich case, stating that the free movement of capital should cover generally any cross-border transfer of money.[9]

It is interesting that the Austrian Supreme Tax Court has not referred to this timing aspect in its request for preliminary ruling. It remains to be seen whether this issue will be raised in the ECJ proceedings.

---

9 Opinion of Advocate General Kokott in *Bouanich* (ECJ C-265/04 *Bouanich*, pending), 14 July 2005, para 26: "Der EG-Vertrag enthält keine Definition des Begriffes Kapitalverkehr. Allgemein kann unter den Kapitalverkehr jede über die Grenzen eines Mitgliedstaats hinweg stattfindende Übertragung von Geld- oder Sachkapital gefasst werden, die nicht im Zusammenhang mit einer Warenlieferung oder Dienstleistung steht und damit unter den freien Zahlungsverkehr fällt .... Außerdem hat die im Anhang I zur Richtlinie 88/361 ... abgedruckte ‚Nomenklatur für den Kapitalverkehr', wenngleich sie keine erschöpfende Auflistung der möglichen Transaktionen enthält, unstreitig Hinweischarakter für die Definition des Begriffs Kapitalverkehr ....“ [no English version available yet].

4.2.3 Free movement of capital and payments vs. right of establishment

For sake of completeness, it is also noted that, in a cross-border dividend case involving two Member States, a dividend resulting from a major investment (e.g. giving economic control over the company) may not only be protected by the freedom of capital and payments but also the right of establishment (Articles 43 et seq of the Treaty).

In its case law, the ECJ has explicitly held in a number of cases that it might well be that a taxpayer is protected by both freedoms at the same time. Specifically, the freedom of capital and payments is not excluded by having additional protection under the right of establishment for the same case.[10] The ECJ has avoided developing a hierarchy of the freedoms, e.g. giving prevalence to the "stronger" or "older" right of establishment over the freedom of capital and payments. Therefore, even in cases where the right of establishment is successfully invoked (and there is no further practical need to invoke also the freedom of capital and payments) it might well be that the freedom of capital and payments provides for additional (although "covert") protection.

Accordingly, the absence of protection under the right of establishment (as it is by nature the case in third-country situations) does not influence the application of the freedom of capital and payments for the third-country investment. Therefore, in a third-country case, dividends are protected (only) by the freedom of capital and payments even if the investment in the third-country company would (if established in another Member State) qualify as an establishment in the meaning of Article 43 of the Treaty. In a sense, in such third-country case the freedom of capital and payments comes "alive".[11]

---

10 Eg, ECJ 21 November 2002, C-436/00 *X and Y* [2002] ECR I-10829; or 4 June 2002, C-483/99 *Commission v France* (Golden Shares) [2002] ECR I-4781, para 56 where it is held that once an infringement of the free movement of capital has been established, there is no need for a separate examination of the measures at issue in the light of the right of establishment.

11 Schön, Der Kapitalverkehr mit Drittstaaten und das internationale Steuerrecht, in Gocke/Gosch/Lang (eds) *Körperschaftsteuer, Internationales Steuerrecht, Doppelbesteuerung – Festschrift für Franz Wassermeyer* (2005) p 501.

4.3 *Is the free movement of capital and payments violated in the Holböck Case?*

4.3.1 The Lenz case

In the Lenz case, the ECJ had to rule on the (non-) compliance of the former Austrian tax regime of domestic and foreign dividends, which is once again in question in the Holböck case. Both cases, Lenz and Holböck, are testing the same domestic legal background against the freedom of capital and payments. In Lenz, the ECJ held that this Austrian system was not in line with the freedom as far as dividends paid by companies resident in other Member States are concerned.

Therefore, in the light of the ECJ's Lenz decision, one might well expect that Austrian tax law violates the freedom of capital and payments in the Holböck case as well. When the ECJ has stated in the Lenz case that it is against the freedom of capital and payments if Austrian tax law applies the preferred (half the average) income tax rate only to domestic dividends while dividends from other Member States are taxed at full rates, it will be difficult to argue that the very same legal situation should not violate the freedom if the foreign dividend is coming from a third country.[12]

4.3.2 Are third-country dividends comparable with intra-Community dividends?

At least arguably, it might be brought forward that there is a difference between the Holböck and the Lenz case. In Lenz, it was assumed that the received cross-border dividend from a Member State is, for purposes of applying the freedom, comparable to a domestic dividend (and therefore the different tax treatment of both dividends is discrimination, as both dividends are to be treated equally).

In the Holböck case, however, the distributing foreign company is resident in a third country (rather than in a Member State). To this extent, one might question whether the Holböck dividend is actually comparable to a domestic dividend (as the Lenz dividend was), as it was received from outside the EU. Such view might be supported by the Opinion of the Advocate General Kokott in the Manninen case, where it is argued that the „comparability test" of domestic and cross-border-situations might

---

[12] Hohenwarter, Vorlagebeschluss des VwGH zur Kapitalverkehrsfreiheit im Verhältnis zu Drittstaaten, *SWI* 2005, p 225 (p 231).

yield different results if applied to third-country cases (compared to domestic cases).[13] In the tax literature it has therefore been argued that domestic and third-country dividends might not be comparable e.g. if the third-country company benefits from a low tax regime in its residence state which is fairly below typical EU standards.[14]

However, it should be seen that this argument has already been dealt with by the ECJ in the Lenz case. In that case, the ECJ was explicitly asked whether the level of taxation in the Member State of the dividend distributing company is of relevance for the freedom of capital and payments. The ECJ held on this point that it might well be that a low level of taxation for the distributing company might create an economic advantage not only for this company but also for its shareholders, but this could not justify a more burdensome treatment of the dividends in the hands of the shareholders as it would take place for domestic dividends.[15] From this reasoning in the Lenz case it can be assumed that the ECJ apparently regards this argument as a (potential) justification argument rather as a comparability issue. Therefore, it seems to be likely that the ECJ will consider this argument also in the Holböck case on the justification level.[16]

4.4 Is the discrimination justified?

4.4.1 No justification in the Lenz case

As a starting point, it seems to be clear that the discrimination between domestic and foreign dividends as foreseen by the Austrian tax system in the Holböck case would not be justified if the dividend had been paid by a company resident in another EU Member State. This was already decided by the ECJ in the Lenz case.

Therefore, a potential justification of the given discrimination could, if at all, only be found in the specific third-country nature of the Holböck case. In other words, in the Holböck case the issue will be whether there are grounds for justification that are specifically based in the third-country context.

---

[13] Opinion of Advocate General Kokott in *Manninen* (ECJ 7 September 2004, C-319/02 *Manninen* [2004] ECR I-74771), 18 March 2004, para 79.

[14] Schön, Der Kapitalverkehr mit Drittstaaten und das internationale Steuerrecht, in Gocke/Gosch/Lang (eds) *Festschrift für Franz Wassermeyer,* pp 512 et seq.

[15] ECJ 15 July 2004, C-315/02 *Lenz* [2004] ECR I-7063, para 43.

[16] See also Hohenwarter, *SWI* 2005, pp 228 and 232.

4.4.2 Loss of Member States' tax revenues?

In intra-Community cases, the ECJ has always rejected to regard a loss of a Member State's tax revenues as a possible justification for discriminatory taxation.[17] Theoretically, a Member State could now argue in a third-country context that a loss of its tax revenues would not be against a corresponding gain in tax revenues for another Member State, but a third country, which could arguably be a much more dangerous situation from an overall EU budgetary perspective.

However, it seems that such argument would go too far since, as a consequence of such argument, there would be no freedom of capital and payments in tax matters with third countries at all.[18] In cross-border tax matters, a loss of a Member State's tax revenues would occur by nature, therefore justifying discrimination of the third-country cross-border case at any time. This seems not to be the intention of the Treaty when expanding this freedom to third-country cases.

4.4.3 Member State's lack of information?

A potential ground for justification could be that Member States have a more limited access to relevant tax information in relation to third countries than they have in relation to other Member States. In fact the ECJ, in a number of cases, has not allowed a Member State's lack of information to levy its taxes as a justification for a discriminatory tax situation.[19] This

---

[17] Eg, ECJ 28 January 1986, 270/83 *Avoir Fiscal* [1986] ECR 273, para 25; 16 July 1998, C-264/96 *ICI* [1998] ECR I-4695, para 28; 21 September 1999, C-307/97 *Saint-Gobain* [1999] ECR I-6161, para 51; 6 June 2000, C-35/98 *Verkooijen* [2000] ECR I-4071, para 59; 8 March 2001, C-397/98 and C-410/98 *Metallgesellschaft/Hoechst* [2001] ECR I-1727, para 59; 18 November 1999, C-200/98 *X and Y* [1999] ECR I-8261, para 50; 12 December 2002, C-324/00 *Lankhorst-Hohorst* [2002] ECR I-11779, para 36; 18 September 2003, C-168/01 *Bosal* [2003] ECR I-9409, para 42; 15 July 2004, C-315/02 *Lenz* [2004] ECR I-7063, para 40; 7 September 2004, C-319/02 *Manninen* [2004] ECR I-7477, para 49.

[18] Schön, Der Kapitalverkehr mit Drittstaaten und das internationale Steuerrecht, in Gocke/Gosch/Lang (eds) *Festschrift für Franz Wassermeyer,* p 516.

[19] Eg, ECJ 28 January 1992, C-204/90 *Bachmann* [1992] ECR I-249, paras 18 et seq; 12 April 1994, C-1/93 *Halliburton* [1994] ECR I-1137, paras 21 et seq; 14 February 1995, C-279/93 *Schumacker* [1995] ECR I-225, paras 43 et seq; 11 August 1995, C-80/94 *Wielockx* [1995] ECR I-2493, para 26; 15 May 1997, C-250/95 *Futura* [1997] ECR I-2471, para 30; 28 October 1999, C-55/98 *Vestergaard* [1999] ECR I-7641, paras 26 et seq; 3 October 2002, C-136/00 *Danner* [2002] ECR I-8147, paras 44 et seq; 26 June 2003, C-422/01 *Skandia and Ramstedt* [2003] ECR I-6817, paras 38 et seq.

was typically based on the argument, that between Member States there are viable tools of exchange of information in tax matters provided by EC law.[20]

In a third-country case, these EC law-based exchange of information tools are not available. Typically, the only source of information for a Member State's tax authority would be a bilaterally agreed exchange of information procedure, as often foreseen in bilateral tax treaties. In a third-country case, however, there will be a number of countries without a tax treaty (or similar exchange of information instrument) with the respective Member State. To this extent, the (non-)availability of exchange of information could potentially be of relevance here.

However, coming back to the Holböck case, it seems doubtful whether such exchange of information argument, even if admissible in principle, could justify the discrimination. The exchange of information argument would only be valid, if information were needed on how the dividend-paying company is taxed in its residence state. Such information need, however, does not exist under Austrian law, as the third-country dividend would be taxed in the hands of the shareholder at full rates irrespective of the actual amount of tax levied on the company level.

4.4.4 The cohesion argument

Finally, there is the cohesion argument, which is also brought forward by the Austrian Supreme Tax Court in the Holböck case. In dividend cases, the typical cohesion argument claims that, when examining potential discrimination in shareholder's taxation of dividends, one should take into account not only the shareholder's individual tax burden but also the underlying tax burden of the dividend on the company level. Under the cohesion argument, both levels should be looked at from an overall perspective.[21]

---

[20] Council Directive 2004/56/EC of 21 April 2004 amending Directive 77/799/EEC concerning mutual assistance by the competent authorities of the Member States in the field of direct taxation, certain excise duties and taxation of insurance premiums; OJ L 127, 29 April 2004, p 70.

[21] Eg, Rust, Renaissance der Kohärenz, *EWS* 2004, pp 450 et seq; Englisch, Fiscal Cohesion in the Taxation of Cross-Border Dividends (Part Two), *ET* 2004, pp 355 et seq; Schnitger, Grenzüberschreitende Körperschaftsteueranrechnung und Neuausrichtung der Kohärenz nach dem EuGH-Urteil in der Rs. *Manninen*, *ÖStZ* 2005, pp 26 et seq.

In the Holböck case, the Austrian Supreme Tax Court is undecided as to whether it can play a role in the cohesion argument (as a ground for justification of discriminatory taxation) if the dividend paying company is low taxed, e.g. by reason of a preferential tax regime in its residence state or its residence state's nature as a tax haven. In other words, the Court raises the following question: Is a discriminatory regime like the Austrian one in the Holböck case justified in a case where the overall tax burden of the distributed dividend (i.e. the underlying corporate income tax of the distributing company and the individual income tax of the shareholder) is lower than it would be in a purely domestic situation (where the distributing company is subject to domestic corporate income tax rate)?

In the Lenz case, the ECJ has explicitly rejected this cohesion argument for a case where the distributing company was resident in another Member State, even if this Member State was taxing the company at a lower level than Austria would.[22] This was based on the ECJ's general understanding that the principle of cohesion could not serve as a justification for discriminatory taxation of dividends in the hands of the shareholders, as this principle is to be applied on an isolated basis on the level of the shareholder or the distributing company. An overall view, taking into account the treatment on both levels, has never been permitted by the ECJ in this respect.[23] The legal literature has criticised the ECJ for its rather narrow view on the cohesion principle.[24] Interestingly, it seems that in most recent case law this issue is apparently again under discussion. In the Manninen case, it was at least proposed by the Advocate General that the ECJ should have a wider perspective when applying the cohesion

---

22 Opinion of Advocate General Tizzano in *Lenz* (ECJ 15 July 2004, C-315/02 *Lenz* [2004] ECR I-7063), 25 March 2004, para 39.

23 Eg, ECJ 11 August 1995, C-80/94 *Wielockx* [1995] ECR I-2493, paras 13 et seq; 16 July 1998, C-264/96 *ICI* [1998] ECR I-4695, para 29; 6 June 2000, C-35/98 *Verkooijen* [2000] ECR I-4071, paras 49 et seq; 26 September 2000, C-478/98 *Commission v Belgium* [2000] ECR I-7587, paras 34 et seq; 8 March 2001, C-397/98 and C-410/98 *Metallgesellschaft/ Hoechst* [2001] ECR I-1727, paras 67 et seq; 21 November 2002, C-436/00 *X and Y* [2002] ECR I-10829, para 72; 12 December 2002, C-324/00 *Lankhorst-Hohorst* [2002] ECR I-11779, paras 40 et seq; 15 July 2004, C-315/02 *Lenz* [2004] ECR I-7063, paras 35 et seq.

24 Eg, Englisch, Fiscal Cohesion in the Taxation of Cross-Border Dividends (Part Two), *ET* 2004, p 355 (pp 356 et seq); Stangl, Der Begriff der steuerlichen Kohärenz nach den Urteilen Baars und Verkooijen, *SWI* 2000, p 463 (pp 465 et seq); Schön, Besteuerung im Binnenmarkt – die Rechtsprechung des EuGH zu den direkten Steuern, *IStR* 2004, p 289 (pp 298 et seq).

argument, looking in dividend cases at both the company's and the shareholder's level.[25]

In a third-country context, like in the Holböck case, the cohesion argument is of much more practical relevance as compared to EU cross-border cases as it might well be that the third country (where the dividend distributing company is resident) provides for a rather low level of tax for its residents or is even a typical tax haven. In such a case, the overall tax burden for the dividend could be significantly lower than it would be in purely domestic case. Against this background, it should not be excluded that the ECJ may further reconsider its view on the cohesion argument.

It might therefore well be that the cohesion argument could justify discriminatory taxation in third-country cases where there actually is a lower overall taxation of dividends in cross-border cases as compared to domestic cases. If that should be the case, the outcome of the Holböck case might give some further perspective on the future of the cohesion argument in general.

4.4.5 The proportionality test

In the Holböck case, however, it will be nevertheless (even if the cohesion argument should be admissible) difficult to justify the Austrian legal system of foreign dividend taxation.

It has to be seen that Austrian law denies the reduced taxation of foreign (in the Holböck case third-country) dividends in general and therefore irrespective of the actual underlying tax burden of the foreign distributing company. In other words, Austria would deny equal treatment with domestic dividends even in cases where the foreign dividend actually suffers a higher or equally high overall tax burden as a domestic dividend. Therefore, it is in fact not the amount of overall tax on the dividend, but the pure residence of the distributing company that is the reason for the discriminatory taxation. It is rather doubtful whether such rule would meet the proportionality test that the ECJ has developed in its case law when testing whether a specific discriminatory rule may be justified.[26]

---

25 Opinion of Advocate General Kokott in *Manninen* (ECJ 7 September 2004, C-319/02 *Manninen* [2004] ECR I-7477); 18 March 2004, paras 50 et seq, in particular paras 61 and 65. Refer also to the statement in the judgment itself; ECJ 7 September 2004, C-319/02 *Manninen* [2004] ECR I-7477, para 46.

26 Eg, ECJ 5 March 2002, C-515/99, 519/99 to 524/99, and 526/99 to 540/99 *Reisch* [2002] ECR I-2157, paras 33 et seq; 15 May 2003, C-300/01 *Salzmann* [2003] ECR I-4899, paras 48-51.

In order to meet this proportionality test, the Austrian regime would have to take in account the actual tax burden suffered by the distributing foreign company, e.g. through making the equal treatment of the foreign dividend with domestic dividends subject to a minimum underlying tax at the level of the foreign company, which is equivalent to the Austrian corporate income tax rate. In fact, Austria has adopted a similar rule as a result of the Lenz case, but these new rules apply only from 2003 on (and were therefore not yet available in the Holböck case).

4.5 The stand-still clause

4.5.1 Article 57 para 1 of the Treaty

The key issue of the Holböck case is the scope of the stand-still clause in Article 57 of the Treaty. Article 57 para 1 of the Treaty allows Member States to keep their discriminatory tax regimes in relation to third countries in place, if these regimes were in existence on 31 December 1993.

In its essence, Article 57 para 1 of the Treaty enables Member States to „grandfather" their discriminatory tax rules to the extent they apply to third countries.[27] To date, scope and content of this grandfathering clause are rather uncertain. To this extent, it can be expected that the Holböck case will clarify some of the issues.

4.5.2 The grandfathering date

First, Article 57 para 1 of the Treaty refers to 31 December 1993 as the grandfathering date. However, in the tax literature it has been argued at least in the case of Austria that for Member States joining the EU after this date, it is the date of accession that is relevant as grandfathering date.[28] Therefore, for Austria, it is 31 December 1994 that is the date to be looked at when determining whether the rules in question were already in place.

Looking at the Austrian tax regime in question, it is interesting that the Austrian Supreme Tax Court obviously assumes that the stand-still clause may apply regardless of the fact that the rules in question have been changed in wording after the grandfathering date (31 December 1993) but without changing the rules in substance. By taking such view, the Court

---

27 Schön, Der Kapitalverkehr mit Drittstaaten und das internationale Steuerrecht, in Gocke/Gosch/Lang (eds) *Festschrift für Franz Wassermeyer*, pp 493 et seq.

28 Schneider in Mayer (ed), *Kommentar zu EU- und EG-Vertrag*, Art 57 mn 10.

supports the argument brought forward in the literature that it should be the substance of the rule that is to exist as of the grandfathering date in order to be covered by the stand-still clause.[29] Later formal changes or amendments to these rules do not affect the application of the clause as long as the rules are in substance the same.

Therefore, in the Holböck case, at first sight, it appears that the Austrian tax regime for dividends is actually grandfathered as the relevant rules were, at least in substance, already in place on the relevant grandfathering date.

4.5.3 Grandfathering for "direct investments"

The issue is, however, that the grandfathering clause in Article 57 para 1 of the Treaty covers only specific cases of capital transfers with third countries, these cases being explicitly listed in the Treaty. Specifically, Article 57 para 1 of the Treaty covers a Member State's rules "in relation to direct investments including real estate investments, to the establishment and exercise of financial services or the admission of securities to capital markets".

In the Holböck case, only the „direct investments" will be relevant. Therefore, the issue is whether the dividend received by Mr Holböck (or his initial investment in shares) is a „direct investment". If this is the case, discriminatory taxation of such direct investment in a third-country company would be grandfathered under Article 57 para 1 of the Treaty and could therefore be upheld by Austria.

The term „direct investment" is defined in Annex I to the Capital Movements Directive. According to this annex, a direct investment is defined, inter alia, as „a participation in new or existing undertaking with a view to establishing or maintaining lasting economic links". Further, it is clarified in the Explanatory Notes to the Directive that there is such participation in the sense of a direct investment "where the block of shares

[29] Eg, Endfellner/Rainer, Austrian Case on Tax Treatment of Inbound Dividends Referred to ECJ, 105(10) *WTD* (2005). The criterion of substantive identity was also a point at issue in ECJ 15 May 2003, C-300/01 *Salzmann* [2003] ECR I-4899. At para 55 the ECJ held that "legislation which is based on an approach which differs from that of the previous law … cannot be treated as legislation existing at the time of accession". Thus, "legislation which includes a number of significant differences when compared with the legislation existing on the date of accession" is not acceptable.

held by a natural person … enables the shareholder, either pursuant to the provisions of national laws relating to companies limited by shares or otherwise, to participate effectively in the management of the company or in its control".

Therefore, it appears to be the key element of a direct investment that the shareholder has the opportunity to either effectively manage or control the company[30]. In the Holböck case (where Mr Holböck held 2/3 of the shares in the distributing company) this management or control element will probably exist. Unfortunately, the Austrian Supreme Tax Court is rather silent on this facts issue in its request for preliminary ruling. Therefore, it might well be that the ECJ will decide the case in general and refer it back to the domestic court to clarify the facts situation. Assuming that Mr Holböck had actual control over the company, the result will likely be that the grandfathering clause of Article 57 para 1 of the Treaty will apply. Accordingly, the Holböck case will be lost by the taxpayer as Austria will be able to grandfather its discriminatory tax regime for foreign dividends in relation to third countries.

Notably, it seems that the result would be different if Mr Holböck had held not a controlling interest in the company but only a portfolio shareholding. In such case, according to the above definitions, no „direct investment" would exist and therefore the grandfathering clause could not be applied. Nevertheless, the portfolio investment would still be protected by the freedom of capital and payments, as the ECJ has clarified that also such portfolio investments would be in the scope of the freedom[31].

5 Conclusions

As a conclusion from the above analysis, it follows that, in third-country dividend cases, due to the standstill clause there is less protection under the freedom of capital and payments for the stronger investment (constituting a „direct investment") as compared to a mere portfolio investment.

---

[30] This is also confirmed by the ECJ's "Golden Share" case law. See, for example, ECJ 4 June 2002, C-503/99 *Commission v Belgium* (Golden Shares) [2002] ECR I-4809, para 6; 4 June 2002, C-483/99 *Commission v France* (Golden Shares) [2002] ECR I-4781, para 6; 13 May 2003, C-98/01 *Commission v UK* (Golden Shares) [2003] ECR I-4641, para 5.

[31] Eg, ECJ 15 July 2004, C-315/02 *Lenz* [2004] ECR I-7063; 15 July 2004, C-242/03 *Weidert and Paulus* [2004] ECR I-7379; 7 September 2004, C-319/02 *Manninen* [2004] ECR I-7477.

At first sight, this result appears somewhat surprising. However, from a Member States' perspective such a result makes perfect sense: Through excluding major investments in companies, the standstill clause secures that third-country cases do not achieve the effects of the other freedoms provided for by the Treaty of Rome, in particular the right of establishment, which would otherwise become available through the „backdoor" of the freedom of capital and payments.

Nevertheless, the Holböck case still leads to a question mark as to the scope of the standstill clause: Assuming that the Austrian tax rules at issue (i.e. the taxation of foreign dividends at full tax rates) are disproportionate, can it be that Member States are actually allowed to apply disproportionate measures to third countries when limiting the scope of the freedom of capital and payments? It appears doubtful whether Member States should be entitled to restrict or even penalise capital movements to and from third countries without any need for objectiveness, necessity and proportionality of the restrictive measure. Future research and case law will have to clarify whether even the standstill clause has implied limitations, e.g. a proportionality test. There seem to be good arguments for it.

Pending Cases Filed by Belgian Courts: The Kerckhaert-Morres Case

Pending Cases involving Belgium: The Belgian Coordination Centres Cases, Commission v Belgium, Commission v Belgium

Pending Cases Filed by French Courts: The Denkavit Case

Jacques Malherbe/Melchior Wathelet

I Belgian Coordination Centres (C-182/03, C-217/03, C-399/03, C-176/03, and C-433/04)

1 Background
2 Description
2.1 Introduction
2.2 Eligibility conditions
2.2.1 Legal form
2.2.2 International group of companies
2.2.3 Authorised activities
2.2.4 "Intra muros" requirement
2.2.5 Employment condition
2.2.6 Recognition by Royal Decree
2.3 Tax treatment
2.3.1 Corporate income tax
2.3.2 Personal property withholding tax (Précompte mobilier – Roerende Voorheffing)
2.3.3 Notional personal property withholding tax
2.3.4 Real estate withholding tax
2.3.5 Registration Duties
2.3.6 Annual tax on coordination centres
2.3.7 Recognition period
2.4 Other advantages
3 Code of Conduct
4 State Aid Action
5 Code of Conduct Report
6 State Aid Procedure before the Commission
7 Reasoning
8 Economic Advantage

9 Exemption from Property Tax
10 Exemption from Capital Duty
11 Exemption from Withholding Tax
12 Notional Withholding Tax
13 Cost plus Assessment
14 Use of State Resources
15 Distortion of Competition and Adverse Effect on Trade between Member States
16 Selectivity
17 Justification on Grounds of the Nature or Structure of the System
18 Decision
19 Belgium´s Appeal
20 Suspension
21 Appeal of the Commission
22 State Aid Procedure in respect of a New Scheme
23 General Replacement Measure: Notional Interest
24 Conclusion

II The Kerckhaert-Morres Case (C-513/04)

III Commission v Belgium (C-433/04)
1 Applicable Belgian Law
2 Alleged Incompatibility with EU Law
2.1 Is there discrimination or an impediment to the freedom to provide services?
2.2 Is this justifiable?
2.3 Proportionality
3 Status of the Proceedings

IV Commission v Belgium (C-522/04)
1 Applicable Belgian Law
2 Incompatibility with EULaw
3 Status of the Proceedings

V Denkavit (C-170/05)
1 Applicable French Law
2 Incompatibility with EC-Law
2.1 Is there discrimination or an impediment to the free movement of capital?
2.2 Is this obstacle justifiable?
3 Status of the Proceedings

I Belgian Coordination Centres (C-182/03, C-217/03, C-399/03, C-176/03, and C-433/04)

1 Background

Coordination centres were introduced in Belgium by Royal Decree N° 187 of 30 December 1982[1].

On 2 May 1984, the Commission decided not to object to the regime if it were amended as per a proposal of the Belgian Government.

As the actual amendments did not correspond to the proposal, the Commission initiated an investigation on 12 December 1985.

The amendments required were enacted on 4 August 1986 and the Commission decided on 9 March 1987 to close the procedure.

2 Description

2.1 Introduction

A special tax regime for coordination centres (centres de coordination/ coördinatiecentra) was introduced by Royal Decree N° 187 of 30 December 1982 ("Royal Decree N° 187"). The Report to the Crown which serves as an introduction to Royal Decree N° 187 indicates that the legislation is designed to make Belgium a more attractive location, primarily from a tax point of view, for coordination and research centres of multinational enterprises. The presence of such centres would stimulate investment and the employment of qualified personnel. Approximately 300 recognised coordination centres representing many of the world's largest multinational groups are active in Belgium.

2.2 Eligibility conditions

A coordination centre may be established as a Belgian company or as a branch of a foreign company. A coordination centre must form part of an international group of companies meeting minimum assets and turnover requirements. It must have as its sole purpose the development and centralisation of qualifying activities that are performed for the sole benefit

[1] For a summary, see among others, Malherbe, *Droit fiscal international* (1994) p 707; Malherbe/François, Die belgischen Koordinierungsstellen, *IStR* 1997, p 105.

of certain members of the group. It must employ, by the end of the two-year period following the commencement of its activities, the equivalent of at least 10 full-time employees. The favourable tax regime and the other advantages made available under Royal Decree N° 187, as amended, do not apply automatically. A group of companies wishing to set up a coordination centre must obtain prior approval (ie, an individual decree granting recognition) from the competent Belgian authorities.

2.2.1 Legal form

A coordination centre must be established either as a Belgian company with separate legal personality in one of the forms provided for in the Company Code or as a Belgian establishment (branch) of a foreign company with separate legal personality.

2.2.2 International group of companies

A coordination centre, established as a Belgian company or as a branch of a foreign company, must be part of an international group of affiliated companies meeting minimum asset and turnover requirements.

A group of companies is defined as all the affiliated companies that are placed under one and the same management as a consequence of their direct or indirect mutual shareholdings. The "one and the same" criterion is deemed to be met if a company holds, either directly or indirectly, at least 20 % of the capital of another company or at least 20 % of the voting rights attached to the shares issued. To determine whether the 20 % threshold is met, shares that several members of a group hold in a company may be aggregated.

The group of companies to which the coordination centre belongs must have consolidated capital and reserves, on a worldwide basis, of at least € 24 million and a consolidated annual turnover of at least € 240,000. Royal Decree N° 187 does not specify the manner in which the consolidated amounts are to be computed. A decision of 27 July 1985 of the Ministry of Economic Affairs suggests that shareholdings and sales between the group members may be excluded, without specifying which consolidation technique should be applied. Arguably, therefore, the consolidation is not required to comply with the Belgian legislation on the consolidated annual accounts of enterprises.

The group of companies to which the coordination centre belongs must qualify as an international group, which means that the following three cumulative conditions must be met:

(i) the consolidated capital of the group, excluding its net worth in Belgium, must be at least € 12 million or 20 % of the consolidated capital and reserves of the group, whichever is lower;

(ii) the group must have a consolidated turnover outside Belgium of at least € 120,000 or 20 % of the total consolidated turnover of the group, whichever is lower; and

(iii) the group must have had at least one subsidiary in each of four different countries since the first day of January of the second year preceding the year during which the request for recognition as a coordination centre was filed.

Banking, leasing, credit and insurance companies are not eligible to establish coordination centres[2]. Moreover, a group that is not predominantly a bank, a leasing, a credit or an insurance enterprise, but that has in its structure one or more banking, leasing, credit or insurance companies, must exclude these companies from the coordination centre group (ie, the group members that are entitled to use the services of the coordination centre).[3]

The tax authorities accept that several coordination centres may be recognised within the same group of companies, provided each of the recognised coordination centres limits its activities to a well-defined separate subgroup and that such segregation is economically justified[4]. In such an event, each subgroup must itself meet the international group requirements described above, which means that a given company cannot be considered to be part of more than one subgroup at the same time[5].

2.2.3 Authorised activities

A coordination centre must have as its sole purpose the development and centralisation of one or more of the activities listed in Royal Decree N° 187. The application for coordination centre status must specify those

2 R.D. No. 187, Art 7.

3 Circular Letter of 29 November 1993 (Bull. Contr., n°733, p 3298, n°26).

4 Parliamentary Question n° 135 of 12 March 1990 (Bull. Bel., 1990, 3121).

5 Circular Letter of 29 November 1993 (Bull. Contr., n° 733, p 3300, n° 31).

activities intended to be carried on by the applicant. The coordination centre can then only engage in those activities enumerated in the specific Royal Decree in which it was recognised.

The authorised activities listed in Royal Decree N° 187 can be divided into two categories, namely headquarters functions and financial functions.

(1) Headquarters functions

Authorised activities cover first general head office services, including:

- advertising and marketing services such as the organisation of advertising campaigns for the group members, centralisation of the purchase of goods, participation in trade fairs, the organisation of seminars for the sales personnel of the group members, the development of promotional materials, coordination in the field of public relations; however, any activities that would result in a direct contact with the customers of the group members aimed at obtaining, realising, accepting or performing supplies of goods or services are excluded;
- the collection and dissemination of information (for example, market surveys, competition surveys, product research, in-house legal services and tax management);
- scientific research (for example, the exploitation of a laboratory for scientific R&D, the coordination of group policies in the field of scientific R&D);
- non-commercial relations with national and international authorities (for example, monitoring and liaising with the institutions of the EU and contacts with governmental bodies other than with a view to obtaining government contracts);
- accounting, data processing and administrative services (for example, the preparation and distribution of customer invoices on behalf of the group members, the collection of invoices, the control of inventories, and the development and creation of software); and
- in general, any and all other preparatory and ancillary activities.

(2) Financial services

The financial services category of authorised activities relates to centralised financial operations and the hedging of foreign exchange and interest rate risks. More specifically, the following types of activities are typical of the activities falling in this category:

- the control of the debit/credit accounts of the group members;
- the collection and payment of commissions and royalties in the name and for the account of the group members;
- the coordination and/or centralisation of the financial and treasury management for the group members (for example, cash-pooling, electronic banking, the centralisation of the group members' financial debit/credit accounts, and negotiations with financial institutions and institutional investors);
- insurance and re-insurance activities (although a review of the individual recognition decrees would appear to suggest that the competent authorities are unlikely to accept that coordination centres are actually engaged in insurance or re-insurance activities as such);
- the coordination and/or centralisation of the long-term and short-term financing needs of the group members. The coordination centre may use its own resources or may enter into loan agreements with Belgian or foreign group members (subject to certain conditions) or with financial institutions in Belgium or abroad; the centre may also finance itself through the issuing of negotiable instruments (for example, bonds and commercial paper). However, the centre is not allowed to deposit funds with third parties if such funds derive from borrowings made by Belgian group members with a view to capitalising the coordination centre;[6]
- support services with respect to negotiations relating to export financing;
- the leasing of personal and real estate property and the sale and lease-back of new fixed assets;
- re-invoicing activities, i.e. activities whereby goods and services invoiced to the centre by group members are re-invoiced to other group members in their own currency;
- factoring activities, i.e. the purchase by the coordination centre of receivables that group members have from other group members or from third parties;
- the hedging of foreign exchange and interest rate risks;
- the granting of security interests or similar instruments to guarantee the financial obligations of the group members; and
- the development of new financial instruments and techniques.

---

6 Royal Decree of 5 August 1991.

A coordination centre may not own shares or any other equity interests in any other companies or enterprises. Hence, a coordination centre cannot act as a holding company.

2.2.4 "Intra muros" requirement

A coordination centre must perform its activities for the sole benefit of the members of the group of companies to which it belongs. The Report to the Crown considers the intra muros requirement to be an essential feature of the coordination centre regime. An additional restriction imposed by the individual decrees granting recognition prohibits a coordination centre from providing services or performing functions for the benefit of group members that receive services from another centre or that are themselves engaged in activities similar to the activities performed by the coordination centre. As indicated in (2), above, neither financial institutions nor insurance companies can qualify as group members that may benefit from the activities performed by a coordination centre. It follows from the intra muros requirement, as well as from the list of authorised activities discussed in (3), above, that a coordination centre may not deal with third parties except on ancillary matters.

2.2.5 Employment condition

A coordination centre must employ, at the latest by the end of the two-year period following the commencement of its activities, the equivalent of at least 10 full-time employees. According to the Belgian social security authorities, these employees are to be subject to the Belgian social security regime. As there appears to be no legal basis for this assertion, there is doubt as to whether it can be upheld in practice. There are no requirements with respect to the functions performed. Employees transferred to a coordination centre from a Belgian group member or from a Belgian establishment of a foreign group member are only taken into account if the employees so transferred are replaced by newly-recruited employees, either at the level of the coordination centre or at the level of the transferring entity.

2.2.6 Recognition by Royal Decree

To benefit from the special tax regime, a coordination centre must be recognised by an individual Royal Decree. An application for recognition must be filed with the Ministry of Finance. The application consists of three parts; (i) a general description of the group, its composition and its activities; (ii) a detailed description of the proposed activities and; (iii) a number of supporting documents (for example, the annual reports published by the group) to establish that the international group requirement is met. Whether the application is to be approved is decided by an inter-ministerial working group consisting of representatives from the Ministry of Finance (verification of the authorised activities), the Ministry of Economic Affairs (verification of the group criteria), the Ministry of Employment and Labour and the Ministry of Middle Classes. After the application is approved, the services of the Ministry of Finance draft a proposal for a Royal Decree. Upon the execution of the Royal Decree, the coordination centre is deemed to be approved for a renewable period of 10 years. The above procedure takes on average more than six months. The individual decree granting recognition is not published, but lists of recognised coordination centres (stating the name of the centre and the group to which it belongs) are published periodically in the Belgian Official Journal.

2.3 Tax treatment

2.3.1 Corporate income tax

A coordination centre is subject to resident or non-resident corporate income tax, depending upon whether it is established as a Belgian company or as a Belgian establishment (branch) of a foreign company.

Corporate income tax is levied on a notional tax base, determined in practice as a percentage of the coordination centre's operating expenses other than personnel and financial costs. For this purpose, personnel costs consist of the salaries and wages and direct social benefits of directors or managers, management personnel, and salaried and hourly personnel; the employer's social security contributions; the employer's premiums for benefit plans; and the old age and survivor pensions. Financial costs are interest, commissions and charges pertaining to debts; booked write-downs on claims other than commercial claims, treasury placements and available securities; depreciation on the sale of assets other than commercial claims, treasury placements and available securities; the discount for the centre's account on the negotiation of claims; and exchange differentials and differences in the conversion of currencies.

The specific percentage mark-up must, in principle, be determined for each coordination centre individually. In practice, however, the percentage corresponds to the mark-up charged by the coordination centre to the group members. In the absence of any objective criteria for determining the profit percentage, it must be fixed at 8 %.[7] It should be noted that certain services of coordination centres may not be charged out to the group members on the basis of the cost-plus method (for example, services such as re-invoicing, factoring, leasing and intra-group financing). The arm's length character of the consideration received by the coordination centre should in these instances be measured by comparing it to the consideration applying between unrelated parties. Where the conditions offered by the coordination centre are not less favourable than those applied between unrelated parties, they should in principle be acceptable to the Belgian tax authorities.

However, a coordination centre's tax base may not be less that the sum of any non-deductible expenses and any abnormal or gratuitous advantages granted to the centre (the "alternative minimum tax base").

Non-deductible expenses relate to all expenditures and charges incurred by the coordination centre that, in conformity with the normal tax rules, are not deductible as business expenses. Elements that, although technically treated as a "disallowed expense" in the tax return, do not have the nature of an expenditure should, arguably, not be included in the non-deductible expenses (for example, abnormal or gratuitous advantages granted by the coordination centre).[8]

The inclusion in the alternative minimum tax base of abnormal or gratuitous advantages granted to the coordination centre is designed to remove any incentive to shift profits realised elsewhere in the group to the coordination centre by way of artificial and non-market conforming arrangements.

2.3.2 Personal property withholding tax (Précompte mobilier – Roerende Voorheffing)

An unconditional exemption from the personal property withholding tax is available for all dividends distributed, for all interest owed (unless the

[7] Circular Letter of 29 November 1993 (Bull.Contr., n° 733, p 3307, n° 44).

[8] Denayer, Enkele forfaitaire regimes, in Joseph/Hinnekens/Malherbe/Van Hoorn Jr (eds) *Het Belgisch internationaal belastingrecht in ontwikkeling in Nieuwe wegen voor het Belgisch internationaal belastingrecht?*, (1993) p 304, n° 22; contra Hinnekens, De coördinatiecentra na de wet van 4 augustus 1986, *A.F.T.* 1987, p 13.

recipient is subject to the individual income tax or to the legal persons income tax) and for all royalties paid by recognised coordination centres.

Any interest paid to recognised coordination centres on cash deposits is exempt from the personal property withholding tax.

Recognised coordination centres qualify as "professional investors" within the meaning of the Royal Decree implementing the Income Tax Code and, hence, any interest on loans paid to such centres is exempt from the personal property withholding tax.

2.3.3 Notional personal property withholding tax

Until 24 July 1991 and subject to certain conditions and limitations, a Belgian beneficiary of dividends distributed or interest paid by a recognised coordination centre was eligible to claim a tax credit for notional personal property withholding tax (précompte mobilier fictif/fictieve roerende voorheffing) equal to one-ninth of the dividend or interest payment, even if no such withholding tax was effectively levied. In the case of interest, Belgian banks were willing to pass the benefit of the tax credit on to the coordination centres in the form of reduced interest rates, which enabled the centre to on-lend the borrowed funds to other group members on more favourable terms. The tax credit for fictitious personal property withholding tax has been „temporarily" reduced to zero for dividends distributed and interest paid by coordination centres after 24 July 1991.

2.3.4 Real estate withholding tax

Coordination centres are exempted from the real estate withholding tax relating to land, buildings and equipment owned and used by them for the exercise of their business activities in Belgium.[9]

2.3.5 Registration duties

The proportional registration or capital duty of 0.5 % is not due on contributions made to the capital of recognised coordination centres. Capital duties levied on contributions and capital increases made prior to the recognition as a coordination centre are reimbursed once the recognition is obtained.[10]

---

9 Law of 11 April 1983, Art 29, 1°.

10 Circular Letter of 12 April 1985 (Rec. Gén. Enr. Not. 1985, n° 23.203).

2.3.6 *Annual tax on coordination centres*

With effect from 1 January 1993, coordination centres are subject to an annual tax of € 10,000 per full-time employee, up to a maximum of € 100,000 annually. The annual tax on coordination centres has (surprisingly) been inserted in the Inheritance Tax Code.[11]

2.3.7 *Recognition period*

In principle, the advantages relating to the notional tax base, the personal property withholding tax, the real estate withholding tax and registration duties are granted for a period of 10 years, starting with the financial year in which the application for recognition is made and ending with the end of the financial year ended during the tenth calendar year following the year in which the application was filed.[12]

On the expiry of the 10-year period, a renewal of the recognition as a coordination centre may be requested for a new period of 10 years. The request must be filed simultaneously with the Minister of Finance and the Minister of Economic Affairs, approximately one year prior to the expiry of the initial recognition period. The granting of the renewal is subject to the same formalities and eligibility conditions as those applying in the case of a first recognition. After verification of the eligibility conditions and approval by the competent authorities, the renewal is granted by a Royal Decree, which enters into force on the first day following the expiry of the initial recognition period.[13]

Coordination centre status will be prematurely terminated in various circumstances. First, the individual coordination centre recognition decrees expressly provide that the special status expires if the coordination centre, without prior ministerial authorisation, develops activities other than those listed in its decree on recognition. The expiry of the recognition automatically triggers the termination of the tax concessions described above, with effect from the financial year in which the coordination centre engaged in non-authorised activities. Second, the coordination centre will be denied the benefit of the tax concessions if the employment requirement ceases to be met. According to the tax authorities, this will apply with retrospective

---

[11] Inheritance Tax Code, Art. 162 *bis*.

[12] Royal Decree n° 187, Art. 4 as introduced by Art. 7A of the Law of 23 October 1991.

[13] Circular Letter of 29 November 1993 (Bull. Contr., n° 733, p 3305, n° 40).

effect (i.e. as of the commencement of the coordination centre's activities) if the centre has not employed, at the latest at the end of the two-year period following the commencement of its activities, the equivalent of at least 10 full-time employees. After the two-year period has elapsed, the tax concessions will be denied with effect from the financial year in which the coordination centre no longer meets the 10-employee requirement. Finally, the coordination centre will lose the benefit of the tax concessions if it ceases to be part of an international group, if its activities are taken over by a new centre (for example, as a result of a group restructuring), or if it ceases its activities due to its being wound-up.

2.4 Other advantages

Other advantages relating to the coordination centre regime concern (i) the availability of the special tax regime for certain foreign executives temporarily working in Belgium (with increased tax deductions); (ii) an exemption from the obligation to obtain work permits, professional cards and employment permits for foreign employees; and (iii) depending on the volume of cash flows between the coordination centre and abroad, special reporting obligations to the Belgian-Luxembourg Foreign Exchange Institute.

3 Code of Conduct

On 1 December 1997, the Council of Ministers adopted a Code of conduct calling for the removal of tax measures which are potentially harmful because they establish a tax level lower than the normal tax level of the State concerned and thus have a significant effect on where economic activities are located.

Deviation from generally accepted transfer pricing principles, including the OECD guidelines, was included in the criteria for considering a tax regime harmful.

The Council noted that some of the tax measures could be considered State aid and acknowledged a commitment on the part of the Commission to publish guidelines on the application of State aid rules to measures in the field of direct business taxation and to examine or re-examine existing or new tax regimes while securing coherence and equality in the application of the Treaty.

4 State Aid Action

On 10 December 1998, the Commission published a notice on the application of State aid rules to measures relating to direct business taxation[14].

A tax measure would be considered aid if it:

- provided an advantage relieving the recipient from a tax charge;
- granted the advantage through State resources, including a loss of tax revenue;
- affected competition and trade between Member States, the mere strengthening of a firm's position vis-à-vis its competitors being sufficient in that respect;
- was selective in favouring certain undertakings or the production of certain goods, if the selectivity was not justified by the nature or general scheme of the tax system.

5 Code of Conduct Report

On 23 November 1999, the Working Group on the Code of conduct, headed by Ms. Dawn Primarolo, delivered its report.

It listed under various headings the tax measures considered harmful. As regards intra- group services, provided under cost-plus or resale minus methods, it took into account the following features:

- possibility of obtaining a comparable uncontrolled price;
- failure to examine the facts of the case and to review the margin regularly against normal commercial criteria;
- requirement for the beneficiary to be part of an international group;
- reduction of the expense base used to determine taxable income[15].

The Belgian coordination centres were included under title A001, thereby "leading the band".

---

14 OJ C 384, 10 December 1998, p 3. See Schön, Taxation and State Aid Law in the European Union, *CMLR* 1999, p 911; Rossi/Maccanico, State Aid Review of Member States, Measures Relating to Direct Business Taxation, *ESTAL* 2004, p 229.

15 Report (SN 4901/99), p 15, No. 43. For a decision of the "harmfulness" of Coordination centres, see Malherbe/Neirynck, National Report Belgium, in Schön (ed) *Tax Competition in Europe* (2003) p 187; Malherbe, Harmful Tax Competition and the Future of Financial Centres in the European Union, *Intertax* 2002, p 219.

6 State Aid Procedure before the Commission

In 1999, the Commission initiated vis-à-vis Belgium the cooperation procedure applying to existing State aid[16].

On 27 February 2002, the Commission initiated the formal procedure under Article 88 (2) EC[17].

The action of the Commission was determined by the deviation from OECD guidelines on the cost-plus method:

- significant costs (financial charges and staff costs) were excluded from the tax base;
- the profit margin was generally set at 8 %, regardless of the work actually performed.

The taxable income so calculated was unlikely to coincide with income determined under ordinary tax law.

The same held true for the exemptions from property tax, withholding tax and capital duty[18].

7 Reasoning

We shall look first at the substantive reasoning which the Commission followed to consider the coordination centres regime State aid[19]. [the structure of the headings is not logical – 8 should be a sub-heading of 7, etc.]

8 Economic Advantage

Applying the rules stated in the 1998 notice, the Commission determined first that an economic advantage was indeed granted to the beneficiaries.

9 Exemption from Property Tax

The exemption from property tax may be of no use to a tenant[20] and may be available to other companies, for instance those located in employment areas which are being judged to have high unemployment levels.

---

16 OJ L 83, 27 March 1999, p 1, Comments in Pinto, *Tax Competition and EU law*, Thesis (2002), Amsterdam, p 136.

17 OJ C 147, 20 June 2002, p 2.

18 Decision of 17 February 2003; OJ L 282, 30 October 2003, p 28 at 23.

19 Commission Decision of 17 February 2003 on the aid scheme implemented by Belgium for coordination centres established in Belgium (2003/755/EC); OJ L 282, 30 October 2003, p 25.

20 According to the Belgian Government, no more than 5 % of the centres own their premises.

Derogations are, however, not the rule as the Belgian Government put it. Besides, the Decision which found the regime of employment areas to be compatible with Article 92 stated first that the exemptions foreseen fell under the prohibition.

10 Exemption from Capital Duty

The same held true for the exemption from capital duty. Although other exemptions exist, the rule is the levy of the tax and not the exemption.

Directive 69/335/EC of 17 July 1969 concerning indirect taxes on the raising of capital[21] as amended by the Act of Accession of Austria, Finland and Sweden, states that exemptions predating 1 July 1984 will be maintained. The Commission failed to consider whether the regime was compatible with the Directive as it held that the aid was incompatible with the Treaty[22].

11 Exemption from Withholding Tax

The exemption from withholding tax is also an advantage. Although other exemptions exist and "professional investors" are in many cases exempt from withholding tax on interest received[23], withholding remains the rule.

The Commission found three instances in which a payer other than a coordination centre would have to withhold. These are when:

- income is paid to company established in a country which has no tax treaty with Belgium;
- income is paid to a Belgian or EU company which does not meet the criteria of the Parent-Subsidiary Directive;
- income is paid to a company in a treaty country when Belgium is entitled to withhold, even at a rate lower than the domestic rate.

There is clearly a certain amount of confusion in the Commission's analysis.The second case relates only to dividends and not to interest, although the Directive on the payment of interest and royalties between associated companies has changed the picture in the meantime.

21 OJ L 249, 3 October1969, p 25.

22 Decision, at 116.

23 On deposits, for instance.

The third case seems to be out of place: even if a country has the right to withhold, it may waive this right in certain economic circumstances: such a waiver exists in Belgium for interest paid by Belgian banks to foreign banks.

Insofar as payments to non-residents are, subject to certain conditions, exempt from withholding tax, this is not relevant in an analysis of tax benefits granted to companies and not to non-resident individuals.

For a Belgian corporate recipient, the absence of withholding is compensated by the need to make advance payments of tax if it wants to avoid a tax increase.

However, unlike withholding tax, those payments can be made at selected dates.

They concern only profit-making companies. A loss-making company subject to withholding tax would have to wait for a refund.

The absence of withholding tax is a benefit to foreign companies which are unable to obtain a credit or a refund in their home country for the foreign tax.

12 Notional Withholding Tax

The notional withholding tax – a credit granted for the withholding which had not taken place – has been reduced to zero in 1991. However, the measure is still in the books and can still apply to long-term loans predating 1991.

13 Cost-plus Assessment

The exclusion from the cost-plus tax base of staff and financial costs is a major concern as these are an essential contribution to the earning of revenue. A profit margin would, therefore, be required under the OECD transfer pricing guidelines.

A comparison cannot be made with companies which are not permanent establishments. Most coordination centres are either permanent establishments or subsidiaries which not only pass on income and expenses but also have a tax base of their own.

The 8 % on cost has indeed been applied in Belgium since 1964 to permanent establishments which had activities making it impossible to determine an accounting profit (control centres, headquarters …). But this was applied to full cost, without exclusion.

The flat base is disadvantageous for a centre that might make a loss. A loss is unlikely for activities such as those of coordination centres, which the Commission too restrictively labels as preparatory or ancillary, a characterisation which could not apply to financing[24].

It is also true that the tax benefit is offset by worldwide taxation in countries which apply it[25]. Finland, Germany and the United States are cited. This is a minority.

The flat tax on staff is restricted to the first 10 staff members. It is not the equivalent of the inclusion of staff costs in the tax base.

The tax base charge does not approximate the prices which would be obtained under free competition as the OECD rules require.

14 Use of State Resources

State Resources are used as Belgium forfeits revenue. The fact that the scheme attracted taxpayers in general cannot be taken into account. The assessment is made on an individual basis. Otherwise, any form of aid could be justified.

15 Distortion of Competition and Adverse Effect on Trade between Member States

The scheme distorts competition and affects trade between Member States. The centres strengthen their competitive position in the sector of services and compete with financial, trust and consulting organisations.

The Commission cannot be expected to it look into comparable systems which may exist in other Member States[26].

It may be true that multinational companies concentrate service provision within a group, including cash-flow management and financing, and may establish such a central unit anywhere. But here the problem is their setting up under a favourable tax regime. Also, the competitors of multinationals are not only other multinationals, but also smaller or local firms.

---

24 Decision, at 92.

25 Compare Kirkpatrick/Garabedian, *Le régime fiscal des sociétés en Belgique*, 3rd edition (2003) p 516.

26 Compare Luja, *Assessment and Recovery of Tax Incentives in the EC and the WTO: A view on State Aids, Trade Subsidies and Direct Taxation* (2003) p 37-38.

Even if the financial institutions determine the conditions made to the group on the basis of a global analysis, not taking into account the existence of a coordination centre, the tax benefits granted strengthen the position of the group and give it access to more favourable conditions.

16 Selectivity

The scheme is selective because it applies only to large multinational groups under specific criteria.

It is true that the tax administration has few discretionary powers in granting approval[27]. The systematic application of the low 8 % rate set out in the applicable tax circular is, however, the exercise of discretion.

17 Justification on Grounds of the Nature or Structure of the System

The nature or structure of the tax system does not "rescue" the scheme.

Withholding tax is a form of taxation and not, as claimed, a tax on persons – natural or legal – who do not have to report income.

Withholding creates a risk of international double taxation: this is true for all enterprises. The risk is minimised by the Belgian network of tax treaties.

The selectivity as applied to withholding may be similar to the effect of the Parent-Subsidiary and Interest and Royalties Directives. The very adoption of those Directives harmonises tax rules in Member States: Those rules can no longer be attributed to one Member State and constitute State aid.

Besides, smaller groups having head offices are excluded from the scheme.

18 Decision

The scheme does not meet any of the conditions making it compatible with the common market. It is in the nature of general operating aid.

The principle of legitimate expectations means that centres holding an approval in 2000 will continue to benefit from the scheme until the end of

27 For instance, insurance and reinsurance activities are excluded because insurance legislation does not allow insurance companies to engage in other activities.

their approval period but at the latest until 2010. The centres have made investments and have entered into contracts based on the prior approval of the schemes.

No renewal will be granted if no justified expectation of such renewal existed.

19 Belgium's Appeal

The Belgian Government and Forum 187, the association of coordination centres, filed appeals to the ECJ against the Commission Decision of 17 February 2003 on the aid scheme implemented by Belgium for coordination centres.

To date this appeal is still pending (September 2005).

20 Suspension

The Belgian Government and Forum 187 also requested a suspension of the Commission Decision in order for the Government to be able to grant renewals until the end of 2005.

The President of the ECJ granted the suspension by an order of 26 June 2003[28].

Procedure before the Council

In the meantime, the Belgian Government filed an application to the Council on 26 May 2005. According to Article 88.2 EC, the Council has the power to decide unanimously that aid, in derogation from Article 87, is compatible with the common market, provided such decision is justified by exceptional circumstances.

The purpose of the request was the grant of the possibility to apply until 31 December 2005 special treatment to coordination centres whose authorisations were due to expire between 17 February 2003 and 31 December 2005.

This would partially overrule the Decision of the Commission of 17 February 2003 and bring the situation within the framework of the outcome of the Council meeting of 26 and 27 November 2000, in which conclusions on the rollback of potentially harmful arrangements were

[28] ECJ 26 June 2003, C-182/03 *Belgium v Commission* [2003] ECR I-6887.

approved, whereby their effects on enterprises subject to such arrangements on 31 December 2000 would cease on 31 December 2005 at the latest.

Belgium had granted to those undertakings temporary but renewable authorisations expiring before 1 January 2006.

The Council considered, by a Decision of 16 July 2003, that exceptional circumstances existed, warranting the granting of the aid[29].

The multinational groups involved had made considerable investments in the centres and might, without the aid, be obliged to cease operating in Belgium, with negative economic and social repercussions for Belgium.

The aid was temporary and intended to prevent an irreversible loss of financial business and jobs to Belgium, and to enable Belgium to introduce other measures for giving the groups involved the possibility to reorganise their investments.

The denial of such temporary aid might lead to a collapse of the multinationals' confidence in Belgium and have economic repercussions in the long term.

The temporary aid was unlikely to distort competition as the Commission Decision allowed existing arrangements to be maintained until expiry dates falling after 31 December 2005 and deadlines had been granted for special arrangements to other Member States until 31 December 2010.

21 Appeal of the Commission

The Commission filed an appeal to the ECJ against the Council Decision on the following grounds:

- lack of Council competence, since the Council has only an exceptional power, subject to strict limitations;
- abuse of power and procedure, in that the exceptional power of the Council was used to neutralise a decision of the Commission and obtain the same effect as a judgment of nullification of the Court of Justice;
- infringement of the power of the Commission and the Court, particularly the institutional balance established by the Treaty;

[29] Council Decision of 16 July 2003 on the granting of aid by the Belgian Government to certain coordination centres established in Belgium (2003) 531/EC; OJ L 184, 23 July 2003, p 17. See the criticism of Luja, Harmful Tax Policy: When Political Objectives Interfere with State Aid Rules, *Intertax* 2003, p 484.

- violation of State aid law and Directive 69/335/EC;
- manifest error of judgement and abuse of power as to the presence of exceptional circumstances[30].

The appeal is pending (September 2005).

22 State Aid Procedure in respect of a New Scheme

Finally, on 16 May 2002 the Belgian Government proposed to the Commission a new scheme for coordination centres, implemented by Article 290 of the Law of 24 December 2002 amending the system for companies with regard to income taxes and instituting a system of advance rulings on tax matters[31]. The date for the entry into force of the provisions was to be fixed by Royal Decree.

After discussion, the Commission approved the scheme subject to certain commitments by Belgium[32].

On 23 April 2003, the Commission approved the main aspects of the new scheme[33].

Only centres approved in advance by Royal Decree that are part of a multinational group meeting size criteria, would qualify. They may conduct certain activities only and only for the benefit of group members.

Approval or renewal is granted for 10 years. The cost-plus method is applied to each centre individually, by an advance ruling of the Federal Public Service Finance – a new name for the Federal Department of Finance- , valid for five years and published without identifying the group by name.

The taxable income would be determined by a flat rate corresponding to a percentage of all operating expenditures, without exception.

Vis-à-vis the previous regime, the major differences are:

- the determination of the cost-plus percentage on a case-by-case basis;

---

30 OJ C, 15 November 2003, p 35.

31 Moniteur Belge, 31 December 2002, 2nd edition, p 58817.

32 Commission Decision of 8 September 2004 concerning the aid scheme which Belgium is proposing to implement for coordination centres (2005/378/EC); OJ L 125, 18 May 2005, p 10.

33 OJ C 209, 4 September 2003, p 2.

– the inclusion of personnel and financial costs in the cost-plus tax base[34].

Also, the annual tax would be creditable against the centre's tax liability, but not refundable.

The notional tax credit is abolished.

The Commission initiated the State aid procedure in respect of three provisions which were subject of commitments by the Belgian Government.

The exemptions from withholding tax would be removed and replaced by general exemption or reduction measures.

A Royal Decree of 16 May 2003 introduced a withholding tax exemption on interest paid to non-resident with savings deposits[35] in "intra-group banks", i.e. companies supplying exclusively or chiefly financial services to group members, a definition broader than the category of coordination centres.

The same would be true for the exemption from capital duty. This duty will be abolished from 1 January 2006.

The Commission was still critical. Belgium then exempted from withholding interest paid by professional investors[36] to banks located in the EEA or in countries with which Belgium has a double tax treaty. This was done by a Royal Decree of 3 July 2005, which retroactive effect from 5 June 2003[37].

The general exemption applies only to interest on debt claims and loans.

The special exemption applying to intra-group banks applies not only to interest on loans but also to interest on nominative bonds.

Under the initial scheme, if abnormal and gratuitous advantages were granted to the centre, they formed, together with non-deductible expens-

[34] Minne/Douénias, *Planification internationale des sociétés belges* (2004) p 503; Malherbe/De Wolf/Schotte, *Les centres de coordination après la réforme fiscale belge pour 2003, l'Année fiscale Paris* (2004) p 184; Vanhaute, *Belgium in International Tax Planning* (2004) p 288; Malherbe/Faes, *Business Operation in Belgium*, 953 T.M. Portfolio, Washington, D.C. (2005) p A-129.

[35] Non-resident savers include non-residents, individuals or corporations, who have not invested their funds in a Belgian business (R.D.-C.I.T., Art 105, 5).

[36] Professional investors include business, whether incorporated or not, and Belgian establishments of non-residents (R.D.-C.I.T., Art 105, 3).

[37] R.D.-C.I.T., Art 107, §2, 5, a (new).

es, an alternative tax base, whereas under general tax law, such advantages are added to the tax base of the recipient.

Belgium agreed that such advantages would be added to the cost-plus tax base of coordination centres.

23 General Replacement Measure: Notional Interest

Finally, the Belgian Government gave up on coordination centres. As a general replacement measure, it introduced a tax deduction for equity, also labelled as deduction of notional interest[38].

The deduction, effective from tax year 2007 (normally accounting year 2006), amounts to a percentage of equity (capital, share premium, retained earnings), after deduction of certain assets.

For instance, participations in the form of fixed assets and net assets of permanent establishments in treaty countries will be excluded to avoid a double deduction.

The percentage of deduction will be determined according to the average interest rate of 10-year Belgian treasury notes without exceeding 6.5 % (in 2005, 3.5 %).

Certain companies are excluded, e.g. coordination centres still enjoying the old regime.

The measure applies to Belgian companies and branches of foreign companies.

24 Conclusion

Given the circumstances, the question whether the coordination centre regime constitutes State Aid will become largely moot and will be relevant only for the transitional period during which the Commission and the Belgian Government were in disagreement.

[38] Law of 22 June 2005 introducing a tax deduction for capital at risk, Moniteur Belge, 30 June 2005; Vanpeteghem/Van Hove, Belgian Parliament Approves Bill on Notional Interest Deduction, 32 *TPIR* 2005, No. 7, p 13.

II The Kerckhaert-Morres Case (C-513/04)

Denial by Belgium of the notional foreign tax credit to foreign dividends

Belgian taxpayers, a married couple, received a dividend from French sources followed by a reimbursement of the French tax credit (avoir fiscal) which is also to be considered a dividend and is subject to a French withholding tax of 15 %. When dividends were taxable in Belgium under the global income tax, at the normal tax rates, a notional tax credit of 15 % was granted on account of the foreign withholding under domestic law. Tax treaties signed by Belgium confirmed, in one way or another, the domestic regime.

The treaty signed with France on 10 March 1964 granted Belgian recipients of French dividends or the notional tax credit under the conditions foreseen by Belgian legislation (Tax treaty between Belgium and France, Article 19, A 1, § 2).

Starting in 1984, Belgium refrained from taxing capital income of individual taxpayers under the global income tax. When such income, in the form of dividends, interest or royalties, was from Belgian sources, the payor had to withhold the "précompte mobilier" of 25 %, later reduced in many instances to 15 %. The income then no longer had to be reported.

When the recipient was not subject to withholding tax, for instance because the income was paid abroad, he had to report the income which was taxed at the same original rate, of 25 % or 15 %, plus municipal surcharge.

Given the modest amount of income tax due, the law abolished the notional foreign tax credit for foreign capital income received by individual taxpayers. The credit was later abolished for dividends received by individuals and shares which were professional assets invested in a business (Law of 23 October 1991).

The situation of a Belgian taxpayer is thus different when he receives income from Belgian or from foreign stock, as the following example shows:

	Belgian shareholders of French company	Belgian shareholder of Belgian company
Dividend	739.50	739.50
French withholding tax, 15 %	–130.50	–
– 25 % Belgian tax	–152.25	–184.88
Net dividend	**456.75**	**554.62**

Before the Court of First Instance of Ghent, the taxpayers argued that this was a violation of Article 56 EC guaranteeing the free movement of capital. By a judgment of 1 December 2004, the Court directed to the European Court of Justice the question whether Article 56.1 prohibited a domestic provision under which dividends on shares of companies established in the country and dividends on shares of companies established abroad were subject to a uniform tax rate but for dividends from foreign sources no credit was granted for tax withheld at source in the other country.

The Belgian taxpayers submitted their observations to the Court. They first pointed out that the comparison concerns only the dividend after it has left the company and that the tax treatment of the company has no bearing on the discussion. The question to be examined is whether the Belgian shareholder who invests in a French company is taxed more heavily than the Belgian shareholder who invests in a Belgian company.

The plaintiffs demonstrated first that the receipt of dividends falls within the movement of capital under Article 56 EC. Movements of capital include financial transactions which aim at investment and not at the remuneration of a service.

The list in annex 1 of Directive 88/361 of 24 June 1988 implementing the old Article 67 EEC is still relevant. Although the payment of dividends is not on the list, the Court has held that it is a capital transaction because it is connected with other forms of capital movements covered by the Directive: the acquisition of a participation in an enterprise in order to create lasting economic ties or the acquisition of securities quoted on a stock exchange.

The taxpayers went on to demonstrate that the denial of the notional tax credit by Belgium is a restriction of the free movement of capital, which is incompatible with Article 56 EC.

French companies will have more difficulty to find capital on the Belgian capital market. Their shares will be less attractive to a Belgian investor than the shares of a Belgian company.

Either of the two consequences is sufficient for there to be a restriction of the free movement of capital. In various decisions, the Court has found that measures discriminating between domestic and foreign dividends from EU Member States for the avoidance of economic double taxation are contrary to Article 57. The same is true for a measure, such as the present one, which discriminates in the field of juridical international double taxation.

When drafting the recent Savings Directive, the European legislator opted for a withholding tax on interest paid to residents of other EU countries in countries which had elected to apply such withholding (Belgium, Luxembourg, Austria). A residence country would be compelled to credit this withholding, which means that this was necessary under the free movement of capital.

Is there a grounds of justification which would make an obstacle to capital movement acceptable?

Article 58 I A EC Treaty, indeed allows, notwithstanding Article 56, Member States to apply the relevant provisions of their tax law, which distinguish between taxpayers who are not in the same situation with regard to their place of residence or with regard to the place where their capital is invested. Prima facie, the measure would be justified because capital is invested in France and not in Belgium. However, Article 58.3 states that the measures and procedures mentioned in paragraph 1 may not constitute the means of arbitrary discrimination or a disguised restriction on the free movement of capital and payments as defined in Article 56.

A difference in treatment must relate to situations which are not objectively comparable and must be justified by overriding reasons of general interest.

The taxpayers emphasised that their situation and the situation of taxpayers receiving Belgian dividends shows no objective difference: in both cases, dividends are taxed under an analytical or schedular system, separately from other income and at a flat rate. Because of the denial of the credit, French dividends are then subject to a higher tax burden than Belgian dividends.

This is not to be attributed to the French withholding, which is allowed by the Treaty. The Treaty, in conformity with the OECD Model Convention, leaves it to the state of residence to avoid double taxation and makes it an obligation.

The Communication of the Commission of 19 December 2003 stated that a Member State fails to apply the Treaty if it does not avoid juridical double taxation on dividends from an EU Member State.

Member States must exercise the taxation rights conferred upon them by a treaty in conformity with the rules aiming at the realisation of the internal market.

No reason of general interest can be put forward by Belgium; in particular, the cohesion of the tax system may not be used as justification grounds. This cohesion implies that a tax charge is compensated by a tax benefit. In the present situation, there is no compensating benefit.

Besides, in the field of interest and royalties, Belgium does grant a foreign tax credit, which is notional for royalties and equal to the real tax withheld abroad for interest. Coherence would warrant the same treatment for dividends.

Also, when domestic dividends are received and the tax rate is lower than the withholding tax, the withholding tax may be imputed in the form of a credit against domestic tax.

Written observations were filed in the procedure.

The European Commission is of the same opinion as the taxpayers.

The Kingdom of Belgium argued that, as long as Belgian shareholders of French companies are entitled to a tax credit for the company tax paid in France (avoir fiscal) they receive a higher return on an investment in French stock than an investment in Belgian stock. The following example illustrates this:

	French dividend	Belgian dividend
Gross dividend	1000.00	1000.00
French withholding (15 %)	–150.00	
	850.00	
Tax credit	500.00	
French withholding	–75.00	
	425.00	
Total subject to Belgian tax	1275.00	1000.00
Belgian tax (25 %)	–318.75	–250.00
Net dividend after tax	956.25	750.00

The Belgian government further states very simply that Belgian dividends are subject to withholding, 15 % or 25 %, whereas French dividends are subject to income tax at the same rate of 25 %. It therefore sees no discrimination.

The solution for the problem of the imputation of the notional tax credit in Belgium will be influenced by three recent decisions of the Court of Justice which have disallowed national discrimination concerning either the treatment of dividends or the treatment of the purchase of shares.

Until 2002, Austria applied a final levy of 25 % to dividends distributed by Austrian companies. Dividends from other States were always subject to the global income tax, which is the ordinary income tax reduced by half.

This distinction was considered an obstacle to the free movement of capital (Article 56, EC). Tax coherence was invoked by the Austrian Government but was set aside. Coherence lies within the avoidance of double taxation[39].

In order to avoid economic double taxation, Finland granted, its residents a tax credit equal to 29.70 % of the amount of dividends distributed by a Finnish company to an individual. A taxpayer received dividends from a Swedish company and claimed that the denial of the credit was a restriction to the free movement of capital.

Once more, the argument of coherence, in the form of the correlation between the tax benefit and the corporate tax levied in Finland, was set aside.

Similarly, the justification of general interest and loss of tax receipts was denied[40].

Finally, in the same line as previous decisions, the Court considered that Luxembourg could not grant a tax rebate for the purchase of shares solely in the event of the purchase of shares of Luxembourg companies, excluding the purchase of Belgian shares[41].

---

39 ECJ 15 July 2004, C-315/02 *Lenz* [2004] ECR I-7063.

40 ECJ 7 September 2004, C-319/02 *Manninen* [2004] ECR I-7477.

41 ECJ 15 July 2004, C-242/03 *Weidert and Paulus* [2004] ECR I-7379; see also ECJ 6 June 2000, C-35/98 *Verkooijen* [2000] ECR I-4071; Ilhi/Malmer/Schonewille/Tuominen, Dividend Taxation in the European Union, *Cahiers de Droit fiscal international*, vol 83A, Trends in Company – Shareholder taxation: single or double taxation?, p 81; Communication from the Commission to the Council, the European Parliament and the European Economic and Social Committee, Dividend taxation of individuals in the Internal Market, 19 December 2003, Com 2003 (810 final).

One may therefore expect a confirmation by the Court of the views of the Belgian reporter to the Sydney Congress of the International Fiscal Association: the imposition of the foreign withholding tax and the Belgian proportional tax is "the main cause of double taxation … which leads the Belgian shareholder to prefer investing in a Belgian company" (our translation)[42].

[42] Malherbe, Ph., Belgian International Fiscal Association 2003, Sydney Congress, op. cit. p 204; see also EFTA Court 23 November 2004, E-1/04 *Fokus Bank ASA*, *Tijdschrift voor Fiscaal Recht* 2005, p 319; Vanden Berghe, Naar een interne markt zonder internationale juridische en economische dubbele belasting, *Tijdschrift voor Fiscaal Recht* 2005, p 271; Larking, Fokus Bank: the end of withholding tax as we know it, *EC Tax Review* 2005, p 69.

III Commission v Belgium (C-433/04)

Infringement procedure against Belgium – Obligation on principals and contractors using co-contractors not registered in Belgium to deduct and to pay to the tax administration 15 % of the amount owed for the work carried out and incur joint liability for these co-contractors' tax debts in Belgium

The freedom to provide services is central to this case combined with, on the one hand, the justification of discrimination or an impediment by the need to fight tax fraud and, on the other hand, the proportionality of the measures adopted to achieve this objective.

1 Applicable Belgian Law

With the aim of fighting tax fraud[43], Belgian law requires principals using contractors not registered in Belgium, or contractors using sub-contractors not registered in Belgium in the construction sector, to:

- be jointly and severally liable for the payment of a non-registered contractor's tax debts up to a limit of 35 % of the total cost of the work, and
- deduct 15 % from the amount owed to the contractor, which is subsequently paid to the Belgian authorities (failing which, an administrative fine may be imposed for double this amount).

2 Alleged Incompatibility with EU Law

In line with standard practice, it is necessary to analyse this type of case in three stages:

1) Is there discrimination or an impediment?
2) If so, can it be justified by an overriding reason of general interest (in this case, the need to fight tax fraud) and
3) If so, are the measures in proportion to the objective sought?

2.1 Is there discrimination or an impediment to the freedom to provide services?

Assuming that it is possible to consider that the provisions of Belgian law indiscriminately apply to all service providers (since the obligations are

[43] These measures were also initially aimed at fighting fraud in relation to the payment of social security contributions but this is no longer the case.

imposed on all persons who contract with a non-registered contractor or sub-contractor, whether Belgian or not, although it is highly probable that the majority of businesses not registered in Belgium are not established there), it appears to be very difficult to object to the fact that the law in question is not likely to discourage principals or contractors from using businesses not registered in Belgium and acts as an impediment for the latter to offering services in Belgium.

2.2 Is this justifiable?

Belgium invoked the combating of tax fraud, which the ECJ has held may justify interference in the exercise of fundamental freedoms of movement. However, the ECJ has very strictly limited this possibility by stating that it may only be invoked vis-à-vis laws specifically targeted at excluding from entitlement to tax benefits purely artificial structures solely aimed at circumventing the tax law[44]. Therefore, any legislation creating a general presumption of tax evasion or fraud, for a given type of operation, whether by forming a foreign branch[45], establishing the parent company's registered office in another Member State for any reason whatsoever[46] or transferring an individual's tax residence outside a given Member State[47] is not permitted.

Belgian law clearly appears to fall within the second category. The two measures clearly form an integral part of a wider system aimed at fighting tax fraud. According to the Belgian authorities, the success of this objective is obviously linked to the pressing need for the fight against tax fraud to be indiscriminately conducted in the whole sector.

In addition to this stated objective, other aspects of Belgian law appear to establish a kind of general presumption of fraud in the given sector. In particular, the obligation to deduct 15 % from the amount owed to the co-contractor, which in theory is aimed at guaranteeing tax debts incurred by non-registered co-contractors (direct tax debts, debts in relation to tax deductions at source from employees' salaries and foreign tax debts for which the Belgian authorities' assistance is requested), applies even though service providers not registered in Belgium are practically never liable for the aforementioned taxes there.

---

44 ECJ 16 July 1998, C-264/96 *ICI* [1998] ECR I-4695, para 26.

45 ECJ 16 July 1998, C-264/96 *ICI* [1998] ECR I-4695, para 26.

46 ECJ 21 November 2002, C-436/00 *X and Y* [2002] ECR I-10829; and 12 December 2002, C-324/00 *Lankhorst-Hohorst* [2002] ECR I-11779.

47 ECJ 11 March 2004, C-9/02 *de Lasteyrie du Saillant* [2004] ECR I-2409.

Moreover, Belgian law provides that the 15 % deduction is also to be allocated to VAT debts, whereas service providers not registered and not established in Belgium are not liable for VAT on services provided, except in exceptional circumstances.

Nevertheless, it should be pointed out that service providers from other Member States may have direct tax or VAT debts in Belgium in exceptional cases (for instance, long-term construction projects, which are treated as permanent establishments subject to tax in Belgium or, alternatively, in the event foreign employees work in Belgium for more than 183 days or live in Belgium, in which case the tax deduction at source is owed, etc). However, the provisions of Belgian law do not in the least exclusively apply to these relatively exceptional cases. Although it is impossible to completely rule out the possibility of tax debts being incurred by service providers from other Member States, it is necessary to point out that the 15 % deduction is always, without any exception, imposed in order to guarantee the payment of very exceptional tax debts. Is the existence of exceptional cases sufficient to justify Belgian law? This issue will be raised in the discussion on proportionality, which should also be a key factor in the assessment of the compatibility of the second measure provided for by Belgian law with EC law, namely, the principal's and contractor's automatic joint and several liability in the event a service provider fails to pay its tax obligations in Belgium. In this respect, it can be noted that by definition joint liability may only be incurred in the event a service provider has tax debts in Belgium.

2.3 Proportionality

ECJ case law does not very often apply the proportionality principle with regard to direct taxation. The ECJ very regularly concludes its rulings by finding that no justification at all exists for the discrimination or for the impediment. Occasionally, it relies on the proportionality principle to corroborate its finding regarding the lack of sufficient justification[48]. The ECJ accepted the justification for a Luxembourg law in a case[49] by the need to improve the efficiency of tax controls, but sanctioned one of its provisions on the basis of the lack of proportionality.

[48] See above.

[49] ECJ 15 May 1997, C-250/95 *Futura* [1997] ECR I-2471.

With regard to the 15 % deduction, the discussion relating to proportionality will focus on the issue of whether the general application of the 15% deduction does not significantly exceed the objective aimed at guaranteeing tax debts incurred and, whether alternatively less restrictive measures could be adopted for the limited cases where non-registered service providers incur tax debts.

It seems difficult to justify a general obligation based on very rare individual cases.

Moreover, in these individual cases, would not alternative, less restrictive measures be just as effective? In particular, possible alternatives could involve using the seizure technique or releasing principals or contractors from the deduction obligation, when they have received confirmation from the Belgian authorities that their co-contractors or sub-contractors do not have tax debts in Belgium. This system currently applies for social security debts in Belgium.

In this respect, it would also undeniably be possible to invoke the measures made available to the Member States by the Directives and Regulations on mutual administrative assistance, with which Member States must comply in relation to the collection of tax debts, whether by referring to Directive 77/799/ECC of 19 December 1977 on income tax or Regulation 1798/2003 of 7 October 2003 on VAT.

With regard to the automatic joint and several liability, this measure appears at first sight to be more proportionate insofar as, by definition, it only applies to non-registered co-contractors' existing tax debts.

However, it is necessary to point out that joint and several liability

- does not only relate to the co-contractors' tax debts for the work carried out for the principals and contractors deemed liable, but also applies to all tax debts for the tax years during which the work was carried out and even to previous tax years, which means that it may apply to tax debts relating to work carried out for other persons, and
- is automatically applied, regardless whether the principal or contractor has made the 15 % deduction or the principal or contractor committed fraud or was an accomplice in this respect, combined with the added complication for the principal or contractor deemed jointly and severally liable of having to check or object to the validity of the amounts claimed by the Belgian tax authorities from the co-contractor.

A final point for discussion regarding proportionality relates to determining whether the actual registration procedure could offer a proportionate alternative to the challenged measures.

There is no doubt that Belgium will argue that the registration procedure is very simple, that it requires minimal formalities, that a service provider established in another Member State could satisfy the legal conditions by producing equivalent documents issued by his/her/its home Member State and that this procedure is likely to achieve the expected objectives with regard to fighting tax fraud.

There is no doubt that the European Commission will attempt to demonstrate that the Belgian registration procedure is, on the contrary, a complicated measure for companies wishing to carry out services in Belgium on an occasional basis and that it will further point out that a Member State is not entitled to make the provision of services in its country contingent on compliance with all conditions applying to establishments. It will certainly emphasise that registration is not automatic but, on the contrary, allows a degree of discretion for the competent bodies, composed not only of State representatives but also representatives of competitors in the given sector and of employee trade unions. The fact that the procedure generally takes between six months and one year, which represents a major obstacle for foreign service providers, will surely be raised during the discussions. The European Commission will probably also highlight the fact that real fraudsters can easily circumvent the registration procedure by finding a front man who has not yet been implicated in fraudulent activities and who, in view of his/her clean background, can obtain registration. In addition, registration does not act as a guarantee that the relevant contractor will effectively pay any future tax debts, which will feed the debate regarding the inappropriateness of the registration formality since it consequently cannot achieve the objective of preventing fraud.

Finally, the European Commission can point out that less complicated measures than the registration procedure are more efficient. For instance, the application of Regulation 1798/2003 of 7 October 2003 on administrative mutual assistance in VAT matters enables Belgium to ask the State of the contractor's establishment whether the latter is in compliance with VAT obligations and to obtain the requested information in a shorter period than that required for the registration procedure.

Moreover, nothing prevents Belgium from making co-contractors solely liable for unpaid tax debts relating to work stipulated in the contract. This system could also apply to national and foreign operators and could also be more effective than the registration procedure, since co-contractors are released from all deductions and all liability under the Belgium system as soon as there is registration.

3 Status of the Proceedings

The written part of the procedure for this case has been completed. The ECJ has not decided yet to hold a hearing. Therefore, the ruling will not be delivered before 2006.

IV Commission v Belgium (C-522/04)

Infringement procedure against Belgium

This case challenges the incompatibility of Belgian law both with regard to the Treaty provisions (on free movement of workers, freedom of establishment, freedom to provide services and free movement of capital) and Council Directive 92/96/EEC on direct life insurance.

1 Applicable Belgian Law

Four Belgian rules are being challenged by the infringement procedure initiated by the European Commission against Belgium:

Pursuant to the Income Tax Code, employer's contributions to supplementary retirement and life insurance policies only constitute business expenses that can be deducted from the employer's taxable income if they are paid to an insurance company established in Belgium except if otherwise provided in some double tax treaties. Similarly, individual contributions to supplementary retirement and life insurance policies paid via the employer by means of salary deductions only trigger entitlement to tax relief under the same conditions as applying to employer contributions.

According to this Code, capital, share buy-backs and savings paid or allocated to a taxpayer who has previously transferred his/her domicile or registered office for his/her assets abroad are deemed to have been paid or allocated on the date prior to such transfer, which results in the obligation on all insurers to withhold income tax at source in the event the payment is made to a non-resident who was previously a Belgian tax resident at a given time.

This Code provides that in the event of a transfer of capital or buyback shares to a pension fund or an insurance company established abroad, such transfers always trigger the immediate taxation of the relevant amounts for the beneficiary of the group insurance or pension fund policy.

Finally, Belgian law provides that the annual tax on insurance policies, for which the insured persons are normally liable, must be paid by the insurance company on behalf of the insured person, if the insurance company is established abroad.

2 Incompatibility with EU Law

According to the European Commission, three breaches exist:

The first relates to the restriction on the freedom to provide services. This results from the limit on the deductibility of individual and employer contributions to professional retirement policies, in the event such contributions are paid abroad. This rule deters persons from taking out insurance policies with foreign companies and foreign companies from offering services on the Belgian market.

Moreover, the general and absolute obligation imposed on foreign insurance companies to appoint a representative domiciled in Belgium, who personally undertakes to pay the annual tax on the insurance policies is disproportionate since the tax payment may be guaranteed by alternative, less restrictive measures, such as requesting information from the foreign company or the Belgian resident insured person, or by applying for mutual assistance between Member States in direct and indirect tax matters pursuant to Directive 2003/93/EC of 7 October 2003, which modified Directive 77/799/EC.

Belgian law is also challenged with regard to the provisions of the 3rd Directive on life insurance (92/96/EEC) since pursuant to Article 4 of this Directive, authorisation granted in one Member State is valid for the entire European Community and allows a company to carry out business either via an establishment or through the free provision of services.

The European Commission also considers that Belgian law restricts the free movement of workers and the freedom of establishment since employees or businessmen who come to work in Belgium are not entitled to the tax benefits for contributions paid to professional retirement policies in the State from which they originate. Similarly, in the event, they want to move or set up business in another Member State, after having worked in Belgium, they are faced with obstacles if they wish to transfer capital or buy back shares abroad.

Moreover, the European Commission considers that the fiction whereby the payment or allocation of capital, share buy backs or savings occurs on the date before the transfer of the domicile or registered office for the assets abroad constitutes an unjustified breach of the freedoms afforded by Articles 39 and 43 of the EC Treaty.

It will be interesting to compare the ECJ's decision on this point with Advocate-General Leger's findings in the Van Hilten case C-513/03 of 5 July 2005. According to the Advocate-General, Dutch inheritance law, which provides for a deemed residence for all Dutch nationals, who die within ten years after leaving the Netherlands, does not constitute an impediment to the free movement of capital or freedom of establishment.

Finally, the European Commission considers that the Belgian provisions in question also constitute unjustified restrictions of the free movement of capital.

Belgium does not object to the various points above. It simply defended its position by stating that Belgian law is currently being adapted in order to comply with the Treaty and the Directive. Moreover, this announcement prompted the European Commission not to submit observations in reply.

Belgium has consequently neither objected to the fact that the relevant Belgian law is an impediment to the exercise of the freedoms of movement guaranteed by the EC Treaty nor attempted to demonstrate that any interference, if established, is justified by an overriding reason of general interest.

3 Status of the Proceedings

The written part of the procedure is completed. As the infringement is not being contested by Belgium, it is probable that there will not be a hearing. Therefore, the judgment could be handed down rather quickly.

It is necessary to point out that this case is similar in some respects to the Bachmann case, in which a Belgian law prohibiting the deduction of insurance contributions paid abroad was at stake. At the time, Belgium justified such interference with the freedom to provide services by the need to maintain the coherence of its tax system, which the ECJ accepted.

It should be noted that even in relation to the most similar aspect with the Bachmann case, namely the non-deductibility of individual contributions to supplementary insurance policies paid via the employer by means of salary deductions to an insurance company or pension fund established abroad, Belgium has not put forward any justification whatsoever.

V Denkavit (C-170/05)

Tax treatment by a Member State of dividends paid by a subsidiary established in this Member State to its parent company established in another Member State (outbound dividends)

The ECJ recently delivered decisions regarding the compatibility of national laws relating to the taxation of inbound dividends, i.e. dividends paid to a resident taxpayer by a company established in another Member State, with the provisions of the Treaty on the free movement of capital.

These decisions related to the Lenz and Manninen cases[50], where the Austrian shareholder in the first case and the Finnish shareholder in the second were only entitled to tax relief on the dividends if they were distributed by a company established in Austria or Finland.

The ECJ very clearly ruled that this was a restriction on the free movement of capital in two directions, since the relevant laws discouraged nationals from investing in companies established in other Member States and complicated the collection of capital by these companies in the relevant Member States, namely Austria and Finland.

Moreover, the ECJ held that these restrictions were not justified by the need to maintain the coherence of the national tax system. Although the challenged national law aimed at avoiding economic double taxation of company profits, firstly through corporate income tax imposed on the company and secondly through dividend tax imposed on the shareholder, the refusal to grant the Austrian or Finnish shareholder any tax relief could counter this stated objective if corporate income tax was paid by the dividend distributing company on its profits in its State of establishment. In a way, the ECJ beat the Austrian and Finnish legislators at their own game: if the objective was truly to avoid economic double taxation on profits, it would be just as necessary to grant a tax benefit to a shareholder who receives dividends from a foreign company taxed in another Member State as to a shareholder in a national company. The following point should not be forgotten in the Denkavit case: the ECJ clearly stated in the Manninen ruling (para. 46) that granting a tax credit to a shareholder who is primarily liable for tax in Finland and who holds shares in

[50] ECJ 15 July 2004, C-315/02 *Lenz* [2004] ECR I-7063; and 7 September 2004, C-319/02 *Manninen* [2004] ECR I-7477.

a company established in Sweden, which would be calculated based on the tax owed by this company for corporate income tax in the latter Member State, would not disturb the coherence of the Finnish tax system. In other words, if the Swedish company in this case did not pay corporate income tax or if Swedish corporate income tax was lower than the applicable tax in Finland, Finnish law could consequently adapt the tax benefit restricted to the Finnish shareholder.

The Denkavit case will give the ECJ the occasion to reach a decision on the national tax treatment of outbound dividends even though, given the facts, the case now only has a historical interest. This case relates to the tax years 1987 to 1998, i.e., prior to the implementation of the Parent-Subsidiary Directive, pursuant to which laws such those challenged in the Denkavit case were automatically incompatible with EC law. However, this case concerning the payment of dividends by French subsidiaries to the parent company established in the Netherlands remains very interesting for determining the correct tax treatment of outbound dividends

1 Applicable French Law

Under the French law at the time, a parent company resident in France was granted an almost total tax exemption on dividends received from a subsidiary and the latter did not apply any tax deduction at source.

For non-resident parent companies, although the French parent company system was not applicable to them and a tax deduction at source was applied upon the payment of the dividends, their situation varied under the double tax treaties concluded by France.

In this case, the treaty concluded with the Netherlands provided for a tax credit to be granted and a reduced rate deduction at source.

In particular, with regard to the Denkavit case, the parent company was not entitled to this tax credit and was not able to offset the tax deduction at source paid to the French tax authorities insofar as the Dutch parent company was exempt from dividend tax in the Netherlands and was in any event liable for less tax than the amount of the tax relief granted by the double tax treaty.

2 Incompatibility with EC law

2.1 Is there discrimination or an impediment to the free movement of capital?

Different treatment clearly seems to occur as a result of the imposition of a tax deduction at source on dividends distributed to a non-resident parent company, whereas such deduction does not exist for dividends distributed to a French resident parent company. In addition, this difference constitutes an impediment for companies resident in another Member State that may discourage them from creating subsidiaries in France. Even if resident companies were only taxed at a tax rate corresponding to the rate of the deduction at source, the foreign companies were at a disadvantage in terms of cash flow as they were obliged to pay the tax at an earlier date.

It is interesting at this stage to mention the EFTA Court's ruling in Fokus Bank ASA of 23 November 2004 (E–1/04, not yet published), which found Norwegian tax law to be incompatible with the Agreement on the European Economic Area. Under Norwegian tax law, Norwegian resident shareholders were entitled to a tax credit on dividend distributions by a Norwegian company, whereas non-resident shareholders were subject to a deduction at source by the distributing company and were not entitled to a tax credit. The EFTA Court considered that such different treatment discouraged non-residents from investing in Norwegian companies and added that the objective situations of residents and non-residents were comparable.

2.2 Is this obstacle justifiable?

It is difficult to see what justification traditionally invoked as an overriding reason of general interest could be put forward in this case, even if recent developments in ECJ case law on the concept of the coherence of the tax system may encourage parties to constantly reopen the debate on this matter.

However, this case raises another issue insofar as the French Conseil d'Etat expressly asked whether or not the national tax system's compatibility with EC law should be assessed with or without taking into consideration a tax treaty concluded by the given Member State with another Member State, in this case the Netherlands.

In other words, if the different treatment is completely neutralised because of the effects of the double tax treaty, would it still be incompatible with EC law?

We shall firstly assume in relation to this case that the effects of the treaty concluded with the Netherlands place French resident parent companies and Dutch resident parent companies on an equal footing from a tax standpoint.

In this respect, two arguments may conflict:

1. The first argument was raised in the EFTA Court's aforementioned ruling in the Fokus Bank case. To a certain extent, Norway not only justified the refusal to grant a tax credit to non-resident shareholders but also justified the tax deduction at source by the distributing company on grounds of the existence of double tax treaties with some countries. These treaties provide for a tax credit in the resident Member State and enable the tax deduction at source carried out in Norway to be offset. The EFTA Court dismissed this argument on the grounds that ECJ case law has always refused to take into account benefits available to non-residents in other Member States to justify obstacles or discrimination under national law.
2. The other argument hinted at to certain extent in the Manninen ruling and very clearly explained in Advocate General Kokott's opinion in the Bouanich case C-265/04 is that when assessing a national system's compatibility with EC law, it is necessary to take into account the entire national tax system, including the applicable provisions of double tax treaties. This would not involve justifying such treatment, as in the case of the Norwegian government before the EFTA Court, by other tax benefits available under other national laws that do not relate to the case in point, but rather considering the effects of the applicable law in France (including therefore the tax conventions) on concrete cases. In the case Denkavit, the double tax treaty with the Netherlands would therefore form part of the legal framework, which must be applied by the French Conseil d'Etat.

Therefore, France would not be able in this respect to "make unconditional rights afforded by the Treaty contingent on the provisions of a treaty concluded with a Member State"[51].

If the second argument is accepted, the ECJ would still have to check whether a different treatment is neutralised by the system provided for by the double taxation convention in the case in point (which does not appear

[51] ECJ 28 January 1986, 270/83 *Avoir Fiscal* [1986] ECR 273.

to be so in the Denkavit case to the extent that the treaty concluded with the Netherlands only provides for limited offsetting of the tax imposed on the Dutch company).

3 Status of the Proceedings

The reference of the French Conseil d'Etat was recorded by the ECJ on 8 February 2005.

The written observations of the parties, the European Commission and the Member States have been submitted to the ECJ but it has not yet decided whether a hearing will be held. Probably no decision can be expected before 2007.

Pending Cases involving Denmark: Commission v Denmark

Niels Winther-Sørensen

1 Existing Case Law of the Court of Justice

2 The Distinction between Tax-Privileged and Not Tax-Privileged Schemes

3 The Commission's Main Arguments

4 Discussion of the Commission's Arguments

4.1 Taxation of investment returns (appreciation in value) of pension schemes

4.2 Example

4.3 The impact of tax on the investment returns (appreciation in value) on the pension scheme

5 Implications of a Judgment Unfavourable to Denmark

The Danish Pension Tax Case (C-150/04)

The issue in the action brought by the Commission against the Kingdom of Denmark (Case C-150/04) is whether it is contrary to the provisions governing the fundamental freedoms enshrined in the EC Treaty that Denmark does not allow tax deductions for payments into foreign pension schemes but allows deductions for payments into Danish pension schemes.

1 Existing Case Law of the Court of Justice

In its judgment in the Bachmann case from 1992, the Court of Justice of the European Communities first addressed the question whether it was contrary to the provisions of the EC Treaty governing the free movement of workers and services to refuse to allow deduction for payments into foreign pension schemes.[1]

Mr Bachmann was a German national, who had moved from Germany to Belgium in order to live and work there. He continued to pay contributions in Germany under sickness and invalidity insurance contracts and a life assurance contract. These contracts had all been entered into before he moved to Belgium. According to Belgian tax law, payments into life insurance schemes may be deducted from occupational income. At the same time, amounts later paid out from such schemes are taxed, and therefore payments into foreign insurance schemes could not be deducted. Mr Bachmann argued that the refusal to allow deductions for payments into foreign schemes was discriminatory and contrary to the free movement of workers and the freedom to provide services, see (now) Articles 39 and 49 of the EC Treaty.

In its judgment the Court of Justice first stated (para 9) that rules like the Belgian ones will normally affect persons who have previously carried on an occupation in another Member State, and who subsequently move to Belgium in order to work. Such persons will normally have concluded their pension and life assurance contracts in their state of origin. As such persons are, as a general rule, nationals of their state of origin, it follows that there is a risk that the provisions in question operate to the particular detriment of foreign nationals. Even though the Belgian rules applied without distinction as to nationality (Mr Bachmann was fully liable to pay

1 ECJ 28 January 1992, C-204/90 *Bachmann* [1992] ECR I-249.

tax), the rules resulted in a hidden discrimination of foreign nationals, and this is, as a general rule, contrary to (now) Article 39 on the free movement of workers.

The Court also addressed the issue whether the non-deductibility was contrary to the provisions of the EC Treaty governing the freedom to provide services (now Article 49). These provisions intend to protect the right of foreign life assurance companies to sell life assurance contracts in Belgium.

The Court found that provisions requiring an insurer to be established in a Member State as a condition of the eligibility of insured persons to benefit from certain tax deductions operate to deter those insured from approaching insurers established in other Member States. Such a requirement constitutes a restriction of the freedom to provide services of such insurers (para 31).

According to the Court of Justice, the Belgian rules were not contrary to the provisions of the EC Treaty, as the Court found that the hidden discrimination was justified by the need to preserve the cohesion of the tax system. This cohesion was ensured by a connection between the deductibility of contributions and the liability to tax of payments etc. under the schemes, when at the same time payments etc. under such schemes are exempt from tax when there has been no deduction of contributions (paras 21 et seq).

Finally, the Court held that, as Community law stands at present, it is not possible to ensure the cohesion of such tax systems by means of measures that are less restrictive. Consequently, the rules were not contrary to the principle of proportionality (para 27).

Since the decision in the Bachmann case, the majority of cases dealing with direct taxes and the freedom of movement that have been heard by the Court of Justice have also dealt with the issue of fiscal cohesion. Even though it has accepted the relevance of the need to ensure cohesion, the Court has, in all its cases since its decision in the Bachmann case, refused to accept that the need to preserve the cohesion of the tax system could justify discrimination or a restriction.

In a Communication from 2001,[2] the Commission argued that the need to ensure the cohesion of the tax system cannot justify the failure to allow

2 COM(2001) 214.

tax deductions and tax exemptions for payments into foreign pension schemes. This implies that, in the opinion of the Commission, the Court of Justice will reach the opposite conclusion if an issue similar to that in the Bachmann case comes before the Court again.

As an important part of its argumentation, the Commission refers to the Wielockx case from 1995.[3] This case involved a person who was resident in Belgium and carried on work as a self-employed person in the Netherlands, the source state. As Mr Wielockx was only subject to limited tax liability in the Netherlands, the Dutch authorities did not grant him deductions for payments into a pension scheme. The Dutch government sought to justify the refusal of the deduction by reference to the need to preserve the cohesion of its tax system. The government argued that the tax treaty between the Netherlands and Belgium granted Belgium, the state of residence, the right to tax the pension benefits payable and therefore, there would not be the necessary connection between deduction and taxation if the Dutch authorities allowed Wielockx to deduct his contributions.

The Court of Justice dismissed that argument on the ground that the cohesion of the tax system was secured by the reciprocity provided by the tax treaty between the Netherlands and Belgium. The Court held (para 24):

> As the Advocate General observed in point 54 of his Opinion, the effect of double-taxation conventions which, like the one referred to above, follow the OECD model is that the State taxes all pensions received by residents in its territory, whatever the State in which the contributions were paid, but, conversely, waives the right to tax pensions received abroad even if they derive from contributions paid in its territory which it treated as deductible. Fiscal cohesion has not therefore been established in relation to one and the same person by a strict correlation between the deductibility of contributions and the taxation of pensions but is shifted to another level, that of the reciprocity of the rules applicable in the Contracting States.

The Commission notes that the majority of tax treaties between Member States grant the right to tax pension benefits to the state of residence, like the treaty concerned in the Wielockx case. Although individual Member States in their treaty negotiations seek to introduce source state taxing rights, not all of their tax treaties make such a provision.

---

3 ECJ 11 August 1995, C-80/94 *Wielockx* [1995] ECR I-2493.

The arguments put forward by the Commission seem logical and convincing. However, it is not yet clear whether the Court of Justice will accept the arguments in a case whose facts are similar to those addressed by the Court in the Bachmann case. In other words: Is the Court of Justice prepared to hold that the judgment in the Bachmann case is no longer valid case law?

2 The Distinction between Tax-Privileged and Not Tax-Privileged Schemes

The Danish rules distinguish between those schemes that are tax-privileged and those that are not.

The fundamental principle of tax-privileged schemes is that the time of taxation is deferred from the time of contribution to the time pension benefits are received. Accordingly, an employee does not pay tax on the share of his earnings that is paid as a contribution to a pension scheme, but the employee is liable to pay tax on the benefits received. The employer may treat the contribution as a deduction for tax purposes, whereas the employee is not liable to pay tax on the share of the pension contribution paid by the employer, nor his own share of the pension contribution.[4]

In the individual private pension schemes that enjoy the tax privilege, the contributor is entitled to tax relief on the contributions and liable to pay tax on the pension benefits. Consequently, the time of taxation is deferred from the time of contribution to the time the benefits are received in a manner similar to that applying to occupational pension schemes.

The tax-privileged schemes may be referred to as ET. Income paid into a pension scheme is exempt from tax or is deductible (i.e. E = Exempt), whereas pension benefits are taxable (i.e. T = Tax).

As for schemes that do not enjoy the tax privilege, no tax relief is granted on contributions and benefits are not subject to tax. In such schemes taxation is not deferred to the time when benefits are received. Such schemes may therefore be referred to as TE schemes (i.e. Tax-Exempt).

---

4 A modification of the principle of deferred taxation is the payment of an 8 % labour market contribution, which is payable during the time contributions are paid to a pension scheme, whereas the labour market contribution is not payable at the time of receipt of pension benefits.

Formally, no distinction is made between Danish and foreign pension schemes, but between those schemes that are tax-privileged (ET) and those that are not (TE). However, foreign pension institutions will not be able to satisfy the requirements for providing tax-privileged schemes (ET) unless they are established in Denmark. The Danish rules de facto affect foreign pension institutions.

Until 1998 the Danish pension tax rules resembled the rules applicable in Finland, which came before the Court of Justice in the Danner case decided in 2002.[5] Prior to 1998, periodical payments out of a pension scheme were subject to tax, irrespective of whether contributions were deductible or not (i.e. neither ET nor TE, but TT!). In its judgment in the Danner case, the Court of Justice held that the need for cohesion of the tax system could not justify such a system, and the failure to allow deductions for payments into a foreign scheme was contrary to Article 49 of the EC Treaty governing the freedom to provide services.

Before the Danner case, Denmark had amended the applicable law in 1998 to ensure the connection between non-deductibility of payments in and tax exemption on payments out.[6] In relation to the connection between deductibility and taxation, or non-deductibility and tax exemption, referred to by the Court in its judgment in the Bachmann case, the Danish rules are now very similar to the Belgian rules that were examined by the Court in the Bachmann case.

3 The Commission's Main Arguments

In its action against Denmark, the Commission argues that the Danish legislation concerning, inter alia, deductions for payments into life insurance and pension schemes is contrary to the provisions of the EC Treaty governing the freedom to provide services, the free movement of workers, right of establishment and the free movement of capital.

In relation to Articles 39 and 43 on the free movement of workers and the right of establishment, the Commission refers to the protection of workers and self-employed persons who move to Denmark. Such persons will (like Mr Bachmann in the Bachmann case) already have set up pension

5 ECJ 3 October 2002, C-136/00 *Danner* [2002] ECR I-8147.

6 See Danish Act no. 429 of 26 June 1998 amending sections 53A and 53B of the Danish Pension Tax Act. For a detailed discussion, see Winther-Sørensen in Skat Udland 2001, p 357.

schemes in other Member States and will therefore be particularly affected by the failure to allow deductions.

In relation to Article 49 on the freedom to provide services, the Commission argues that the failure to allow deductions and exemptions for payments to foreign pension schemes leads to a situation where policy-holders residing in Denmark are precluded from setting up pension schemes with pension institutions established in Member States other than Denmark. Foreign pension institutions are de facto precluded from offering their services on the Danish market. The requirement of being established in Denmark therefore constitutes a restriction on the freedom to provide services from Member States other than Denmark.

The Commission further argues that the Danish provisions lead to a situation where restrictions are placed on the free movement of capital in the form of payments into and out of pension schemes.

The Danish Government has argued in particular that the Danish rules can be justified by the need to ensure effective fiscal supervision and the need to ensure the cohesion of the tax system.

There can be no doubt that the central issue is whether the Danish rules can be justified.

The Commission considers that effective fiscal supervision can be ensured by less restrictive measures. The Commission points out that the Member States may require that the taxpayers provide the necessary information as a precondition for obtaining the tax deduction and that the Member States may have recourse to the Mutual Assistance Directive.[7] The Commission argues that the Danish rules are contrary to the principle of proportionality. It must be expected that the Court of Justice will accept the Commission's arguments on this issue.

As for the argument that the need to ensure the cohesion of the tax system justifies the Danish rules, the Commission repeats the arguments set out in its Communication from 2001. It points out that Denmark can tax all payments out from schemes to policy-holders residing in Denmark, regardless of whether the scheme has been set up in Denmark or elsewhere. Denmark only loses that right if the policy-holder moves his or her place of residence to another country.

---

7 Council Directive 77/799/EEC of 19 December 1977.

The Commission further argues that Denmark has entered into a number of tax treaties conferring the right to tax pension benefits – as in the OECD Model – on the country of residence. The Commission argues that it follows from these tax treaties that the coherence of the tax system is not attained for individual taxpayers in terms of a close connection between deductions for payments in and taxation of payments out of the scheme.

It should be noted that, when entering into tax treaties, Denmark's policy is to try to ensure that the right to tax pension benefits is conferred on Denmark as the source state.[8] Not all countries have been willing to confer the right to tax pension benefits on Denmark, however. For example, it has not been possible for Denmark to get the right to tax under the tax treaties with Spain and France. If a pensioner moves from Denmark to Spain or France, Denmark will not be able to tax pension benefits regardless of whether contributions were paid into a Danish or a foreign pension scheme.

Finally, the Commission argues that some of Denmark's tax treaties contain provisions which allow policy-holders to deduct payments to foreign pension schemes. People who move to Denmark from one of those countries can thus maintain their pension schemes in their home country and deduct the payments into the schemes from their taxable income in Denmark.[9] The Commission argues here that these provisions show that the Danish rules not allowing for tax deductions for payments to foreign pension schemes are not consistent.

4 Discussion of the Commission's Arguments

Taken in isolation, the Commission's arguments in the action against Denmark automatically lead one to call the case "Bachmann 2". The Commission only finds it important whether payments to the pension scheme are deductible or not, and whether there is a connection between deductions and taxation (TE/ET).

It is not yet clear whether the Court of Justice will accept the arguments of the Commission. On the one hand, the judgment in the Bachmann case

---

8 See Ulstrup in SU 2001, p 69, for a discussion of the Danish "Model Convention".

9 See e.g. Article 18 of the Nordic tax treaty, which generally confers the right to tax pensions on the source state; and Article 18(1) and (2) of the UK/Denmark tax treaty containing a special provision introducing tax at source in the case of persons moving to or from the two contracting states.

is difficult to understand when it is compared to the Court's subsequent case law, in particular its judgment in the Wielockx case. On the other hand, the Court has, on numerous occasions, referred to its judgment in the Bachmann case as an example where the cohesion of the tax system may be justify discriminatory rules.

4.1 Taxation of investment returns (appreciation in value) of pension schemes

Apparently, the Commission has not considered the taxation of the investment returns (appreciation in value) – often called yield tax – on the pension schemes concerned. Pension institutions invest the contributions in assets which may generate income and appreciate in value. In its Communication from 2001, the Commission pointed out that most Member States provide for exemption of any income and capital gains in the hands of pension institutions. The Commission recommends that Members States consider introducing such tax exemption generally in the EU.

Several Member States, however, levy a yield tax on this income, including Denmark. The Danish tax levied on the investment returns de facto discriminates against TE schemes compared to ET schemes. And as indicated above, foreign pension institutions may only offer TE schemes to persons in Denmark. If the Court of Justice also addresses the issue of taxation of investment returns, there is little doubt, in my opinion, that the Danish rules will be found to be contrary to the provisions of the EC Treaty governing the fundamental freedoms. This is the case regardless of whether the judgment in the Bachmann case is considered correct or not.

Under the Danish rules, investment returns are, in principle, taxed both when the scheme is tax-privileged (ET) or not tax-privileged (TE). But where the returns on an ET scheme are "only" taxed at a rate of 15 % (yield tax),[10] the return on a TE scheme is treated as investment income and subject to tax at a rate ranging from 32 % to 59 %.[11] In addition, the owner or the beneficiary is liable to pay tax on the return on an ET scheme, which places heavy demands on liquidity.

[10] See section 2 of the Danish Pension Investment Returns Tax Act.

[11] See section 53A(3) of the Danish Pension Tax Act, and section 4(1), no. 15, of the Danish Personal Tax Act.

The fact that the appreciation in value of a tax-privileged scheme (ET) is subject to tax when the pension benefits are paid does not eliminate this difference. The reason is that, due to the tax exemption of contributions to the scheme, larger sums may be paid into the schemes. A simple example may illustrate this.

4.2 Example

It is assumed that, in every year, a taxpayer is liable to pay tax at a rate of 50 %, provided, however, that the return on an ET scheme is only subject to tax at the rate of 15 %. The Danish labour market contribution is disregarded. It is finally assumed that the taxpayer is allowed to withdraw a sum each year from the TE scheme to pay the investment return tax so that the ET scheme and the TE scheme are treated equally in this respect. The investment return is estimated at 6 % per year and, for the sake of simplicity, it is assumed that the scheme runs for 3 years before benefits become payable.

	Tax-Privileged Scheme (ET)	Not Tax-Privileged Scheme (TE)
Earned/occupational income	100	100
Tax on earned/occupational income	0	50
Sum for payment into pension scheme	100	50
Return year 1	6 (6 % of 100)	3 (6 % of 50)
Tax on return year 1	0.9 (15 %)	1.5 (50 %)
Return year 1 after tax	5.1	1.5
Return year 2	6.31 (6 % of 105.1)	3.09 (6 % of 51.5)
Tax on return year 2	0.95 (15 %)	1.55 (50 %)
Return year 2 after tax	5.36	1.55
Return year 3	6.63 (6 % of 110.46)	3.18 (6 % of 53.04)
Tax on return year 3	0.99 (15 %)	1.59 (50 %)
Return year 3 after tax	5.64	1.59
Total sum for payment out	116.10	54.63
Tax on payment out	58.05 (50 %)	0
Pension after tax	58.05	54.63

4.3 The impact of tax on the investment returns (appreciation in value) on the pension scheme

The difference in the tax levied on the investment return in an ET scheme and a TE scheme constitutes a significant restriction for persons in

Denmark who want to set up TE schemes. As indicated above, foreign pension institutions may only set up tax-privileged schemes (ET schemes) if they are established in Denmark and foreign pension institutions may not offer schemes whose returns are subject to the low tax at 15 %.

This difference in the taxation of the investment returns cannot reasonably be justified by reference to the cohesion of the tax system. In relation to the connection between deductions and taxation, there is both an advantage and a disadvantage. In relation to the taxation of the investment returns, there is only a disadvantage (ie increased taxation).

I am not aware of the reason why the Commission apparently has not included the issue of taxation of the investment returns on pension schemes in the action against Denmark. There may be (at least) three possible reasons. Firstly, the Commission may be unaware of the significance of the difference in the taxation of the investment returns in the complex Danish pension tax system. Secondly, the Commission may have decided to limit the action to the issue of the failure to allow deductions for contributions for procedural reasons. Finally, the reason may be political, including the intention, once and for all, to find out whether the Court of Justice will now take a different view of rules similar to the Belgian rules in the Bachmann case from 1992.

5 Implications of a Judgment Unfavourable to Denmark

It must be assumed that the existing difference in the tax levied on the investment returns on pension schemes is contrary to the provisions of the EC Treaty governing the fundamental freedoms. A reduction of the tax rate levied on the investment returns on pension schemes enjoying no tax privilege (TE schemes) to 15 % will lead to complex problems of delimitation in relation to the taxation of the investment returns on ordinary savings, which are subject to tax at a rate ranging from 32 % to 59 %.

If the Court of Justice holds that it is contrary to the provisions of the EC Treaty governing the fundamental freedoms to refuse to allow deductions for payments into foreign pension schemes when deductions are granted for payments into Danish schemes, this will result in additional problems for Denmark.

Firstly, there will be an increased risk that Denmark will have to waive the right to tax payments from pension schemes even though Denmark has previously granted deductions for contributions.

As long as a person receiving pension benefits remains resident in Denmark, Denmark has the right to tax unless the right to tax the pension benefits has been conferred on the source state under a tax treaty. The Nordic Convention is an example showing that pension benefits may only be taxed in the source state. It must then be expected that this and similar tax treaties will be amended. In addition, there will be practical control problems because Denmark will have difficulties imposing on the foreign pension institutions the same obligations to submit the necessary information to the Danish tax authorities.

If a person, with reference to EC law, is entitled to deductions for payments into a foreign scheme, he may avoid paying Danish tax by moving to another country before the pension benefits become payable. This problem already occurs nowadays when a person moves from Denmark to, for instance, Spain or France as a result of the existing tax treaties, but the problem will be extended to cover every situation where a person moves from Denmark to another country before pension benefits become payable. The Danish government may consider introducing a tax imposed when the taxpayer moves his tax residence abroad in order to solve the problem, but such a tax may be contrary to the provisions of the EC Treaty, see the judgment in the de Lasteyrie du Saillant case.[12]

Another solution to the problem in relation to EC law may be to abolish deductions for payments into the schemes, i.e. change to a system that generally has only TE schemes. Danish economists have supported such a solution,[13] but Danish politicians have so far decided to maintain tax deductions and tax exemptions for pension schemes.

Secondly, it is necessary to resolve the problem how the Danish pension yield tax can be maintained. The tax sums involved are in reality paid by the Danish pension institutions. It may be difficult to require foreign pension institutions to pay the tax. One solution could be to require the individual to pay the tax relating to his pension scheme. However, this will be more complicated than the existing system. For example, it will be difficult to ensure that an individual who withdraws the return on his pension scheme on an ongoing basis will have the liquidity necessary to pay the tax.

---

12 11 March 2004, C-9/02 *de Lasteyrie du Saillant* [2004] ECR I-2409.

13 See Det økonomiske Råd: Dansk Økonomi, spring 2001, pp 174 et seq.

Pending Cases Filed by Finnish Courts: The Turpeinen Case and the Esab Case

Marjaana Helminen

I The Turpeinen Case (C-520/04)

1 Tax Treatment of Pensions in Finland
2 The Facts in the Turpeinen Case
3 The EC Treaty
4 Directive 90/365/EEC
5 Justifications
6 Concluding Remarks

II The Esab Case (C-231/05)

1 The Finnish Group Contribution Regime
2 The Question Asked in the Esab Case
3 The Marks & Spencer Case
4 The EC Treaty Freedoms
  4.1 Introduction
  4.2 Contribution from parent to subsidiary
  4.3 Contribution from subsidiary to parent
  4.4 Contribution between sister companies
5 The Parent-Subsidiary Directive
6 Justifications
7 Concluding Remarks

I The Turpeinen Case (C-520/04)

1 Tax Treatment of Pensions in Finland

A Finnish resident is subject to unlimited tax liability in Finland.[1] Pensions of a Finnish resident are taxed as earned income in accordance with the progressive income tax scale. A pension based on voluntary pension insurance may also constitute investment income. A Finnish resident must pay a sickness insurance fee on his pensions. A resident is entitled to deductions for the costs of acquiring the pension income[2] and to a pension income allowance.[3]

A non-resident is subject to taxes in Finland only for Finnish and not for foreign-source pensions.[4] A public sector pension is Finnish-source income, if it is paid by or if it is based on work for the state of Finland, a municipality of Finland or any other domestic statutory body. A private sector pension is Finnish-source income, if it is based on employment which was exercised solely or primarily in Finland for a private sector employer, which is in Finland.[5] The gross amount of the Finnish-source pensions of a non-resident is subject to a 35 % withholding tax in Finland.[6]

The tax treatment of a pension in a tax treaty situation depends on whether the pension is based on a private or public sector employment. A private sector pension is taxable only in the state of residence of the taxpayer whereas a public sector pension is taxed only in the source state.[7] However, many Finnish tax treaties, unlike the OECD Model, also give the source state a taxing right with respect to the private sector pensions. Also, the nationality of the taxpayer may have impact on the tax treatment. [8] If Finland has the right to tax a Finnish-source pension of a non-

1 Sec 9(1) of the Income Tax Act (TVL).

2 Sec 29 TVL.

3 Secs 100, 101, and 107 TVL.

4 Sec 9(1) TVL.

5 Sec 10(1)(4) and 10(1)(5) TVL. A private sector employee pension is not Finnish-source income if the employment was exercised mainly abroad. See KHO 1990/3922.

6 Secs 3 and 7 of the Act on the tax treatment of income and wealth of a person subject to limited tax liability (LähdeVL).

7 See Arts 18 and 19(2) of the OECD Model.

8 Some treaties preclude Finland from taxing Finnish-source public sector pensions if the pension was earned from work relating to the business of the public sector employer or if the taxpayer is a national and a resident of the same state. Some treaties prevent Finland from taxing a Finnish-source public sector pension if the pension was not earned by a public official or if the taxpayer is not a national of Finland.

resident, Finland usually levies the 35 % withholding tax in a tax treaty situation as well.[9] Only a small number of tax treaties require the application of a lower tax rate.

2 The Facts in the Turpeinen Case

In case KHO 2004/3330 (106), the Supreme Administrative Court of Finland (Korkein hallinto-oikeus) was confronted with the question of the EC law-compatibility of the Finnish tax system, including the different treatment of pensions of non-residents and of residents.

The case concerns Mrs Pirkko Marjatta Turpeinen, a Finnish national who lived in Finland until 1998 and who then moved first to Belgium and thereafter to Spain. The only income Mrs Turpeinen receives yearly is a Finnish-source pension based on her previous employment with a Finnish public sector employer.[10] Until the end of year 2001 Mrs Turpeinen was treated as a resident subject to unlimited tax liability in Finland.[11] In 2001 the personal progressive tax rate applied to her was 28.5 %. From the beginning of year 2002 the tax office of Uusimaa in Helsinki began to treat Mrs Turpeinen as a non-resident subject to limited tax liability in Finland. Because of the non-resident status, the pension was subject to a 35 % withholding tax in Finland levied on the gross amount of the pension. Mrs Turpeinen had no right to any tax deductions. Because of the tax treaty between Finland and Spain Mrs Turpeinen did not have to pay taxes on the same pension in Spain.

In this case, the 35 % tax levied on the gross mount of the pension was higher than the tax she used to pay as a resident and higher than the tax that she would pay on the same income if she were a Finnish resident. As a consequence, Mrs Turpeinen claimed that the tax treatment is not be in accordance with EC law and that she should be taxed in the same way as she was taxed as a resident, in accordance with the progressive tax rates. Because the tax office did not change the treatment, Mrs Turpeinen brought her case before the Administrative Court.

---

9 Secs 3 and 7 LähdeVL.

10 Mrs Turpeinen used to work as a child psychiatrist employed by the state or municipalities of Finland.

11 The residence treatment was based on a Finnish tax rule according to which a Finnish national who moves abroad is treated as a resident for tax purposes for the three calendar years following the removal year (sec 11 TVL). See Helminen, *Finnish International Taxation*, 2nd edition (2005), WSOY, pp 65-69 about the three-year rule.

The Administrative Court did not change the decision, because the Court did not see any conflict with EC law. According to the court, Mrs Turpeinen had not exercised the freedoms guaranteed by Article 39 of the EC Treaty (free movement of workers) or Article 43 of the EC Treaty (freedom of establishment), because she was a retired person. The Court was also of the opinion that the Finnish tax treatment was not contrary to the general non-discrimination article of the EC Treaty (Article 12), because it is based on residence and not on nationality. The Court did not refer to Article 18. Finally, the Court mentioned that Council Directive 90/365/EEC on the right of residence for employees and self-employed persons who have ceased their occupational activity does not have any relevance in this case. As a consequence, Mrs Turpeinen had to refer her case to the Supreme Administrative Court of Finland.

Because of the EC law involved was unclear, the Supreme Administrative Court of Finland made a reference to the European Court of Justice for a preliminary ruling in the case of Pirkko Marjatta Turpeinen[12]on the following questions:

> Is Article 18 of EC Treaty on the right of a citizen of the Union to move and reside freely in the territory of the Member States, or Article 39 on ensuring the freedom of movement of workers within the Community, to be interpreted as meaning that one or both of them preclude national legislation under which, in the case of a person who resides abroad and is a person subject to limited tax liability in the Member State, the withholding tax charged on the taxpayer's pension based on a public-law service relationship paid from that Member State exceeds in certain cases the tax which the taxpayer would be charged as a person resident and hence a taxpayer subject to unlimited tax liability in the Member State?

Is Council Directive 90/365/EEC on the right of residence for employees and self-employed persons who have ceased their occupational activity to be interpreted as precluding national legislation such as that described in question 1 above?

3 The EC Treaty

Although direct taxation does not as such fall within the purview of the Community and the tax treatment of cross-border pensions is not har-

[12] ECJ C-520/04 *Turpeinen*, pending.

monised in the Community, the powers retained by the Member States must be exercised consistently with Community law.[13]

The EC Treaty prohibits any direct or indirect discrimination on grounds of nationality (Article 12). Tax provisions of the EU Member States must not treat nationals of two different EU Member States under the same circumstances differently or under different circumstances similarly with the result that one is disadvantaged compared to the other.[14]

The general non-discrimination article (Article 12) is applicable only if the special articles of the EC Treaty, which guarantee the basic freedoms, are not applicable.[15] Article 39 of the EC Treaty prohibits taxation which restricts free movement of workers. It is established case law that the free movement of workers article also applies to pensions, if the person used the right to free movement of workers while still working.[16] Nevertheless, it does not apply to employment in the public service.[17]

In any case, the situations falling within the scope of Community law include those involving the exercise of the freedom to move and reside within the territory of the Member States, as conferred by Article 18 of the EC Treaty.[18] Article 18 of the EC Treaty prohibits taxation which restricts free movement of any EU citizens, including the free movement of retired citizens. Every citizen of the EU has the right to move and reside freely within the territory of the EU Member States. The fact that a person makes use of this right must not lead to a disadvantage.

---

13 See for example, ECJ 14 February 1995, C-279/93 *Schumacker* [1995] ECR I-225, para 21; 7 September 2004, C-319/02 *Manninen* [2004] ECR I-7477, para 19; 11 August 1995, C-80/94 *Wielockx* [1995] ECR I-2493, para 16; and 14 September 1999, C-391/97 *Gschwind* [1999] ECR I-5451, para 20.

14 See for example ECJ 14 February 1995, C-279/93 *Schumacker* [1995] ECR I-225; 21 September 1999, C-307/97 *Saint-Gobain* [1999] ECR I-6161; 27 June 1996, C-107/94 *Asscher* [1996] ECR I-3089; 16 July 1998, C-264/96 *ICI* [1998] ECR I-4695; and 12 May 1998, C-336/96 *Gilly* [1998] ECR I-2793.

15 See for example, ECJ 12 April 1994, C-1/93 *Halliburton* [1994] ECR I-1137; and 29 April 1999, C-311/97 *Royal Bank of Scotland* [1999] ECR I-2651.

16 See for example, ECJ 15 June 2000, C-302/98 *Sehrer* [2000] ECR I-4585, which concerned a retired resident of Germany who had worked earlier both in Germany and in France and therefore received pensions both from Germany and France. The French pension was subject to social security payments in France as well as in Germany. This German rule was found to infringe Article 39 of the EC Treaty on the free movement of workers, because it leads to heavier payments for residents who have worked in addition to Germany also in other Member States.

17 Art 39(4) of the EC Treaty.

18 See ECJ 29 April 2004, C-224/02 *Pusa* [2004] ECR I-5763, para 17; and 11 July 2002, C-224/98 *D'Hoop* [2002] ECR I-6191, para 29.

A citizen of the Union must be granted in all Member States the same treatment as that accorded to the nationals of those Member States who find themselves in the same situation. It is incompatible with the right of freedom of movement if a citizen in the Member State of which he is a national receives treatment that is less favourable than he would enjoy if he had not availed himself of the opportunities offered by the Treaty in relation to the freedom of movement.[19] A national of a Member State must not be deterred from availing himself of the right to free movement by obstacles raised to his residence in the host Member State by legislation of his State of origin that penalise the fact that he has used the right.[20]

National legislation which places at a disadvantage certain of its nationals because they have exercised their freedom to move and to reside in another Member State gives rise to inequality of treatment, contrary to the principles which guarantee the same treatment in law in the exercise of the citizen's freedom to move. Such legislation may be justified only if it is based on objective considerations independent of the nationality of the persons concerned and proportionate to the legitimate aim of the national provisions.[21]

The Commission mentioned in its official notice to the Government of Finland on 19 April 2001 (SG(2001)D/287914) that the 35 % withholding tax for non-residents may be contrary to the EC Treaty, because it restricts the free movement of retired people. This opinion is based on the fact that with respect to low pensions the 35 % tax is higher than the progressive tax a resident owes. The Commission repeated its opinion in its statement on 14 December 2004 (C(2004) 2000/4995).

A different treatment based on the residence of a taxpayer may conflict with the EC Treaty because most non-residents are foreign nationals and the treatment, therefore, may indirectly include discrimination based on nationality. The treatment may also otherwise restrict the free movement.

Because Mrs Turpeinen is a Finnish national, her tax treatment is not based on her nationality but only on her being a non-resident. Because

---

19 See ECJ 29 April 2004, C-224/02 *Pusa* [2004] ECR I-5763, para 19; and 11 July 2002, C-224/98 *D'Hoop* [2002] ECR I-6191, para 31.

20 See ECJ 29 April 2004, C-224/02 *Pusa* [2004] ECR I-5763, para 17; and 11 July 2002, C-224/98 *D'Hoop* [2002] ECR I-6191, para 29.

21 See ECJ 29 April 2004, C-224/02 *Pusa* [2004] ECR I-5763, para 20; and 11 July 2002, C-224/98 *D'Hoop* [2002] ECR I-6191, paras 34-36.

Mrs Turpeinen has exercised the right to free movement by moving abroad, it is relevant in her case whether the Finnish tax treatment restricts the free movement principle. The different tax treatment of residents and non-residents places Mrs Turpeinen at a disadvantage simply because she has exercised her right to move freely. In other cases, as regards other non-residentswho are not Finnish nationals, the Finnish tax treatment may constitute also discrimination based on nationality.

Based on the decisions of the European Court of Justice, residents and non-residents may be treated differently unless they are regarded as being in a similar situation. Because residents and non-residents are in many respects in different situations, different treatment is often acceptable.[22] The tax treatment of a resident and a non-resident, for example, may be based on different provisions.[23]

A different treatment of residents and non-residents is prohibited if a resident and a non-resident are in a similar situation.[24] For example, a taxpayer who resides and works in two different Member States and derives most or all of his income from the source state, which is not his state of residence, may not be subject to a more severe tax treatment in the source state than the residents of that state. In such a situation the source state has the better, or the only, possibility to take into account the personal situation of the taxpayer. In such a situation the taxpayer must have the same right to personal deductions as a resident even though he is a non-resident.[25] In the Turpeinen case, all of Mrs Turpeinen's income is from

---

22 See for example, ECJ 12 June 2003, C-234/01 *Gerritse* [2003] ECR I-5933; 14 February 1995, C-279/93 *Schumacker* [1995] ECR I-225; 14 September 1999, C-391/97 *Gschwind* [1999] ECR I-5451; 16 May 2000, C-87/99 *Zurstrassen* [2000] ECR I-3337; 1 July 2004, C-169/03 *Wallentin* [2004] ECR I-6443; 11 August 1995, C-80/94 *Wielockx* [1995] ECR I-2493; and 26 January 1993, C-112/91 *Werner* [1993] ECR I-429.

23 See for example, ECJ 12 June 2003, C-234/01 *Gerritse* [2003] ECR I-5933.

24 See for example, ECJ 11 August 1995, C-80/94 *Wielockx* [1995] ECR I-2493; 28 January 1986, 270/83 *Avoir Fiscal* [1986] ECR 273; 8 May 1990, 175/88 *Biehl* [1990] ECR I-1779; 27 June 1996, C-107/94 *Asscher* [1996] ECR I-3089; 13 July 1993, C-330/91 *Commerzbank* [1993] ECR I-4017; 14 February 1995, C-279/93 *Schumacker* [1995] ECR I-225; 12 June 2003, C-234/01 *Gerritse* [2003] ECR I-5933; 1 July 2004, C-169/03 *Wallentin* [2004] ECR I-6443; and 11 December 2003, C-364/01 *Barbier* [2003] ECR I-15013.

25 See ECJ 14 February 1995, C-279/93 *Schumacker* [1995] ECR I-225; 26 October 1995, C-151/94 *Biehl II* [1995] ECR I-3685; 11 August 1995, C-80/94 *Wielockx* [1995] ECR I-2493; and 1 July 2004, C-169/03 *Wallentin* [2004] ECR I-6443. See also the recommendation of the Commission regarding frontier workers (Commission Recommendation of 21 December 1993 on the taxation of EC, OJ 39/1994 p 22) according to which an indi-

Finland and is taxed only in Finland. In such a situation, the personal situation of Mrs Turpeinen can be taken into account for tax purposes only in Finland. As a consequence, she should be entitled to taxation similar to the taxation of residents.

A different treatment of residents and non-residents may be prohibited even if most of the income of the non-resident taxpayer is not from the state concerned and is not taxable there.[26] For example, the withholding tax levied on the gross income of a non-resident should not be higher than the progressive tax levied on the net income of a resident.[27] As a consequence, the tax levied on Mrs Turpeinen should not exceed the tax that would be levied on her if she were still a Finnish resident.

As a consequence of the decisions of the European Court of Justice, it seems that the costs for the acquiring of income should be deductible for a non-resident if they are deductible for a resident, regardless whether the taxpayer has most of his income from the source state or not. In contrast, deductions that do not relate directly to the income but to the personal situation of the taxpayer must be available to a non-resident only if most of his income is from the source state. The tax rate of a non-resident on the income calculated in this way may not be higher than the tax rate of a resident would be.

4 Directive 90/365/EEC

In its reference of the Turpeinen case to the EC Court, the Supreme Administrative Court also mentioned Council Directive 90/365/EEC on the right of residence for employees and self-employed persons who have ceased their occupational activity. The reference was made because the Directive had already been mentioned by the Administrative Court, and because the Commission has mentioned in its official notice to the Government of Finland on 19 April 2001 (SG(2001)D/287914) that the 35 % withholding tax of non-residents may be contrary to the Directive. It seems, however, that, unlike the EC Treaty, the Directive does not have direct relevance in the Turpeinen case.

vidual should get resident treatment even though he is a non-resident in a country, if at least 75 % of his income is from the state that is not the residence state. See ECJ 14 September 1999, C-391/97 *Gschwind* [1999] ECR I-5451 for an example of a situation in which most of the income was not from the source state and the non-resident, therefore, was not regarded as being in a similar situation as a resident and in which equally advantageous treatment was not required.

26 See ECJ 12 June 2003, C-234/01 *Gerritse* [2003] ECR I-5933.

27 See ECJ 12 June 2003, C-234/01 *Gerritse* [2003] ECR I-5933.

5 Justifications

Because the Finnish distinction between the tax treatment of pensions of residents and non-residents seems to be a restriction of the free movement principles of the EC Treaty, whether there is a justification for such a restriction has to be examined. Direct discrimination on grounds of nationality is prohibited unless the EC Treaty expressly allows it in a specific situation. Indirect discrimination or a restriction may be justified on the grounds of an objectively acceptable reason. According to the rule of reason principle established by the EC Court, a mandatory requirement of public interest may constitute an acceptable reason (necessity test).[28] Any discriminatory or restrictive provision, however, must be appropriate for the protection of the recognised public interest and the restrictive effect must be proportionate in relation to the goal pursued (proportionality test). The provision must be the least restrictive possible (less restrictive test).[29]

Indirect discrimination may, for example, be allowed on grounds of a public policy, security or health reason[30] or in order to prevent infringements of domestic law.[31] In principle, an acceptable reason may also be, for example, the need to safeguard the effectiveness of fiscal supervision[32], prevention of abuse[33] or the necessity to safeguard the cohesion of the domestic tax system. [34] There are, however, no direct tax cases in which the EC Court has accepted discriminatory or restrictive tax treatment on these grounds.[35]

---

28 See ECJ 20 February 1979, 120/78 *Cassis de Dijon* [1979] ECR 649. See also for example, ECJ 29 April 1999, C-311/97 *Royal Bank of Scotland* [1999] ECR I-2651, para 32.

29 See for example, ECJ 15 May 1997, C-250/95 *Futura* [1997] ECR I-2471, para 26.

30 Art 46 of EC Treaty.

31 Art 58 of EC Treaty.

32 See ECJ 15 May 1997, C-250/95 *Futura* [1997] ECR I-2471.

33 See for example, ECJ 28 January 1986, 270/83 *Avoir Fiscal* [1986] ECR 273.

34 See ECJ 28 January 1992, C-204/90 *Bachmann* [1992] ECR I-249.

35 See for example, ECJ 15 May 1997, C-250/95 *Futura* [1997] ECR I-2471; 11 August 1995, C-80/94 *Wielockx* [1995] ECR I-2493; 28 April 1998, C-118/96 *Safir* [1998] ECR I-1897; 28 October 1999, C-55/98 *Vestergaard* [1999] ECR I-7641; 3 October 2002, C-136/00 *Danner* [2002] ECR I-8147; 28 January 1986, 270/83 *Avoir Fiscal* [1986] ECR 273; 16 July 1998, C-264/96 *ICI* [1998] ECR I-4695; 26 October 1999, C-294/97 *Eurowings* [1999] ECR I-7447; 8 March 2001, C-397/98 and C-410/98 *Metallgesellschaft/Hoechst* [2001] ECR I-1727; 15 July 2004, C-315/02 *Lenz* [2004] ECR I-7063; 13 July 1993, C-330/91 *Commerzbank* [1993] ECR I-4017; 27 June 1996, C-107/94 *Asscher* [1996] ECR I-3089; 13 April 2000, C-251/98 *Baars* [2000] ECR I-2787; 6 June 2000, C-35/98 *Verkooijen* [2000] ECR I-4071; and 7 September 2004, C-319/02 *Manninen* [2004] ECR I-7477. The Bachmann case (ECJ 28 January 1992, C-204/90 *Bachmann* [1992] ECR I-249) is an exception, but no very far-reaching conclusions should be drawn from such an old case.

The Court has repeatedly held that reduction in tax revenue cannot be regarded as an overriding reason of public interest which may be relied on to justify a measure which is in principle contrary to a fundamental freedom.[36]

It may be argued that the fiscal principle of territoriality and the necessity of ensuring the cohesion of the Finnish tax system would justify the different treatment of residents and non-residents. However, the territoriality principle or the cohesion requirement, in the autho's opinion, is not a reason to allow the Member States to evade their obligations under Community law.[37] The national tax rules must be neutral in regard to the exercise of the freedoms of movement. In any case, the Finnish rules that treat non-residents and residents differently with no regard to the fact which country has the best possibilities to take into account the situation of the taxpayer go well beyond what is necessary.

6 Concluding Remarks

It seems clear that the Finnish 35 % withholding tax levied on gross pensions of non-residents is contrary to the EC Treaty principle of free movement of persons, because it may lead to higher tax burden for retired persons who exercise the right to move abroad from Finland. There seems to be no acceptable justification for a treatment that does not take the situation of a non-resident compared to the situation of a resident into account in any way. As a consequence, it appears that Finland will have to change its tax system.

Nevertheless, it is clear that Finland will replace its system of taxing pension of non-residents no matter what the decision in the Turpeinen case will be. The government has proposed[38] that from 1 January 2006 Finnish-source pensions of all non-residents will be subject to the progressive tax system, in the same way as the pensions of resident.

---

36 See for example, ECJ 7 September 2004, C-319/02 *Manninen* [2004] ECR I-7477, para 49.

37 See also the Opinion of Advocate General Maduro in *Marks & Spencer* (ECJ C-446/03 *Marks & Spencer*, pending), 7 April 2005, para 62.

38 Government proposal HE 104/2005.

II The Esab Case (C-231/05)

1 The Finnish Group Contribution Regime

The companies in a group are treated as separate tax subjects for Finnish tax purposes. The results of the group companies are not consolidated. Finnish domestic tax law, however, includes a special group regime, the Act on Group Contribution.[39] Accordingly, Finnish corporate entities belonging to the same group of companies have the possibility for an open group contribution that allows the balancing of profits and losses between the group companies. A Finnish company may make a group contribution to one of the other Finnish companies belonging to the same group. The recipient may be a parent company, a subsidiary company or a sister company.

There has to be a direct or indirect holding of at least 90 % between the contributor and the recipient companies or the same parent company must hold directly or indirectly at least 90 % of the contributor and the recipient.[40] A group contribution is treated as taxable income of the recipient and as a tax-deductible contribution of the contributor.[41]

The Act on Group Contribution requires that both the contributor and the recipient of a group contribution be Finnish corporate entities.[42] Foreign companies are not taken into account even when determining whether the group relationship required for a group contribution exists between a Finnish contributor and a Finnish recipient of a group contribution.[43] In the case of dual resident companies it is required that the group contribution is made for the purpose of business conducted in Finland.[44] Accordingly, a group contribution is not possible for a Finnish company that has its tax treaty residence abroad unless the company conducts business in Finland from a permanent establishment.

39 Laki konserniavustuksesta verotuksessa 21.11.1986/825 (KonseerniavustusL).

40 Sec 3 KonserniavustusL. There are also certain other requirements that have to be met in order for a group contribution to be tax-deductible. See Secs 2-7KonserniavustusL.

41 Sec 1 KonserniavustusL.

42 Sec 3 KonserniavustusL. A European company (SE) that has its place of registration and the place of management in Finland is treated as a domestic corporate entity (KVL 2004/35).

43 KVL 1989/351.

44 This requirement is based on decision KHO 2003/1484 (33) of the Supreme Administrative Court of Finland.

Despite the strict wording of the Act on Group Contribution based on the non-discrimination provisions of tax treaties and the EC Treaty and the decisions of the Supreme Administrative Court of Finland (Korkein hallinto-oikeus), it is clear that a company of a tax treaty state or of an EU or EEA Member State with a permanent establishment in Finland has the right to make or receive a tax-deductible group contribution under the same circumstances as a Finnish company.[45] In the same way, the non-discrimination provisions of the tax treaties and the EC Treaty require that companies of the tax treaty states and the EU and EEA Member States be taken into account when determining the required holding between the group companies.[46] A group contribution may be possible between two Finnish companies because of a tax treaty non-discrimination article even if there are companies of non-treaty states interposed, provided that the parent of the whole group is from a tax treaty state.[47]

Despite the non-discrimination provisions of tax treaties and the EC Treaty, until now there have been no cases in which a company of another tax treaty state or of an EU Member State that has no permanent establishment in Finland has been allowed to make or receive a tax-deductible group contribution under the Finnish system.[48] It has, however, been often discussed whether the freedom of establishment principle of the EC Treaty requires that a group contribution from a Finnish company to a company of another EU or EEA Member State be deductible for the Finnish company.[49]

---

45 Arts 24(3) and 24(5) of the OECD Model, Art 43 of the EC Treaty and KHO 2003/2773 (79). See also ECJ 16 July 1998, C-264/96 *ICI* [1998] ECR I-4695.

46 A tax-deductible group contribution is possible, for example, between two Finnish sister companies, which are both wholly owned subsidiaries of a foreign parent from an EU Member State or a tax treaty state. The same treatment concerns a group contribution from a Finnish parent of a foreign EU or tax treaty state subsidiary to a Finnish subsidiary of the same foreign subsidiary. See KHO 1992/536-537 (B 509 and 510), 2000/864 and 2003/2773 (79) and KVL 1996/290 and 1998/31. See also ECJ 18 November 1999, C-200/98 *X and Y* [1999] ECR I-8261.

47 KHO 2004/1525 (65). See also Hintsanen/Viitanen, Supreme Administrative Court Ruling on the Finland-US Tax Treaty Non-Discrimination Clause, *European Taxation* 2004, pp. 460-462.

48 See for example, KVL 1995/304 in which the question was dealt with. According to the preliminary ruling of the Central Board of Taxes of Finland on this case, a group contribution that a Finnish company wanted to make to a Netherlands company belonging to the same group was not tax-deductible for the Finnish company. Finland has been a Member of the European Union only since 1995, so the EC law aspect was not considered in the case.

49 See Art 43 of the EC Treaty and ECJ 18 November 1999, C-200/98 *X and Y* [1999] ECR I-8261 and 16 July 1998, C-264/96 *ICI* [1998] ECR I-4695. See also the pending case C-446/03 *Marks & Spencer* and Helminen, *Finnish International Taxation*[2], pp. 164-165.

2 The Question Asked in the Esab Case

In case KHO 2005/1215 (29) the Supreme Administrative Court of Finland was finally confronted with the much-discussed question in the final instance. The case concerned an appeal on a preliminary ruling of the Central Board of Taxes of Finland[50] requested by a Finnish company Esab Oy.[51] The Court was asked whether a Finnish company has the right to make a tax-deductible group contribution to a company registered in Great Britain belonging to the same group of companies, if all other requirements of the Act on a Group Contribution except the requirement of the company being a Finnish company are met, even though the British company does not have a permanent establishment for its business in Finland.[52] Because the EC law involved was unclear the Supreme Administrative Court of Finland made a reference to the European Court of Justice for a preliminary ruling on the question.[53]

The Supreme Administrative Court of Finland asked the European Court of Justice whether Article 43 of the EC Treaty on the freedom of establishment and Article 56 of the EC Treaty on the free movement of capital and payments, having regard to Article 58 of the Treaty and the Parent-Subsidiary Directive[54], has to be interpreted as precluding a system such as that of the Finnish group contribution legislation in which a condition for the deductibility in taxation of a group contribution is that both the contributor and the recipient of the group contribution are domestic companies[55]. The question is quite broadly formulated, including all possible group contribution relations even though the preliminary ruling of the Central Tax Board of Finland on the case actually concerns only a group contribution from a Finnish subsidiary to a foreign parent company.

50 KVL 39/2004, not yet published.

51 Esab Oy is the world's largest producer of welding supplies and equipment.

52 The Finnish Esab Oy is a sub-subsidiary (owned via two Netherlands companies) of the British company to which Esab Oy wanted to give a tax-deductible group contribution.

53 ECJ C-231/05 *Esab*, pending.

54 Council Directive 90/435/EEC on the common system of taxation applicable in the case of parent companies and subsidiaries of different Member States, 23 July 1990.

55 In the English language translation of the Notice for the OJ, the word "resident" was used incorrectly as the translation of the Finnish language word kotimainen, which means domestic. Under Finnish domestic tax law, however, only domestic companies, ie companies established or registered under Finnish law, are treated as resident companies for the Finnish tax purposes. As a consequence, the relevance of the error is minor but meaningful nevertheless. See for the Finnish domestic tax law residence concept, Helminen, *Finnish International Taxation*[2], Chapter 3.

3 The Marks & Spencer Case

The decision in the Marks & Spencer case[56], pending before the European Court of Justice, will be made before the decision on the Finnish Esab case. That decision will have great relevance with respect to the Esab case. In the Marks & Spencer case the EC Court was called upon to clarify the effect of the EC Treaty provisions concerning the freedom of establishment on the British tax regime governing groups. The question is whether EC law precludes legislation such as that in force in the United Kingdom on group relief under which the transfer and off-setting of losses within a group is subject to the condition that those companies are resident or carry on an economic activity in the United Kingdom. According to the Opinion of Advocate General Poiares Maduro, the British regime is in conflict with the freedom of establishment principle of the EC Treaty.[57]

The purpose of the Finnish group contribution, in the same way as the British group relief system, is to limit the negative effects from a tax point of view of establishing groups. The purpose is to avoid penalising companies which, rather than establishing branches, decide to expand their activities by setting up subsidiaries. The special regimes are specifically intended to make the taxation of groups more neutral compared to enterprises organised in a single company, without making the separately taxable group companies a single unit.

Despite similar purposes, the British group relief legislation differs from the Finnish group contribution legislation in many respects. The British legislation deals with off-setting of losses whereas the Finnish group contribution regime does not require the existence of any losses. Under the Finnish system, a tax-deductible contribution may be made to any domestic group company despite the receiving company's profitability. Many times a group contribution, however, is granted by a profitable company to a loss company, which effectively means the same for the group as the possibility for off-setting losses would. The taxes of the whole group will decrease compared to a situation in which the group companies are treated for tax purposes totally separate from each other.

The cross-border application of the British group relief system and the Finnish group contribution system with regard to companies from EU

56 ECJ C-446/03 *Marks & Spencer*, pending.

57 Opinion of Advocate General Maduro in *Marks & Spencer* (C-446-03 *Marks & Spencer*, pending), 7 April 2005.

Member States is basically the same. The application of the British regime is subject to the condition that the companies are resident or carry on an economic activity in the United Kingdom through a branch or agency. The application of the Finnish regime is subject to the condition that the companies are domestic, ie resident for tax purposes in Finland or that the companies conduct economic activities through a permanent establishment situated in Finland. The benefits of the regimes are not available to non-resident companiesthat do not carry on an economic activity in the country concerned.

4 The EC Treaty Freedoms

4.1 Introduction

The EC Court has already ruled on several cases involving the application of the basic freedoms of the EC Treaty in relation to the treatment of foreign losses[58] and the tax treatment of companies having secondary establishments in other Member States[59]. A clear answer with respect to the Marks & Spencer case or the Esab case, however, cannot be derived from these decisions.

Although direct taxation does not as such fall within the purview of the Community and the tax treatment of groups is not harmonised in the Community, the powers retained by the Member States must be exercised consistently with Community law.[60] The tax treatment of groups must not restrict the freedom of establishment of nationals of one Member State in another Member State or the free movement of capital from one Member State to another.

The EC Treaty guarantees free movement of EU nationals in the Community including the freedom of establishment. Article 43 of the EC

58 See for example, ECJ 15 May 1997, C-250/95 *Futura* [1997] ECR I-247; 16 July 1998, C-264/96 *ICI* [1998] ECR I-4695; 18 November 1999, C-200/98 *X and Y* [1999] ECR I-8261; and 14 December 2000, C-141/99 *AMID* [2000] ECR I-11619.

59 See for example, ECJ 13 July 1993, C-330/91 *Commerzbank* [1993] ECR I-4017; 29 April 1999, C-311/97 *Royal Bank of Scotland* [1999] ECR I-2651; 21 September 1999, C-307/97 *Saint-Gobain* [1999] ECR I-6161; 8 March 2001, C-397/98 and C-410/98 *Metallgesellschaft/Hoechst* [2001] ECR I-1727; and 18 September 2003, C-168/01 *Bosal* [2003] ECR I-9409.

60 Compare ECJ 14 February 1995, C-279/93 *Schumacker* [1995] ECR I-225, para 21; and 7 September 2004, C-319/02 *Manninen* [2004] ECR I-7477, para 19.

Treaty on the freedom of establishment guarantees to a Community national access to and the pursuit of activities as a self-employed person as well as the right to set up and manage undertakings under the conditions laid down for its own nationals by the law of the Member State where such establishment is effected. Together with Article 48 of the EC Treaty, Article 43 ensures that companies constituted according to the law of one Member State and having their registered office, central administration or principal place of business within the Community are entitled to carry on their business in the Member State concerned through the intermediary of a subsidiary, branch or agency.[61]

Both Article 43 on freedom of establishment and Article 56 on free movement of capital may be applicable in a case involving a direct investment. Article 43 on the freedom of establishment, however, has priority in the cases involving direct investments and Article 56 on the free movement of capital has relevance only if Article 43 on the freedom of establishment is not applicable in the case concerned.[62]

The freedom of establishment principle limits the competences exercised by the Member States, while the Member States remain free to determine the organisation of their tax system[63] and to determine the need to allocate between themselves taxation rights in tax treaties[64]. As long as group taxation is not harmonised, the difficulties caused by the mere differences in tax regimes between Member States are outside the scope of the EC Treaty.[65] The differences in treatment resulting from legislative disparities between the Member States do not constitute discrimination prohibited by the EC Treaty.[66] However, the Member States must ensure that cross-border situations associated with the exercise of the freedom of movement between the Member States are not disadvantaged.

The Member States must accord nationals of the other Member States the same tax treatment as they do their own nationals.[67] Basically, any dis-

61 See for example, ECJ 21 September 1999, C-307/97 *Saint-Gobain* [1999] ECR I-6161, para 35.

62 See for example, ECJ 13 April 2000, C-251/98 *Baars* [2000] ECR I-2787, para 22.

63 See for example, ECJ 28 January 1992, C-204/90 *Bachmann* [1992] ECR I-249, para 23.

64 See for example, ECJ 21 September 1999, C-307/97 *Saint-Gobain* [1999] ECR I-6161, para 57.

65 See for example, ECJ 12 May 1998, C-336/96 *Gilly* [1998] ECR I-2793, para 47.

66 See for example, ECJ 15 July 2004, C-365/02 *Lindfors* [2004] ECR I-7183, para 34.

67 See for example, ECJ 29 April 1999, C-311/97 *Royal Bank of Scotland* [1999] ECR I-2651, para 29.

crimination, based either directly or indirectly on nationality, is prohibited.[68] Also, tax restrictions on the freedom of establishment are prohibited irrespective of any discrimination. Such restrictions cover measures which prohibit, impede, or render less attractive the exercise of the EC Treaty freedoms. The freedom of establishment prohibits the Member State of origin from hindering the establishment in another Member State of one of its nationals or of a company incorporated under its legislation.[69] The Member States may not restrict the use of the right to free establishment. A cross-border situation with no objective differences compared to a domestic situation may not be subjected to more burdensome tax treatment compared to the domestic situation.[70]

The refusal of a tax advantage such as a tax-deductible group contribution may constitute a restriction contrary to the freedom of establishment principle of the EC Treaty if it is associated with the exercise of the right of establishment.[71] The Finnish group contribution regime creates a specific disadvantage for operators willing to move or establish themselves within the Community. The regime includes discrimination against those Community nationals wishing to assert their right to free establishment.[72] If the situation of the group is seen as a whole, it is clear that the application of the Finnish group contribution regime constitutes a tax advantage for a group that consist of only Finnish companies compared to a group which includes, in addition to Finnish companies, companies from other Member States. As a consequence of a tax deduction to which a Finnish company is entitled if it makes a group contribution to a Finnish loss company, the taxable profit of the whole group is reduced during the course of a given tax year. If the Finnish company makes a contribution to a foreign company, the deduction is not available and the group with foreign companies thus has a disadvantage compared to the group with only Finnish companies.

---

[68] See for example, ECJ 14 February 1995, C-279/93 *Schumacker* [1995] ECR I-225, para 26.

[69] See for example, ECJ 16 July 1998, C-264/96 *ICI* [1998] ECR I-4695, para 16.

[70] See for example, ECJ 14 February 1995, C-279/93 *Schumacker* [1995] ECR I-225; 11 August 1995, C-80/94 *Wielockx* [1995] ECR I-2493; and 27 June 1996, C-107/94 *Asscher* [1996] ECR I-3089 on the concept of objective differences.

[71] See for example, ECJ 13 April 2000, C-251/98 *Baars* [2000] ECR I-2787, paras 30 and 31; and 27 June 1996, C-107/94 *Asscher* [1996] ECR I-3089, para 42.

[72] Compare to the opinion of Advocate General Maduro in *Marks & Spencer* (ECJ C-446/03 *Marks & Spencer*, pending), 7 April 2005, para 28.

Three basic situations may be evaluated with respect to the Finnish group contribution regime: the situation where Finnish parent companies make a contribution to their Finnish or foreign subsidiaries, the situation where Finnish subsidiaries make a contribution to their Finnish or foreign parent companies, and the situation where Finnish subsidiaries make a contribution to their Finnish or foreign sister companies. In each of these examples only the domestic and not the cross-border contribution is tax-deductible for the Finnish contributor. The Finnish regime places groups wishing to establish themselves abroad at a disadvantage in relation to groups that want to establish only in Finland.

4.2 Contribution from parent to subsidiary

The Finnish regime treats differently two Finnish parent companies that use the freedom of establishment either in Finland or abroad. Only the group contribution from the Finnish parent to the Finnish subsidiary is tax-deductible for the parent, even though the situation of the Finnish parent companies is different only because of the place of establishment of their subsidiaries. The denial of the deduction stems from the sole fact that the Finnish parent company has availed itself of the right to freedom of establishment. It is a measure that restricts the use by Finnish nationals of the right to move freely within the Community. The refusal constitutes a restriction including unfavourable treatment of companies wishing to establish subsidiaries in other Member States. The advantages the subsidiaries may be entitled to in their residence state have no relevance because the Finnish treatment by itself creates an obstacle such as to dissuade companies established in Finland from establishing subsidiaries in other Member States.[73] A comparison may be made to the Bosal case[74] in which the European Court of Justice held that a system in which a parent company has no right to deductions with respect to costs relating to holdings in non-resident subsidiaries but has the right with respect to costs relating to domestic subsidiaries is in conflict with the freedom of establishment.

4.3 Contribution from subsidiary to parent

The Esab case concerns a situation in which a Finnish subsidiary wishes to make a tax-deductible group contribution to its British parent compa-

---

73 This notion was also made by Advocate General Maduro in his Opinion in *Marks & Spencer* (ECJ C-446/03 *Marks & Spencer*, pending), 7 April 2005, para 53.

74 See ECJ 18 September 2003, C-168/01 *Bosal* [2003] ECR I-9409.

ny.[75] The Finnish group regime treats Finnish subsidiaries of Finnish or foreign parent companies differently. Only a Finnish subsidiary of a Finnish parent can make a tax-deductible group contribution to its parent. The Finnish Esab Oy, thus, according to the wording of the Finnish group contribution regime, cannot make a group contribution to its British parent.

Subsidiaries of Finnish companies are favoured over Finnish subsidiaries of foreign parent companies under the Finnish group contribution regime. This difference makes the establishment of a foreign parent to Finland in the form of a subsidiary less attractive than the establishment of a Finnish parent, because only the subsidiary with the foreign parent is allowed to make a tax-deductible group contribution. The situation of the subsidiaries is different only becasue of the place of the parent's establishment.

The different treatment of resident subsidiaries with resident or non-resident parent companies was at issue in the Metallgesellschaft case.[76] The case involved a British subsidiary with a German parent company. The companies could not make the British group income election because the parent company was a non-resident. Because group income election was not possible, the British company had to pay advance corporate tax (ACT) under the British dividend imputation credit system (avoir fiscal) unlike resident companies with resident parents that have made the group income election. Consequently, the British tax system subjected resident subsidiaries with non-resident parents to a worse tax treatment compared to resident companies with resident parents. Such a treatment was found to conflict with the freedom of establishment principle. Based on the Metallgesellschaft case it seems that the Finnish group contribution system is also in conflict with the freedom of establishment principle.

It is also established case law that it does not have to be the taxpayer with the disadvantageous treatment that has exercised the freedom of movement but it is enough that the tax treatment of the taxpayer is affected by the fact that somebody, in this case the parent company, exercised the right.[77] As a consequence, it is enough that the British parent company exercised the right of establishment in Finland via its Netherlands subsidiaries.

75 The British company owns 100 % of the Finnish company via two Netherlands companies.

76 ECJ 8 March 2001, C-397/98 and C-410/98 *Metallgesellschaft/Hoechst* [2001] ECR I-1727.

77 See for example ECJ 12 July 2005, C-403/03 *Schempp*, not yet reported.

Even if it could be argued that the freedom of establishment article does not apply to Esab, because Esab did not exercise the right, but only its parent company did[78], the Finnish treatment may be contrary to the EC Treaty. The Finnish regime, after all, restricts the possibilities of Finnish subsidiaries to move capital from Finland to other Member States, because a group contribution is tax-deductible only if it is paid to a Finnish company.

Broadly interpreted, the Finnish regime that denies the tax deduction with regard to a group contribution may even be regarded to be contrary to the non-discrimination provisions of tax treaties on the lines of Article 24(5) of the OECD Model. According to this article, a state must not treat less favourably its resident companies owned by resident companies of the other contracting state compared to the resident companies owned by residents of the same state. Under the group contribution system, Finland treats less favourably Finnish subsidiaries owned by foreign companies compared to Finnish subsidiaries of Finnish companies.

4.4 Contribution between sister companies

Finally, the Finnish regime treats differently two Finnish subsidiaries that have sister companies, ie subsidiaries of the same parent company, in Finland or abroad. Only the Finnish subsidiary with a Finnish sister company can make a tax-deductible contribution to its sister company. The Finnish regime makes it less attractive for Finnish or foreign parent companies to establish subsidiaries in other Member States and not only in Finland. The situation of the two Finnish subsidiaries is different only because of the place of the sister company's establishment.

5 The Parent-Subsidiary Directive

The Supreme Administrative Court of Finland also referred in its question to the EC Court to the Parent-Subsidiary Directive in addition to the basic freedoms of the EC Treaty. The Parent-Subsidiary Directive clearly indicates the Community's desire to eliminate the disadvantage resulting from the fact that the tax provisions governing relations between parent companies and subsidiaries in Member States are in general less favourable

[78] This argument has been made by certain Finnish authors. See Penttilä, Seppo/Mattila, Pauli K/Ranta-Lassila, Hannele (2005) Suomen konserniavustusjärjestelmä – EY-oikeuden vaatimukset täyttävä vai ei? – Verotus 4/2005 p 363.

than those applicable to relations between parent companies and subsidiaries in one Member State.[79] However, the Parent-Subsidiary Directive concerns distributions of profits between subsidiaries and their parent companies, and it does not cover the question of the treatment of the transfer of losses or the transfer of other contributions within groups of companies or group taxation in other respects.[80] In the author's opinion, the Directive, therefore, is not relevant in the Esab case.

It may be argued that a group contribution is comparable to a profit distribution when it is made by a subsidiary to its parent company. A situation could be imagined where the state of residence of the recipient of the contribution would treat the contribution as a profit distribution qualifying under the Parent-Subsidiary Directive and would therefore exempt the contribution from tax.[81] If the contribution were tax-deductible in Finland the part of the profit that was distributed to the parent company as a group contribution would then not be taxed at all.

In any case, the Parent-Subsidiary Directive does not require that the profits from which a tax-exempt distribution was made had to have been subject to tax in the source state. The Directive does not apply to totally tax-exempt entities, but it does not exclude entities that may have certain tax-exempt profits nor does it require that the specific part of the profit from which the distribution was made had to have been subject to tax. As a consequence, the Parent-Subsidiary Directive in the opinion of the author is not an argument for a different treatment of a domestic and a cross-border contribution in Finland.

At the moment there is no secondary Community legislation that covers the transfer of profits and losses between group companies.[82] It is clear

79 See for example, ECJ 18 September 2003, C-168/01 *Bosal* [2003] ECR I-9409, para 22.

80 Advocate General Maduro also mentioned this notion in his Opinion on *Marks & Spencer* (ECJ C-446/03 *Marks & Spencer*, pending), 7 April 2005, para 2.

81 According to Esab Oy, this would not be the case with respect to Great Britain but the contribution would be treated as a taxable item there.

82 A consolidated profit regime, taking into account the losses of subsidiaries of different Member States, had already been proposed by the Commission of the European Communities in 1969, but the proposed regime never saw the light of day (Proposal for a Council Directive on the common tax regime applicable to parent and subsidiary companies of different Member States (OJ 1969 C 39, p 7). On 6 December 1990, the Commission submitted a proposal for a Council directive concerning arrangements for the taking into account by enterprises of the losses of their permanent establishments and subsidiaries situated in other Member States (91/C 53/03, OJ 1991 C 53, p 30). This proposal was not successful, either.

that the absence of provisions on cross-border offset of the losses of groups of companies in the Community constitutes a major obstacle to the proper functioning of the internal market.[83] Until some further approximation of laws, the problem, however, has to be dealt with by the application of the EC Treaty freedoms. The lack of harmonisation does not prevent nationals of the Member States from enjoying the freedoms of the EC Treaty.[84]

6 Justifications

Because the Finnish group contribution regime seems to mean a restriction of the EC Treaty freedoms, it has to be examined whether there is a justification for such a restriction. Direct discrimination on grounds of nationality is prohibited unless the EC Treaty expressly allows it in a specific situation. Indirect discrimination or a restriction may be justified also on the grounds of an objective reason. According to the rule of reason principle established by the EC Court, a mandatory requirement of public interest may constitute an acceptable reason (necessity test).[85] A discriminatory or restrictive provision, however, must be appropriate for the protection of the recognised public interest and the restrictive effect must be proportionate in relation to the goal pursued (proportionality test). The provision must be the least restrictive possible (less restrictive test).[86]

Indirect discrimination may be allowed, for example, on grounds of a public policy, security or health reason[87] or in order to prevent infringements of domestic law.[88] In principle, an acceptable reason may also be, for example, the need to safeguard the effectiveness of fiscal supervision[89], prevention of abuse[90] or the necessity to safeguard the cohesion of the domestic tax system.[91] There are, however, no direct tax cases in

83 See for example, Communication by the Commission to the Council, European Parliament and the Economic and Social Committee – An Internal Market without Company Tax Obstacles (COM (2003) 726 final).

84 See for example, ECJ 28 January 1992, C-204/90 *Bachmann* [1992] ECR I-249, para 11; and 28 January 1986, 270/83 *Avoir Fiscal* [1986] ECR 273, para 24.

85 See ECJ 20 February 1979, 120/78 *Cassis de Dijon* [1979] ECR 649. See also for example 29 April 1999, C-311/97 *Royal Bank of Scotland* [1999] ECR I-2651, para 32.

86 See for example, ECJ 15 May 1997, C-250/95 *Futura* [1997] ECR I-2471, para 26.

87 Art 46 of EC Treaty.

88 Art 58 of EC Treaty.

89 See ECJ 15 May 1997, C-250/95 *Futura* [1997] ECR I-2471.

90 See for example, ECJ 28 January 1986, 270/83 *Avoir Fiscal* [1986] ECR 273.

91 See ECJ 28 January 1992, C-204/90 *Bachmann* [1992] ECR I-249.

which the EC Court has accepted discriminatory or restrictive tax treatment on these grounds.[92] The Court has repeatedly held that reduction in tax revenue cannot be regarded as an overriding reason in the public interest which may be relied on to justify a measure which is in principle contrary to a fundamental freedom.[93]

It may be argued that the fiscal principle of territoriality and the necessity of ensuring the cohesion of the Finnish tax system would justify the denial of a tax-deductible group contribution in cross-border situations. It could be argued that Finland should not be forced to offer a tax advantage where it has no power to tax the recipient of the contribution. Finland has the power to tax the recipient of a group contribution only if the recipient is a Finnish company or a foreign company with a permanent establishment in Finland. In these situations the contribution is deductible for the contributor. However, the territoriality principle or the cohesion requirement, in the author's opinion, is no reason to allow the Member States to evade their obligations under Community law.[94] It cannot be accepted that a national tax system be structured in the way that it favours national situations.[95] The national tax rules must be neutral in regard to the exercise of the freedoms of movement. Only wholly artificial arrangements with the sole purpose of abusively evading national laws or exploiting the differences between those laws may be out of the scope of the right of free movement and establishment.

---

92 See for example ECJ 15 May 1997, C-250/95 *Futura* [1997] ECR I-2471; 11 August 1995, C-80/94 *Wielockx* [1995] ECR I-2493; 28 April 1998, C-118/96 *Safir* [1998] ECR I-1897; 28 October 1999, C-55/98 *Vestergaard* [1999] ECR I-7641; 3 October 2002, C-136/00 *Danner* [2002] ECR I-8147; 28 January 1986, 270/83 *Avoir Fiscal* [1986] ECR 273; 16 July 1998, C-264/96 *ICI* [1998] ECR I-4695; 26 October 1999, C-294/97 *Eurowings* [1999] ECR I-7447; 8 March 2001, C-397/98 and C-410/98 *Metallgesellschaft/Hoechst* [2001] ECR I-1727; 15 July 2004, C-315/02 *Lenz* [2004] ECR I-7063; 13 July 1993, C-330/91 *Commerzbank* [1993] ECR I-4017; 27 June 1996, C-107/94 *Asscher* [1996] ECR I-3089; 13 April 2000, C-251/98 *Baars* [2000] ECR I-2787; 6 June 2000, C-35/98 *Verkooijen* [2000] ECR I-4071; and 7 September 2004, C-319/02 *Manninen* [2004] ECR I-7477. The Bachmann case (ECJ 28 January 1992, C-204/90 *Bachmann* [1992] ECR I-249) is an exception, but not very far-reaching conclusions should be made from this old case.

93 See for example, ECJ 7 September 2004, C-319/02 *Manninen* [2004] ECR I-7477, para 49.

94 See also Opinion of Advocate General Maduro in *Marks & Spencer* (ECJ C-446/03 *Marks & Spencer*, pending), 7 April 2005, para 62.

95 See also Opinion of Advocate General Maduro in *Marks & Spencer* (ECJ C-446/03 *Marks & Spencer*, pending), 7 April 2005, para 66.

The Esab case concerns a deduction for a Finnish domestic resident company that is subject to unlimited tax liability in Finland.[96] Nobody is asking Finland to allow a tax deduction to a foreign company that it cannot tax. The companies in a group of companies are separate tax subjects despite the special group contribution possibility and the tax treatment of the recipient company is thus not a justification for a denial of a tax benefit for the Finnish company making a contribution. There is no direct link between the tax deductions of a Finnish company that is taxable separately in Finland and the taxation of a foreign recipient (which is separately taxable) of a group contribution abroad.[97] Based on the decisions of the EC Court, a direct link exists only in the context of the same tax and in the case of the same taxpayer.[98]

However, it may be argued, that cohesion should be adjudged in light of the aim and logic of the tax regime at issue.[99] The aim of the group contribution scheme is to ensure fiscal neutrality for the effects of the creation of a group. Its purpose is not to create an advantage for a group compared to a single entity. Therefore, the advantage of the tax deductibility conferred on the contributor should be neutralised by the tax to be charged to the recipient company. As a consequence, it may be argued that a group contribution needs to be deductible in Finland only if the contribution is treated as a taxable item for the recipient in its state of residence. As a consequence, a group contribution made by a Finnish company to a company of another EU Member State should be deductible in Finland at least where the state of residence of the recipient treats the contribution as a taxable item for the recipient.[100] On the other hand, it could be argued that

---

96 Compare ECJ 7 September 2004, C-319/02 *Manninen* [2004] ECR I-7477, para 38.

97 A Direct link was the requirement IN the Bachmann case where the cohesion principle was accepted as a justification. See ECJ 28 January 1992, C-204/90 *Bachmann* [1992] ECR I-249.

98 See for example, ECJ 18 September 2003, C-168/01 *Bosal* [2003] ECR I-9409, para 30.

99 See for example, ECJ 7 September 2004, C-319/02 *Manninen* [2004] ECR I-7477, para 43; and 11 March 2004, C-9/02 *de Lasteyrie du Saillant* [2004] ECR I-2409, para 67. See also opinion of Advocate General Maduro in *Marks & Spencer* (ECJ C-446/03 *Marks & Spencer*, pending), 7 April 2005, paras 71-74.

100 Compare to ECJ 7 September 2004, C-319/02 Manninen [2004] ECR I-7477, para 54, in which the EC Court mentioned that the taxes paid by a dividend distributing company in Sweden may be taken into account when determining the amount of a dividend imputation credit of the dividend recipient in Finland. In the Esab case, the group contribution would according to Esab Oy be treated as a taxable item in Britain and should therefore be deductible in Finland.

based on the more broadly understood cohesion concept, the deductibility of a contribution could be denied if the state of residence of the recipient of the contribution does not treat it as a taxable item.

A Finnish measure that denies a deduction of a group contribution in all cases without regard to the tax treatment abroad goes well beyond what is necessary in order to protect the cohesion of Finland's group system. It results from objectives that are foreign to the rationale of the group contribution regime. Such a broad denial of the deductibility can be understood only as a measure to protect Finland's tax revenue or to favour Finnish groups compared to multinational groups. Such objectives are not in accordance with the EC Treaty.

7 Concluding Remarks

It seems that the Finnish group contribution regime in its present form is not in accordance with Community legislation. The regime goes too far in restricting the free movement and establishment of Finnish companies abroad and in protecting the tax revenues.

It is clear that allowing the deduction of a group contribution made to a foreign company may lead to a situation in which contributions are made to foreign loss-making companies or to companies in states with low corporate taxes. However, the possibility of minimising or avoiding taxes by group contributions between Finnish companies was already possible. The fact that the same possibility would be available to multinational groups is completely in accordance with the principle of an internal market. It is, however, clear that the budgetary concerns of Finland may force Finland to abolish the group contribution system all together, if the group contributions made to foreign companies become deductible.

In any case, there is a crying need for positive harmonisation of group taxation in the Communities. Something new has to be developed to replace the various domestic group taxation systems. A possibility of balancing profits and losses between the companies in a group of companies is also necessary in the future. It is to be hoped that a new EU-wide system taking the cross-border situation better into account will be introduced irrespective of the decision of the European Court of Justice in the Esab case.

Pending Cases Filed by German Courts I: The Meilicke, CLT-UFA, Keller Holding, Lasertec, Rewe Zentralfinanz, Ritter-Coulais, Kolumbus Container Services, and Stauffer Cases

*Jürgen Lüdicke**

I Meilicke (C-292/04)

1 Introduction
2 Relevant German Legislation
3 Facts of the Case
4 German Court Proceedings and Referral to the ECJ
5 Observations
5.1 Amount of credit and/or refund of foreign corporation tax
5.2 Restriction on the retrospective application of ECJ judgments

II CLT-UFA (C-152/03)

1 Introduction
2 Relevant German Legislation
3 Facts of the Case
4 German Court Proceedings and the Referral to the ECJ
5 Opinion of the Advocate General
6 Observations
6.1 Free choice of form of secondary establishment
6.2 Withholding tax according to the Parent-Subsidiary Directive 90/435/EEC compatible with the freedom of establishment?

III Keller Holding (C-471/04)

1 Introduction
2 Relevant German legislation
3 Facts of the Case
4 German Court Proceedings and Questions Referred to the ECJ
5 Observations
5.1 Denial of imputation credit for dividends from non-resident companies decisive for Keller Holding?

* I would like to thank StB Caroline Naumburg, LL.M., and RA Dr. Florian Haase, M.I.Tax, for the preparation of this manuscript.

5.2 Other pending cases in Germany in respect of deductibility of expenses connected to foreign shareholdings

IV Lasertec (C-492/04)
1 Introduction
2 Relevant German Legislation
3 Facts of the Case
4 German Court Proceedings and Questions Referred to the ECJ
5 Observations

V Rewe Zentralfinanz (C-347/04)
1 Introduction
2 Relevant German Legislation
3 Facts of the Case
4 German Court Proceedings and Questions Referred to the ECJ
5 Observations

VI Ritter-Coulais (C-152/03)
1 Introduction
2 Relevant German Legislation
3 Facts of the Case
4 German Court Proceedings and Questions Referred to the ECJ
5 Opinion of the Advocate General
6 Observations

VII Kolumbus Container Services (C-298/05)
1 Introduction
2 Relevant German Legislation
3 Facts of the Case
4 German Court Proceedings and Questions Referred to the ECJ
5 Observations

VIII Stauffer (C-386/04)
1 Introduction
2 Relevant German Legislation
3 Facts of the Case
4 German Court Proceedings and Questions Referred to the ECJ
5 Observations

I Meilicke (C-292/04)

1 Introduction

The Meilicke case is the German pendant to the Finnish ECJ case Petri Manninen[1], which was decided on 7 September 2004.

The latter was a landmark ruling for all Member States that apply some sort of imputation system for dividend taxation. In this case, profits distributed by Finnish companies were subject to corporate tax and also in principle to income tax at the same rate in the hands of Finnish shareholders. In order to avoid double taxation, the shareholders were granted an imputation credit amounting to their income tax liability on the dividend, with the result that the only tax paid on the profits was the company's corporate tax.

Dividends received by Finnish resident shareholders from companies outside Finland were equally subject to income tax, but with no equivalent imputation credit. The claimant, Petri Manninen, who had to pay income tax on dividends received by a Swedish company in which he had shares, argued that the difference in treatment between dividends from a Finnish company and a Swedish company due to the lack of imputation credit infringed Article 56 EC and the matter was referred to the ECJ for preliminary ruling.

The ECJ held that the unequal treatment was likely to both deter Finnish investors from investing in equity in other countries as well as to deter companies in other Member States from raising capital in Finland. The relevant legislation was therefore in principle contrary to Article 56 EC. Article 58(1) (a) EC is to be interpreted restrictively and does not mean that all legislation making distinctions by reference to the place of investment of capital is compatible with Articles 56 and 58(3) EC. Article 58 EC can justify different treatment if the situations are not comparable, but in the Manninen case the situation of a shareholder receiving dividends from Finnish companies is comparable to the situation of a shareholder receiving dividends from non-Finnish companies, as in both cases the profits were at risk of being taxed twice.

Furthermore, the unequal treatment could not be justified by the need to maintain the coherence of the tax system, since even if there were a nec-

1 ECJ 7 September 2004, C-319/02 *Manninen* [2004] ECR I-7477.

essary link between a taxation of the profits of the company and a countervailing tax deduction at the shareholder level, the treatment was disproportionate as the granting of an imputation credit to the claimant to offset the corporate tax payable in Sweden would be less restrictive of the free movement of capital than the Finnish practice.

The ECJ made it very clear that the EC Treaty generally precludes any national provisions where the right to an imputation credit is excluded unless dividends are paid by a company established in the same country as the shareholder. This holds true equally for the former German imputation system for dividend taxation, which was abolished as of 2001/2002 and onwards.

The ECJ now has the chance to give its first explicit ruling with respect to a possible infringement of Article 56 EC by the former German imputation system in the case Wienand Meilicke, Heidi Christa Weyde und Marina Stöffler, hereinafter Meilicke[2]. The case was referred to the ECJ by the German Tax Court of Cologne on 24 June 2004[3]. The Court had doubts about the compatibility of the German provisions with the free movement of capital. This view is shared by German academic literature[4].

2 Relevant German Legislation

In order to understand the Court's reasoning, one has to understand how the former German imputation system worked. Until 2001, Germany applied an imputation system for dividend taxation. It aimed at taxing dividends only at the level of the individual shareholder at his personal income tax rate. Germany also applied a split corporate tax rate, one for retained profits at 45 % until 1998 and 40 % until 2000, and another one for distributed profits, which was 30 %.

The imputation system worked as follows: If a German resident company made a profit of 100 in 1999, it paid 40 corporate tax. Upon distribution to its parent company, the tax was reduced to the rate applicable for distributed profits, namely 30. As a result, 70 could be distributed on to the parent company as a dividend.

The parent company received the dividend of 70 and was at the same time granted an imputation credit amounting to the underlying corporate tax of

[2] ECJ C-292/04 *Meilicke*, pending.

[3] Case no 2 K 2241/02; EFG 2004, p 1374.

[4] For example, Schnitger/Papantonopoulos, Deutsche Vorabentscheidungsersuchen zu den direkten Steuern des Jahres 2004, *BB* 2005, p 407.

30 that the subsidiary had paid, or 3/7 of the dividend. This imputation credit was taxable, so that the taxable income of the parent company added up to 100. Again, 40 corporate tax was levied. The imputation credit of 30 could be offset against the corporate tax and so the parent company paid a tax of 40 less 30, ie 10. As a result, the parent company had 60 left after tax. Upon further distribution of the dividend, the corporate tax was again reduced from 40 to 30 and the company could pass on a dividend of 70 to its shareholders.

Dividends could thus float through a chain of companies economically tax-exempt at the level of a receiving and redistributing company. The individual shareholder at the end of the chain also received an imputation credit with the dividend, which were both taxed at his personal income tax rate. He could both offset the imputation credit against this income tax as well as – if there was no tax burden – get the imputation wholly refunded. The refund applied to companies as well as to individuals. A company could receive such a refund in a loss situation.

However, the German imputation system only applied when a German resident company distributed dividends to a German resident shareholder. Consequently, a German resident shareholder receiving foreign dividends was not granted an imputation credit (see sec 36 para 2 no 3 German Income Tax Act before the imputation system was abolished). The same applied to non-resident shareholders – these were not entitled to imputation credits on dividends from German companies.

3 Facts of the Case

The German resident individual Meilicke received dividends from Danish and Dutch shareholdings in the years 1995 through 1997. These dividends were taxed in Germany in accordance with the principle of taxation on the basis of worldwide income as income from capital investments (sec 2 para 1 no 5, 20 para 1 no 1 German Income Tax Act). As the dividends were not distributed by companies resident in Germany, Meilicke was not granted an imputation credit for the Danish and Dutch corporate income tax.

The claimants, heirs of Meilicke, filed an objection against his tax assessment with the local tax authority and asked for an imputation credit of 3/7 of the foreign dividends. They argued that the denial of an imputation credit according to the restriction in sec 36 para 2 no 3 German Income Tax Act solely because the distributing companies were resident outside Germany constituted a breach of the free movement of capital in Article 56 EC.

4 German Court Proceedings and Referral to the ECJ

In its decision of 24 June 2004 the German Tax Court of Cologne questioned the compatibility of sec 36 para 2 no 3 German Income Tax Act with the free movement of capital in Article 56 EC. The Court's reasoning was pretty much straightforward, and stated that dividends distributed from resident corporations were tax-privileged whereas dividends from non-resident corporations did not fall within the scope of the imputation system. It is obvious in this respect that there is a difference between the treatment of dividends from a German and a foreign company.

The Court held that despite the fact that the ECJ basically recognises coherence of the tax system as a valid justification of a restriction the coherence argument is not applicable here.

Moreover, the Court held that the denial of an imputation credit on foreign dividends cannot be justified by the loss of revenue or by difficulties in obtaining information and the verifiability of the same from other Member States, thereby citing the Advocate General in the Manninen case[5].

The Court thus referred the following question to the ECJ:

> Is sec 36 para 2 no 3 German Income Tax Act (in the version in force during the relevant years), whereby only corporation tax payable by a fully-taxable corporation or association amounting to three sevenths of the income within the meaning of sec 20 para 1 no 1 or 2 German Income Tax Act is offset against income tax, compatible with Articles 56

para EC and 58 para 1 lit a and para 3 EC?

5 Observations

5.1 Amount of credit and/or refund of foreign corporate tax

After the ECJ decision in the Manninen case it cannot be doubted that the German imputation system contravenes EC law. The legal issue is obviously the same as in the Manninen case, so that the Meilicke case will have a similar outcome, even though the German government argued in the hearing of the case on 8 September 2005 that the situations in Manninen and Meilicke were completely different.

5 Opinion of Advocate General Kokott in *Manninen* (ECJ 7 September 2004, C-319/02 *Manninen* [2004] ECR I-74771), 18 March 2004, paras 71et seq.

There are, however, a couple of remaining questions about the credit of foreign corporate tax that were not raised in the original referral in Meilicke, namely credit of foreign tax where the foreign corporate tax rate is higher than the domestic imputation credit and the question of refund rather than simply a credit of the foreign tax.

In Manninen, the Swedish corporate tax rate on the underlying profits was lower than the Finnish corporate tax rate. In the Meilicke case, the Dutch and probably also the Danish underlying corporate tax on the dividends was higher than the German corporate tax rate on distributed dividends, but lower or equal to the German corporate tax rate on retained profits. This issue was raised in the hearing by Meilicke and the European Commission. If the foreign underlying corporate tax rate is higher than the domestic imputation credit, must a Member State give an imputation credit for the whole amount, or is the obligation limited to the domestic credit? That is, can Meilicke claim not only 3/7 of the dividend as an imputation credit, but for example 2/3 of the dividend, if the foreign underlying corporate tax is 40 %?

In the hearing of the Meilicke case, the European Commission submitted that it was of the opinion that regardless of whether the foreign underlying corporate tax is higher or lower than the domestic rate, the actually paid foreign corporate tax must be credited[6]. I share that view, as the rate on distributed dividends was in a purely domestic case irrelevant due to the full imputation or refund of the actually paid German corporate tax. In fact, it had been 36 % before 1994. It was reduced with regard to non-resident shareholders, as these were not entitled to the imputation credit; resident shareholders did not benefit from the reduction.

Both the Manninen and the Meilicke cases concern individuals, but the underlying principles are equally applicable to corporations. A denial of an imputation credit to a corporation in a cross-border case is therefore to the same extent in breach of either the freedom of establishment or the free movement of capital as in the case of an individual.

The third issue that is of interest in respect of imputation credits is unfortunately not subject to the referral in Meilicke. This question is probably of more relevance to corporations than to individuals, namely the question of a refund rather than only a credit of foreign tax. Since Germany not

6 Report of the hearing, 8 September 2005, para 24.

only credited, but also refunded domestic corporate tax, was it equally obliged to refund foreign corporate tax if there was no or merely a low tax burden in Germany?

Here two situations must be distinguished: The first one is that of a loss in Germany. Must Germany refund foreign underlying corporate tax in the case of a loss of the shareholder? Personally, I doubt that a State has to refund foreign tax before it can actually charge tax on the relevant income, ie before the losses are used up. In my view, it is more likely that a State has to grant some sort of credit carry forward in such cases, to be set off against future tax potential.

Here two situations must be distinguished: The first one is that of a loss in Germany. Must Germany refund foreign underlying corporate tax in the case of a loss of the shareholder? Personally, I doubt that a State has to refund foreign tax before it can actually charge tax on the relevant income, ie before the losses are used up. In my view, it is more likely that a State has to grant some sort of credit carry forward in such cases, to be set off against future tax potential.

The second situation is where the personal income tax rate of an individual or the corporate tax rate of the company receiving the dividend is lower than the imputation credit, if such credit is granted to the full extent of the foreign underlying corporate tax. In this case, we are simply dealing with differences in tax rates of two Member States. According to previous ECJ case law and more specifically, the Gilly case[7], the fact that a cross-border activity is taxed higher than a domestic one merely due to different tax rates in the Member States is not a breach of the fundamental freedoms, as tax rates are not harmonised. This implies that a Member State does not have to refund or credit excess tax, where a full credit could not take place due to differences in tax rates.

I do not share the opposite view that the foreign tax has be wholly refunded just because the distributed profits have been subject to taxation by way of corporate tax, irrespective of whether those dividends come from domestic or from foreign companies[8]. If the German imputation system aimed at levying the shareholder's individual tax rate on the dividends received and thereby on the profits made by the distributing company, the

---

7 ECJ 12 May 1998, C-336/96 *Gilly* [1998] ECR I-2793.

8 ECJ 7 September 2004, C-319/02 *Manninen* [2004] ECR I-7477.

company was finally treated as a transparent vehicle. If in such a situation a foreign state chose to tax the foreign profits (in its view as profits of the foreign corporation) at a higher rate than the shareholder's individual tax rate in his home state, this was a result of different tax rates in a not yet harmonised market. Similarly, the home state would not be obliged to refund a higher foreign tax if it was levied on the shareholder's own income in that state derived from a transparent vehicle like a partnership or from an own permanent establishment in that state.

5.2 Restriction on the retrospective application of ECJ judgments

Another issue of utmost interest to taxpayers was raised in the hearing of the Meilicke case: It is the question of restriction on the judgment's period of application. The German government argued that should the German practice be considered to be in breach of the free movement of capital, the applicability of the judgment should be limited to the future, more precisely the Member States have to be granted a suitable transitional period to abolish the discriminatory legislation[9]. Alternatively, the government asked the application to be restricted to the future without a transitional period and thirdly, to the period after the ECJ's judgment in Verkooijen[10].

The German government thereby stated that the ECJ has in certain cases granted such limitation of the retroactive effect of a judgment and that the requirements for this are met in the present case[11]. The government argued that the Member States were at least in good faith with respect to the scope of Articles 56 and 58 EC until the judgment in the Verkooijen judgment in 2000[12]. This statement was, however, proved wrong by the claimant, as he showed that the European Commission had in 1995 already addressed the German government in respect on an infringement of the EC by the same provision of the German Income Tax Act now being challenged in the Meilicke case[13]. In addition, the government had officially announced its intent to abolish the imputation system already in

9 Report of the hearing 8 September 2005, para 22.

10 ECJ 6 June 2000, C-35/98 *Verkooijen* [2000] ECR I-4071.

11 ECJ 8 April 1976, 43/75 *Defrenne* [1976] ECR 455; and 17 May 1990, 262/88 *Barber* [1990] ECR 1889.

12 Report of the hearing, 8 September 2005, para. 20.

13 Portner, ECJ Conducts Oral Hearing in German Tax Case, *Tax Analysts* 20 September 2005.

December 1999[14], which is before the Verkooijen judgment. Finally, depending on the shareholder quote, the denial of a credit for foreign corporate tax may infringe the freedom of establishment. It is difficult to see how the Member States could be in good faith insofar as Article 58 EC is not applicable.

The second argument of the German government in this respect at the hearing, namely that a retrospective application would cost Germany around nine billion EURO, seems questionable. There is no statement as to how this amount has been calculated. Moreover, this was stated to be the amount that would have to be paid out if foreign corporate tax must be credited back to 1994. The report of the hearing does not say whether the German government mentioned that Germany changed its procedural rules last year as a consequence of the Manninen decision, so that claims based on Manninen/Meilicke could only be made within the normal period of statute of limitations, which is regularly 4 to 7 years.[15]

One should bear in mind that a limitation on the retrospective application of ECJ judgments would deprive EU nationals of an effective legal protection when relying on the EC Treaty. Member States could feel tempted to "test" how far to go without having to bear respective budgetary risks.

The last issue that was addressed in the hearing deals with the question of third-country relationships, ie whether dividends from companies in States outside the EU should also give rise to an imputation credit. It was requested that the ECJ state an opinion on this issue, in order to avoid more referrals[16].

---

14 Bundesministerium der Finanzen, Referat Presse und Information, 21 December 1999, Steuerreform 2000, p 10/11: „Das Halbeinkünfteverfahren verdient in mehrfacher Hinsicht den Vorzug vor dem Anrechnungsverfahren: Es ist **wettbewerbsneutral** und damit **europatauglich**, weil es den – noch – existierenden steuerlichen Fokus auf dem nationalen Markt durchbricht."

15 Reference is made to sec 175 para 2 sentence 2 German General Tax Code (Abgabenordnung).

16 Report of the hearing, 8 September 2005, para 15.

II CLT-UFA (C-152/03)

1 Introduction

The case concerns the special corporate tax rate of 42 % that applied to profits of permanent establishments of non-resident corporations, ie corporations without seat or management in Germany, under the former German imputation system[17]. At a first glance, the case is a Royal Bank of Scotland[18] look-alike and the referral by the German Supreme Tax Court seems dispensable, as the compatibility of the national regulations in question with the freedom of establishment seems to be a case of an acte claire. However, there is more to this case than just different tax rates for non-residents and residents; the technique of the former German imputation system needs to be accounted for when deciding on the matter and certain points on the free choice of legal form for a secondary establishment made by the Advocate General in his Opinion leaves room for discussion.

2 Relevant German Legislation

Under the German imputation system, split tax rates for retained and distributed profits of a German resident corporation were applied. In 1994, the relevant year in CLT-UFA, the rate for retained profits was 45 %. The corporate tax rate on distributed profits amounted to 30 %. Profits of a German permanent establishment of a non-resident corporation were by contrast subject to a final corporate tax rate of 42 %.

The Parent-Subsidiary Directive (90/435/EEC) applied in 1994 to profit distributions from a German subsidiary to its foreign EU parent company. By way of derogation in Article 5 para 3 Parent-Subsidiary Directive (90/435/EEC), Germany was allowed, as long as it charged corporate tax on distributed profits at a rate at least 11 % lower than the rate applicable to retained profits and at the latest until 30 June 1996, to impose a compensatory withholding tax of 5 % on profits distributed by German subsidiaries to foreign EU parent companies. Distributed profits would as a result be subject to a corporate tax of 33.5 %.

After 30 June 1996, Germany did not levy any withholding tax on distributions from a German subsidiary to its foreign EU parent company where the requirements of the Parent- Subsidiary Directive (90/435/EEC) were met.

---

17 Abolished by Steuersenkungsgesetz of 23 October 2000, BGBl. I, p 1433.

18 ECJ 29 April 1999, C-311/97 *Royal Bank of Scotland* [1999] ECR I-2651.

Moreover, as stated under I.2, the technique of the German imputation system led to an economic exemption of dividends at the level of a company receiving and distributing dividends. This was achieved by the granting of an imputation credit on received dividends and the reduction in corporate tax rate upon distribution of profits. As a result, corporate profits could flow through a chain of companies without effective taxation on intermediate levels.

A 25 % withholding tax rate (and additional solidarity surcharge) was levied on dividends paid to German resident companies. This was, however, a prepayment of the receiving company's corporate tax on the dividend and was credited against the mainstream corporate tax or refunded in case the receiving company had no tax burden.

3 Facts of the Case

The claimant CLT-UFA is a societe anonyme (S.A.) with seat and management in Luxembourg that maintained a permanent establishment in Germany in 1994. It was assessed for the taxable income of the German permanent establishment in accordance with the special tax rate of 42 % applying to companies merely being subject to limited tax liability in Germany at that time.

CLT-UFA filed an objection against this treatment and argued that the special tax rate for non-residents is discriminatory and infringes the freedom of establishment in Article 52 of the EC Treaty (now Article 43 EC). The Tax Court decided to the disadvantage of CLT-UFA, which appealed against the judgment and applied for cancellation of the Tax Court's judgment and alteration of the tax assessment to the extent that the tax rate should be reduced to 30 %.

4 German Court Proceedings and the Referral to the ECJ

The German Supreme Tax Court initially stated that the treatment of the permanent establishment was in accordance with German national law and that the underlying computation of the taxable income in Germany was undisputed between the parties. It then went on to observe that even though direct taxation lies within the Member States' competence, these nevertheless have to exercise this competence in accordance with Community law, thereby citing the ECJ judgment in the Eurowings case[19].

[19] ECJ 26 October 1999, C-294/97 *Eurowings* [1999] ECR I-7447.

The Court held that CLT-UFA was entitled to rely on the freedom of establishment in the year in question, as it was a company founded under the laws of a Member State, had its seat in Luxembourg and carried on business both through its activities in the Member State of its seat as well as through a branch in Germany. In accordance with ECJ jurisprudence, the Court moreover held that the freedom of establishment grants the companies the right to freely chose the form of their establishment in another Member State and that this right may not be limited by discriminatory national tax regulations[20].

Due to its seat and management outside Germany, CLT-UFA was treated differently in respect of its German branch profits than had it carried out its German activities in the form of a limited company with seat and/or management in Germany (subsidiary). Profits that a subsidiary in Germany had wholly distributed in 1994 would not have been taxed at 42 %, but at the most at 33.5 %, in accordance with the German legislation in force at that time (see II.2).

The disadvantage that CLT-UFA was subject to was neither compensated for by favourable computation rules nor by the fact that a German resident subsidiary had suffered 45 % corporate tax until its profits were actually distributed.

The tax rate on a permanent establishment applied regardless of whether profits were transferred to the head office or they were left and thus "retained" in the permanent establishment. The Court pointed out that the higher tax rate on retained profits in a subsidiary could be avoided by distribution of the profits to the parent company. If the subsidiary was in need of funding for its business, the distributed profits were simply transferred back by the parent company as equity or as shareholders' loan.

The Court furthermore held that the aim of the former German imputation system did not exclude the comparison between the corporate tax rates on distributed profits (ie 30 %) and profits of permanent establishments of non-residents. The imputation system could also not justify that profits of a permanent establishment of a foreign EU company are taxed higher than profits of a domestic subsidiary.

The major aim of the imputation system was the avoidance of multiple taxation of profits of a company, subject to unlimited taxation in

20 ECJ 13 July 1993, C-330/91 *Commerzbank* [1993] ECR I-4017, para 14.

Germany. This was achieved by the reduction in tax rate on distributed profits and the imputation credit. The corporate tax thus had the character of a prepayment of the tax burden of the shareholder and was not final. The taxation of the profits of a permanent establishment of a non-resident however, led to a final burden.

This difference in treatment would be possible to justify, had the reduced tax rate on distributed dividends only been applied on distributions to shareholders resident in Germany. This, however, was not the case; the reduced tax rate also applied to distributions from a German resident subsidiary to a non-resident shareholder. Against the opinion of the tax authorities, there was thus no obvious link between the reduced tax rate on distributed profits and the taxation of the shareholder.

The Court moreover held that a loss of revenue in Germany in the case of a lower tax rate on profits of a permanent establishment was not capable of justifying this different treatment[21]. The fact that CLT-UFA could have avoided the higher tax rate by forming a subsidiary rather than a permanent establishment in Germany cannot serve as a justification either. And finally, the higher tax rate for permanent establishments cannot be justified by a further taxation of dividends from a German subsidiary to its Luxembourg parent company, as such dividends are – as the profits of a German permanent establishment – exempt from taxation in Luxembourg.

Should the corporate tax rate on permanent establishments constitute an infringement of Articles 43 and 48 EC, a tax rate of 33.5 % might be sufficient to end this breach, based on the following argumentation: CLT-UFA could dispose over the profits of the permanent establishment in the year in question, i.e. in 1994. It was therefore in a situation comparable to that of a non-resident EU company receiving an interim or regular dividend right after year end from its German subsidiary. The corporate tax plus withholding tax suffered had in such a case been 33.5 %.

Finally, the Court pointed out that there is a difference between the present case and Royal Bank of Scotland[22], as in the latter the question was simply whether different tax rates could be applied to resident and non-resident companies. In the present case, however, the discrimination

---

21 ECJ 21 September 1999, C-307/97 *Saint-Gobain* [1999] ECR I-6161, para 51.

22 ECJ 29 April 1999, C-311/97 *Royal Bank of Scotland* [1999] ECR I-2651.

against non-resident companies only occurs if the comparison is based on the fact that – as a rule rather than as an exception – a subsidiary distributed all its profits, as the tax rate on retained profits in a subsidiary was 45 % in 1994 and thus was higher than the 42 % imposed on a permanent establishment of a non-resident company.

Based on these doubts, BFH referred the following questions to the ECJ:

1. Is Article 52 in conjunction with Article 58 of the EC Treaty to be interpreted as meaning that charging the profits made in 1994 by a company from another Member State through a branch in Germany to German corporation tax at the rate of 42 % (the „place of business tax rate“) constitutes an infringement of the right of freedom of establishment, given that
   - the profits would have been charged to German corporation tax at the rate of only 33.5 % if they had been made by a company subject to unlimited corporation tax in Germany which was a subsidiary of a capital company from another Member State and had distributed all the profits to its parent by the end of 30 June 1996,
   - the profits would initially have been charged to German corporation tax at the rate of 45 % if the subsidiary had retained them until the end of 30 June 1996, but the liability to corporation tax would have been reduced retrospectively to 30 % if the profits had been distributed in full after 30 June 1996?
2. If the place of business tax rate infringes Article 52 in conjunction with Article 58 of the EC Treaty, is it necessary to reduce it to 30 % for the year in dispute in order to cure the infringement?

5 Opinion of the Advocate General

On 14 April 2005, Advocate General Philippe Legér issued his Opinion in the CLT-UFA case. He thereby started by analysing the arguments brought forward by the German tax authorities and the German government.

The German government and the tax authorities had stated that the situation of a subsidiary and a permanent establishment in Germany were not objectively comparable: The transfer of profits from a permanent establishment cannot be compared to a distribution of profits of a subsidiary. Whereas upon profit transfer from a permanent establishment to its head office, the profits remain within the company, the situation of a distributing subsidiary is different as the profits actually leave the company upon distribution. Other than the national tax regulations questioned in the cases Commission v France, Royal Bank of Scotland and Saint Gobain[23], the German tax rule did not depend on the seat of the company, but on a profit distribution. The reduction is, moreover, connected with the former imputation system, which aimed at avoiding the double taxation of the profits that would occur if the profits were both taxed at the level of the distributing company as well as at the level of the receiving shareholder. Accordingly, the system could only apply to companies whose profits led to taxable income at the level of the shareholder. Thus, the tax rate of 42 % not only applied to non-resident companies, but also to resident corporations that were not part of the imputation system.

Moreover, the general application of a tax rate of 30 % on profits of a permanent establishment of a non-resident company is not justified, as it would lead to an advantage for non-resident compared to resident companies. The tax authorities added that the tax rate of a distributing subsidiary could be higher due to non-deductible expenses and mentioned a case where the tax rate of a distributing subsidiary amounted to 35.59 %.

The Advocate General did not share these views. He concluded that the German practice seemed to limit the right of free choice of establishment for non-resident companies that wanted to invest in Germany. Moreover, the situations in which this differentiating treatment applied seem to be objectively comparable.

The Advocate General cited the above mentioned cases of Commission v France and Saint Gobain to substantiate his arguments. He stated that the free choice of legal form for a secondary establishment is an integral part of the freedom of establishment in Articles 43 and 48 EC. These articles prohibit all restrictions that are the result of a treatment, which is not in accordance with Article 43 EC, due to it being an obvious discrimination on the grounds of a company's seat. From Saint Gobain it follows that the right to choose the best form of secondary establishment is infringed where a branch is not granted the same tax benefits as a subsidiary. It also follows that this right to choose the best form of establishment implies that a branch of a company with seat in another Member State must receive the same benefits as a subsidiary of a company with seat in another Member State.

23 ECJ 28 January 1986, 270/83 *Avoir Fiscal* [1986] ECR 273; 29 April 1999, C-311/97 *Royal Bank of Scotland* [1999] ECR I-2651; 21 September 1999, C-307/97 *Saint-Gobain* [1999] ECR I-6161.

The Advocate General concluded that the tax rate of 42 % of a permanent establishment was definite and thus irrespective of a profit distribution. Even though, as the tax authorities argued, the tax rate of a distributing company could under circumstances be higher than the tax rate for a permanent establishment, it cannot seriously be contested that a reduction to 33.5 % or 30 % leads to a more favourable treatment than taxation at a 42 % rate. Finally, can the disadvantage that occurs due to the different tax rates applicable to a permanent establishment and a subsidiary not be avoided by the tax treaty between Luxembourg and Germany, as this convention does not foresee any credit of the taxes levied in Germany on the profits of a permanent establishment? Luxembourg exempts these profits from taxation.

The Advocate General continued by stating that even though the analysis in this case is different from that in Commission vs. France and Saint-Gobain due to the fact that the benefit in CLT-UFA is of importance to the parent company rather than to the subsidiary, as was the case in Commission vs. France and Saint-Gobain, it does not change the fact that the German practice cannot be an infringement in the sense that it limits the right of free choice of secondary establishment.

As for the analysis of whether objective comparable situations are at hand, the Advocate General makes a clear point. He states that the normal argument used by governments that residents and non-residents are generally not in comparable situations cannot be extended to the taxation of companies. This argument has been accepted regarding the taxation of non-resident individuals. However, in respect of individuals residence and nationality may differ from each other and so the criterion residence for individuals can merely lead to indirect discrimination, whereas in respect of companies, the seat constitutes the nationality. The ECJ has held that Article 48 EC would be carved out, if it were possible for the host state to treat situations differently, merely because the seat of a company is in another Member state.

When analysing national regulations that have imposed different treatment on companies due to their seat, the Advocate General held that seat as a connecting factor has been applied differently in respect of deciding on the taxation of a company than in respect of benefits associated with this taxation. In other words, the infringement of Community law arises because the Member State in question within one and the same set of rules treats the company with a seat in another Member State as a domestic company for purposes of the computation of tax, but at the same time, in respect of the assessment of these taxes, excludes the company with a seat in another Member State from benefits connected with this very taxation.

From the information by the referring Court, it becomes clear that the profit derived by a permanent establishment of a company with a seat in another Member State than Germany is computed according to the same set of rules. There are indeed cases where special agreements between a parent company and its subsidiary may lead to a higher profit in the subsidiary situation than in the permanent establishment situation. However, this is the exception rather than the rule. According to this information, the Advocate General assumed that there is no difference in the computation of taxable income between a subsidiary and a permanent establishment. The fact that non-resident companies are only subject to taxation on income from Germany, whereas resident companies are subject to taxation on their world-wide income does not alter the conclusion that they are in objectively comparable situations in respect of the German income.

On the question of whether the fact that the reduction in tax rate was only granted to subsidiaries in the case of a distribution of profits could mean that a permanent establishment of a foreign company and a German subsidiary are not in comparable situations, the Advocate General concluded that this is not the case. He substantiated this by analysing the aim of the rules. According to the tax authorities, the reduction of the tax rate upon distribution was a part of the imputation system, in order to avoid double taxation of the profits. The imputation system, however, did not apply to foreign companies that received a distribution from their German subsidiaries. Such parent companies are, however, subject to tax on their income in another Member State. This also applies to foreign companies with a permanent establishment in Germany. In both these cases, the possibility for foreign companies to deduct or credit the taxes paid in Germany depends on the tax treaty of the foreign state with Germany or on the national law of the state of the foreign company.

The tax treaty between Germany and Luxembourg provides for an exemption of the profits of a German permanent establishment as well as of dividends distributed by a German subsidiary to its qualifying Luxembourg parent company. The fact that the profits of both types of secondary establishments in Germany are treated equally in Luxembourg also confirms that the parent companies are in objectively comparable situations.

Moreover, the Advocate General did not agree with the argument that a profit transfer from a permanent establishment is not comparable with a profit distribution from a subsidiary to its parent company because the profits actually do not leave the company in the case of a transfer between permanent establishment and head office. He held that, even though the permanent establishment does not have a separate legal personality, for tax purposes it may be possible to assume separate assets and profits of the permanent establishment that remain with the permanent establishment until the actual transfer to the head office. This is supported by the OECDModel Convention, Article 7 para 2, (similar to Article 5 of the tax treaty between Germany and Luxembourg) which considers the relationship between a head office and a permanent establishment equal to the relationship between legally separate entities. Furthermore, the Advocate General concluded that this argument is not decisive, especially taking into consideration the practice explained by the German Supreme Tax Court of distributing profits and contributing these to the subsidiary in order to enjoy the lower tax rate on distributed profits.

As concerns practicalities, the Advocate General held that it should not be more difficult for the national tax authorities to use a similar set of rules for profits transfers than it is to use these rules for profit distributions.

The Advocate General opined that the first question of the BFH should be answered as follows:

> Article 52 in conjunction with Article 58 EC treaty are to be interpreted as precluding national tax provisions of a Member State, according to which the profits of a permanent establishment of a company of another Member State are taxed with 42 % without possibility of reduction, whereas a company in that Member State, for example a subsidiary, that distributes its entire profit to its parent company in another Member State, is taxed with a rate of 33.5 % in case of a distribution before 30 June 1996 and with 30 % in case of a distribution after 30 June 1996.

As concerns the second question referred, the Advocate General concluded that it is – depending on whether the ECJ follows the proposed answer to the first question – up to the referring Court to decide the total tax rate that would have applied, had a subsidiary distributed the entire profit to its parent company.

6 Observations

6.1 Free choice of form of secondary establishment

There are certain points in the Advocate General's opinion that need some deeper analysis. The first issue is whether the free choice of form of the secondary establishment is the right comparison here. One could well argue that the free choice of form of secondary establishment is simply a part of the prohibition of discriminatory treatment[24].

The right comparison here would then have been the one between a German resident company and CLT-UFA, had CLT-UFA been resident in Germany. This is also the comparison carried out in Royal Bank of Scotland[25]. Indeed, both in Commission v France and in Saint-Gobain, the form of secondary establishment was the decisive point; however, only as means to show discrimination[26].

That the question here is not one of the right form of secondary establishment is also suggested if we substitute CLT-UFA for an individual that is resident in Luxembourg. In such a case, the idea of treating the individual's permanent establishment in Germany as a subsidiary, paying corporate tax rather than the individual paying his personal income tax rate on the profits of the permanent establishment, sounds almost ludicrous. If the ECJ would thus compare CLT-UFA to a resident company, the reduced tax rate on distributed profits would only have to be granted once CLT-UFA carried out a distribution to its shareholders. Unlike in Commission v France and Saint-Gobain, the ECJ will therefore need to expressly decide whether Article 43 EC only prohibits discrimination against the foreign corporation compared to a domestic one or whether the foreign corporation must not be treated worse because it has chosen a permanent establishment instead of a subsidiary.

6.2 Withholding tax according to the Parent-Subsidiary Directive (90/435/EEC) compatible with the freedom of establishment?

Moreover, the answer to the second question referred by the German Supreme Tax Court did not receive proper attention: Does Germany have

24 Taking the same opinion, Schnitger, EuGH: Schlussantrag – Früherer fester Betriebsstättensteuersatz von 42 % KSt EU-widrig?, *IStR* 2005, p 379 (p 388).

25 ECJ 29 April 1999, C-311/97 *Royal Bank of Scotland* [1999] ECR I-2651.

26 ECJ 28 January 1986, 270/83 *Avoir Fiscal* [1986] ECR 273, para 22; 21 September 1999, C-307/97 *Saint-Gobain* [1999] ECR I-6161, paras. 42 and 43.

to reduce the corporate tax rate to 33.5 % or to 30 %? Due to the exception in the Parent-Subsidiary Directive (90/435/EEC) that Germany was granted, it was allowed to levy 5 % withholding tax until 30 June 1996. The Advocate General's statement seems to indicate that there was no information in the case indicating when the profits were actually transferred from the German permanent establishment to the Luxembourg head office and that he therefore left it to the referring Court to decide on this.

The analysis in CLT-UFA is solely carried out as a comparison between a subsidiary distributing profits to its parent company in another Member State and a permanent establishment transferring profits to its head office in another Member State.

This analysis might, however, be taken one step further: If it is established that a permanent establishment must be treated as a German subsidiary in respect of the tax rate, must the fictive subsidiary then not be treated as if it had a German parent company, in order to make the comparison complete? This consideration also holdsif the above "correct" comparison, ie between CLT-UFA and a resident German distributing company, had been carried out.

In the case of a German subsidiary distributing dividends to its German parent company, the tax rate would be reduced to 30 % for the subsidiary. At the same time, 25 % withholding tax would be levied as a prepayment of the tax burden of the parent company. As previously described, the parent company did economically not pay any tax on the dividend from the subsidiary, once it was distributed further. Effectively, the withholding tax was credited against other mainstream corporate tax or simply refunded where there was no tax burden. The taxation on domestic dividend flows was thus entirely eliminated.

Until 30 June 1996 there was, however, a 5 % final withholding tax on dividends to foreign EU parent companies.

Such a system, ie a system that avoids double taxation on dividends in domestic but not in cross-border cases, has been considered an infringement of the free movement of capital in Article 40 of the EEA Agreement[27].

The conclusion would thus be that Germany was not allowed to impose the 5 % withholding tax on profit distributions from a German subsidiary

---

27 EFTA Court 23 November 2004, E-1/04 *Fokus Bank ASA*.

to a foreign EU parent company, even though this is expressly provided for in the Parent-Subsidiary Directive (90/435/EEC), since primary EC law takes precedence over secondary EC law.

If Germany was thus not allowed to levy such tax in the subsidiary scenario, it is indeed possible to claim that a reduction of the corporate tax rate to 33.5 % on the profits of the permanent establishment even before 30 June 1996 is not enough to put an end to the breach of the freedom of establishment. In order to achieve a treatment which is completely equal to the treatment of a purely domestic German situation, the corporate tax rate would have to be reduced to 30 %[28].

This kind of comparison would force the ECJ to take a position on the applicability of the Parent/Subsidiary Directive (90/435/EEC), where the Directive might be contrary to primary EC law. This is something the ECJ would probably be reluctant to hold, as Germany was expressly allowed to levy withholding tax under the Directive. However, the ECJ has, indeed, held in one case that the Parent/Subsidiary Directive must be interpreted in the light of the fundamental freedoms[29]. Even though an exception is stated in a Directive, be it only for Germany or generally for all Member States, the implementation of the exception may be exercised only in compliance with the fundamental provisions of the EC, ie the freedom of establishment.

---

28 On this, see also Schnitger, Früherer fester Betriebsstättensteuersatz von 42 % KSt EU-widrig?, *IStR* 2005, p 379 (p 388) and on the Fokus Bank decision, Cordewener, Körperschaftsteueranrechnung für Gebietsfremde versus Kapitalverkehrsfreiheit – Zum Gutachten des EFTA-Gerichtshofs in Sachen Fokus Bank ASA, *FR* 2005, p 345.

29 ECJ 18 September 2003, C-168/01 *Bosal* [2003] ECR I-9409, para 43.

III Keller Holding (C-471/04)

1 Introduction

The Keller Holding case[30] concerns the deductibility of shareholders' expenses connected with tax-exempt dividends from non-resident subsidiaries. This issue is at issue at issue in several other cases currently pending before German courts, both before lower courts and with the German Supreme Tax Court. As with the previously discussed cases, the underlying questions are again the result of the former German imputation system.

To some extent, the case has similarities to the Dutch ECJ case Bosal Holding[31]. Here the ECJ held that the Parent-Subsidiary Directive (90/435/EEC), interpreted in the light of the freedom of establishment of Article 43 EC precluded a Dutch national provision that, when the taxable income of a Dutch parent company was determined, made the deductibility of expenses connected to this company's shareholding in a subsidiary in another Member State subject to the condition that such expenses be indirectly instrumental in making profits taxable in the Netherlands. The deduction of expenses connected to a shareholding in a Dutch company was not subject to such restriction.

2 Relevant German Legislation

Expenses that have an immediate economic connection with tax-exempt income are disallowed for deduction for tax purposes in Germany, sec 3c para 1 German Income Tax Act (former sec 3c German Income Tax Act). The precondition "immediate" requires that the expenses not only be economically connected with the income in question, but also that they be incurred in the same year the tax-exempt income is derived. Expenses are only immediately connected with the income insofar as they do not exceed that income. Accordingly, if expenses are incurred in a fiscal year in which no tax-exempt income is derived, expenses are wholly deductible.

Dividends from non-resident shareholdings were exempt from taxation in Germany under the former German imputation system if this was regulated in a DTC, which was generally the case if the shareholding amount-

30 Referral by BFH 14 July 2004, I R 17/03.

31 ECJ 18 September 2003, C-168/01 *Bosal* [2003] ECR I-9409.

ed to at least 25 % of the share capital in a non-resident subsidiary. Moreover, according to national German law, dividends from such shareholdings were tax exempt if the shareholding was at least 10 %, regardless of the level agreed upon in the DTC, sec 8b para 5 German Corporate Tax Act before the abolishment of the German imputation system.

Such tax-exempt dividends remained exempt when passed on through a multi-tier structure of corporations in Germany, sec 8b para 1 German Corporate Tax Act before the abolishment of the imputation system, and were merely taxed at the level of the individual shareholder. This treatment was introduced as of the fiscal year 1994[32]. Before that, a German resident company distributing dividends that were tax exempt under a DTC was subject to an increase of corporate tax upon distribution, which could however, be imputed to a resident shareholder or be reimbursed to a foreign shareholder upon application. With the 1994 legislative changes, the legislator thus sought to establish a neutrality of redistributed foreign and domestic profits at the level of the redistributing company.

As a consequence of the tax exemption of the dividends, expenses related to such a shareholding incurred in a year in which tax-exempt dividends were received were disallowed for deduction. The common practice for avoiding this was to let profits remain with the subsidiary and only make a distribution in years in which no or merely low expenses had been incurred.

Dividends from German resident subsidiaries were, on the other hand, taxed at the level of a corporate shareholder under the imputation system. However, as described under, the technique of the imputation system (namely, the granting of an imputation credit to be set off against the corporate tax and reduction of corporate tax upon distribution) led to an economic tax exemption at the corporate shareholder level, once the dividends had been further distributed. Even so, expenses connected with such shareholdings were wholly allowed for deduction and were not subject to sec 3c of the German Income Tax Act.

3 Facts of the Case

Keller Holding GmbH (hereafter Keller Holding) was a German resident company with a German resident subsidiary, Keller GmbH. This, in turn, had a substantial shareholding in a company resident in Austria. This sec-

32 Standortsicherungsgesetz, 13 September 1993, *BGBl.* 1993 I p 1569.

ond-tier subsidiary distributed dividends to Keller GmbH. The dividends were in accordance with Article 10a para 1 and Article 15 para 2 3rd sentence of the tax treaty between the Federal Republic of Germany and the Republic of Austria tax exempt in Germany[33].

In the years 1993 through 1995, the dividends were passed on to Keller Holding GmbH and remained tax exempt in accordance with sec 8b para 1 of the German Corporate Tax Act before the abolishment of the imputation system. Despite this, Keller Holding deducted both interest paid on the loans that had been taken up to finance the acquisition of Keller GmbH as well as administrative expenses. The local tax authorities denied the deduction of these expenses insofar as they were attributable to the shareholding in Keller GmbH.

Keller Holding filed an objection against the assessment and argued that the non-deductibility of expenses constituted a breach of the freedom of establishment, as expenses incurred in connection with German shareholdings were wholly deductible.

The Tax Court of Hessan dismissed the appeal for 1993, since Austria was neither a part of the EEA nor of the EU in that year and the freedom of establishment was accordingly not yet applicable.

However, the appeal was successful for the years 1994 and 1995 and the Tax Court of Hessan held that the different treatment of expenses in respect of dividends from resident and non-resident shareholdings was in breach of the freedom of establishment in Article 43 EC and the free movement of capital in Article 56 EC. The tax authorities appealed against this decision.

4 German Court Proceedings and Questions Referred to the ECJ

In its decision of 14 July 2004, the German Supreme Tax Court expressed doubts about the compatibility of the German provisions with Community law, and more specifically with the freedom of establishment in Article 43 EC and the free movement of capital in Article 56 EC. It thereby cited the above-mentioned Bosal Holding judgment and the doubts expressed in the German tax literature on the German provisions in question[34].

---

33 DTC in the amended version of 1992, *BSBl.* 1994 II, p 123.

34 For example *Meilicke*, Anmerkung zu C-168/01 *Bosal*, *DB* 2003, p 2100.

The Court held that the German legal position was comparable to the Dutch one in Bosal Holding. Expenses in both cases were disallowed for deduction due to the tax exemption of dividends from non-resident shareholdings.

Unlike in the Bosal Holding case, however, the Court held that the denial of deduction in sec 3c of the German Income Tax Act in this particular case was not linked to expenses incurred because of having a subsidiary resident in another Member State, but to expenses incurred by the shareholding of a subsidiary resident in Germany (ie Keller GmbH). The case could thus be seen as a purely domestic situation. The connection to the second-tier subsidiary in Austria was only indirect and was based merely by the fact that the profits of the second-tier subsidiary were distributed tax exempt through the first-tier subsidiary to the ultimate parent Keller Holding.

Another difference with Bosal Holding was, according to the Court, that sec 3c of the German Income Tax Act requires that tax-exempt dividends actually be distributed for the rule to apply. The disadvantage, compared to the shareholding in a German resident company, thus only occurred upon actual distribution of dividends.

Unlike the distribution from a German resident subsidiary, the distribution from a non-resident subsidiary was, moreover, tax exempt. The disadvantage of non-deductibility of expenses at the level of the parent company thus corresponded to the tax exemption of the dividends. Accordingly, the Court held that it can be argued that a direct link existed in the case of one and the same taxpayer, between the granting of a tax advantage (ie tax exemption of the dividend) and the offsetting of that advantage by a fiscal levy (ie the denial of deduction of expenses), both of which related to the same (corporate) tax. The Court noted that the ECJ accepts such an argumentation of coherence of national tax systems as justification for a restriction of the fundamental freedoms[35].

This argument can, however, according to the Court, be countered by the fact that the shareholding in a non-resident subsidiary was ultimately treated worse only due to the fact that its profits were not taxed in Germany. This has to be seen against the background that a corporate shareholder of a German resident subsidiary indeed initially paid tax on

[35] ECJ 18 September 2003, [2003] ECR I-9409, para 29 with further references.

the distributed profits. However, the shareholder was granted an imputation credit that it could offset against its own tax liability. The lack of tax exemption on dividends from resident shareholdings was thus economically compensated by the technique of the imputation system. Nonetheless, the deduction of expenses was not restricted in respect of such shareholdings.

From an economic point of view, the shareholding in a foreign subsidiary was consequently treated less favourably than a shareholding in a German subsidiary.

The Court, however, held that comparability of the qualifying shareholding in a resident and a non-resident subsidiary requires objectively similar situations. This would be the case only if the denial of imputation credit of foreign underlying tax against domestic corporate tax is in breach of the fundamental freedoms.

In this regard, the Court held that this question is controversial and currently pending in the Meilicke case (see above). The Court also cited the ECJ judgment in Manninen in this context, which is somewhat surprising as the Manninen judgment was delivered on 7 September 2004 and the referral in Keller Holding was made on 14 July 2004. In any case, the Court shares the doubts on the compatibility of the imputation system that were stated in the referral in Meilicke and in the Manninen judgment.

The Court further held that the denial of an imputation credit for dividends from foreign shareholdings under the imputation system cannot be successfully justified by the coherence of the tax system, as the taxation of the distributing company and the shareholder concerns two different persons. Other justifications would, in the Court's view, not be applicable either.

Based on this analysis, the Court referred the following question to the ECJ:

> Is it contrary to Article 52, in conjunction with Article 58, of the Treaty establishing the European Community and to Article 73b of that Treaty if financing costs incurred by a corporation which have a direct economic link to profits, not subject to tax in Germany, derived from a holding in a capital company established in another Member State may be deducted as operating expenditure only in so far as no profits from that holding are distributed on a tax-free basis?

5 Observations

5.1 Denial of imputation credit for dividends from non-resident companies decisive for Keller Holding?

One interesting point in the Keller Holding referral is that the German Supreme Tax Court made reference to Meilicke and Manninen in respect of the comparability of the investment in a non-resident and a resident subsidiary.

It is difficult to see why the comparability of the shareholding in a resident and a non-resident subsidiary should be dependent on whether the denial of an imputation credit on foreign dividends under the former German imputation system is in breach of the fundamental freedoms: In several cases, the ECJ has clearly stated that a taxpayer investing in a non-resident shareholding is in an objectively comparable situation to a taxpayer investing in a resident shareholding[36]. The comparability of the situations in Keller Holding can thus not be dependent on the former German imputation system.

Moreover, at issue in Keller Holding is not the denial of an imputation credit in respect of dividends from a non-resident subsidiary, as these dividends were tax exempt in Germany in this case. It is the question of whether the tax exemption of the foreign dividends justifies the denial of deduction for expenses connected with the underlying shareholding that has to be decided upon. This matter is not related to the denial of an imputation credit for these dividends, but to how domestic dividends were taxed. As the German Supreme Tax Court held, domestic dividends were also eventually economically tax exempt due to the technique of the imputation system. The question therefore boils down to whether domestic and foreign dividends that were both ultimately tax exempt can be treated differently in respect of the deduction of expenses.

It is, moreover, interesting that the Tax Court of Hessen held the German provisions to be in breach of the freedom of establishment and the free movement of capital without referring the case to the ECJ[37].

---

[36] ECJ 6 June 2000, C-35/98 *Verkooijen* [2000] ECR I-4071; 18 September 2003, C-168/01 *Bosal* [2003] ECR I-9409; 15 July 2004, C-315/02 *Lenz* [2004] ECR I-7063.

[37] FG Hessen 10 December 2002, 4-K-1044/99.

5.2 *Other pending cases in Germany in respect of deductibility of expenses connected to foreign shareholdings*

Two other cases are pending before the Supreme Tax Court in Germany regarding the same issue.

In 1999, the German legislation changed so that sec 3c German Income Tax Act was no longer applicable to foreign tax-exempt dividends. Instead a flat 5 % add-back of the dividend was introduced for tax-exempt dividends from non-resident shareholdings, sec 8b para 7 German Corporate Tax Act before abolishment of the imputation system. Again, such tax-exempt dividends were treated differently in respect of the deduction of expenses: Recipients of such dividends were now indeed allowed to deduct expenses, but they were always subject to the 5 % add-back. The 5 % add-back of dividends from non-resident shareholdings still constituted a disadvantage compared to the receipt of dividends from resident shareholdings, for which no restriction as regards the deduction of expenses applied.

On 29 February 2004, the Tax Court of Hamburg held this unfavourable tax treatment of foreign dividends to be an infringement of the Parent Subsidiary Directive (90/435/EEC), interpreted in the light of the freedom of establishment of Article 43 EC. The tax authorities – not surprisingly – appealed the decision and the case is now pending before the Supreme German Tax Court[38].

The German imputation system was abolished in 2001/2002[39]. The new German system regularly exempts dividends from resident shareholdings as well as from non-resident shareholdings from taxation in the hands of a corporate shareholder from 2002 and onwards, sec 8b para 1 German Corporate Tax Act, after the imputation system was abolished.

In accordance with this, sec 3c para 1 German Income Tax Act applied to dividends from resident shareholdings in 2002, ie expenses having an immediate economic connection with exempt income were disallowed for deduction. For exempt dividends from non-resident shareholdings, however, the legislation still contained the add-back of 5 % of dividends, although it was now obvious that foreign and domestic dividends were both exempt and should be subject to the same restrictions regarding

38 FG Hamburg 29 February 2004, VI 53/02; BFH pending I R 78/04.

39 Steuersenkungsgesetz of 23 October 2000, *BGBl.* I 2000, p 1433.

deductions of expenses. For a claimant with a non-resident shareholding and expenses lower than the 5 % add-back, the treatment thus was still less favourable than that for the receipt of a domestic dividend.

On 29 April 2005, the Tax Court of Hamburg again took the position that such less favourable tax treatment of foreign dividends is in breach of the Parent-Subsidiary Directive (90/435/EEC) and decided in favour of the taxpayer. Again, the tax authorities appealed against the judgment and the case is currently pending with the Supreme German Tax Court[40].

From fiscal year 2004, this differentiated treatment of the deductibility of expenses for dividends from resident and non-resident companies was abolished and both types of dividends are now generally subject to a flat 5 % add-back[41].

[40] FG Hamburg 29 April 2005, III-58/04; BFH pending I R 50/05.

[41] Gesetz zur Umsetzung der Protokollerklärung der Bundesregierung zur Vermittlungsempfehlung zum Steuervergünstigungsabbaugesetz of 22 December 2003, *BGBl.* I 2003, p 2840.

IV Lasertec (C-492/04)

1 Introduction

The case concerns the German provision on thin capitalisation in the wording before the abolishment of the German imputation system. The ECJ has already decided on this provision in a different context, namely in the Lankhorst-Hohorst case in 2002[42]. Lankhorst-Hohorst concerned the application of the thin capitalisation provision where a Dutch resident shareholder had granted the loan. The German provision was considered to be in breach of the freedom of establishment in Article 43 EC (at that time, Article 52).

The question in the present case is whether the free movement of capital in Article 56 EC prohibits a disadvantageous treatment of interest paid from a German resident company to its shareholder, where the latter is resident in a third state. The case further deals with the requirement of a rule "existing" on 31 December 1993 in the stand-still clause in Article 57 EC and whether the former German thin capitalisation rule is covered by the scope of this article.

2 Relevant German Legislation

The former German thin capitalisation rule applied a 3:1 debt/equity ratio as a safe haven not only to short-term loans bearing an interest based on capital borrowed from substantial shareholders or affiliated persons not entitled to participate in the German imputation system, sec 8a German Corporate tax Act before abolishment of the imputation system: The rule also applied to third party loans where the third party lender had recourse to such shareholder or affiliated person. Interest paid on the part of a loan exceeding this debt/equity ratio was characterised as a constructive profit distribution to the shareholder and disallowed for deduction at the level of the borrowing company.

The equity decisive for calculating the safe haven was determined on the basis of the equity at the end of the previous accounting period. Not yet paid-in contributions to equity did not count as equity for thin capitalisation purposes, sec 8a para 2 2nd sentence German Corporate Tax Act before abolishment of the imputation system.

---

[42] ECJ 12 December 2002, C-324/00 *Lankhorst-Hohorst* [2002] ECR I-11779. For previous coverage of this case, see Cordewener, Pending Cases Filed by the German Courts, in Lang (ed) *Direct Taxation: Recent ECJ Developments* (2003) p 35.

Only companies that were subject to tax on received dividends and where these dividends were included in a tax assessment were able to participate in the German imputation system, sec 51 German Corporate Tax Act before abolishment of the imputation system. The thin capitalisation rule thus basically applied only to non-residents. Some German organisations were also excluded from the benefits of the imputation system; however, as these were mainly tax-exempt institutions, they were not comparable with regular commercial companies. The application of the thin capitalisation rules to non-residents only was therefore considered by the ECJ in Lankhorst-Hohorst a prohibited indirect discrimination of non-residents and a breach of the freedom of establishment in (at that time) Article 52 of the EC Treaty, now Article 43 EC[43].

3 Facts of the Case

The claimant Lasertec is a German resident company established on 12 September 1994. The registered capital amounted to DEM 300,000, of which Mr S.R. held a share of DEM 3,000, Mr U.G.P. a share of DEM 97,000 and the company L-AG, with a seat in Switzerland, DEM 200,000. S.R. immediately sold his share in the claimant to Mr U.G.P. On the same day, Mr S.R. sold his sole trading business to the claimant for a price of DEM 1,000,000, which was to be paid on 10 January 1995.

According to the shareholders' agreement, the registered capital had to be paid in immediately to 25 % and the rest when the management of the claimant so required. The balance sheet for the stub accounting period ending on 31 December 1994 showed outstanding contributions to registered capital of DEM 225,000. The balance sheet for the accounting period ending on 31 December 1995 showed no outstanding equity amounts. According to the facts of the case, the management of the claimant had required payments of the remaining equity before 31 December 1994.

On 5 January 1995, L-AG in Switzerland granted the claimant a loan without security, amounting to DEM 700,000, which was paid out on 10 January 1995. The mortgage term was two years and the loan bore interest at a variable rate of 8 %. The balance sheet on 31 December 1995 contained liabilities to affiliated companies amounting to DEM 612,132.64 and the financial statements record interest expenses for this loan amounting to DEM 48,132.64.

43 ECJ 12 December 2002, C-324/00 *Lankhorst-Hohorst* [2002] ECR I-11779, para 28.

In the course of a tax audit in 1997, the tax auditor stated that the equity attributable to L-AG on 31 December 1994 for thin capitalisation purposes amounted to DEM 50,000, due to the fact that the outstanding part of the equity had to be deducted from L-AG's share of equity. The whole loan granted in 1995, amounting to DEM 700,000, was considered to be debt within the meaning of the thin capitalisation provision. From this, three times the equity was deducted, ie DEM 150,000. The part of the interest paid on the exceeding amount (DEM 37,818) was treated as a constructive dividend in accordance with the thin capitalisation rule and was accordingly denied deduction.

Apart from this, the auditor correctly assessed that the rest of the equity had been paid in on 10 January 1995. However, as the equity at the end of the last accounting period (here, 31 December 1994) is decisive for the calculation of the safe haven for thin capitalisation purposes, this instalment was not considered.

As a result of the tax audit, the taxable income of the claimant was reassessed and the corporate tax was increased to include tax on the interest for which deduction had been denied in the new assessment from 15 June 1998. The claimant filed an objection against these assessments, which was rejected by the tax authorities. The claimant lodged an appeal with the Tax Court of Baden-Wuerttemberg from this negative decision,

4 German Court Proceedings and Questions Referred to the ECJ

The claimant argued that in this specific case that there was not a wholly artificial constructionwhereby a resident subsidiary was financed by debt instead of equity. The obligation to pay Mr S.R. was due on 10 January 1995. The management of the claimant had therefore prompted the non-resident shareholder to pay in his part of the equity. The payment was effected a few days after end of the accounting period, due to the fact that the transfer was slightly delayed. This delay did not justify the assumption of a constructive profit distribution according to the thin capitalisation provisions. In fact, the calculation of the equity must take into consideration the total equity of L-AG, not reduced by the outstanding contribution.

Moreover, due to the fact that the claimant was established in 1994, the 1994 accounting period was a stub period and the actual activity of the claimant was only initiated with the purchase of the business in January 1995. The thin capitalisation provision should grant planning reliability and especially with a view to the thin capitalisation provision, the shareholder loan was granted and paid back so that it at the end of 1995 amounted to roughly DEM 600,000.

The claimant further argued that the thin capitalisation provision led to a disadvantage due to the granting of capital by a non-resident shareholder. This is not in accordance with the free movement of capital in Article 56 EC. Apart from that, the tax treaty between the Federal Republic of Germany and the Swiss Confederation contains an anti-discrimination article in Article 25 that has to be considered.

The tax authorities applied to have the appeal rejected and argued that is it uncertain whether the free movement of capital in Article 56 EC applies to the present situation. Moreover, the stand-still clause in Article 57 EC has to be considered, as this allows for restrictions on the free movement of capital towards third states that existed on 31 December 1993 to continue to apply. Since the German thin capitalisation provision was enacted on 13 September 1993 – even if it applied only to accounting periods starting after 31 December 1993 – it still "existed" before 31 December 1993. Decisive for the term "existing" must be the legislation enacted and not the time of the first application. Article 25 of the tax treaty between the Federal Republic of Germany and the Swiss Confederation is a special provision that is not necessary for the actual aim of the treaty, namely the avoidance of double taxation, and is therefore to be interpreted narrowly.

During the proceedings in the Tax Court of Baden-Wuerttemberg, the claimant and the respondent (tax authorities) agreed that the thin capitalisation rules were applicable to the claimant's situation.

The Court, however, held that the application of the thin capitalisation rule is questionable as to the matter of the decisive equity, ie should the equity on 31 December 1994 be decisive, or did the circumstances of the case allow the equity on 31 December 1995 to be decisive? Moreover, it is debatable whether the equity of L-AG on 31 December 1994 was to be reduced by the outstanding contributions, as the payment had already been requested before 31 December 1994.

However, the Court held that the outcome of the proceedings is primarily subject to clarification on whether the German thin capitalisation regulations "existed" on 31 December 1993 within the meaning of Article 57(1) EC.

The loan granted by the shareholder in Switzerland can be considered to be a direct investment that is covered by the scope of Article 57 EC. Restrictions in respect of direct investment towards third states that existed on 31 December 1993 can therefore basically still be applied. Sec 8a German Corporate Tax Act, regulating thin capitalisation, was introduced on 13 September 1993. This legislation went into force on the day after enactment, ie on 14 September 1993 and was thus effective before 31 December 1993.

However, the same Act states that sec 8a applies to accounting periods beginning after 31 December 1993. The Court held that even though several arguments point toward sec 8a "existing" on 31 December 1993, e.g. that it had been published before that date and that the taxpayers thus had the chance to change their conduct well before that date, the fact that the effective legal consequences of the rule could not apply on the decisive date, nevertheless points to the fact that the rule did not "exist" on 31 December 1993.

The Court then went on to state that even though the question of whether Article 57 EC can be applied to sec 8a German Corporate Tax Act should be answered in the negative, decisive will be if Article 56 EC can be interpreted as prohibiting the application of a national rule like sec 8a, since it limits the movement of capital with third states and further, whether this limitation can be justified by Article 58 EC.

The Court decided to stay proceedings and refer the case to the ECJ for a preliminary ruling, thereby posing the following questions:

1. Is Article 57 (1) of the EC to be interpreted as meaning that the restrictions on the movement of capital to or from third countries which "exist" on 31 December 1993 are those for which the legislative process has already been completed by the national legislature on that date, or those which under the national legislation are already applicable on that date to existing factual situations?
2. Is Article 56 (1) EC in conjunction with Article 58 EC to be interpreted as meaning that the – partial – taxation as the distribution of profits of payments of interest by a capital company resident in a Member State to a loan provider in a third country who is at the same time shareholder in the capital company is thereby prohibited because this is arbitrary discrimination or a disguised restriction of the free movement of capital between a Member State and a third country?

5 Observations

Apart from the question for which the entire tax community is awaiting an answer, namely whether the free movement of capital in Article 56 EC will have an impact on direct taxes in respect of third states, which is currently pending before the ECJ in several cases[44], the question of the applicability of the stand-still clause in Article 57 EC where legislation had been previously enacted, but was not applicable on 31 December 1993, is equally of interest[45].

One matter that the Tax Court of Baden-Wuerttemberg should have dealt with before referring the case to the ECJ is whether the discrimination article in the tax treaty between the Federal Republic of Germany and the Swiss Confederation prohibited the applicability of the German thin capitalisation provision. This not least against the background that the French Conseil d'Etat in 2003 held that the French thin capitalisation rules were not compatible with the tax treaty between France and Austria, which contains an article similar to that in the German/Swiss tax treaty[46].

Before the Lankhorst-Hohorst judgment by the ECJ, the German tax literature considered the German thin capitalisation rule not in conflict with the non-discrimination provision in Article 24 para 5 OECD Model Convention[47]. This was based on the fact that the German rule did not openly discriminate on grounds of the residence of the shareholder, but merely differentiated between persons covered by the old German imputation system and persons excluded from this. This was, according to the prevailing opinion, therefore not discrimination of companies due to the residence of their shareholders, as some German resident organisations could also not participate in the German system. Thus, the thin capitalisation provision could also apply in these cases.

As stated above, in the Lankhorst-Hohorst judgment (see IV.1), the ECJ, however, opined that the German thin capitalisation regulation constituted covert discrimination against non-residents. The German resident

44 For example, ECJ C-101/05 *Skatteverket v A*, pending; C-102/05 *Skatteverket v A and B*, pending; C-201/05 *Test Claimants in the CFC and Dividend Group litigation*, pending.

45 On this question, see Prinz, Verstößt der "alte" § 8a KStG gegen die europäische Kapitalverkehrsfreiheit (Art. 56 EG)?, *FR* 2005, p 370.

46 Conseil d'Etat 30 December 2003, no 233894, *SA Andritz*: Reveue de droit fiscal 2004, no 16, comm. 427; *International Tax law Reports* 2004, p 582.

47 Wassermeyer in Debatin/Wassermeyer (eds.) *DBA* (1997) Art 24 MA, para 98.

organisations that could not be part of the imputation system were mostly tax exempt non-profit institutions, carrying out activities of general public interest and could not be compared with regular profit-making companies subject to corporate tax.

Since the ECJ held that the distinction between persons entitled to the imputation system and persons not entitled to it in respect of application of the former thin capitalisation rule to be covert discrimination due to its applicability in most cases to non-resident shareholders and thus a breach of the freedom of establishment, it is questionable whether the distinction between shareholders entitled to the imputation system and shareholders not entitled to the same can still be upheld as an argument as to why the non-discrimination provision in Article 24 para 5 OECD Model Convention should not apply in a thin capitalisation situation where the former German rule applies[48].

This issue was ignored by the Tax Court of Baden-Wuerttemberg – it did not express an opinion on the application of Article 25 DTC between the Federal Republic of Germany and the Swiss Confederation. It is arguable whether the Court could refer the question of the applicability of Articles 56 and 57 EC to the ECJ at all, as it had not yet made a statement on the application of national law – it might very well be that the application of the tax treaty precludes the application of the thin capitalisation rule and the referral is thus unnecessary.

---

48 Lüdicke, Darf im internationalen Steuerrecht noch differenziert werden?, in Gocke/Gosch/Lang (eds), *Festschrift für Franz Wassermeyer*, p 473 (pp 486 et seq).

V Rewe Zentralfinanz (C-347/04)

1 Introduction

The Rewe Zentralfinanz case (herafter Rewe) deals with tax-effective write-downs on foreign investments before abolishment of the German imputation system in 2001. The underlying issue is the treatment of negative foreign passive income in a set of German tax rules introduced in 1983. In several cases, the ECJ has held that a different treatment of foreign investments compared to domestic investments can be in breach of the freedom of establishment[49]. This particular German rule has, moreover, been subject to criticism in the German tax literature as infringing the fundamental freedoms of the EC Treaty[50].

2 Relevant German Legislation

Sec 2a German Income Tax Act provides that certain negative foreign passive income may only be offset against positive income of the same kind from the same foreign state; it may not be used to reduce other taxable income in Germany. If it is not possible to deduct such passive negative foreign income against positive income of the same kind from the same state in one year, it reduces such positive income from the same foreign state in subsequent years. Reduction of profit counts as negative income for these purposes, so that write-downs are also covered.

Write-downs to current value on non-resident shareholdings (sec 2a para 1 no 3a German Income Tax Act) count as such passive negative income, unless the shareholding qualifies as active. This is the case where the shareholding in the said company is an immediate one and amounts to at least 25 % of the share capital and the company is active within the meaning of sec 2a para 2 1st sentence German Income Tax Act.

Due to the wording of the law (sec 2a para 2 1st sentence second half together with sec 2a para 2 2nd sentence), the treatment as active extends

---

[49] See, for example, ECJ 18 November 1999, C-200/98 *X and Y* [1999] ECR I-8261; 14 December 2000, C-141/99 *AMID* [2000] ECR I-11619.

[50] For example Cordewener, Auslandsverluste und EG-Grundfreiheiten: Kurskorrektur am falschen Fall?, *IStR* 2003, p 413; Dautzenberg, EG-rechtswidrige Behandlung von negativen ausländischen Einkünften nach den EuGH-Entscheidungen Vestergaard und AMID, *FR* 2001, p 809; Kellersmann/Treisch, *Europäische Unternehmensbesteuerung* (2002) p 180; Lüdicke, Baars: Weigerung der Anerkennung des Vermögensteuerfreibetrages als Verletzung der Niederlassungsfreiheit, *IStR* 2000, p 337.

to the shareholding in a non-resident holding company that in turn has an active subsidiary. The criteria "immediate" shareholding, means, according to the prevailing opinion in the German tax literature that only a two-tier foreign structure may qualify as active, whereas a more than two-tier structure is considered a passive investment.

The underlying reason for the write-down on the foreign shareholding is irrelevant for the treatment as passive negative income – it could very well be that, for example, the write-down was caused by too high a purchase price for the foreign shareholding and had very little to do with the profitability of foreign shareholding itself. In such cases a mere participation in the foreign shareholding was enough to trigger the application of sec 2a German Income Tax Act – if the participation was profitable or not was irrelevant for purposes of sec 2a German Income Tax Act.

Sec 2a German Income Tax Act, as previously mentioned, was introduced in 1983. The reasoning behind the rule was – in cases where the utilisation of foreign losses was not already excluded by a tax treaty – that it should only be possible to offset foreign negative income without restriction against German income where the foreign income was active. The German legislator was trying to curb the effect of loss-making schemes for tax purposes unless the German economy could visibly profit from these[51], ie collect the revenue from them.

Until the abolishment of the German imputation system in 2001, capital gains on foreign shareholdings were tax exempt if a tax treaty in which dividends on substantial shareholdings were exempted from German taxation applied[52], unless a write-down on the shareholding had been carried out tax effective in previous years and had not been balanced by a write up on the same shareholding. This exemption of capital gains was introduced in 1994[53].

Accordingly, losses incurred on the disposal of such shareholdings were not tax deductible[54]. Write downs on such shareholdings, however, were still basically tax effective[55].

51 Draft bill by the Government BR-Drs. 334/82, printed in Flick/Wassermeyer/Baumhoff, *Außensteuerrecht*, Vol II, § 2a EStG, legislative material.

52 Sec 8b para 3 1st sentence German Corporate Tax Act before abolishment of the German imputation system.

53 Standortsicherungsgesetz of 13.09.1993, *BStBl. I* 1993, 774, *BGBl.* I 1993, p 1569.

54 Sec 8b para 3 3rd sentence German Corporate Tax Act before abolishment of the German imputation system.

55 Sec 6 para 1 no 2 2nd sentence German Income Tax Act.

Capital gains, losses and write-downs on German shareholdings were tax effective before the abolishment of the German imputation system.

3 Facts of the Case

Rewe had a subsidiary in another EU Member State. The subsidiary was a holding company with a multi-tier structure where only the lowest-tier subsidiary carried out business that was "active" in the sense of the sec 2a German Income Tax Act. This business was loss making and, as a result, Rewe wrote down the value of the shareholding in the first-tier foreign subsidiary in the years 1993 and 1994.

Rewe filed objection and later appealed before the Tax Court of Cologne from the non-recognition of the write-down in its tax assessment and claimed that the different treatment of write-downs on resident and non-resident shareholdings is discriminatory and prohibited by Community law.

4 German Court Proceedings and Questions Referred to the ECJ

On 15 July 2004, the Tax Court of Cologne decided to refer the case to the ECJ[56]. The referring division held that it is likely that the different treatment of write-downs on German or foreign shareholdings according to sec 2a of the German Income Tax Act is in breach of Community law, thereby citing the vast amount of German tax literature on this question[57]. However, the Court held that the interpretation of the EC Treaty is not so entirely clear in this case that no doubts remain in respect of the application of Community law. It thereby mentioned the referral of the German Supreme Tax Court now pending with the ECJ in the Ritter-Coulais case[58].

The Court went on to state that the freedom of establishment was applicable in the present case, as Rewe had a 100 % shareholding in a company with its seat in another Member State. Such a 100 % shareholding means that the articles concerning the freedom of establishment are applicable[59]. It moreover stated that not only does the freedom of establishment protect non-residents in the state of secondary establishment; it also

---

56 13 K 1908/00.

57 For example, Rädler/Lausterer, *Festschrift Welf Müller* (2000) p 339; Cordewener, *IStR* 2003, p 413.

58 ECJ C-152/03 *Ritter-Coulais*, pending; referral by the German Supreme Tax Court on 13 November 2002, I R 13/02.

59 The Court hereby cited ECJ 13 April 2000, C-251/98, *Baars* [2000] ECR I-2787.

prohibits the state of origin from impeding the possibility of its own companies of establishing themselves in another Member State.

In the view of the Court, the limitation of the tax effectiveness of write-downs on certain shareholdings constitutes such impediment. As a result of the German rule, the shareholding in a foreign subsidiary is disadvantaged compared to the shareholding in a German subsidiary. In addition, the shareholding in a foreign multi-tier structure is disadvantaged. Where active business by second-tier subsidiaries is acknowledged and thus opens up the possibility to deduct losses, active business in third- and lower-tier subsidiaries is not accepted as an active investment.

The Tax Court of Cologne did not see any arguments that could justify this different treatment: The disadvantageous treatment of foreign subsidiaries, according to the legislative material (see V.2), is purely carried out for economic reasons, and this has never been accepted by the ECJ as valid justification of a restriction[60]. Moreover, the loss of revenue also mentioned in the legislative material on the German rule may not, according to prevailing ECJ case law, be applied to justify restrictions[61]. The in itself valid justification grounds that sec 2a of the German Income Tax Act is a provision needed in order to curb tax avoidance does not apply, as sec 2a goes far beyond the aim of combatting tax avoidance. The fact that a subsidiary has its seat in another Member State is in itself not tax avoidance. Furthermore, fiscal supervision does not play a role in sec 2a, as, firstly, the rule was not introduced for this purpose and, secondly, the ECJ has accepted the applicability of rules that concern the determination of the amount of business expenses; however, the deduction of expenses in the own Member State and other Member States may not be subject to different requirements[62].

On the more important argument, the coherence of the tax system, the Court held that coherence as the Court understands it means that a current tax advantage is connected with a future payment of the deferred tax to the same tax creditor by the same tax subject. The Court then went on to decide that the tax exemption of capital gains upon disposal of foreign

---

60 The Court thereby cited for example ECJ 6 June 2000, C-35/98 *Verkooijen* [2000] ECR I-4071, para 48.

61 For example ECJ 18 September 2003, C-168/01 *Bosal* [2003] ECR I-9409, para 42.

62 The Court hereby cites ECJ 28 October 1999, C-55/98 *Vestergaard* [1999] ECR I-7641, para 21.

subsidiaries may not serve as a coherence argument for the first year in question in the case, namely 1993, as the exemption for capital gains was introduced only in 1994. For the second year in question, namely 1994, the Court held, firstly, that is it questionable whether coherence can be accepted as argument, as the exemption of capital gains was only granted where no write-down in previous years had reduced the tax base and, secondly, there is no immediate connection between a tax deduction and a future taxation of a capital gain, as it is not certain if a gain will actually arise before disposal has taken place.

5 Observations

The Rewe case is a quite straightforward situation of a restriction on foreign investments and, therefore, it is to be expected that the ECJ will decide that the freedom of establishment prohibits such a provision as sec 2a German Income Tax Act.

The ECJ's holding on a worse treatment of foreign income or income with a cross-border element due to classification by the German legislator of the nature of this income as passive will be interesting. This will – at least indirectly – show where the ECJ is heading in respect of the various CFC cases that are currently pending before the ECJ[63].

63 For example ECJ C-196/04 Cadbury Schweppes, pending; C-201/05 Test Claimants in the CFC and Dividend Group litigation, pending ; C-298/05 Kolumbus Container Services, pending; and C-203/05 *Vodafone 2*, pending.

VI Ritter-Coulais (C-152/03)

1 Introduction

The Ritter-Coulais case was referred before Rewe Zentralfinanz and was thought to be the groundbreaking case for deciding on the German tax treatment of not only negative foreign passive income, but also the question of whether the exemption method in a tax treaty allows for an exemption of not only foreign profits, but equally of foreign losses.

Unfortunately, the facts in Ritter-Coulais are not suited to answering the question of whether the German practice is in breach of one of the fundamental freedoms of the EC Treaty for several reasons.

2 Relevant German Legislation

Not only resident individuals, but also German non-resident citizens that are employed by a German state institution and derive salary from the German state, are subject to unlimited taxation in Germany, if they have no income or income that does not exceed a certain threshold abroad, sec 1 para 1 no 2 and para 3 German Income Tax Act.

In 1987, the year of the Ritter-Coulais case, the mere ownership and own use of real estate (Wohnung im eigenen Haus) was taxable in Germany and, accordingly, expenses incurred in connection with such real estate were deductible, sec 21 para 2 1st sentence, sec 52 para 21 2nd sentence German Income Tax Act in 1987. Ownership of real estate counted as leasing income according to this provision[64].

Negative foreign income of a passive nature was subject to the restrictions of sec 2a German Income Tax Act described under V.2, ie that such negative foreign income may only be set off against positive income of the same kind from the same foreign state; it may not be used to reduce other taxable income. If it is not possible to deduct such passive negative foreign income against positive income of the same kind from the same state in one year, it reduces such positive income from the same state in subsequent years.

Leasing of real estate falls under the scope of income with a passive nature within the meaning of sec 2a para 1 sentence 1 no 4 German Income Tax Act. Thus, this also included negative income incurred by the ownership of real estate.

64 BFH 26 March 1991, IX R 162/85, *BStBl. II* 1991, p 704.

Article 3 para 1 and 4 of the tax treaty between the Federal Republic of Germany and the French Republic grants France the taxation of income from real estate situated in France. Article 20 para 1 lit a 1st sentence of the treaty provides for an exemption of such income from taxation in Germany, where Germany is the state of residence.

According to national law, Germany applies the exemption method with progression, ie the progressive tax rate on the income taxable in Germany is determined on the basis of world-wide income, including exempted income. This also applies in case the foreign exempt income is negative, ie the German tax rate may be reduced by exempt negative income, sec 32b para 1 no 3 German Income Tax Act.

The negative progression is, however, according to case law of the German Supreme Tax Court[65], not applicable where the foreign income falls under sec 2a German Income Tax Act, ie is of a passive nature.

3 Facts of the Case

Hans-Juergen and Monique Ritter-Coulais are two German citizens that lived in France but worked at a state school in Germany in 1987. Since they were German citizens, worked for a state institution and had no income or only a low income abroad, they were subject to unlimited taxation in Germany and were taxed on their worldwide income.

In their 1987 income tax return, Ritter-Coulais applied to have their negative income incurred by the ownership of real estate in France considered for purposes of calculating their income tax rate, ie a negative progression in accordance with sec 32 b German Income Tax Act.

The tax authorities denied this and referred to sec 2a para 1 sentence 1 no 4 German Income Tax Act, which classifies such income as passive and thus as not eligible for reducing the income tax rate by way of progression. Ritter-Coulais objected to this decision and later appealed to the Tax Court, which followed the opinion of the tax authorities. Ritter-Coulais appealed to the German Supreme Tax Court.

4 German Court Proceedings and Questions Referred to the ECJ

The German Supreme Tax Court first held that the decision of the tax authorities and the Tax Court are in accordance with German national law.

---

65 BFHE 162, p. 307, *BStBl. II* 1991, p 136.

The statements made by the Court on the question of German national law seem to indicate that Ritter-Coulais were resident in Germany within the meaning of the tax treaty between the Federal Republic of Germany and the French Republic, as the Court holds that according to the tax treaty, France has the right to tax real estate situated in France and that income derived therefrom is tax exempt in Germany according to Article 20 of the treaty. As Article 20 deals with the method to avoid double taxation in the State of residence, the Court must have been of the opinion that Ritter-Coulais, even though they were living in France, had their centre of vital interests in Germany.

In accordance with German jurisprudence, the Court held that the exemption method in a tax treaty not only applies to positive, but also to negative foreign income. Hereby it referred to the judgment by the Austrian Supreme Court, in which the Austrian Court interpreted the exemption method as only applying to foreign positive income and holding that negative foreign income must be deductible in Austria[66]. The German Supreme Tax Court held that this does not apply in the relation between Germany and France, as the tax treaty between the Federal Republic of Germany and the Republic of France expressly exempts income from French sources from German taxation. By holding in this way, the Court makes it clear that not only positive, but also negative income is included in the exemption.

However, the German Supreme Tax Court expressed doubts as to whether the different treatment of, on the one hand, foreign negative leasing income and, on the other hand, domestic negative leasing income when calculating the taxable income when deciding the tax rate according to sec 32 b German Income Tax Act is compatible with Community law. The Court held that this could constitute a breach of Articles 43 and Art 56 EC (at that time, Article 52 and Article 73b).

In the present case it is obvious that negative income from the ownership of real estate in another Member State is disadvantaged compared to the ownership of real estate in Germany: The negative foreign income is explicitly excluded from being deducted or from being considered by way of negative progression as opposed to positive foreign exempt income. A cross-border investment that is protected by Community law may, however, neither be restricted nor be treated economically less advantageously. The Court did not find any arguments that could justify this differentiating treatment.

66 öVwGH 25 September 2001, 99/14/0217 E.

The Court thus referred the following questions to the ECJ:

> Is it contrary to Art 43 and 56 of the Treaty establishing the European Community if, when determining his taxable income, a natural person who has full tax liability in Germany and who receives employment income there is not allowed to deduct in Germany losses incurred in another Member State from leasing and letting property?
>
> If that question is answered in the negative: is it contrary to Art 43 and 56 of the Treaty establishing the European Community if such losses cannot be taken into account for the purposes of the negative tax progression clause (negativer Progressionsvorbehalt)?

5 Opinion of the Advocate General

On 1 March, Advocate General Philippe Legér gave his Opinion on the Ritter-Coulais case. The outcome was somewhat unexpected.

The Advocate General starts by concluding that Article 43 is not applicable in the Ritter-Coulais case, as the couple worked as employees in Germany and had not established themselves there in the way necessary to be covered by the scope of the freedom of establishment.

Secondly, the Advocate General concludes that the free movement of capital may not be applied either, as in the relevant year 1987 Council Directive 88/361/EEC of 24 June 1988 for the implementation of Article 67 of the Treaty was not yet in force. Moreover, the facts of the case contain nothing that implies a cross-border capital movement in connection with the purchase of real estate.

Mr Legér then points out that ECJ case law allows for an interpretation of other Community law provisions than the ones referred by the national courts, where this is of relevance for the referring court to decide on the matter. He thus opined on the applicability of the free movement of workers in Article 39 EC (at that time, Article 48), as Ritter-Coulais were employees within the meaning of Article 39 EC. However, here he comes to the conclusion that even though Ritter-Coulais are indeed theoretically protected by Article 39 EC, the same article is not applicable in this specific case. He hereby analyses the differences from the Gilly case[67] in order to show why Article 39 cannot be applied:

> In the Gilly case, Mrs Gilly was a German citizen that lived in France. She later on acquired the French citizenship due to her marriage and

[67] ECJ 12 May 1998, C-336/96 *Gilly* [1998] ECR I-2793.

she was working in Germany. The French authorities were in this case of the opinion that Mrs Gilly was not exercising her rights according to Article 39 (at that time Article 48) EC, as she was actually working in her own Member State. The ECJ countered this argument by stating that Mrs Gilly, after she acquired the French citizenship but continued working in Germany, had in France to be regarded as a worker making use of her right to free movement.

The situation in Ritter-Coulais has to be analysed from a different view, namely that of the German authorities. From a German perspective, Ritter-Coulais worked in Germany and moved to France only in order to take up residence there, as opposed to working there. The Advocate General also added that in the year of the Ritter-Coulais case, 1987, there was no provision in Community law protecting mere residence in another Member State.

Community law at that time treated free movement purely from an economic aspect and it was thus necessary to carry on employment in another Member State to be protected. There is, however, nothing in the files implying that Ritter-Coulais took up residence in France to carry out activities in France; on the contrary it seems as if they moved to France for private reasons only. In accordance with this, they worked in the Member State in which they were citizens and the only cross-border element was their French residence[68]. This is the difference with the Gilly case.

Article 18 EC, providing for the right to move and reside freely within the EU, was only introduced in 1992 and was thus not yet applicable in the present situation. This freedom would, however, according to the Advocate General, constitute the cross-border connection necessary for EU citizens to fall within the scope of Community law protection, where these are citizens of one Member State but regularly reside in another Member State.

Until this point, the Advocate General's Opinion seems well reasoned and the outcome in line with what had been expected.

Once the AG had stated that the fundamental freedoms were basically not applicable to the present case, he went on to state that the ECJ is obliged to answer questions referred by national courts where it is not obvious that the national court is in no need of interpretation of Community law in

68 The Advocate General hereby referred to the *Werner* case to emphasise this point, ECJ 26 January 1993, C-112/91 *Werner* [1993] ECR I-429.

order to answer the referred questions. This approach by the ECJ is indeed subject to discussion, but the Advocate General proposed that the ECJ analyse the referred questions.

He then rephrased the question referred by the German court as to whether it is contrary to Article 48 (now Article 39) EC where German citizens, subject to unlimited taxation in Germany and deriving income from employment in Germany, may not consider leasing losses incurred in another Member State because they use their own real estate, either when calculating the taxable income in Germany or when calculating the applicable income tax rate in Germany.

In this respect, the Advocate General first stated that the situations of residents and of non-residents are generally not comparable, because the income received in the territory of a Member State by a non-resident is in most cases only a part of his total income, which is concentrated at his place of residence, and because a non-resident's personal ability to pay tax, determined by reference to his aggregate income and his personal and family circumstances, is easier to assess at the place where his personal and financial interests are centred, which in general is the place where he has his usual abode[69].

The Advocate General then referred to the Schumacker jurisprudence, according to which Article 48 (now Article 39) EC must be interpreted as precluding the application of rules of a Member State under which a worker who is a national of, and resides in, another Member State and is employed in the first state is taxed more heavily than a worker who resides in the first state and performs the same work there when, as in the main action, the national of the second state obtains his income entirely or almost exclusively from the work performed in the first state and does not receive in the second state sufficient income to be subject to taxation there in a manner enabling his personal and family circumstances to be taken into account[70].

The Advocate General then stated – in brief – that the state of residence is primarily obliged to grant tax relief for personal circumstances. In this case, the state of employment may deny the kind of advantageous treatment that it grants its own residents.

---

69 For example, ECJ 1 July 2004, C-169/03 *Wallentin* [2004] ECR I-6443.
70 ECJ 14 February 1995, C-279/93 *Schumacker* [1995] ECR I-225.

This, however, requires that the state of residence actually levies tax so that such circumstances can be considered. If the taxpayer does not have any income subject to taxation in the state of residence, this obligation is transferred to the state of employment.

The ECJ case law ultimately means that the taxation of a taxpayer in the state of employment or in the state of residence may not result in the complete or partial non-recognition of his personal circumstances and family status.

In the Advocate General's view, this means that the tax ability of a non-resident, which is not only the result of his personal circumstances but also a result of taking into consideration his aggregate income and losses, may not be judged differently only due to residence, if the resident and non-resident persons derive their income entirely or almost exclusively in the state that taxes the income.

This is, however, exactly the result of a national provision that denies non-residents the deduction of foreign negative leasing income either by deduction from the taxable income or as a reduction of the applicable tax rate, where such deduction is granted resident persons.

The Advocate General thus concluded that Article 39 EC (at that time Article 48) must be interpreted as prohibiting national provisions that constitute such discrimination against non-resident workers. He hereby emphasised that this approach only applies where the non-resident taxpayer obtains his income entirely or almost exclusively in the state of taxation.

The arguments by the German government in respect to coherence of the tax system and especially with respect to the tax treaty between the Federal Republic of Germany and the French Republic were rejected by the Advocate General. He held that the German government missed the point of dividing of taxing rights, as had been respected in the Gilly case[71]. In Ritter-Coulais, the question is not, as it was in Gilly, about which state is granted the taxing right, but about the computation of the taxable income, which is a product not of the tax treaty, but of national law. Secondly, the Advocate General cannot see any immediate connection between the deduction of losses incurred by leasing in the state of employment and the taxation of the leasing in the state in which the real

---

71 ECJ 1 July 2004, C-169/03 *Wallentin* [2004] ECR I-6443.

estate is situated. Ceteribus paribus, nothing indicates that the losses incurred by the leasing may be taken into account in the state of residence in subsequent years.

6 Observations

The Advocate General's opinion is surprising: First, because he transformed what the German tax literature until his Opinion had treated as an outbound case with respect to the deductibility of foreign losses into an inbound case. Second, his conclusion seems to be limited to the situation where negative income is incurred due to the ownership of real estate, ie to a rule that is no longer applicable.

From a German tax point of view, Ritter-Coulais could have been resident in France or in Germany – they were subject to unlimited taxation in Germany in either case due to their German citizenship and the employment with a German state institution from which they derived (basically) their whole income. Moreover, the German Supreme Tax Court seems to have regarded them as resident for tax treaty purposes in Germany. With respect to their negative passive foreign income, they were thus not in a different situation than a German resident individual with foreign negative passive income, which was also not considered.

What the Advocate General did, and what may be correct in this specific situation, is to fictitiously transfer the real estate to Germany in order to create a situation of residence. The fact still remains that the relevant provision of German tax law is concerned with foreign negative passive income and that it applies only in situations of unlimited taxation in Germany, ie in the overwhelming majority of cases it will apply as an outbound restriction rule rather than an inbound discrimination rule.

VII Kolumbus Container Services (C-298/05)

1 Introduction

Several cases regarding the British CFC regulations are already pending with the ECJ[72]. Kolumbus Container Services is the first case referred by a German court in respect of the German CFC rules. Unfortunately, it might not be the ideal referral to receive clear answers to the German CFC legislation.

The question of whether a Member State may treat foreign, passive income differently than other income is already pending in the above Rewe Zentralfinanz referral (see above). However, that case concerned the treatment of negative passive foreign income, whereas CFC legislation is primarily aimed at taxing positive passive foreign income before it is distributed to resident shareholders.

2 Relevant German Legislation

Germany's CFC legislation, regulated in the International Transactions Tax Act[73], aims at protecting German revenue by preventing residents from avoiding or deferring German taxation by means of foreign low taxed corporations. The provisions only apply to foreign passive low taxed income, leaving active low taxed income unaffected, sec 7 and 8 International Transactions Tax Act.

In short, an application of the CFC regulations is triggered if the following prerequisites are cumulatively met: German residents (individuals or corporations subject to unlimited taxation) hold (in total) a participation of more than 50 % of the capital or voting rights of a corporation (as defined in the German Corporate Tax Act), which has neither its seat nor its place of management in Germany (Section 7 paras. 1 and 2 International Transactions Tax Act), the foreign controlled corporation (intermediate company) is subject to a low taxation (Section 8 para. 3 International Transactions Tax Act) and it derives passive income.

There is a separate set of rules in respect of passive income of a capital investment character, sec 7 para. 6a International Transactions Tax Act (former sec 10 para. 6). Such income is: Income of the foreign corpora-

---

72 ECJ C-196/04 *Cadbury Schweppes*, pending; C-201/05 *Test Claimants in the CFC and Dividend Group litigation*, pending; and C-203/05 *Vodafone 2*, pending.

73 Introduced by the Act of 8 September 1972, *BGBl.* 1972 I, p 1713.

tion derived from the possession, administration, preservation of the value of, or the increase in the value of, legal tender, receivables, stocks and bonds, shares or similar assets. Here, a participation of 1 % is basically sufficient to trigger the application of the rules.

The legal consequence of an application of the CFC provisions is (technically) not the treatment of the foreign entity as transparent, but instead the fiction of a profit distribution from the foreign entity at the earliest possible time, which is taxed in the hands of the resident shareholder.

An exception was made for income derived in the CFC for accounting periods starting earlier than or on 31 December 2002, where dividends would have been exempt in Germany due to provisions in a tax treaty, sec 10 para 5 International Transactions Tax Act. Such income was exempt from taxation in Germany. As an exception to this exception, no exemption was granted (with a few exceptions) where the CFC derived income with capital investment character.

As the German CFC rules only apply to foreign corporations, a provision was added in sec 20 para. 2 International Transactions Tax Act, stating that the regulations regarding income with a capital investment character also apply to foreign permanent establishments, if these would have applied to the permanent establishment, had this been a corporation. The consequence is that the exemption method, stated in most German tax treaties regarding foreign permanent establishments, ceases to apply and, instead, the foreign tax on the profits of the permanent establishment is credited. The same applied according to sec 20 para. 3 International Transactions Tax Act for wealth tax purposes.

For business years starting before 1 January 2001, low taxation was defined as a taxation of less than 30 %. In the course of the German tax reform and the reduction of the federal corporate tax rate, this changed to taxation of less than 25 % for business years starting after the 31 December 2000 (Section 8 para 3 International Transactions Tax Act)[74].

Germany treats partnerships as transparent for tax purposes; profits of a partnership are thus normally taxed in the hands of the partners. According to the tax treaty between the Federal Republic of Germany and the Kingdom of Belgium, profits from and the net assets of a Belgian part-

---

74 Act (Unternehmensteuerfortentwicklungsgesetz) of 20 December, 2001 *BGBl.* 2001 I, p 3858.

nership are taxed in Belgium where these are attributable to a permanent establishment in Belgium, Article 3 para 1 no 5 and Article 7 of the tax treaty. Such profits are exempt from taxation in Germany according to Article 23 para 1 no 1 of the tax treaty.

3 Facts of the Case

German resident individuals together held 100 % of a Belgian limited partnership (a BVBA) as limited partners, either directly or indirectly, in a German partnership. The unlimited partner was a Belgian resident company.

This Belgian partnership was treated as a corporation for tax purposes in Belgium and was also recognised as a coordination centre. As a result, the profits of the partnership were subject to taxation lower than 30 %. The activities of the partnership consisted, among other things, of financing of subsidiaries and branches.

Even though the profits in the Belgian permanent establishment of the partnership were tax exempt in Germany according to Article 23 para 1 no 1 of the tax treaty, the German tax authorities assessed the profits and net assets of the Belgian partnership in Germany in 1996 for income tax and wealth tax purposes, due to the provision in sec 20 para 2 and 3 International Transactions Tax Act. As the partnership derived income with a capital investment character, the CFC legislation would have applied if the partnership had been a corporation. The partnership filed objection against this assessment and later appealed against the negative decision to the Tax Court of Münster.

4 German Court Proceedings and Questions Referred to the ECJ

After stating that the treatment of the profits of the Belgian permanent establishment was in accordance with German national law, the Tax Court of Münster expressed doubts as to whether the treatment was in accordance with the freedom of establishment in Article 43 EC and the free movement of capital in Article 56 EC.

The Court held that a breach of the freedom of establishment cannot be excluded, as German national law makes investment in a foreign permanent establishment difficult. The provisions in question, sec 20 para 2 and 3 International Transactions Tax Act, seek to prevent resident taxpayers from establishing themselves abroad in the form of a permanent establishment in order to avoid the application of the German CFC legislation.

Due to the additional German tax on low taxed passive income from another Member State, Germany deters its residents from taking up activities that are aimed at deriving income in other Member States. Hereby financing companies are especially affected, as merely certain activities are characterised as passive. In addition, there are additional administrative requirements that the resident shareholder has to meet, e.g. the obligation to compute the profits of the foreign company according to German tax law and the burden of proof.

The Court further stated that the reason for the introduction of sec 20 para 2 and 3 International Transactions Tax Act was the loss of revenue that would have resulted had the provisions not been enacted[75]. This has as such never been acknowledged by the ECJ as a justification for a restriction. Moreover, the Court held that it is irrelevant whether the Belgian coordination centres constitute prohibited state aid. This does not allow Germany to levy a compensatory tax. Sec 20 para 2 and 3 International Transactions Tax Act are probably also in breach of the requirement to fulfil the obligations of the Treaty, Article 10 EC. The Court was of the opinion that Germany is not entitled to sanction possible prohibited state aid granted by another Member States.

As to the tax authorities' argument that sec 20 para 2 and 3 International Transactions Tax Act is an acceptable means to counter tax avoidance, the Court held that the mere fact that a permanent establishment is situated outside Germany does not constitute tax avoidance.

The argument that the foreign low tax may be a justification for the national higher tax could be of relevance in the context of a supranational comparison of tax burdens (the Court hereby referred to the judgment in Manninen, see I.1). Other justification grounds were, according to the Court, not applicable.

The Court then analysed a possible breach of the free movement of capital and came to the same conclusion as for the freedom of establishment.

Consequently, the Tax Court of Münster stayed proceedings and referred the question of the compatibility of sec 20 para 2 and 3 International Transactions Tax Act with the freedom of establishment in Article 43 EC and the free movement of capital in Article 56 EC to the ECJ. Under this provision, contrary to the tax treaty between the Federal Republic of

75 BT-Drs 12/1596.

Germany and the Kingdom of Belgium, Germany avoids double taxation by crediting foreign tax instead of exempting the foreign income.

5 Observations

As stated above, this is not the ideal referral in respect of the German CFC legislation. This is because we are not dealing with the classic different treatment between a foreign and a domestic investment.

The comparison between the German taxation of a Belgian permanent establishment in the context of the CFC legislation and the regular taxation of a German permanent establishment shows that both situations will be taxed in the year the profits are generated. They are both subject to the same German tax rate and, in respect of the Belgian permanent establishment, the foreign tax is credited. The difference is that in the case of a Belgian permanent establishment, additional administrative requirements are placed on the taxpayer, but substantively, there is no difference in taxation that could constitute a restriction.

The key question here is quite a different one: Is Germany allowed, under EC law principles, to switch from the exemption method for profits of a permanent establishment agreed in a tax treaty to a mere tax credit if the foreign branch income is subject to low taxation abroad and stems from certain „passive“ sources?

The provisions in question serve to put foreign permanent establishments and partnerships on a par with foreign subsidiaries in terms of penalising foreign investment in low tax countries. The referral therefore raises, at least prima facie, high expectations of eliciting more about the ECJ's attitude towards the German CFC rules in their by far more prominent field of application, ie with respect to foreign subsidiaries.

According to the Tax Court of Münster, it cannot be excluded that the provisions in question infringe the freedom of establishment by simply rendering difficult certain economic activity in a foreign branch or partnership. Although not it did explicitly put it that way, the Tax Court of Münster may have identified a direct barrier in the fact that the provisions are exclusively intended to prevent such activity abroad.

Whether the ECJ will follow this route remains to be seen. Another question the ECJ might consider, although not posed in the referral, is whether Germany (and other Member States) is permitted to exert investment control within the European Union by penalising passive investments in

Member States at a tax rate of less than 25 % and leaving completely unaffected passive investments in Member States taxed at a rate of 25 % or more.

It cannot be excluded, however, that the question in this case may also boil down to the rather general question whether treaty overrides are permitted under EC law principles. After the judgment in the D case[76], it seems questionable whether treaty overrides within the EU are permissible, since it was held in the D case that the different benefits of a tax treaty are integral parts of the treaty and contribute to its overall balance. Must it be possible for a Member State to refer to the tax treaty when it comes to excluding others than residents from the contracting states to benefit from the same on grounds of the overall balance in the tax treaty, but at the same time to disturb this balance by not applying the provision agreed in the treaty towards the other contracting state?

[76] ECJ 5 July 2002, C-376/03 *D.*, not yet reported.

VIII Stauffer (C-386/04)

1 Introduction

The impact of the fundamental freedoms on direct taxation of non-profit making organisations (charitable trusts, foundations, etc) is still unclear.

The ECJ will have the chance to give an explicit ruling with respect to a possible infringement of the EC Treaty by certain provisions of the German General Tax Code and the German Corporate Tax Act in the case Centro di Musicologia Walter Stauffer, hereinafter Stauffer.

The pending case has led to an echo in academic writing only to a moderate extent, since it shifts the European focus onto a very special group of taxpayers, ie non-profit making organisations. So far, all authors seem to reach conclusions in favor of Stauffer[77] despite the fact that Article 48 para. 2 EC excludes organisations that are non-profit making from protection against discriminatory treatment under the freedom of establishment.

2 Relevant German Legislation

The German Corporate Tax Act exempts charitable organisations from corporate tax in Germany, sec 5 para 1 no 9 German Corporate Tax Act. This exemption however, is according to sec 5 para 2 German Corporate Tax Act not applicable to taxpayers merely subject to limited taxation in Germany in the sense of sec 2 no 1 German Corporate tax Act. Sec 2 no 1 defines limited liability to corporate tax for taxpayers that neither have their seat nor their management in Germany. As a result, non-resident charitable organisations are excluded from the German exemption from corporate tax.

Decisive for the classification as a tax-exempt entity for resident institutions is that they comply with the provisions of the German General Tax Code, sec 51 et seq.

---

77 Buciek, Anmerkung, Die Information für Wirtschaftsprüfer und Steuerberater, 2004, p 764; Eicker, Anmerkung, IWB 1999 F. 11 Gr. 2, p 365 et seq;
Helios/Müller, Vereinbarkeit des steuerlichen Gemeinnützigkeitsrechts mit dem EG-Vertrag, *BB* 2004, p 2332 et seq; Höreth, Ausschluss der Steuerbefreiung für beschränkt steuerpflichtige gemeinnützige Stiftung gemeinschaftsrechtswidrig?, *DStZ* 2004, p 698 et seq; Schäfers, Steuerliche Gemeinnützigkeit ausländischer Körperschaften?, *IStR* 2004, p 752 (p 755 et seq); Schnitger/Papantonopoulos, Deutsche Vorabentscheidungsersuchen zu den direkten Steuern des Jahres 2004, Betriebs-Berater 2005, p 407 et seq; Wachter, Gemeinnützigkeit von Stiftungen mit Sitz im EU-Ausland, *FR* 2004, p 1220 et seq.

3 Facts of the Case

The plaintiff Stauffer is a charitable and non-profit making Italian foundation with its statutory seat and place of management in Italy. It is under state supervision of an Italian authority and is exempt from Italian corporate tax under Italian tax law.

According to sec 2 of the articles of association, the sole purpose of the foundation was schooling, education and promotion in the field of music theory and history as well as the manufacture of classical string instruments. The articles provided for scholarships for study visits in Italy that were exclusively granted to young students from Switzerland and particularly the city of Bern.

In the year in question, 1997, Stauffer owned real estate and premises in Germany from which it derived rental income.

Stauffer was subject to corporate tax in Germany on the German rental income, sec 2 no 1, 8 para 1 German Corporate Tax Act, sec 49 para 1 no 6 German Income Tax Act and Article 6 para 1 of the tax treaty between the Federal Republic of Germany and the Italian Republic and was thus assessed by the tax authorities on the German income. The income was solely used for charitable activities. The objection against the assessment and the appeal to the Tax Court of Munich were unsuccessful[78].

4 German Court Proceedings and Questions Referred to the ECJ

On 14 July 2004, the German Supreme Tax Court decided to stay proceedings and refer a question to the ECJ[79], due to doubts of the compatibility of the German provisions with the freedom of establishment in Article 43 EC, the freedom to provide services in Article 49 EC and the free movement of capital in Article 56 EC.

The German Supreme Tax Court held that – in principle – the articles of association of the Stauffer foundation satisfied the German requirements in sec 51 et seq. German General Tax Code for a charitable, non-profit-making organisation. The fact that scholarships for study visit purposes were only granted to young students from Switzerland and particularly to those from the city of Bern was not regarded as being harmful within the meaning of sec 52 para 1 German General Tax Code, since the young peo-

78 FG München 30 October 2002; file no 7 K 1384/00; *EFG* 2003, p 481.
79 File no I R 94/02; *BFH/NV* 2004, p 1575.

ple of Switzerland or even Bern could well be interpreted as the „general public". Even the fact that the purposes of the foundation were basically fulfilled in a foreign country (Switzerland) and that the articles of association did not expressly state that the application of funds was exclusively linked to the purposes of the foundation, did not deter the German Supreme Tax Court from characterising the foundation as being non-profit making.

Certain conditions for a tax exemption under German law were, however, not fulfilled, such as the appropriation of assets in the case of liquidation of the foundation, but these requirements are dispensable when a German resident institution is state-supervised. As the Stauffer foundation was supervised by an Italian authority, the Court held that this must be sufficient for purposes of the German tax exemption.

Due to the above-mentioned doubts on the compatibility of the German provisions with the fundamental freedoms, the German Supreme Tax Court referred the following question to the ECJ:

> Is it contrary to Article 52 EC, in conjunction with Article 58 EC, Article 59 EC, in conjunction with Articles 66 EC and 58 EC, and Article 73b EC for a charitable foundation established under private law in another Member State, with limited liability to tax on its rental income in Germany, unlike a charitable foundation established in Germany, with unlimited liability to tax and receiving similar income, not to be entitled to exemption from corporate tax?

5 Observations

The main question of interest is whether non-profit organisations are covered by the freedom of establishment or the freedom to provide services. Article 48 EC extends these freedoms to include companies. These are defined to cover companies governed by private or public law, save for those that are non-profit making (Article 48 para 2 EC). This seems to indicate that charitable institutions may not rely on the freedom of establishment or to provide services, since they are inevitably non-profit making.

However, German academic writing on this subject defines „profit making" as all market participants, apart from when these are exercising sovereign rights. The term profit-making thus has to be interpreted broadly. All activities that form part of economic life should be included in this definition when carried out for money.

Accordingly, when leasing real estate in a commercial way, charitable organisations also fall within the scope of the term "company" and should be able to make use of the freedom of establishment and the freedom to provide services.

The next question, of course, is whether in this specific case, Stauffer can be considered to have made use of the freedom of establishment, as it merely derived rental income in Germany. The Commission expressed the opposite view in the hearing of the Stauffer case on 13 October 2005, a position that seems reasonable.

The free movement of capital does, however, not contain the requirement that a company must be profit making, so that this freedom may be applied in any case. This freedom is also applicable in the Stauffer case, as investment in real estate is covered by the scope of the free movement of capital.

The second main question the ECJ will have to decide is whether the coherence argument applies. The ECJ has until now recognised coherence of a tax system as a valid justification for discriminatory rules when and if advantages and disadvantages concern the same tax and the same taxpayer. However, the coherence argument does not fit the Stauffer case since the non-resident foundation is not compensated in any way for the less advantageous treatment in Germany.

The German government and the tax authorities argued at the hearing on Stauffer that resident foundations more often fulfil their aims in Germany and thus contribute to the relief of the German state finances, hence the exemption from German corporate tax. Organisations resident outside Germany, however, mostly provide their benefits outside Germany and it is therefore not justified to exempt these from German taxation. Whether the ECJ will pick up this type of argument remains to be seen. On the other hand, since Article 27 of the tax treaty between the Federal Republic of Germany and the United States of America provides for an exemption of non-resident profit making organisations, this argument by the German government seems somewhat hollow, as Germany obviously accepts that non-residents can be tax exempt in Germany, even though no activities that correspond to the tax exemption are carried out in Germany to relieve the German state finances.

Moreover, sec 5 para 2 no 2 German Corporate Tax Act does not differentiate between the fulfilment of foundation purposes in Germany (possible reason for coherence) and outside Germany, but merely between resident and non-resident taxpayers.

A decision in favour of Stauffer by the ECJ will not only be relevant for the future application of sec 5 para 2 no 2 German Corporate Tax Act, but also for similar provisions in the German Inheritance and Gift Tax Act that make voluntary grants to non-resident charitable organisations less attractive than grants to resident organisations (sec 13 para 1 no 16 lit b and c, 29 para 1 no 4 German Inheritance and Gift Tax Act).

Further, the recognition of the applicability of the fundamental freedoms for non-profit making organisations and specifically the tax exemption of non-residents will in most Member States have an impact on the taxation of dividends paid to such non-resident institutions.

Whereas dividends to resident non-profit making institutions – such as pension funds – are generally exempt from withholding taxes or the taxes are refunded, non-resident equivalents suffer a final withholding tax on dividends from other Member States. The EFTA Court already decided (in brief) with respect to regular profit-making companies that tax exemption on domestic dividends must be extended to cross-border dividend flows in order to be compatible with the free movement of capital in the EEA Agreement[80].

[80] EFTA Court 23 November 2004, E-1/04 *Fokus Bank ASA*.

Pending Cases Filed by German Courts II: The Scorpio, Centro Equestre, Conijn, Schwarz, and Meindl Cases

Pending Cases involving Germany: Commission v Germany

Alexander Rust

I The Scorpio Case (C-290/04)

1 Facts of the Case and Relevant German Legal Provisions
2 Question Referred to the ECJ
3 Possible Approach to Answering the Question Referred

II The Centro Equestre Case (C-345/04)

1 Facts of the Case and Relevant German Legal Provisions
2 Question Referred to the ECJ
3 Possible Approach to Answering the Question Referred

III The Conijn Case (C-346/04) – R.H. Conijn v FA Hamburg-Mitte-Altstadt

1 Facts of the Case and Relevant German Legal Provisions
2 Question Referred to the ECJ
3 Possible Approach to Answering the Question Referred

IV The Schwarz Case (C-76/05) – Schwarz and Gootjes-Schwarz v FA Berg. Gladbach

1 Facts of the Case and Relevant German Legal Provisions
2 Question Referred to the ECJ
3 Possible Approach to Answering the Question Referred

V Commission v Germany (C-152/05) – Eigenheimzulage

1 Facts of the Case and Relevant German Legal Provisions
2 Possible Approach to Answering the Question Referred

VI The Meindl Case (C-329/05) – G. Meindl v FA Dinslaken

1 Facts of the Case and Relevant German Legal Provisions
2 Question Referred to the ECJ
3 Possible Approach to Answering the Question Referred

I The Scorpio Case (C-290/04)

1 Facts of the Case and Relevant German Legal Provisions

The German Corporation Scorpio Konzertproduktionen GmbH organized pop concerts in Germany. Some of the pop artists were managed by an individual resident in the Netherlands whose firm had the name Europop. The nationality of the individual is unknown[1]. In 1993 Scorpio paid the professional fees for the artists to Europop but did not levy a withholding tax on the fees. Pursuant to Sec. 50a (4) 3 ITA[2], the debtor of the artist fees had to withhold a tax of 15 % on the gross amount of the fees. In accordance with Sec. 50a (4) 6 ITA a deduction of operating expenses was not permitted during the withholding procedure. In the taxable year 1993 the withholding tax was final, operating expenses were never taken into account (see Sec. 50 (5) 1 ITA[3]).

If the debtor of the fees refrains from his withholding obligation he can be made liable for the taxes he should have withheld.

Due to Article 5 of the Germany-Netherlands tax treaty, the income earned by Europop is exempt from tax in Germany[4]. Despite the tax treaty obligation to exempt the income Germany nevertheless levies a withholding tax and refers the taxpayer to a refund procedure (Sec. 50d (1) ITA). The debtor of the payments is only allowed to abstain from levying

1 According to Dick Molenaar, the individual is of Dutch nationality. The Bundesfinanzhof as court of appeal only discusses questions of law and is not allowed to inquire the facts. The Lower Court of Hamburg did not ask about the nationality as it considered the question of the nationality as irrelevant. Therefore, the Bundesfinanzhof had to leave the question of the nationality open and refer alternative questions to the ECJ: the first assuming the nationality of a Member State and the second assuming the individual not to be a national of a Member State.

2 Version in force in the year 1993; currently the tax rate varies from 0 % to 20 % depending on the amount of fees paid.

3 A refund procedure was introduced in 1997 with retroactive effect for the year 1996 (see Heinicke in Schmidt, *Einkommensteuergesetz*, München, 24th edn (2005), Sec 50 ITA mn 13. In accordance with Sec 50(5) 2 N°3 ITA, operating expenses may now be taken into account if they exceed 50 % of the gross income. In this case taxes are levied at a rate of 50 % on the net income. Taxes overpaid are refunded.

4 The tax treaty between Germany and the Netherlands does not contain an artist clause similar to Art 17(2) OECD MC. Art 9(2) 2 of the Germany-Netherlands tax treaty, which allows taxation of independent artists in the source state, is only applicable if the artist himself performs an activity in the source state. Europop only managed the artist and did not perform himself. As Europop has not set up a permanent establishment in Germany, Germany is not allowed to tax the income.

a withholding tax if he has asked the tax administration for a certificate of exemption prior to the payment (Sec. 50d (2) ITA).

Scorpio did not have a certificate of exemption and was, therefore, made liable for the taxes it had refused to withhold. Scorpio did not accept liability for the taxes and went to court, arguing that due to Community law operating expenses have to be taken into account already in the withholding procedure and that the withholding tax is unlawful because Germany is obliged to refrain from taxing under the Germany/Netherlands tax treaty. The Lower Court of Hamburg[5] held the German provisions to be in conformity with EC law. Scorpio finally appealed to the Bundesfinanzhof and the Bundesfinanhof was uncertain about the conformity of the provisions with EC law[6].

2 Question Referred to the ECJ

The Bundesfinanzhof referred the following question to the ECJ[7]:

1. Must Articles 59 and 60 of the EC Treaty be interpreted as meaning that they are infringed if a payment debtor established in Germany of a payment creditor established abroad within the Community (in this case: in the Netherlands), who holds the nationality of a Member State, can be held liable under the fifth sentence of Paragraph 50a(5) of the Einkommensteuergesetz 1990 in the version in force in 1993 (Law on Income Tax, hereinafter: "the EStG") because he has failed to deduct tax at source pursuant to Paragraph 50a(4) of the EStG, whereas payments to a payment creditor liable without limitation to income tax in Germany (that is, a German resident) are not subject to any deduction of tax at source pursuant to Paragraph 50a(4) of the EStG and therefore no liability of the payment debtor for non-deduction or insufficient deduction of tax at source can arise?
2. Is the answer to Question 1 different if, at the time of providing his service, the payment creditor established abroad within the Community is not a national of a Member State?
3. If the answer to Question 1 is in the negative:
   (a) Are Articles 59 and 60 of the EC Treaty to be interpreted as meaning that business expenses incurred by a payment creditor estab-

5 FG Hamburg 26.07.2001, EFG 2001, 1553 seq.

6 BFH 28.04.2004, IStR 2004, 583 seq.

7 OJ C 228, 11 September 2004, p 54.

lished abroad within the Community and economically connected with his activities in Germany giving rise to the payments must be taken into account in reduction of tax by the debtor at the time of deducting tax at source pursuant to Paragraph 50a(4) of the EStG because, as is also the case with German residents, only the net income remaining after deduction of business expenses is subject to income tax?

(b) Is it sufficient for the purpose of avoiding an infringement of Articles 59 and 60 of the EC Treaty if, in deducting tax at source pursuant to Paragraph 50a(4) of the EStG, only the business expenses economically connected with the activity in Germany giving rise to the claim for payment and which the payment creditor established abroad within the Community has reported to the payment debtor are taken into account in reduction of tax, and any further business expenses can be taken into account in a subsequent refund procedure?

(c) Are Articles 59 and 60 of the EC Treaty to be interpreted as meaning that they are infringed if the tax exemption to which a payment creditor established in the Netherlands is entitled in Germany under the double taxation convention between the Federal Republic of Germany and the Kingdom of the Netherlands is initially disregarded in the deduction of tax at source pursuant to Paragraph 50a(4) in conjunction with Paragraph 50d(1) of the EStG and only allowed in a subsequent procedure for exemption or refund and the payment debtor is likewise not entitled to rely on the tax exemption in proceedings concerning liability, whereas German residents' tax-free income is not subject to any deduction of tax and therefore no liability for non-deduction or insufficient deduction of tax at source can arise either?

(d) Are the answers to Questions 3(a) to (c) different if the payment creditor established abroad within the Community is not a national of a Member State at the time of providing his service?

3 Possible Approach to Answering the Question Referred

In Germany resident and non-resident artists are treated in a different way. A withholding tax is only levied on non-resident artists whereas resident artists are assessed at the end of the year. The debtor of the payments suffers from additional administrative costs; he can even be made liable if he does not fulfil his withholding obligation correctly. The creditor of the payments suffers at least from a liquidity disadvantage. If the withholding tax is higher than the tax a resident artist would have to pay, the liquidity disadvantage turns into a definite tax disadvantage[8].

In 1993 it was very difficult to execute a tax claim abroad. The Directive on mutual assistance for the recovery of claims[9] did not apply to claims concerning income tax and only a few tax treaties or conventions on legal assistance contained provisions similar to Article 27 OECD Model Convention[10]. Once the artist left Germany an effective tax collection was no longer possible. As a result, the withholding tax procedure as such should be justifiable by the need of an effective tax collection[11].

However, this does not mean that the German withholding tax procedure in concreto is in conformity with Community law. Regarding the deductibility of operating expenses, resident and non-resident taxpayers are in a similar situation[12]. The non-deductibility of expenses leads at least to a liquidity disadvantage for non-resident taxpayers. As the withholding tax is aimed at securing the collection of the tax claim it should not go beyond the amount which is actually due. By not allowing the deduction of expenses, Germany clearly overtaxes the non-resident. This violates the principle of proportionality, since overtaxation is not necessary for securing the tax claim[13]. Besides, Germany has already recognised in other provisions that expenses may be taken into account for the withholding procedure by the debtor of the payments[14]. Thus, the non-deductibility of expenses cannot be justified.

---

8 In 1993 a tax refund procedure had not yet been introduced.

9 Council Directive 76/308/EEC of 15.03.76. The scope of the Directive was extended to income tax claims by Directive 2001/44/EC.

10 See Engelschalk in Vogel/Lehner, *Doppelbesteuerungsabkommen*, 4th edn (2003), Art 27 OECD MC, mn 11.

11 This statement is no longer correct in the current situation in which the Directive on mutual assistance for the recovery of tax claims applies to income tax claims. See Haarmann/Fuhrmann, Konsequenzen aus der EU-Rechtswidrigkeit der abgeltenden Abzugsbesteuerung auf Bruttobasis für beschränkt Steuerpflichtige innerhalb der Europäischen Union, *IStR* 2003, pp 558 et seq (p 559) who cal for either the abolition of the withholding procedure to non-resident artists or for the extension of the withholding system to resident artists. See also Cordewener, Das EuGH-Urteil "Gerritse" und seine Umsetzung durch das BMF-Schreiben vom 3.11.2003 – Steine statt Brot für die Besteuerungspraxis!, *IStR* 2004, pp 109 et seq (p 116).

12 ECJ 12 June 2003, C-234/01 *Gerritse* [2003] ECR I-5933, para 27.

13 Jorewitz, *Die Prüfung der EG-Konformität des deutschen Ertragsteuerrechts* (2004) p 232.

14 See Sec 50a(3) ITA which allows the deduction of expenses in the case of the restitution of travel costs.

The deduction of expenses should not be made compulsory during the withholding procedure. The creditor should have the choice of deducting his expenses either during the withholding procedure or during a subsequent restitution procedure. Otherwise, he would be obliged to reveal his profit margin to the debtor of the payments. The German legislator will have to introduce an option for the non-resident artist to take into account his expenses during the withholding procedure.

The next question regards tax-exempt income. Residents do not have to pay taxes on tax-exempt income whereas tax-exempt income is included for calculating the tax base of the withholding tax. The debtor is not allowed to disregard tax-exempt income unless he obtained a certificate of exemption from the tax administration prior to the withholding. The requirement of a certificate of exemption allows the tax administration to control whether the tax treaty interpretation of the debtor of the payments is correct. As tax treaty law is very difficult there is an imminent danger of mistakes. If the debtor of the payments makes a mistake it is quite difficult to collect the correct tax from the creditor of the payments. Therefore, I believe that the necessity of a certificate of exemption is not disproportionate[15].

Concerning the last question, the freedom to provide services applies only to nationals of a Member State. According to Article 59 (2) of the ECTreaty (now Article 49 (2) EC) the Council may extend the freedom to provide services to nationals of a third country who provide services and who are established within the Community. Up to now the Council has not yet adopted such a resolution[16]. Therefore, Europop could not rely on the freedom to provide services unless he was a national of a Member State. The freedom to provide services, however, not only has an active dimension. The active dimension protects the person who provides the service; the passive dimension protects the person who receives the service. If the recipient of the service is a national of a Member State the freedom becomes applicable irrespective of whether the person providing the service is a national of a Member State[17]. Due to the passive dimension of the freedom to provide services, the nationality of the service provider is irrelevant for answering the first three questions.

---

15 The Commission regards Sec 50d ITA as violating Community law, see opinion of 26 October 2004, JURM (2004) 10039, mn 42.

16 Müller-Graff in Streinz, *Kommentar zum EUV/EGV* (2003) Art 49 mn 131.

17 Müller-Graff in Streinz, *Kommentar zum EUV/EGV* (2003) Art 49 mn 55. See also the opinion of the Commission of 26 October 2004, JURM (2004) 10039, mn 47 et seq.

II The Centro Equestre[18] Case (C-345/04)

Centro Equestre de Lezíria Grande Lda v BfF

1 Facts of the Case and Relevant German Legal Provisions

The Centro Equestre de Lezíria Grande Lda is a Portuguese corporation which organised horse shows in several European cities. Eleven out of fourteen events took place in Germany; the other three performances were organised in Ireland and the UK. In accordance with Sec. 50a (4) ITA Germany as the source state withheld corporate tax of 25 % on the gross receipts. Generally, the withholding tax is final. However, Sec. 50 (5) N° 3 ITA allows the taxpayer to claim a refund if the operating expenses which have a direct economic connection with domestic income exceed 50 % of the receipts. The underlying idea behind this provision is that non-resident artists should pay a 50 % tax on the net income. The expenses are estimated to amount to 50 % of the receipts. As a result, a 25 % tax on the gross income should equal a 50 % tax on the net income[19]. Whenever this estimate turns out to be wrong and the expenses are higher than 50 % of the receipts the non-resident taxpayer is entitled to get a refund of the taxes overpaid.

Centro Equestre's operating expenses that were directly attributable to the domestic activities did not exceed 50 % of the receipts. The overall costs including the overhead costs[20], however, were even higher than the receipts. Centro Equestro wanted to deduct 11/14 of the overhead costs in Germany as 11 out of 14 shows were performed in Germany. Despite the loss situation the German tax administration did not grant a refund of the taxes paid. Centro Equestre went to court but the Lower Court of Cologne[21] confirmed the decision of the tax administration. The Court held that Germany is not obliged to take the overhead costs into account as overhead costs are not directly linked with domestic income. As the overhead costs may be deducted in the residence country the requirement of a direct economic link does not violate the freedom to provide services. The judgment of the Lower Court of Cologne was appealed and the

[18] In the Official Journal one finds the term „Equestro". According to the Portuguese national Ricardo Borges, the term is "Equestre". I am very grateful for his correction.

[19] Heinicke in Schmidt, *Einkommensteuergesetz*, 24th edn (2005), Sec 50 ITA mn 13.

[20] E.g. expenses for a veterinarian, depreciation of the horses, wages for all the events.

[21] FG Köln 18.09.2003, EFG 2004, 49 et seq.

Bundesfinanzhof[22] had doubts about the compatibility of Sec. 50 (V) N°3 ITA with Community law.

2 Question Referred to the ECJ

The Bundesfinanzhof referred the following question to the ECJ[23]:

> Is it contrary to Article 59 of the Treaty establishing the European Communities if a person with restricted tax liability in Germany who is a national of a Member State may claim repayment of tax deducted at source on his income in Germany only when the operating expenses that have a direct economic connection to that income are higher than half of the income?

3 Possible Approach to Answering the Question Referred

Resident taxpayers may deduct all expenses caused by the activity that generates the taxable income whereas non-resident taxpayers are only allowed to deduct the expenses which are directly linked to the generation of domestic income. Therefore, non-resident taxpayers are treated worse[24]. Concerning the tax rate and the deduction of expenses, the ECJ has ruled that resident and non-resident taxpayers are in comparable situations[25].

However, it can be argued that the requirement of a direct economic link can be justified by the principle of territoriality. In the Gerritse judgment[26] the ECJ explicitly stated that the expenses were directly linked to domestic income and, therefore, had to be taken into account: *It is to be noted that the business* expenses in question are directly linked to the activity *that generated* the taxable income in Germany, so that residents and non-*residents are placed in a comparable situation in that respect.*

---

22 BFH 26.05.2004, IStR 2004, 867 et seq.

23 OJ C 273, 6 November 2004, p 20.

24 Haarmann/Fuhrmann, Konsequenzen aus der EU-Rechtswidrigkeit der abgeltenden Abzugsbesteuerung auf Bruttobasis für beschränkt Steuerpflichtige innerhalb der Europäischen Union, *IStR* 2003, p 558 et seq. (559) regard the non-deductibility of expenses that are not directly connected to a domestic income as violating Community law.

25 ECJ 12 June 2003, C-234/01 *Gerritse* [2003] ECR I-5933.

26 ECJ 12 June 2003, C-234/01 *Gerritse* [2003] ECR I-5933, para 27.

As early as in the Futura judgment[27] the ECJ accepted the principle of territoriality as a justification for unequal treatment:

> *For the purpose of calculating the basis of assessment for non-resident taxpayers, only profits and losses* ***arising from their Luxembourg activities*** *are taken into account in calculating the tax payable by them in that State.*
>
> *Such a system, which is in conformity with the fiscal* ***principle of territoriality****, cannot be regarded as entailing any discrimination, overt or covert, prohibited by the treaty.*

The principle of territoriality and the principle of free allocation of taxing rights[28] between the Member States seem to work in the same direction: The Member States are allowed to extend or withdraw the geographical scope of their taxing rights without violating the ECTreaty. If the principle of territoriality is applied in a consistent way, the source state is probably not even obliged to consider parts of the expenses that are not directly attributable to domestic income[29] by means of an apportionment of the company's overhead costs.

A consistent application of principle of territoriality demands the same rules for positive and negative income. Germany is not allowed to split up positive overall income, ie tax parts of receipts which are not directly attributable to domestic activities while disregarding all overhead expenses. The mere fact that the overhead expenses will be taken into account in the residence state cannot justify the non-deductibility in the source state.

---

27 ECJ 15 May 1997, C-250/95 *Futura* [1997] ECR I-2471, paras 21 et seq. See Thömmes, European Court of Justice Releases Branches of EU Companies from Duplication of Bookkeeping Requirements, *Intertax* 1997, p 322 (p 322): In its decision, the Court also addressed the question whether Luxembourg tax law may require that the losses carried forward be economically connected with an activity conducted by the non-resident company within the Luxembourg territory. The Court answered this question in the affirmative and stated that this requirement flows directly from the principle of territoriality which governs the tax systems of all EU Member States. However, in order to determine whether this requirement has been met, the tax authorities may not impose excessive formal requirements, such as the requirement to keep separate accounts in the branch in Luxembourg.

28 See ECJ 12 May 1998, C-336/96 *Gilly* [1998] ECR I-2793.

29 In the *de Groot* decision of 12 December 2002, C-385/00 *de Groot* [2002] ECR I-11819 the ECJ held that the source state is not obliged to partially grant personal allowances in proportion to the domestic income. Like the *Schumacker* judgment of 14 February 1995, C-279/93 *Schumacker* [1995] ECR I-225 the ECJ seems to prefer pass or fail results.

Whenever the credit method is applied[30], the possibility of a deduction in two countries does not lead to a double-dip situation. If the taxpayer suffers a loss due to its high overhead costs the expenses cannot be taken into account in the residence state[31] and taxation in the source state leads to overtaxation.

As long as Germany treats positive and negative income in the same way the non-deductibility of overhead costs will probably be justified by the principle of territoriality[32].

30 As in the case of Centro Equestre due to Art 24 of the Germany-Portugal tax treaty.

31 At least not immediately, a loss carry-forward might be possible in the following years.

32 One could argue that the overhead expenses have to be taken into account at least for calculating the applicable tax rate. Concerning the tax rate, resident and non-resident taxpayers must not be treated differently; see ECJ 12 June 2003, C-234/01 *Gerritse* [2003] ECR I-5933, para 53. See also Schön, Besteuerung im Binnenmarkt – die Rechtsprechung des EuGH zu den direkten Steuern, *IStR* 2004, pp 289 et seq (pp 294 et seq). Regarding individuals, Germany has to introduce a proviso safeguarding progression in order to implement the Gerritse judgment. However, a proviso safeguarding progression is not applicable to corporate tax as the corporate tax rate is not progressive; see Vogel in Vogel/Lehner, *Doppelbesteuerungsabkommen*, 4th edn (2003), Art 23 para 224; Wassermeyer in Debatin/Wassermeyer, *Doppelbesteuerung*, Looseleaf (2002), Art 23 OECD MC para 124.

III The Conijn Case (C-346/04)

R.H. Conijn v FA Hamburg-Mitte-Altstadt

1 Facts of the Case and Relevant German Legal Provisions

Mr Robert Hans Conijn, a Dutch national resident in the Netherlands, was partner of a German limited partnership. Through his partnership he earned business income in Germany. The domestic German income was less than 90 % of his worldwide income. The taxation of a partner in Germany is a two-step process[33]. Although the partnership is regarded as a pass-through entity for tax purposes, the total income of the partnership is calculated on the level of the partnership in a first step. In a second step, the income of the partnership is attributed to the partners in accordance with their share in the partnership.

Mr Conijn wanted to deduct the costs paid to his tax advisor as special expenditures. According to Sec. 10 (1) N°6 ITA, resident taxpayers are entitled to deduct all costs incurred for obtaining tax advice and filling in the tax return. Non-residents may only deduct payments to the tax advisor that are business related. If the costs can be attributed to the earning of income, eg tax advice for a transaction or for calculating the income, they are deductible for non-residents as well. If the costs are connected with the filling in of the tax return or if they concern the personal and family circumstances they are characterised as special expenditures[34] and deductible for resident taxpayers only[35]. Therefore, Mr Conijn as a non-resident could not deduct his costs paid to the tax advisor for filling in his tax return, as they only concerned the profit already calculated on the level of the partnership and his personal and family circumstances. The Court of First Instance did not see a violation of the EC Treaty and dismissed his claim[36]. The Court of Appeals (Bundesfinanzhof) had doubts about the compatibility of the German provisions with the EC Treaty and asked the ECJ for a preliminary ruling[37].

---

33 See Secs 179, 180(1) N° 2 lit. a GTC, Sec 15(1) 1 N°2 ITA.

34 Jakob, *Einkommensteuergesetz*, 3rd ed. (2003), mn 893.

35 Sec 50(1) 5 ITA 1997 excludes the application of Sec 10 ITA for non-resident taxpayers. According to the coalition contract between the CDU and SPD the deductibility of tax advisor fees as special expenditures will be abolished for resident taxpayers as well.

36 FG Hamburg 11.11.2003, EFG 2004, 563.

37 BFH 26.05.2004, BStBl. II 2004, 994 seq.

2 Question Referred to the ECJ

The Bundesfinanzhof referred the following question to the ECJ[38]:

Is a situation whereby a national of another Member State with restricted tax liability in Germany, unlike a person with unrestricted tax liability, may not deduct from his total income as special expenditure the costs incurred by him in obtaining tax advice contrary to Article 52 of the Treaty establishing the European Community.

3 Possible Approach to Answering the Question Referred

According to the Schumacker judgment[39] the situations of residents and of non-residents are not, as a rule, comparable. Here, Mr Conijn does not earn the majority of his income in Germany. As a result, Germany is not obliged to grant him all tax benefits resulting from the taking into account of the personal and family circumstances. Nevertheless, the businessrelated expenses of a non-resident have to be deductible in the same way as the expenses of a resident taxpayer[40]. The question is whether Germany is allowed to disregard all private expenses that cannot be characterised as business expenses or whether the Schumacker judgment only concerns the narrow scope of the taxpayer's personal and family circumstances. The Schilling judgment[41] seems to differentiate between these two categories, allowing the taxpayer to deduct private expenses which do not fall within the narrow scope of the taxpayer's personal and family circumstances.

The fees of the tax advisor paid by Mr Conijn have to be attributed to one of the two categories. If they are more closely related to expenses for pure personal and family circumstances, Germany is not obliged to grant deductibility. If they are more closely related to other private expenses (or even business expenses) they should be deductible. Predominantly, the completion of Mr Conijn's tax return concerned his personal circumstances. The tax advisor had to fill in his address, his family situation and to transcribe the profit already calculated on the level of the partnership. The fees for the tax advisor are, therefore, more closely related to the narrow scope of non-deductible personal expenses. As a result, EC law does not require the fees to be deductible.

---

[38] OJ C 251, 09 October 2004, p 16.

[39] ECJ 14 February 1995, C-279/93 *Schumacker* [1995] ECR I-225, para 31.

[40] ECJ 12 June 2003, C-234/01 *Gerritse* [2003] ECR I-5933.

[41] ECJ 13 November 2003, C-209/01 *Schilling* [2003] ECR I-13389. However, the Schilling judgment concerned resident taxpayers.

Another argument was brought forward by the Bundesfinanzhof[42]. The Court argued that the deductibility of tax advisor fees has the character of a subsidy. As Germany forces the majority of taxpayers to fill in a tax return and the normal taxpayer is reliant on tax advice in order to fill in his tax return, Germany mitigates theses consequences by allowing deduction of the costs incurred in obtaining professional tax help. If one follows this view, each person obliged to fill in a tax return should consequently benefit from the deductibility of the costs. According to this view, Mr Conijn should be allowed to deduct his costs as he was obliged to fill in a tax return.

Overview of the deductible expenses for non-resident taxpayers:

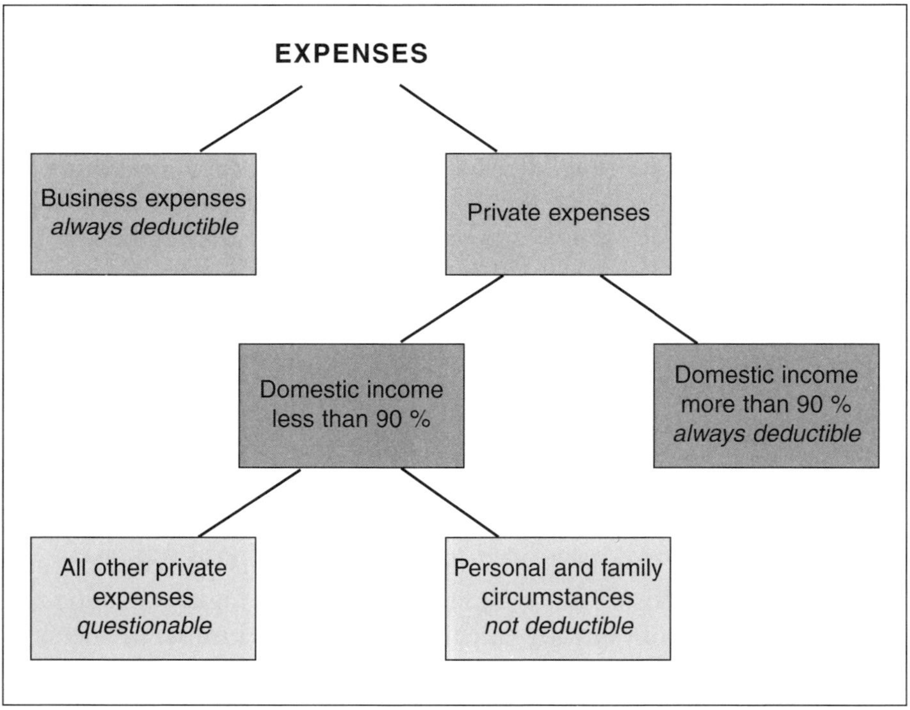

42 BFH 26.05.2004, BStBl. II 2004, 994 et seq.

IV The Schwarz Case (C-76/05) – *Schwarz and Gootjes-Schwarz v FA Berg. Gladbach*

1 Facts of the Case and Relevant German Legal Provisions

Mr Schwarz and Mrs Gootjes Schwarz, a married couple resident in Germany, sent their children to an international school in Scotland. They wanted to deduct the school fees from their tax base as extraordinary expenses (außergewöhnliche Belastungen) according to Sec. 33 ITA and as special expenditures (Sonderausgaben) according to Sec. 10 (1) N°9 ITA. The tax administration denied the deductibility of the school fees and the couple went to court. The Lower Court of Cologne decided that school fees can never be characterised as extraordinary expenses[43]. The requirements of German domestic law were not fulfilled for the deductibility as special expenditures. According to German domestic law[44], 30 % of the school fees paid to a school situated in Germany[45] are deductible as special expenditures. Payments to a foreign school do not benefit from the deductibility. By strictly applying the German provision, the Court had to dismiss the claim. The Court had doubts about the compatibility of this provision with EC law and requested a preliminary ruling in January 2005[46]. Concerning the non-deductibility of payments to foreign private schools, the Commission had already decided to send Germany a formal request to eliminate discrimination[47].

---

43 This question is only of domestic concern. The claimants argued that their children were highly gifted and bored by normal schools. If sent to a normal school they would suffer psychological problems. Therefore, by paying the school fees the parents avoided medical costs. The claimants wanted to characterise the school fees as anticipated medical costs. This characterisation was denied by the court. The school fees could not be deducted in accordance with Sec 33(2) 2 ITA, either. This provision only applies to school fees during a treatment of an illness s. Drenseck in Schmidt, *Einkommensteuergesetz*, 24th edn (2005), Sec 33 ITA mn 4.

44 See Sec 10(1) N°9 ITA.

45 The wording of the provision requires approval by the German State. Only schools situated in Germany can get this approval.

46 FG Köln 27.01.2005, EFG 2005 709 et seq.

47 See Document IP/04/20 of 7 January 2005 http://europa.eu.int/rapid/pressReleasesAction.do?reference=IP/04/20&format=HTML&aged=1&language=EN&guiLanguage=fr

2 Question Referred to the ECJ

The Lower Court of Cologne (FG Köln) referred the following question to the ECJ[48]:

> Is it contrary to Articles 8(a)/18 (freedom of movement), 48/39 (freedom of movement for workers), 52/43 (freedom of establishment) or (59/49 (freedom to provide services) of the EC Treaty to treat payments of school fees to certain German schools, but not payments of school fees to schools in the rest of the European Community area, as special expenditure leading to a reduction of income tax, pursuant to Paragraph 10 (1) N°9 of the Einkommensteuergesetz (Law on Income Tax) as applicable in 1998 and 1999?

3 Possible Approach to Answering the Question Referred

In the tax literature the German provision is regarded as violating the EC Treaty[49]. The courts have already had to decide several times about the compatibility of the German tax provision with EC law[50]. The courts did not see any incompatibility and did not even refer the question to the ECJ. The courts held that the deductibility of school payments would not influence the parents' decision to give or not to send their children to a private school[51]. The Bundesfinanzhof held that the non-deductibility of school payments did not represent overt discrimination,[52] and disregarded the fact that hidden discrimination may be a violation of the EC Treaty as well. In the latest decision, the Bundesfinanzhof avoided a preliminary ruling because the foreign private school charged very high fees. The Court held that a German private school charging the same fees would not be entitled to tax benefits and that the fees paid to that school would not be deductible either. As a result, the foreign school was not treated worse than a domestic school.

---

48 Official translation in the OJ C 93, 4 April 2005, p 27. The German term „Einkommensteuergesetz" normally is translated as "Income Tax Act".

49 Meilicke, Unvereinbarkeit des § 10 Abs. 1 Nr. 9 EStG mit Europarecht, *DB* 1994, pp 1011 et seq; Meilicke/Weyde, Unvereinbarkeit des § 10 Abs. 1 Nr. 9 EStG mit Europarecht, *DStZ* 1996, pp 97 et seq; Gonnella, Nochmals: Unvereinbarkeit des § 10 Abs. 1 Nr. 9 EStG mit Europarecht, *DB* 1994, pp 1395 et seq; Thömmes, IWB Fach 3a Gruppe1 pp 1077 et seq.

50 FG Rheinland-Pfalz 17.03.1995, EFG 1995, 747; BFH 11.06.1997, BStBl. II 1997, 617 et seq; BFH 14.12.2004 BStBl. II 2005, pp 473 et seq.

51 FG Rheinland-Pfalz 17.03.1995, EFG 1995, 747 content of the judgement cited from Thömmes, IWB Fach 3a Gruppe1 p 1077 (p 1080).

52 BFH 11.06.1997, BStBl. II 1997, 617 et seq.

It seems to be quite probable that the ECJ will interpret the EC Treaty as not allowing a differentiation between foreign and domestic schools. Germany will have to extend the deductibility of school payments to private schools within the EU. The violation of the EC Treaty can be explained by two different approaches.

a) Point of view of the parents

The non-deductibility of payments to foreign schools does not represent overt discrimination as it applies to German nationals as well as to nationals of other Member States. But typically the non-deductibility only affects foreign nationals. If foreign nationals move to Germany in order to work there and make use of the free movement guaranteed in the EC Treaty, they will often leave their children at home and send them to a school at home. By doing so, their children have the chance to stay in the environment they are accustomed to. As typically only foreign nationals are affected by the tax rules, the provisions can be characterised as hidden discrimination.

The discrimination cannot be justified on grounds of coherence. Though Germany can only tax the private schools situated in Germany, there is no direct link between the deductibility of the payments, on the one hand, and the taxation of the recipient of the payments (the schools), on the other hand. A coherent provision requires the tax advantage and tax disadvantage to be on the level of the same taxpayer[53]. Besides, Germany exempts private schools from tax and therefore has already destroyed the link between deductibility and taxability.

b) Point of view of the foreign schools

Private schools benefiting from Sec. 10 (1) N°9 ITA are generally non-profit organisations[54]. Thus, it is doubtful whether the freedom to provide services will be applicable[55]. As schooling, education and tuition can be offered for a fee, schools also provide services within the meaning of Article 49 EC. At the very least, private schools that are not non-profit organisations may rely on Article 49 EC.

---

[53] ECJ 28 January 1992, C-204/90 *Bachmann* [1992] ECR I-249, para 28; 6 June 2000, C-35/98 *Verkooijen* [2000] ECR I-4071, para 57.

[54] Sec 10(1) N° 9 ITA refers to Art 7(4) Grundgesetz (Basic Law).

[55] According to Jorewitz, *Die Prüfung der EG-Konformität des deutschen Ertragsteuerrechts* (2004) p 212 the freedom to provide services is not applicable.

Foreign schools suffer from a competitive disadvantage if school fees for German schools are deductible but not those for foreign schools. Due to the deductibility, German schools are more attractive than foreign schools for the parents. For the foreign schools it is more difficult to provide their services to German clients.

This case is quite comparable to the situation in the Danner judgment of the ECJ[56]. The Danner case dealt with Finnish tax provisions regulating the deductibility of payments for an old-age pension. According to Finnish law, contributions paid to a pension insurance scheme were only deductible if the insurance company was based in Finland. Contributions to a foreign insurance company were not deductible. The ECJ held that the Finnish rules were contrary to the freedom to provide services (Article 49 EC). If one replaces "contributions to insurance companies" by "payments to schools", it becomes apparent that the German rules violate the freedom to provide services as well.

c) Possible justification

In Germany the majority of pupils go to public schools. Private schools are quite exceptional in Germany. They only benefit from the provision in Sec. 10 (1) N°9 ITA if they are approved by the state. A school only gets approval if it does not select according to the financial situation of the parents. A school that charges high fees and therefore excludes children from a poor financial background will not get approval. Germany wants to ensure equal opportunities for all children. If Germany was obliged by Community law to extend the deductibility of school fees to foreign private schools it would be forced to financially support schools that do not comply with its concept of education[57]. According to Article 149 (1) EC, the Community has to fully respect the responsibility of the Member States for the content of teaching and the organisation of the educational system. This provision could be regarded as a justification for the different treatment of domestic and foreign schools. However, Article 149 (2) EC requires the Member States to encourage the mobility of students and the development of youth exchanges. By discriminating against foreign schools, Germany makes it more difficult to achieve these targets. As a result I do not believe that the discrimination can be justified[58].

---

56 ECJ 3 October 2002, C-136/00 *Danner* [2002] ECR I-8147.

57 See Schenke, Urteilsanmerkung, *JZ* 2005, pp 946 et seq (p 948).

58 Schenke, Urteilsanmerkung, *JZ* 2005, pp 946 et seq (p 948) fn 34 proposes to limit the deductible fees to a maximum amount. This way schools with high fees (foreign schools) will not be treated better than schools with low fees (German schools).

V Commission v Germany (C-152/05) – *Eigenheimzulage*

1 Facts of the Case and Relevant German Legal Provisions

In order to stimulate the building of houses in Germany and to support families to build their own home, the German state grants a subsidy for self-occupied houses (Eigenheimzulage). In the past, the owner of a house could deduct parts of the acquisition costs from the tax base[59]. Due to the progressive tax rates, higher-income earners benefited more from the allowance than persons who earned less income. Therefore, the system was changed with effect on 1 January 1996[60]. Now, every homeowner receives a fixed amount of money for eight years[61] after the construction or the purchase of the house. This may be as much as € 1,250 per year[62]. The housing grant is subject to three main conditions:

- The income of the homeowner in the year of the purchase and the year before the purchase[63] may not exceed € 70,000[64].
- The applicant must be subject to unlimited tax liability.
- The house must be situated in Germany.

The Commission started proceedings for failure to fulfil an obligation against Germany in January 2004[65]. According to the view of the Commission, the German government did not adequately answer the formal request. Therefore, on 5 April 2005, the Commission brought an action against the Federal Republic of Germany before the European Court of Justice[66]. The Commission claimed that the Court should:

---

59 See Sec 10e ITA old version.

60 See Sec 19(1) EigZulG (Law on allowances for owner-occupied homes).

61 See Sec 3 EigZulG.

62 Sec 9 EigZulG: 1 % of the purchase price, not exceeding € 1,250. For every child of the-homeowner another grant of € 800 is added.

63 Thus, the income of two years will be added together.

64 See Sec 5 EigZulG. For a married couple the limit is € 140,000. Every child increases the limit by € 30,000.

65 See Document IP/04/20 of 7 January 2005 http://europa.eu.int/rapid/pressReleasesAction.do?reference=IP/04/20&format=HTML&aged=1&language=EN&guiLanguage=fr

66 See Document IP/04/950 of 19 July 2004 http://europa.eu.int/rapid/pressReleasesAction.do?reference=IP/04/950&format=HTML&aged=1&language=EN&guiLanguage=en and OJ 2005/C 232/33 of 28 May 2005.

a) declare that by excluding, in the first sentence of Paragraph 2 (1) of the Eigenheimzulagengesetz (Law on allowances of owner-occupied homes), the grant, to persons subject to unlimited taxation, of owner-occupied home allowance in respect of properties situated in other Member States irrespective of whether comparable assistance an be claimed there, the Federal Republic of Germany has failed to fulfil its obligations under Articles 18, 39 and 43 of the EC Treaty.
b) order the Federal Republic of Germany to pay the costs.

According to the Commission, the owner-occupied home allowance has discriminatory features. Only persons subject to unlimited taxation in Germany who acquire a house situated in Germany are entitled to the home allowance. That means that persons – although subject to unlimited tax liability – who live outside Germany and want to acquire a property there do not benefit from the home allowance. The Commission believes that three groups of people are discriminated against by the German rules: (i) state employees who are resident abroad; (ii) frontier workers who earn at least 90 % of their income in Germany; and (iii) diplomats and European officials from Germany. The Commission regards the German home allowance as infringing the freedom of movement for workers (Article 39 EC), freedom of establishment (Article 43 EC) or freedom of movement under Article 18 EC. A justification of this infringement is – in its view – not possible. Taxpayers may not benefit at the same time from the Eigenheimzulage and from a comparable State aid in another Member State. If the other Member State grants a similar aid, the German Eigenheimzulage is excluded, pursuant to Sec. 6 (3) EigZulG[67].

The compatibility of the German home allowance with the EC Treaty was also discussed in court[68]. The claimant lived in France and worked in Germany. He earned nearly all of his income in Germany and opted for the fictitious unlimited tax liability[69]. Having bought a house in France, he applied for the housing grant in Germany. The German tax administration rejected his application in conformity with German domestic law because his house was not situated in Germany. The claimant argued that the requirement of the location of the house in Germany violated the EC

67 For further details, see Häußler, Eigenheimzulage auch für im EU-Ausland belegene Häuser und Wohnungen?, *FR* 2005, pp 872 et seq (p 875).

68 FG Baden-Württemberg, 12 K 434/00, 18.07.2001, not officially published, Juris Document STRE20027160.

69 According to Sec 1(3) ITA.

Treaty. A double dip was not possible in his case as France does not support the building of houses in its domestic tax law. The Lower Court decided that Germany cannot be obliged to support the purchase of a house situated in another Member State if the other Member State does not have a comparable system of granting a home allowance. The French taxpayer appealed against the judgment of the Lower Court. The case is now pending at the Bundesfinanzhof[70]. The judgment of the Bundesfinanzhof has, however, been postponed until after the decision of the ECJ in the proceedings for failure to fulfil an obligation[71].

2 Possible Approach to Answering the Question Referred

The Commission is of the opinion that the reasoning of the Schumacker judgment[72] can be easily transferred to the present case. In the Schumacker case the ECJ decided that resident taxpayers and non-resident taxpayers are normally not in the same situation. Only if the non-resident obtains the major part of his taxable income in the state of employment, with the result that the state of residence is not in a position to grant him the benefits from the taking into account of his personal and family circumstances, must non-residents and residents be treated alike[73]. As a result of this jurisprudence, frontier workers who earn at least 90 % of their income in Germany must be treated in the same way as resident taxpayers. However, a resident taxpayer does not benefit from the home allowance either if he purchases a house outside Germany. The German rules require the house to be located in Germany. Therefore, the Commission by demanding a home allowance for houses situated outside Germany is claiming that frontier workers be treated in a better way than resident taxpayers. The EC Treaty does not grant a better treatment. Germany treats the frontier workers in exactly the same way as it treats its own residents. As soon as the frontier workers buy a house in Germany, they are entitled to the home allowance. With the purchase of the house they are regarded as resident taxpayers and as a resident with a house situated in Germany they – of course – benefit from the house allowance.

The Commission also argues that every person who pays tax on his worldwide income in Germany – as do the frontier workers who opt for the fic-

70 See file number IX R 73/02.

71 BFH IX R 73/02, 18.08.2005, not yet published.

72 ECJ 14 February 1995, C-279/93 *Schumacker* [1995] ECR I-225.

73 ECJ 14 February 1995, C-279/93 *Schumacker* [1995] ECR I-225, para 36.

titious unlimited tax liability – and in this way participates in the financing of German society must be able to benefit from advantages financed out of taxation in the same way as a person resident in Germany. The argument is thus that everybody who pays taxes must get something back and, therefore, be entitled to the home allowance. This argument would have been convincing if Germany had created a link between the payment of taxes and the entitlement to the home allowance in its domestic legislation. However, for entitlement to the home allowance it is irrelevant whether the applicant effectively pays taxes. People without any income may receive the home allowance as well and people earning too high an income are excluded from the entitlement. As there is no link between tax payment and entitlement to benefits, Germany does not have to support the purchase of houses abroad[74].

Concerning the outbound situation (Germans working abroad), a taxpayer who buys a home in another Member State normally leaves his former home in Germany. If he does so, he is no longer subject to unlimited tax liability. The European Court of Justice has already held that the Treaty offers no guarantee to a citizen of the Union that transferring his activities to a Member State other than that in which he previously resided will be neutral as regards taxation. Given the disparities in the tax legislation of the Member States, such a transfer may be to the citizen's advantage in terms of taxation or not, according to circumstances.[75] Non-resident taxpayers may be treated less favourably than resident taxpayer without violating the ECTreaty. It is, therefore, not contrary to EC law to deny the housing grant to non-resident taxpayers who have left Germany. If the taxpayer keeps his home in Germany und purchases a second home in another Member State, he remains subject to unlimited tax liability. The purchase of a second home, however, is not supported by the home allowance.

The only problematic case seems to be an outbound situation, in which the taxpayer remains subject to unlimited tax liability and buys his first home in another Member State. This could be a diplomat who remains subject to unlimited tax liability under Sec. 1 (2) ITA. Had he stayed in Germany and built a house there, he would have benefited from the allowance. Due to his work in another Member State the purchase of his house at his working place is not supported by the German state. This case is similar

[74] See Bilsdorfer, Ausländischer Wohnsitz und inländische Wohnungsbauförderung – zwei Dinge, die nicht zusammengehen?, *IStR* 2001, p 403.

[75] ECJ 12 July 2005, C-403/03 *Schempp*, not yet reported.

to the situation in the Schilling judgment[76]. Mrs and Mr Schilling moved from Germany to Luxembourg in order to work for the European Communities. In accordance with Sec. 1 (2) ITA, they remained subject to unlimited tax liability. The wages paid by the European Communities were tax exempt in Germany. They only had to pay taxes on their income from renting immovable property in Germany. They wanted to deduct the payments for a cleaning lady who worked for them in Luxembourg. Pursuant to Sec. 10 (1) N° 8 ITA[77], only payments for a cleaning lady working in Germany were deductible. The European Court of Justice decided that the deductibility of the payments must not be made dependent on the fact that the cleaning lady works in Germany. Replacing payments to a cleaning lady in Germany by payments for a house in Germany, it becomes obvious that an allowance only for houses situated in Germany would violate Community law as well. However, the difference between the Schilling case and the Eigenheimzulage is that the Eigenheimzulage is not an allowance but a grant.

The entitlement to the housing grant does not depend on whether the applicant effectively pays taxes. A person subject to unlimited tax liability may claim the allowance although he does not earn any income. Conversely, persons exceeding the income limit do not benefit from the housing grant. There is no link between the payment of taxes and the entitlement to the housing grant. Therefore, the housing grant no longer has anything to do with taxes and should not be examined in the light of the jurisprudence concerning taxes. I believe that the State aid provisions[78] would fit this case better.

In any case, due to severe budgetary constraints, Germany will completely abolish the Eigenheimzulage next year.

[76] ECJ 13 November 2003, C-209/01 *Schilling* [2003] ECR I-13389.

[77] This provision has already been abolished.

[78] However, as Frans Vanistendael correctly pointed out during the discussion, classification as State aid does not mean that the fundamental freedoms are no longer applicable.

VI The Meindl Case (C-329/05) – *G. Meindl v FA Dinslaken*

1 Facts of the Case and Relevant German Legal Provisions

Another interesting case the ECJ has to deal with concerns the requirements of a joint assessment. In Germany couples may opt for a joint assessment[79]. If a couple elects joint assessment, the income earned by wife and husband will be aggregated[80]. The tax burden of the couple will be calculated by doubling the tax on the half of the joint income (the "splitting tariff")[81]. Due to the progressive tax rate, twice the tax burden on half a tax base normally is more advantageous than a single tax on a regular tax base[82]. Therefore, most couples opt for a joint assessment.

However, joint assessment is only possible if the couple complies with the following three requirements: the couple has to be married, they have to live together at least one day within the taxable year and both spouses have to be subject to unlimited tax liability[83].

In consequence of the Schumacker judgment of the ECJ[84], the requirement of the unlimited tax liability of both spouses was facilitated. Nowadays[85] it is sufficient if one of the two spouses is subject to unlimited tax liability[86] in Germany and the other spouse is a resident of an EU or an EFTA country. Additionally, at least 90 % of their joint income must be domestic income or their joint income not taxable in Germany may not exceed DEM 24,000[87].

---

79 See Sec 26 ITA.

80 See Sec 26b ITA.

81 See Sec 32a(5) ITA.

82 For some exceptions, see Seeger in Schmidt, *Einkommensteuergesetz*, 24th edition (2005), Sec 26 ITA mn 17. For example, the separate assessment is more beneficial if one spouse has high tax-exempt income which is taken into account for proviso safeguarding progression, or if one spouse is entitled to a loss carry-forward.

83 See Sec 26(1) ITA.

84 ECJ 14 February 1995, C-279/93 *Schumacker* [1995] ECR I-225.

85 Sec 1a(1) N° 2 entered into force in the year 1996; the provision could be also applied with retroactive effect if the tax assessment was not yet definitive.

86 Unlimited tax liability according to Sec 1(1) ITA (depending on residence) or fictitious unlimited tax liability according to Sec 1(3) ITA (if more than 90 % of the income is earned in Germany). Independent of whether Sec 1(1) ITA or Sec 1(3) ITA is applicable, the 90 % domestic income requirement has to be fulfilled.

87 Currently, the threshold of € 12,272 may not be exceeded.

In the taxable year 1997 the Austrian national G. Meindl was living and working in Germany. His wife and his newborn child were living in Austria. Mr Meindl earned all his income (DEM 138,422) in Germany. His wife received wage continuation and maternity benefits from the Austrian state. In 1997 the payments of the Austrian state amounted to ATS 189,703 (DEM 26,995) and were not taxable in Germany. Therefore, the joint income not taxable in Germany was above the threshold of DEM 24,000. The 90 % requirement was not met neither as less than 90 % (138,422/165,417 = 84 %) of their joint income was domestic income. Mr Meindl opted for joint assessment but the German tax administration rejected the option as, according to German domestic law, the conditions for joint assessment were not fulfilled.

The issue of the case is that the maternity benefits paid by the Austrian state were tax exempt in Austria, whereas Germany taxed[88] the foreign maternity benefits. Mr Meindl argued that the Austrian state payments should not be taken into account for calculating the joint income of the couple as Germany had to follow the characterisation given by of Austria.

Mr Meindl filed a suit against the rejection of the German tax administration to grant a joint assessment. The Lower Court of Düsseldorf[89] decided in favour of the taxpayer. It interpreted the 90 % rule in the light of the right of establishment, ruling that the income of the spouse living outside Germany has to be calculated in accordance with the domestic tax law of the residence state. As Austria exempted the wife's income, it should not be taken into account for determining the 90 % threshold. The tax administration appealed against the judgments. The Court of Appeals, the German Bundesfinanzhof, requested a preliminary ruling on the correct interpretation of the right of establishment.

2 Question Referred to the ECJ

The following question has been referred to the ECJ by the Bundesfinanzhof[90]:

---

88 They would have been taxed if Mrs Meindl had lived in Germany. As Mrs Meindl was non-resident they were only taken into account for the 90 % threshold. However, German maternity benefits are tax exempt in Germany.

89 FG Düsseldorf 14.10.2004, *EFG* 2005, pp 612 et seq with remarks by Müller, *EFG* 2005, p 616 and Jahn, *PIStB* 2005, pp 220 et seq.

90 Own translation of BFH 28.06.2005, *DB* 2005, 2002 et seq. An official translation is not yet available. The German wording is the following: "Liegt ein Verstoß gegen Art. 43 EG

Is it contrary to Article 43 EC if a resident taxpayer is not allowed to opt for a joint assessment with his spouse, who lives in Austria and from whom he does not live separately, just because the spouse earned an amount higher than DEM 24,000 representing more than 10 % of the joint income, even if that income is tax exempt according to Austrian law?

3 Possible Approach to Answering the Question Referred

The first question is whether Germany is allowed to fully tax maternity benefits paid by the Austrian state while exempting similar payments paid by the German state[91]. There is no justification for this different treatment[92]. If Germany had exempted the Austrian maternity benefits from taxation all the taxable income would have been earned in Germany and the couple could have benefited from joint assessment.

Even if the first question is answered in the affirmative, it has to be asked whether the maternity benefit has to be taken into account for allowing a joint assessment. If the purpose of the joint assessment is to grant the personal allowance twice and to ensure that the minimum living wage is not taxed, one could argue that this aim is already achieved. The maternity benefit of Mrs Meindl remains untaxed and Mr Meindl is allowed to deduct his personal allowance. Thus, the minimum living wage is not taxed in the hands of Mrs or Mr Meindl. As Mrs Meindl receives her maternity benefit, which exceeds the margin of subsistence, there is no need to make the maintenance payments of Mr Meindl to his wife deductible. On the other hand, it seems to be possible to apply the Wallentin doctrine[93]. In this judgment the European Court of Justice decided that the source state is obliged to grant all personal deductions if the taxpayer only earns tax-exempt income in his residence state. Transferring this doctrine to the Meindl case leads to the conclusion that Germany has to grant the personal deductions twice if the couple only earns tax-exempt income in Austria. This means that Mrs and Mr Meindl must be jointly assessed in Germany.

---

vor, wenn einem gebietsansässigen Steuerpflichtigen die Zusammenveranlagung zur Einkommensteuer mit seinem in Österreich wohnenden Ehegatten, von dem er nicht getrennt lebt, mit der Begründung versagt wird, dieser habe sowohl mehr als 10 % der gemeinsamen Einkünfte als auch mehr als DEM 24,000 erzielt, wenn diese Einkünfte nach österreichischem Recht steuerfrei sind?“

91 Sec 3 N° 1, d ITA.

92 Different opinion BFH 14.08.1991, BStBl. II 1992, 88 et seq.

93 ECJ 1 July 2004, C-169/03 *Wallentin* [2004] ECR I-6643.

I believe that one should go even one step further by completely ignoring the 90 % requirement contained in Sec. 1a (1) N°2, Sec. 1 (3) ITA. Joint assessment not only grants the personal allowance twice but also gives access to the split rate. In situations in which the 90 % requirement is not met access to the split rate is also necessary in order to avoid discriminatory treatment. A double dip can be avoided by applying a proviso safeguarding progression on the total income of the couple.

Pending Cases Filed by Italian Courts: The Banca Popolare di Cremona Case

Pasquale Pistone

1 **Introduction**

2 **The Facts**

3 **The Issues**

3.1 The conflict between IRAP and the common VAT system

3.2 On the retrospective application of a decision in favour of the taxpayer

4 **Some Arguments for a Decision**

5 **The Possible Consequences**

Banca Popolare di Cremona v Agenzia Entrate Ufficio Cremona (C-475/03)

1 Introduction

Nihil novi sub sole from Italian tax courts for European direct taxation.

The Italian legislator is still far from discovering the secret formula for drafting perfectly EU-proof statutes and often ignores direct tax decisions of the ECJ on cases referred from other EU Member States. However, Italian tax courts still do not refer direct tax cases to the European Court of Justice (hereafter: ECJ), thus leaving taxpayers in fact without the protection of rights to which they would be entitled on the basis of the EC Treaty.

However, an interesting situation currently arises from a case referred by the Tax Court of First Instance (*Commissione Tributaria Provinciale*) of Cremona on the compatibility of the Italian business tax (IRAP – *Imposta Regionale sulle Attività Produttive*) with the EU VAT system, which may mainly affect direct taxes.

The case is also important because a decision declaring IRAP incompatible with VAT would have unprecedented repercussions on the Italian state budget, estimated at as much as EUR 120 billion if there is a retrospective application of such decision to other similar claims made by taxpayers.

After analysing the relevant facts and problems of the compatibility of IRAP, we should therefore focus on whether the retrospective effects of a decision by the European Court of Justice in favour of the taxpayer should not apply to other similar claims made by taxpayers.

The outcome of such an analysis will make it possible to draw the arguments on which a decision by the European Court of Justice could be based and then evaluate the possible repercussions of such a decision for Italy and the other Member States, especially those applying at present a business tax.[1]

2 The Facts

IRAP is levied on the net value of goods and services produced by taxpayers carrying out a business activity in Italy. Having regard to its main

[1] On 22 June 2005 the Local Court of Komárom-Esztergom has referred to the ECJ a preliminary ruling procedure (now filed as case C-261/05 Lakép et aa.) on the compatibility of the Hungarian business tax with Article 33 of the Sixth VAT directive.

features, IRAP could be considered an income-type value-added tax. Unlike a consumption-type value-added tax (such as the EU common VAT system), IRAP allows for depreciation of fixed assets and taxes the annual aggregate value added without permitting any deduction of cost for labour and interest expenses. IRAP is levied on goods and services upon production, though VAT will in fact duplicate it once such goods and services are actually supplied.

After its introduction, the Italian government amended IRAP with a view to making it compatible with the common EU VAT system and obtained the preliminary approval of the European Commission on 10 March 1997.

Nevertheless, the plaintiff challenged IRAP before the Tax Court of First Instance of Cremona by arguing that it is incompatible with the general prohibition contained in Article 33(1) of the Sixth VAT Directive. According to this provision, as interpreted by the European Court of Justice, Member States may not maintain or introduce turnover taxes, since such taxes would possibly interfere with the common VAT system.

The plaintiff supported the view that IRAP is charged on all goods and services at every stage of production or distribution. Deduction of costs from proceeds throughout the various stages until consumption ensures an equivalent effect to that which may result by deducting input tax from output tax on a transaction-by-transaction basis for VAT purposes.

The national court shared the plaintiff's doubts concerning the compatibility of IRAP with the common VAT system and thus made reference for a preliminary ruling procedure before the European Court of Justice. The approach taken by the Tax Court of First Instance of Cremona seems indeed the most appropriate one that a national court has to follow whenever a reasonable doubt arises as to whether a specific tax may be incompatible with European law. By contrast, other Italian courts have decided that IRAP is manifestly incompatible (Tax Court of Second Instance of Turin[2], or manifestly compatible (Tax Court of First Instance of Padova[3] with VAT. In both cases I feel that such courts have indeed exceeded their function as national judges in a situation that indeed seems far from being clear at present.

Italian scholars have long debated about this case, supporting opposite views as to whether IRAP in fact infringes the common EU VAT system.

2 Tax Court of Second Instance of Turin, decision 19.5.2005, n. 15.

3 Tax Court of First Instance of Padova, decision 19.9.2005, n. 34.

Some have argued in favour of the compatibility, by underlining that IRAP is a direct tax and is neither levied upon supply of goods and services, nor based on deduction of input tax from output tax as VAT is. Others have instead argued against the compatibility, by underlining that regardless of whether IRAP is a direct or an indirect tax, its levy may supplement VAT once goods and services are actually supplied.

The debate in major tax specialised reviews and newspapers induced most Italian taxpayers to file tax reimbursement requests, thus gradually giving the indirect implications of the decision much bigger dimensions than those immediately affecting the case presented before the European Court of Justice[4].

Consequently, the Italian government, besides requesting the European Court of Justice to reject the plaintiff's arguments, also invoked good faith with a view to excluding a possible retrospective application of a decision in favour of the taxpayer. According to the Italian government the latter request could be justified by the preliminary approval that IRAP received by the European Commission in March 1997.

Advocate General Jacobs supported the view that IRAP interferes with the common EU VAT system, since it shares the four main elements of turnover taxes, such as (i) being generally applicable to supplies of goods and services, (ii) being proportional to the price of those goods and services regardless of the actual number of transactions carried out, (iii) being charged at each stage of the production and distribution process and (iv) being imposed on the value added to the goods and/or services in question[5].

However, Advocate General Jacobs acknowledged that Italy relied on the comfort letter of the European Commission and therefore invited the European Court of Justice to analyse whether the retrospective effects of a decision in favour of the taxpayer could be limited, taking into account the serious financial difficulties that such decision would imply for a state that acted in good faith[6].

---

4 According to the Italian statute of limitation rules, reimbursement could be claimed by taxpayers in respect of payments of tax made in the four years preceding the request.

5 Opinion of Advocate General Jacobs in *Banca Popolare di Cremona* (ECJ C-475/03 *Banca Popolare di Cremona*, pending), 17 March 2005, para 70.

6 Opinion of Advocate General Jacobs in *Banca Popolare di Cremona* (ECJ C-475/03 *Banca Popolare di Cremona*, pending), 17 March 2005, para 80.

Upon request of nine EU Member States the Grand Chamber of the European Court of Justice issued an order on 21 October 2005 to reopen the procedure and further discuss the notion of turnover taxes[7] and the problems related to the limitation of retrospective effects of the decision.

3 The Issues

Several Member States have a business tax sharing some of the features of IRAP.

Consequently, the interest for the issues of this case should not be confined to the plaintiff and similar situations regarding Italian taxpayers, but also concern other countries which levy a business tax, such as, in particular, France, Germany, Hungary and Spain, since a decision in favour of the taxpayer could anticipate a possible procedure of compatibility concerning business taxes levied by other Member States. By contrast, should IRAP be declared compatible with the common EU VAT system, then proceedings on the compatibility of other business taxes with European law would become more unlikely.

The two main issues of the case will now be analysed. First, the focus will be on the conflict between IRAP and the common VAT system; then we will deal with the problems of limiting retrospective application of a decision in favour of the taxpayer.

3.1 The conflict between IRAP and the common VAT system

Italy has levied IRAP since 1998. Italian tax scholars have long debated as to whether IRAP should be regarded as a direct or indirect tax. Nevertheless, changes introduced in 1997 to the original draft persuaded many to regard it is an income-type VAT and thus as a new kind of direct tax, joining those already levied at the state level on income[8] and at the municipal level on immovable property[9].

Characterisation of IRAP as a direct tax under domestic law is nevertheless not decisive from the perspective of ascertaining whether it is compatible

---

7 The first preliminary question referred in ECJ C-261/05, Lakép et aa., pending, exactly addresses the criteria that characterise a tax as a turnover tax.

8 Italy currently levies two taxes on income, namely *Imposta sul Reddito delle Persone Fisiche* (IRPEF) on individuals and *Imposta sul Reddito delle Società* (IRES).

9 *Imposta Comunale sugli Immobili* (ICI).

with an indirect tax like VAT, since European courts normally address such issue by making reference to the main features of each tax[10].

Furthermore, as Advocate General Jacobs underlined in his Opinion, incompatibility does not require a tax to be identical to VAT, but only to share its four main elements, such as it seems to be the case with IRAP.

It is now time to analyse such elements more in details, following the order adopted by Advocate General Jacobs in the Banca Popolare di Cremona pending case.

First, as the Tax Court of First Instance of Cremona has indicated, IRAP generally applies to all supplies of goods and services. Since the European Court of Justice never interferes with how the national court interprets domestic law and Advocate General Jacobs has provided for further elements to support this view[11], the Italian government shoult not be able to to succeed in arguing – as it did at the first hearing – that interference may not arise just because IRAP is a direct tax levied on wealth created (ie goods and services), rather than on the actual supply of the goods and services produced.

The difference between direct and indirect taxes is not decisive with a view to ascertaining the compatibility with the common VAT system. The moment at which IRAP is levied is totally immaterial. After all, one should not forget that insofar as IRAP is levied on goods and services produced without deductions for labour and financial costs related thereto, no goods and/or services may be supplied from Italy without bearing IRAP. In other words, as the Italian *Corte Costituzionale* has mentioned[12], the economic burden of IRAP is normally shifted to goods and services supplied, which in turn are liable to VAT.

Second, IRAP is levied on the value added to goods and services supplied. No one doubts that IRAP and VAT clearly differ as to how such value is calculated; IRAP's taxable base being the difference between costs and proceeds of production in a given year, whereas VAT due is calculated on a transaction-by-transaction basis. Nevertheless, such difference seems to

---

10 ECJ 27 October 1998, C-4/97 *Manifattura Italiana Nonwoven* [1998] ECR I-6469, para 19; 13 February 1996, C-197/94 and 252/94 *Bautiaa and Société Française Maritime* [1996] ECR I-505, para 39.

11 Opinion of Advocate General Jacobs in *Banca Popolare di Cremona* (ECJ C-475/03 *Banca Popolare di Cremona*, pending), 17 March 2005, paras 30-31.

12 Corte Costituzionale, Order 286/2001.

be negligible on an aggregate basis, as both the national court and Advocate General Jacobs highlighted. Furthermore, in the Dansk Denkavit case[13] the ECJ also concluded that a national measure could be regarded as incompatible with ,the common VAT system even when the national measure does not calculate the value added on a transaction-by-transaction basis.

Third, just like VAT, IRAP is also levied at each stage of production and distribution. Once more, Advocate General Jacobs and the national court agree on this point, whereas the Italian government has not provided for arguments to counter this conclusion.

Fourth, IRAP is exactly proportional to the value added of goods and services produced, regardless of the actual number of transactions carried out. Not being labour costs and interest expenses deductible from the taxable base, the economic burden of IRAP may be shifted to the consumer[14], thus presenting all the main features of VAT and in general of turnover taxes, as described by the Court in the Careda[15] decision.

In other words, it is submitted that such common elements prove some relevant degree of similarity between IRAP and VAT, on which basis the European Court of Justice should ascertain the possible interference between the two taxes and thus declare the former incompatible with the common system of turnover taxes established by the European directives. Not surprisingly, both the Italian national court and Advocate General Jacobs have made clear statements to support this view.

By contrast, the position taken by the European Commission in early 1997 – when Italy submitted IRAP's preliminary draft (or IREP as it was called at that stage) for approval – could or should be a surprise. One could wonder why the European Commission asserted that "in the present state, the proposal for this new tax does not appear incompatible with the legislation applicable in the field of value added tax". Would it be possible to conclude that it did so just because the Italian Government was presenting it as a direct tax on wealth produced? Or was this conclusion reached

[13] ECJ 31 March 1992, C-200/90 *Dansk Denkavit* [1992] ECR I-2217, paras 13-14.

[14] A legally structured shifting of the tax burden down to the final consumer would instead not be possible in respect of income or corporation tax, albeit market forces could in some instances achieve this result.

[15] ECJ 26 June 1997, C-370/95, 371/95, and 372/95 *Careda* [1997] ECR I-3721, paras 15, 18, and 26.

because the Commission really believed that IRAP was not interfering with the common VAT system? Whatever the right answer to such question is, one should not forget that already in those days of 1997 the Commission was well aware of the relevant precedents of the European Court of Justice, since the Dansk Denkavit decision was issued long before 1997 and Advocate General Jacobs presented his Opinion on the Careda joined cases more than two weeks before the Commission gave its final consent to IRAP.

This dilemma directly affects the second relevant issue of the Banca Popolare di Cremona case, since the Italian government invoked good faith for the purpose of excluding the retrospective application of a decision in favour of the taxpayer. Itis not just a matter of saying whether the Commission expressed its view formally or informally, as it has held at the hearing on the pending case. It is a much more complex issue, involving whether the Commission may authorise a Member State to introduce a measure that is in conflict with principles already stated by the single interpreter of European law, ie the European Court of Justice.

3.2 On the retrospective application of a decision in favour of the taxpayer

The order for a second hearing may provide further elements to clarify the notion of taxes that are incompatible with Article 33 of the Sixth VAT Directive. However, insofar as the Grand Chamber of the European Court of Justice decide that IRAP interferes with VAT, then it would be obliged to state on a very delicate – issue, such as the limitation of retrospective effects of the desision.

The impact of such decision on the Italian state would go far beyond the obligation to repay IRAP to the plaintiff. Since most Italian taxpayers liable to IRAP have meanwhile filed reimbursement requests for payments of such tax made within the previous 48 months, this decision could turn out to be the one having the highest impact ever on the Italian public budget and possibly in general on the budget of an EU Member State.

The retrospective effects of a decision of the European Court of Justice on similar cases arising in the same Member State that referred a request of preliminary ruling –may be excluded only in exceptional circumstances, since this limitation would affect the homogeneous application of principles under European law.

According to the case law of the European Court of Justice, retrospective effects could only be excluded when this would cause serious consequences for a Member State that has acted in good faith.

Although there is little doubt that the first condition is met in the Banca Popolare di Cremona case, some more problems could arise in respect of ascertaining whether the second condition is also met.

The Italian government has invoked good faith, based on the comfort letter received by the European Commission in March 1997.

Regardless of whether such approval was given by the Commission in the proper formal way[16], one should not forget two important points. It is for the European Commission to carefully scrutinise whether Member States exercise their prerogatives in a way that does not interfere with secondary law, although it is only for the European Court of Justice to determine what complies with European law and what does not.

In other words, the European Court of Justice may decide that a tax is incompatible with VAT even when the European Commission has taken a different position on the same point[17]. Should this be the case, however, the principle of good faith would still represent an important instrument to differentiate between Member States that have deliberately infringed European law from those that did not.

Nevertheless, the homogeneous application of European law, as interpreted by the European Court of Justice, is a likewise important goal, which should normally prevail over the interest of Member States that have exercised their prerogatives in a way that conflicts with European law.

The precedents invoked by Advocate General Jacobs in the Banca Popolare di Cremona case seem to suggest that the Court could now declare IRAP incompatible with VAT on the basis of principles already existing at the time when the tax was introduced. Should this occur, then one could reasonably argue that IRAP was not declared incompatible until now

16 This point is rather unclear in para 78 of the Opinion delivered by Advocate General Jacobs. Nevertheless, the Court will certainly take into account two main factors, namely from what specific perspective of compatibility the European Commission analysed IREP and to what extent such position may raise legitimate expectations.

17 This problem could be easily avoided by obliging Member States to refer a preliminary request to the European Court of Justice (instead of the Commission) on whether a change in their existing taxes or the introduction of a new tax may interfere with a provision of European law.

simply because the case never made its way to the European Court of Justice before.

The European Court of Justice normally applies two criteria for the purpose of limiting the circumstances in which Member States may invoke good faith. First, acting in good faith may neither reduce the objectiveness of European law, nor compromise its application in the future[18] and, second, it may not affect the rights of persons that have already initiated judicial proceedings when the decision was issued[19].

Advocate General Jacobs pleaded for limiting the retrospective application of a decision in favour of the taxpayer because of the serious consequences that this would imply for Italy: a country that acted in good faith, since it relied on the position expressed by the European Commission in March 1997. Nevertheless, it seems that a decision of this kind would in fact affect the objectiveness of European law. It would become an important precedent to allow Member States to keep revenue collected through taxes that for their objective characteristics should not have been cleared by the European Commission and that meanwhile have substantially reduced the competitiveness of economic operators established in a Member State.

The Opinion of Advocate General Jacobs raises some controversial issues insofar as he invites the European Court of Justice to follow the approach taken by the German *Bundesverfassungsgericht* with a view to excluding the right to reimbursement in a more general way until new legislation is enacted.

In general terms, it is submitted that the Court should technically not be in a position to apply such an approach in a procedure where parties did not request it.

Nevertheless, should the Court take a different view, also in the light of the new hearing, then one should wonder to what extent the retrospective effects may be limited for taxpayers that had duly filed a request for reimbursement and initiated a judicial procedure or equivalent claim at the date on which the decision of the European Court of Justice is released, or even whether the same restitution rights of the plaintiff could be scrutinised.

---

[18] ECJ 9 March 2000, C-437/97 *Evangelischer Krankenhausverein Wien* [2000] ECR I-1157, para 57.

[19] ECJ 9 March 2000, C-437/97 *Evangelischer Krankenhausverein Wien* [2000] ECR I-1157, para 60.

I feel that both such approaches would be wrong from a general perspective.

The former approach would create some degree of unfairness among the taxpayer who succeeded in being the first to bring the case before the European Court of Justice and all other taxpayers, which duly filed a request for reimbursement and initiated a judicial procedure[20]. This situation would become even more complicated if the reimbursement agreed by national courts in a similar case not referred to the European Court of Justice (as in the case of the Tax Court of Second Instance of Turin) were no longer appealable on the date in which the European Court issues a decision on the Banca Popolare di Cremona case against the plaintiff.

The latter approach would instead more generally discourage taxpayers from claiming those rights to which they would be entitled on the basis of European law but that they could in fact not enjoy because of the measures introduced by a Member State.

In other words, I believe that, in case the European Court ascertains that IRAP interferes with the common VAT system, they should not only declare the right to reimbursement for the plaintiff, without limiting the retrospective application, since homogeneous application of European law seems to require equal treatment between the case decided and those already pending before courts.

Following the case law of the European Court of Justice, possible limits to retrospective application of a decision should thus only concern reimbursement requests filed after the decision was released.[21]

4 Some Arguments for a Decision

The European Court of Justice should declare IRAP incompatible with the common VAT system, since it provides an anticipated duplication of the

20 However, some Member States apply this principle domestically for the purpose of limiting the obligation to repayment.

21 In his Opinion delivered on 10 November 2005 on the Meilicke case (ECJ C-292/04 *Meilicke*, pending), Advocate General Tizzano addressed the issue of limiting retrospective application of the decision in a situation matching that already decided in the Verkooijen case. According to Advocate General Tizzano (paras 60-63), retrospective application should in such circumstance be limited to the sole taxpayers who diligently supported their rights until the date of publication of the order for reference of the Meilicke case in the Official Journal. This innovative proposal should be positively evaluated by the European Court of Justice in the Meilicke case, where tax payers had almost four years to claim reimbursement since the European legal framework became clear with the Verkooijen decision. However, I doubt that it could achieve a likewise important degree of fairness in a case like Banca Popolare di Cremona, whereas the problem of compatibility is at present still highly uncertain.

tax burden borne by consumer goods and services. Despite being levied at different times and with different methods for calculating the taxable base, no goods or services may escape liability to IRAP upon production and to VAT upon supply and consumption.

Should the European Court follow this argument, then a third dimension would be added to the international phenomenon of double taxation. Besides juridical and economic double taxation, we should thus also consider that a duplication of the tax burden could result from the interference of a (business) tax – frequently included among the direct taxes – with an indirect tax, such as VAT.

Insofar as one agrees that retrospective application should also not be excluded for the purpose of ensuring homogeneous application of European law when a State acted in good faith and suffers some serious consequences from the decision, then reimbursement should be allowed to the plaintiff, as well as to all other taxpayers that had duly requested it and brought a claim before a judicial instance in Italy.

5 The Possible Consequences

Many are currently discussing the possible effects of the Banca Popolare di Cremona case, should the European Court of Justice decide in favour of the taxpayer.

Direct effects would, of course, concern Italy, which would have to eliminate IRAP and provide for refunds as previously indicated. Shifting of tax on the consumer is, in my opinion, the key element for considering IRAP as interfering with the common VAT system, since the total value added produced of goods and services in Italy would also be subject to VAT.

By contrast, the decision should not affect all other taxes – like those levied on income and corporations – in which shifting is driven by market forces and does not necessarily occur in all circumstances: a matter that remains largely controversial among experts of public finance and tax policy.

Indirect effects would concern various other Member States, which include or plan to include a business tax. Nevertheless, it seems that some countries in particular, such as France, Germany, Hungary and Spain, will be more clearly exposed to the effects of the decision on the Banca Popolare di Cremona case.

The French *taxe professionnelle*, as it currently stands, would probably not suffer, in my opinion, from any immediate consequences from a decision of the European Court of Justice declaring IRAP incompatible with the VAT system. However, plans to reshape the taxe professionnelle along the pattern of IRAP have been abandoned since Advocate General Jacobs delivered his Opinion on the Banca Popolare di Cremona case. Meanwhile, the present debate in France seems to focus on alternative forms of levies, capping *taxe professionnell*e to a maximum 3.5 % of the value added on production, or requiring a minimum tax due of 1.5 % of the value added on production. For both measures one could legitimately wonder whether some kind of interference arises between taxe professionnelle and the common VAT system, especially after the Banca Popolare di Cremona case. Nevertheless, such doubts should not be addressed by the national court, but rather referred to the European Court of Justice.

Even if strong similarities could also be drawn between the taxable base of IRAP and the German *Gewerbesteuer*, the most immediate repercussions from the Banca Popolare di Cremona should affect the Hungarian business tax, which has been modelled after IRAP, and the Spanish *Impuesto sobre Actividades Económicas* (IAE), which could have been the true model for IRAP. IAE is levied on those taxpayers that exercise economic activities and produce goods or services, even in the absence of actual profits. Consequently, goods and services supplied would likewise not escape a duplication of taxes, except for special exemption regimes provided by domestic law[22] or tax treaties[23].

For all such reasons the decision in the case Banca Popolare di Cremona is important regardless of whether it will ascertain an infringement and include a time-limitation on its effects.

Should the Court declare IRAP incompatible with the common VAT system, then many more cases should follow in respect of business taxes levied in other Member States.

By contrast, should the Court declare IRAP compatible with the common VAT system, then it is unlikely that other business taxes would be refer-

22 The authority to introduce exemptions from IAE currently exist in some Spanish regions with special regimes (*fueros*), a special geographical location (Canary Islands, Ceuta and Melilla), as well as in the most important cities (Barcelona and Madrid).

23 See in this respect the Treaty on Economic Relations between Spain and the Vatican City, signed on 3 January 1979.

red to the European Court, since IRAP probably is the business tax with the closest similarity to VAT.

As for limiting the effects if there are serious consequences for countries that have acted in good faith, should the Court accept this request, then it would automatically have created a very far-reaching precedent, strongly influenced by arguments based on the loss of revenue.

By contrast, should the European Court reject this limitation or keep it within the boundaries of claims requested at the date of the decision, they would condemn a Member State to an unprecedented reimbursement.

Meanwhile, the Tax Court of First Instance of Cremona has succeeded right where most other Italian courts (and the Commission) have not, ie to refer a case before the European Court of Justice that may affect the field of direct taxation in Italy. For sure, many more cases will have to make their way from Italy to Luxembourg, possibly in the near future. We all may help in catalysing this process so that its natural and fair goal, namely ensuring the homogeneous application of European law throughout Europe, is reached.

Pending Cases Filed by Dutch Courts I: The Van Dijk and Bujura Cases

Eric Kemmeren

I Introduction

II Van Dijk (C-470/04): Exit for Dutch Exit Charge

1 Facts, Circumstances, and Assumptions

2 Domestic Law

3 Preliminary Questions

4 Possible Answers

4.1 Can Van Dijk rely on Article 18 EC?

4.2 If Van Dijk cannot rely on Article 18, can he rely on Article 43 EC?

4.3 If Van Dijk has access to Articles 18/43 EC, do they preclude the Dutch exit charge?

4.3.1 Two separate obstacles

4.3.2 Test of tax treaty precedes test of fundamental freedoms

4.4 If Articles 18/43 EC preclude the Dutch exit charge because security must be provided, can the obstacle be removed with retroactive effect through the release of the security?

4.5 If Articles 18/43 EC preclude the Dutch exit charge and the obstacle cannot be removed with retroactive effect, can the obstacle be justified?

4.5.1 Imperative reasons in the public interest: Preventing tax avoidance and ensuring fiscal coherence

4.5.1.1 Preventing tax avoidance accepted

4.5.1.2 Ensuring fiscal coherence not accepted

4.5.1.3 Other imperative reasons in the public interest not accepted

4.5.2 Exit charge not proportionate to its aim

5 Proportional alternative system: the residence-based compartimentalisation system

5.1 Appealable order to fix income on which state of departure wants to preserve tax jurisdiction
5.2 The compartimentalisation of tax jurisdiction
5.3 The decrease of value after departure taken into account in state of departure if not included in taxable base in new state of residence
5.4 Subsequent emigration may trigger taxable event
5.5 Mutual assistance in tax collection
III Bujura (C-8/04): Most-favoured-nation Treatment Not Favoured
1 Facts, Circumstances, and Assumptions
2 Domestic and Tax Treaty Law
3 Preliminary Question
4 Possible Answer
4.1 Untenable opinion of Advocate General Colomer in the D. case
4.1.1 The aim of bilateral tax treaties
4.1.2 Article 25 (3) NL-Belgium (1970) is a general rule not only applicable to Net Wealth Tax
4.1.3 Article 25 (3) NL-Belgium (1970) is based on reciprocity
4.1.4 Personal allowances, concessions, and reductions are integral parts of ability to pay and not privileges
4.1.5 Residents of Belgium are not comparable to residents of Germany
4.1.6 Other observations
4.2 Sound decision of ECJ on 5 July 2005, Case 376/03 (D.)
4.2.1 Criticism
4.2.2 Appreciation
4.2.3 Member States do not have complete liberty to include any rule in a bilateral tax treaty
5 Future of Most-favoured-nation Treatment?
IV Conclusions

I Introduction

In this contribution, I will discuss two cases currently pending before the Court of Justice of the European Communities: Van Dijk[1] and Bujura[2]. The first case deals with an exit charge of a substantial shareholder in various corporations who transferred his residence from the Netherlands to the United Kingdom. Indeed, the case is highly comparable with the French case of De Lasteyrie du Saillant[3], which has already been decided. Therefore, the latter case will be used as a touchstone to give potential answers to the questions raised by the Dutch court. In addition, some other issues will be addressed: access to the EC Treaty under Article 18 EC will be addressed and whether an obstacle can be removed with retroactive effect. In the conclusion of this part, I will present a proportional alternative system to the widely implemented exit charges in EU Member States, which makes them superfluous and which safeguards the tax claims of states of departure on the latent increase in value which have been built up by its residents. The Bujura case addresses the issue of whether EC law implies a most-favoured-nation (hence also: MFN) treatment under tax treaties concluded by EU Member States. This issue has been extensively discussed in the tax literature already for many years.[4] For the potential answer to the Bujura case, another decision is highly relevant: the D. case.[5] Therefore, this case, which is also a Dutch case, will be discussed in order to find guidance for a potential answer. In this respect, not only the judgment, but also the Opinion of Advocate General Colomer will be critically discussed.[6] This part will be concluded with a view on the future of MFN treatment in respect of tax treaties under European law. The main conclusions will be summarised in the final section.

---

1 See ECJ C-470/04 *Van Dijk*, pending.

2 See ECJ C-8/04 *Bujura*, pending.

3 See ECJ 11 March 2004, C-9/02 *de Lasteyrie du Saillant* [2004] ECR I-2409.

4 See for references, for example, Kemmeren, *Principle of Origin in Tax Conventions, A Rethinking of Models*, diss. (2001), Katholieke Universiteit Brabant, Tilburg, pp 127-131; Weber, Most-Favoured-Nation Treatment under Tax Treaties Rejected in the European Community: Background and Analysis of the *D.* Case, *Intertax* 2005, pp 429-445; and Hofbauer, *Das Prinzip der Meistbegünstigung im grenzüberschreitenden Ertragsteuerrecht* (2005).

5 See ECJ.

6 See Opinion of Advocate General Colomer in *D* (ECJ 5 July 2002, C-376/03 *D.*, not yet reported), 26 October 2004.

II Van Dijk (C-470/04): Exit for Dutch Exit Charge

1 Facts, Circumstances and Assumptions

Van Dijk, a Dutch national, was born in 1946. On 22 January 1997, he transferred his residence from the Netherlands to the United Kingdom . It was not clear or plausible from the outset that he would pursue an economic activity in the UK. In any case, from 2002, Van Dijk has exploited a farm with an apple orchard in the UK. At the moment of emigration in 1997, Van Dijk was the single shareholder of three corporations, incorporated under Dutch company law: A BV, B BV, and C BV. ABV is a private limited company. The effective place of management of these corporations was in the Netherlands Antilles from 22 January 1997 as well. Van Dijk filed a tax return, in which he reported a deemed capital gain on his substantial interest shareholdings of approximately € 7,000,000; a tax and social contributions assessment was imposed for an amount of approximately € 1,778,000. In addition, Van Dijk owed assessment interest for an amount of approximately € 104,000. Upon his request, deferment of payment was granted for both the amount of the tax assessment and the assessment interest. The deferment was granted only upon the condition that Van Dijk would set up sufficient guarantees for the payment of these amounts. For that purpose, he pledged the shares in C BV on 19 February 2001. On 7 June 2004, the security was released by the tax collector based on a statement of practice[7] issued because of the De Lasteyrie du Saillant ruling.[8]

2 Domestic Law

The Dutch exit charge on substantial interest shareholders was and is a rather complicated system. Below, I will only highlight the domestic tax law as it was applied in 1997. Van Dijk reported the deemed capital gain on his substantial interest shareholdings solely because of the transfer of his residence from the Netherlands to the UK. Under Dutch domestic tax law, this transfer triggers a deemed alienation of the shares in A BV, B BV, and C BV, which constitute substantial interest shareholdings.[9] The deemed capital gain amounts to the fair market value of the shares at the moment

7 See letter of 13 April 2004, no. WDB 2004/188U, *Vakstudienieuws* (hence: *V-N*) 2004/21.8.

8 See ECJ 11 March 2004, C-9/02 *de Lasteyrie du Saillant* [2004] ECR I-2409.

9 See Article 20a, para 1, under h. Personal Income Tax Act 1964 (*Wet op de inkomstenbelasting 1964*; PITA 1964).

of emigration minus their acquisition price.[10] The capital gain is deemed to be realised directly before the moment of emigration.[11] After emigration, a substantial interest shareholder in Dutch resident corporations continues to be liable to tax as a non-resident taxpayer.[12] However, a step-up in basis is granted if the emigrant has been taxed upon emigration.[13]

In addition to the taxes and social contributions due because of the transfer of residence outside the Netherlands, assessment interest will be due if the assessment is imposed more than fifteen months after the end of the taxable year.[14] For both the assessment and the assessment interest, the emigrant may file a request for deferment of payment. The deferment is for a maximum period of ten years.[15] After that period, the assessment will be nullified.[16] The deferment of payment is conditional. The taxpayer must set up sufficient guarantees for the payment of the personal income tax, social contributions, and assessment interest due. The tax collector may impose other conditions as well.[17] The deferment of payment is cancelled upon actual or deemed alienation of the shares. The unpaid taxes must be paid at that moment.[18] Upon dividend distribution, the deferment is cancelled equal to the amount of dividend withholding tax due on that dividend.[19]

---

[10] See Article 20c, paras 1, 2, and 4 PITA 1964.

[11] See Article 20h, para 3 PITA 1964.

[12] See Article 49, para 1, under b. PITA 1964.

[13] See Article 49, para 5 PITA 1964.

[14] See Article 30f, paras 1 and 3 under a. General Taxes Act (*Algemene wet inzake rijksbelastingen*; GTA).

[15] See Article 25, paragraph 6, under a. Tax Collection Act 1990 (*Invorderinswet 1990*; TCA 1990) in conjunction with Article 4 Regulation implementing the Tax Collection Act 1990 (*Uitvoeringsregeling Invorderingswet 1990*; RITCA 1990).

[16] See Article 26, para 2, under c. TCA 1990.

[17] See Article 25, para 6, under a. TCA 1990 in conjunction with Article 2 RITCA 1990. As of 11 March 2004, the deferment of payment is granted automatically and unconditionally for emigrations to an EU Member State. Initially, this automatic and unconditional deferment of payment was granted by virtue of a statement of practice. See letter of 13 April 2004, no. WDB 2004/188U, *V-N* 2004/21.8. From 2005, this deferment has been included in statutory law. Initially, the automatic and unconditional deferment of payment was also admitted for emigrations to EEA Member States by virtue of the statement of practice. Under the statutory law, this policy has not been continued, based on the legislator's assumption that tax collection was not secured by virtue of effective Community law in respect of mutual assistance on tax collection. The legislator's position can be challenged, but it is outside the scope of this contribution to elaborate further on this issue.

[18] See Article 25, para 6, under a. TCA 1990 in conjunction with Article 2 RITCA 1990.

[19] See Article 26, para 2, under a. TCA 1990.

After a period of ten years after the end of the taxable year, the deferment is cancelled as well, but then the unpaid taxes need no longer paid.[20] Over the period of deferment, no collection interest is due.[21]

Immigrants to the Netherlands receive a step-up in basis.[22] However, it will not be granted in case of re-emigration into the Netherlands within a period of ten years. Nevertheless, a step-up will be granted in such a situation if the state of departure has charged an exit tax upon re-emigration into the Netherlands.[23] If this is not the case, the tax assessment, which was imposed upon emigration out of the Netherlands and for which deferment of payment was granted, will be cancelled up to the amount of unpaid taxes. This implies also a cancellation of the deferment itself. Nonetheless, in such a case a specific step-up in basis will be granted for certain costs and taxes paid. [24] For transients, who reside in the Netherlands for a period not exceeding eight years, a special rule applies. They will not be taxed upon emigration from the Netherlands.[25]

3 Preliminary Questions

The Arnhem Court of Appeals has asked for a preliminary ruling in this case on the following questions.[26]

1. Can a resident of a Member State who ceases to reside in that Member State in order to establish himself in another Member State rely, in proceedings against the Member State which he is leaving, on the application of Article 18 EC, solely on the ground that the serving of a tax assessment linked with his departure entails, or may entail, an obstacle to that departure?
2. If the answer to question 1 is negative, can a resident of a Member State who ceases to reside in that Member State in order to establish himself in another Member State rely, in proceedings against the

20 See Article 26, para 2, under c. TCA 1990.

21 See Article 28, para 2 TCA 1990.

22 See Article 20c, para 7 PITA 1964.

23 See Article 3d Implementation Regulation Personal Income Tax 1990 *itvoeringsregeling inkomstenbelasting 1990*; IRPITA 1964)

24 See Article 4 RITCA 1990

25 See Article 20a, para 8 PITA 1964.

26 See Hof Arnhem 27 October 2004, no. 00/00191, *V-N* 2004/59.8, and the case of N. (later on known as "Van Dijk") against Inspecteur van de Belastingdienst Oost/Kantoor Almelo; ECJ C-470/04 *Van Dijk*, pending, OJ C 31, 5 February 2005, p 5.

Member State which he is leaving, on the application of Article 43 EC if it is not clear or plausible from the outset that he will be pursuing in the other Member State an economic activity as referred to in that article? Is it relevant to the answer to the previous question that that activity will be pursued within a foreseeable period? If so, how long may that period be?

3. If the answer to questions 1 or 2 is affirmative, do Articles 18 or 43 EC preclude the relevant Dutch legislation by virtue of which an assessment of income tax and social insurance contributions is served in respect of the deemed enjoyment of profit from a substantial shareholding, solely on the ground that a resident of the Netherlands who ceases to be a domestic taxpayer because he has moved his place of residence to another Member State is deemed to have disposed of those of his shares which form part of a substantial holding?

4. If the answer to question 3 is affirmative because of the fact that security has to be provided to enable a deferment of payment of the tax assessed, can the existing obstacle then be removed with retroactive effect through the release of the security provided? Does the answer to this question depend on whether the security is released on the basis of legislation or a rule of policy, whether or not adopted in the context of enforcement? Does the answer to this question depend on whether compensation is provided for any loss incurred as a result of the provision of security?

5. If the answer to question 3 is affirmative and the answer to the first question in 4 is negative, can the obstacle which then exists be justified?

4 Possible Answers

Below, I will give possible answers to the questions of the Dutch Court of Appeals, which, in my opinion, the European Court of Justice will likely give. I will follow the order of the questions. Each of the five groups of questions will be addressed in separate subsections. The result of the analysis below is that, in my opinion, the Court of Appeals should not have asked any of the preliminary questions, because based on the existing body of case law of the European Court of Justice, it should have concluded that 1997 exit tax charge is incompatible with the fundamental right to move and reside freely within the territory of Member States.

4.1 Can Van Dijk rely on Article 18 EC?

The first question refers in substance to the issue of whether Van Dijk has access to the EC Treaty solely by virtue of Article 18 EC. On 22 January 1997, Van Dijk transferred his residence from the Netherlands to the UK. If only because of this transfer, I believe that Van Dijk may indeed rely on Article 18 EC. This follows from settled case law: from Sala to Schempp.[27] Van Dijk has exercised his right to move and reside freely within the territory of Member States as laid down in this provision by establishing his residence in the UK. In Elsen, in which case Mrs Elsen had moved her residence from Germany to France, the Court formulated the exercise of this fundamental freedom as follows:

> "34. Provisions such as those at issue in the main proceedings are disadvantageous to Community nationals who have *exercised* their right to move and reside freely in the Member States, *as guaranteed* in Article 8a of the EC Treaty (now, after amendment, *Article 18 EC*). *By transferring his residence to another Member State* [italics added] while continuing to work in Germany, a Community national would (under the legislation of that State) automatically lose credit for periods of child-rearing completed in the State of residence.

This interpretation was confirmed in Schempp, in which case not Mr Schempp but his former spouse had moved her residence form Germany to the Austria:

> "23 While it is correct that Mr Schempp has not exercised such a right, it is nevertheless common ground that his former spouse, *by establishing her residence in Austria*, *exercised* the right granted by *Article 18 EC* [italics added] to every citizen of the Union to move and reside freely in the territory of another Member State.

It is clear that Van Dijk's situation must be characterised as a transnational situation. It is clearly not a purely national one.[28] However, it should be

[27] See, for example, ECJ 12 May 1998, C-85/96 *Sala* [1998] ECR I-2691; 23 November 2000, C-135/99 *Elsen* [2000] ECR I-10409; 11 July 2002, C-224/98 *D'Hoop* [2002] ECR I-6191; 17 September 2002, C-413/99 *Baumbast* [2002] ECR I-7091; 2 October 2003, C-148/02 *Garcia Avello* [2003] ECR I-11613; 29 April 2004, C-224/02 *Pusa* [2004] ECR I-5763; 7 September 2004, C-456/02 *Trojani* [2004] ECR I-7573; and ECJ 12 July 2005, C-403/03 *Schempp*, not yet reported. Compare also, for example., Meussen in his annotation to the ruling *De Lasteyrie du Saillant*, *Beslissingen in belastingzaken Nederlandse Belastingrechtspraak* (*BNB*) 2004, pp 2561-2562.

[28] Compare, for example, Opinion of Advocate General Maduro in *Marks & Spencer* (ECJ C-446/03 *Marks & Spencer*, pending), 7 April 2005, paras 24 and 37.

noted that Article 18 EC is not relevant in the case of a transfer to third countries, because this provision only provides a right to move and reside freely within the territory of Member States. For instance, in the case of a transfer of residence to Switzerland, Article 18 EC may not be invoked by a Community national. The mere transfer of residence to a third country does not give access to Article 56 EC either, according to Advocate General Léger.[29] Indeed, I believe as well that the mere transfer of residence does not constitute a movement of capital. Nevertheless, in practice it will not be too difficult to combine a transfer of residence with a movement of capital, e.g., a transfer of a bank account from a branch of a bank established in the state of departure to a branch established in the new state of residence. However, it should be noted that the exit charge as at issue in Van Dijk is triggered by the emigration of the substantial shareholder and not by the transfer of the bank account. Thus, it may well be argued that the transfer of the bank account implies a capital movement, but that this capital movement is not restricted by virtue of the exit charge on the substantial interest shareholding. Nonetheless, I feel that, under different circumstances, such a restriction may be at issue, for instance, if a person wants to start up a business in a third country, which constitutes a direct investment. If it were appropriate for that person to be close to that business and if that implies that he has to transfer his residence close to his business for sound reasons, then the movement of capital and the transfer of residence may be connected so closely that they have to be evaluated as a whole for the interpretation of Article 56 EC. In such a case, a transfer of residence may give access to Article 56 EC and the exit charge may constitute (indirectly) a restriction of the free movement of capital. To a certain extent, a parallel can be draw between such a case and the De Lasteyrie du Saillant ruling, in which case a transfer of residence was at issue in conjunction with the interpretation of Article 43 EC. Whether an exit charge does create a restriction will be discussed below.

I feel that the transfer of the effective place of management of the BVs, in which van Dijk held a substantial interest, from the Netherlands to the Netherlands Antilles is not relevant for the question of whether he can rely on Article 18 EC. His own transfer of residence is sufficient to invoke this fundamental freedom. Therefore, I believe that the answer to the question of whether Van Dijk may rely on Article 18 EC must be in the affirmative.

---

[29] See Opinion of Advocate General Léger in *Van Hilten* (ECJ C-513/03 *Van Hilten*, pending), 30 June 2005, paras 57 and 58.

I would even argue that this answer is so clear that question 1 of the Arnhem Court should not have been raised. Reading the Court's ruling, it seems that the question at issue has also been based on the idea that Article 18 EC may be subordinated to the other fundamental freedoms. However, this idea is not in line with the case law of the Court of Justice. In Elsen, the Court explicitly tested the German rule against not only Article 18 EC, but also against Articles 39 and 42 EC.[30] Therefore, I come to the conclusion that it is clear from the Court of Justice's case law that Van Dijk may rely on Article 18 EC and that question 1 should not have been raised.

4.2 If Van Dijk cannot rely on Article 18, can he rely on Article 43 EC?

As Van Dijk has already access to the EC Treaty by virtue of Article 18 EC, I believe that the Court of Justice will not answer question 2. Since no economic activity is required for the application of Article 18 EC, the scope of this provision is much wider than the scope of Article 43 EC. Both are part of the fundamental freedoms and these fundamental freedoms have very much in common. Although each freedom covers its own field, they are based on the same principles.[31] Therefore, I believe that if the Dutch exit charge were to constitute a restriction under Article 43 EC, it will certainly constitute a restriction under Article 18 EC, because of the wider scope of the latter. As a result, I believe that question 2 should not have been raised by the Arnhem Court, either.

4.3 If Van Dijk has access to Articles 18/43 EC, do they preclude the Dutch exit charge?

4.3.1 Two separate obstacles

Considering the above, question 3 boils down to the question of whether the Dutch exit charge does constitute a restriction of the right to freely move and reside in the territory of another Member State under Article 18 EC. It is obvious the ECJ's ruling in De Lasteyrie du Saillant should be

30 See ECJ 23 November 2000, C-135/99 *Elsen* [2000] ECR I-10409, para 36.

31 See, eg, van Themaat, *Het recht van de Europese Unie en van de Europese Gemeenschappen*, zesde, geheel herziene druk (2003) pp 488-489 and 500-501; and Kemmeren, *Principle of Origin in Tax Conventions, A Rethinking of Models*, diss. (2001), Katholieke Universiteit Brabant, Tilburg, pp 160-162.

taken into account when looking for an answer to the Arnhem Court.[32] In De Lasteyrie du Saillant, the European Court of Justice ruled that a French exit charge on an individual substantial interest shareholder, who moved his residence from France to Belgium in order to start up a business there, is incompatible with Article 43 (formerly Article 52) EC. This taxation is solely based on the transfer of the taxpayer's residence outside France.[33] A transfer of residence inside France is not taxed. The exit charge is a taxation of the latent increase in value, whereas French resident substantial interest shareholders are taxed on the increase in value when it is actually realised. Upon request and provided that certain conditions are met, the payment of the French taxes due may be deferred. The Court of Justice identifies two separate obstacles: the exit charge assessment itself and the non-automatic and conditional deferment of payment.[34] This follows from the following considerations:

> 46 A taxpayer wishing to transfer his tax residence outside French territory, in exercise of the right guaranteed to him by Article 52 of the Treaty, is subjected to disadvantageous treatment in comparison with a person who maintains his residence in France. That taxpayer *becomes liable, simply by reaso*n of such a transfer, *to tax* on income which has not yet been realised and which he therefore does not have, whereas, if he remained in France, increases in value would become taxable only when, and to the extent that, they were actually realised. *That difference in treatment* concerning the taxation of increases in value, which is capable of having considerable repercussions on the assets of a taxpayer wishing to transfer his tax residence outside France, *is likely to discourage* a taxpayer from carrying out such a transfer.
>
> 47 An examination of the rules for applying that measure *confirms that conclusion*. Although it is possible to benefit from *suspension*

32 See ECJ 11 March 2004, C-9/02 *de Lasteyrie du Saillant* [2004] ECR I-2409.

33 From 2005, this exit charge has been removed from French statutory law.

34 Compare also, for example, Meussen in his annotation to the ruling *De Lasteyrie du Saillant*, *BNB* 2004/258, pp 2564-2565, van der Spek/van der Linde, Is de uiterste houdbaarheidsdatum van de conserverende aanslag verlopen?, *Weekblad Fiscaal Recht* (*WFR*) 2004, pp 747-748; and te Boekhorst/Ganzeveld, Exitheffingen na Lasteyrie du Saillant, in Nederlandse Orde van Belastingadviseurs, *Alle wegen leiden naar Brussel*, NOB/Reed Business Information (2004) p 45. Dissenting, for example, Rijkers, Conserverende aanslag en Europees recht, in Aardema and others, *Tribuut aan Europa*, NFB/Sdu Fiscale & Financiële Uitgevers (2004) pp 394-396; and Albert, Verdragsrechtelijke complicaties bij intrekking van het betalingsuitstel van een conserverende aanslag na emigratie, *WFR* 2004, pp 756-757.

> *of payment*, that is *not automatic* and it is *subject to strict conditions* such as those described by the Advocate General in points 36 and 37 of his Opinion, including, in particular, conditions as to the *setting up of guarantees*. Those guarantees in themselves constitute a *restrictive effect* [emphasis added], in that they deprive the taxpayer of the enjoyment of the assets given as a guarantee.

Any restriction, even if of limited scope or minor importance, is prohibited.[35] The French taxation discourages a taxpayer from transferring his residence outside France and as a consequence constitutes a restriction on the fundamental right of establishment.

The Dutch 1997 exit charge imposed on Van Dijk is, in my opinion, comparable to the French exit charge imposed on De Lasteyrie du Saillant. Van Dijk, being an individual substantial interest shareholder, is taxed solely because of the transfer of his residence outside the Netherlands. A transfer of residence inside the Netherlands is not taxed. The Dutch exit charge is also a taxation of the latent increase in value, whereas Dutch resident substantial interest shareholders are taxed on the increase in value when it is actually realised. Upon request and provided that certain conditions are met, the payment of the Dutch taxes owed may be deferred as well. Like De Lasteyrie du Saillant, Van Dijk had to set up a guarantee. That was done in 2001. Since the Dutch exit charge discourages a taxpayer from transferring his residence outside the Netherlands, it constitutes a restriction on the fundamental freedom to freely move and reside in the territory of another Member State. Like the French exit charge, the Dutch 1997 exit charge creates two separate obstacles: the exit charge assessment itself and the non-automatic and conditional deferment of payment. Therefore, I believe that it is clear from the De Lasteyrie du Saillant ruling that Article 18 EC precludes the Dutch exit charge, unless it can be objectively justified. The issue of a possible justification will be discussed below. As a result, I believe that the third question should not have been raised, either.

4.3.2 Test against tax treaty law precedes test of fundamental freedoms

The conclusion that the third question should not have been raised is certainly true if the Arnhem Court of Appeals would have followed the analysis

[35] See 11 March 2004, C-9/02 *de Lasteyrie du Saillant* [2004] ECR I-2409, para 43.

of a very recent ruling of the 's-Hertogenbosch Court of Appeal, in which this Court tested the introduction of the Dutch 1997 exit charge firstly against a tax treaty before addressing EC law.[36] It has ruled that the introduction of the 1997 exit charge is an infringement of the principle of good faith as laid down in Article 31 of the Vienna Convention on the Law of Treaties:[37] a treaty must be interpreted in good faith. In this case, the tax treaty between Belgium and the Netherlands of 1970 was at issue. In a nutshell, the Court of Appeals ruled that, by virtue of the introduction of the exit charge after conclusion of the tax treaty, the Netherlands has unilaterally extended its tax jurisdiction on capital gains from the alienation of substantial interest shares from five to ten years. Such an extension is only possible by means of amending the tax treaty itself and not by only amending Dutch domestic tax law, according to the Court. The Court nullified the exit charge tax assessment.[38] This assessment was also challenged under EC law, but the Court ruled that it did not need address this issue, because the tax assessment was already incompatible with the 1970 tax treaty between Belgium and the Netherlands.

This line of reasoning is consistent with the approach of Advocate General Kokott in Bouanich.[39] In order to assess whether taxation constitutes a restriction of one of the fundamental freedoms which cannot be justified, not only domestic tax law but also the relevant tax treaty should be taken into account. I believe this a sound approach, because the ultimate tax position of a person or a person's income or capital gain in a transnational situation is not only determined by virtue of domestic tax law, but also by virtue of the relevant tax treaty. Therefore, both sets of rules should be taken into account in order to assess whether an unjustified restriction of a fundamental freedom is at issue. For example, if a state may tax a person's income or capital gain based on domestic tax law, but if it may not do so

---

36 See Hof 's-Hertogenbosch 15 September 2005, *V-N* 2005/47.11. Without doubt, the tax administration will lodge an appeal with the *Hoge Raad* (the Netherlands Supreme Court) against this ruling.

37 Concluded in Vienna, 23 May 1969.

38 I believe that the Court's decision is indeed correct, but that its reasoning is not. However, it is beyond the scope of this contribution to go into further detail. For a further analysis, I refer to my contribution to be published in the *Weekblad Fiscaal Recht*, entitled: Nederlandse exitheffingen anno 2005 zijn onhoudbaar, maar een passend alternatief is denkbaar.

39 See Opinion of Advocate General Kokott in *Bouanich* (ECJ C-265/04 *Bouanich*, pending), 14 July 2005, paras 44-69

based on a tax treaty, the ultimate result is that this state does not impose any tax and as a consequence the exercise of a fundamental freedom may not be hindered by virtue of the domestic tax rules involved. The same is true for a situation in which unequal treatment based on domestic tax law between resident and non-resident taxpayers detrimental to the latter is equalised by virtue of the rules of a tax treaty.

If the Arnhem Court in the Van Dijk case had applied under the 1980 tax treaty between the UK and the Netherlands, a similar approach as the s-Hertogenbosch Court did under the 1970 tax treaty between Belgium and the Netherlands, Van Dijk's tax assessment would have been nullified as well. As a result, no EC law issue would have been left and no preliminary questions would have been asked.

4.4 If Articles 18/43 EC preclude the Dutch exit charge because security must be provided, can the obstacle be removed with retroactive effect through the release of the security?

As discussed, the Dutch 1997 exit charge, like the French one, creates two separate obstacles: the exit charge assessment itself and the non-automatic and conditional deferment of payment. One of the conditions is setting up a guarantee. The 1997 Dutch domestic law includes the condition of setting up sufficient guarantees for the payment of the personal income tax, social contributions, and assessment interest due. For that purpose, Van Dijk pledged the shares in C BV on 19 February 2001. On 7 June 2004, the security was released by the tax collector based on a statement of practice issued because of De Lasteyrie du Saillant ruling.[40] This release implies that the tax collector only removed the second obstacle; the first obstacle – the exit tax assessment itself – remained intact. Therefore, the 1997 Dutch exit charge is still restrictive only for that reason, since it is settled case law that any restriction, even if of limited scope or minor importance, is prohibited.[41] In line with this case law, it must be concluded as well that only the law applicable to the year of emigration is relevant to assess whether a restriction is at issue.[42] In 1997, it was only

40 See letter of 13 April 2004, no. WDB 2004/188U, *V-N* 2004/21.8.

41 See ECJ 11 March 2004, C-9/02 *de Lasteyrie du Saillant* [2004] ECR I-2409, para 43.

42 See also Hof 's-Hertogenbosch 15 September 2005, *V-N* 2005/47.11, for the assessment of whether the introduction of the 1997 Dutch exit charge is incompatible with Article 31 of the Vienna Convention on the Law of Treaties and the 1980 tax treaty between the UK and the Netherlands.

that set of rules that could discourage Van Dijk from transferring his residence the Netherlands in the UK.[43] In 1997, only that set of rules could be taken into account when Van Dijk was contemplating whether or not he would transfer his residence. Future tax rules, unknown in 1997, cannot have had any impact on that decision. Therefore, the release of the security in 2004 can have had no impact on the Van Dijk's decision in 1997. For this reason alone, the release in 2004 is not relevant for assessing whether or not the 1997 Dutch exit tax constituted a restriction in 1997. Therefore, in my opinion, the release itself can never remove the second obstacle with retroactive effect. In this respect, it is irrelevant whether the release was based on legislation or on policy although it must be acknowledged that based on the Court's ruling in the Biehl case, a removal of discrimination or a restriction must be based on a statutory obligation. It is insufficient that a taxpayer should rely on a statement of practice by virtue of which an obstacle is removed.[44] Furthermore, an obstacle created by virtue of the applicable rules in 1997 cannot remove the second obstacle in case a rule is implemented later on to provide compensation for any loss incurred as a result of the provision of security. Here, the same reasoning is valid as the reasoning in respect of the release of the security itself. As a result, I believe that the fourth question should not have been raised, either.

4.5 If Articles 18/43 EC preclude the Dutch exit charge and the obstacle cannot be removed with retroactive effect, can the obstacle be justified?

It is settled case law that a measure which may hinder a fundamental freedom may be justified only by virtue of a specific provision of the EC Treaty itself or if it pursues a legitimate objective compatible with the EC Treaty and is justified by imperative reasons in the public interest. It is further necessary, in such a case, that its application must be appropriate to ensuring the attainment of the objective thus pursued and must not go beyond what is necessary to attain it.[45] Article 18 EC allows the limitations and conditions laid down in the EC Treaty and on the basis of the measures adopted to give it effect. In this case, no specific provision allows the limitation of the freedom to move and reside freely within the territory of

43 Compare ECJ 11 March 2004, C-9/02 *de Lasteyrie du Saillant* [2004] ECR I-2409, para 46.

44 See ECJ 8 May 1990, 175/88 *Biehl* [1990] ECR I-1779, para 18.

45 See, for example., ECJ 11 March 2004, C-9/02 *de Lasteyrie du Saillant* [2004] ECR I-2409, para 49.

the Member States created by the 1997 Dutch exit charge. Therefore, this exit charge must be tested in line with the rule of reason case law of the Court of Justice. Again, it is obvious that the De Lasteyrie du Saillant ruling must be taken into account, since the French and Dutch exit charges are comparable.

4.5.1 Imperative reasons in the public interest: preventing tax avoidance and ensuring fiscal coherence

Firstly, it should be tested whether the 1997 Dutch exit charge can be justified by imperative reasons in the public interest. Whether this is the case must be assessed in the light of the objective of the exit charge.

4.5.1.1 Preventing tax avoidance accepted

The objective of preventing tax avoidance as such has been accepted as an imperative reason in the public interest. The French administration claimed that the French exit charge, which was at issue in the De Lasteyrie du Saillant ruling, was justified because its aim is to prevent a substantial interest shareholder from transferring temporarily his residence outside France exclusively for tax reasons.[46] The general tax avoidance structure at issue would be the transfer of the taxpayer's residence to a new state of residence, in which the alienation of the substantial interest shareholding is not taxed or taxed more advantageously than in the state of departure, and to benefit from a tax treaty concluded between the state of departure and the new state of residence, which allocates the tax jurisdiction on the capital gain on these shares to the new state of residence. Although the Dutch tax inspector claimed in the Van Dijk case before the Arnhem Court that the objective of the Dutch 1997 exit charge was not the prevention of tax avoidance and that, therefore, the De Lasteyrie du Saillant ruling was not relevant for the Van Dijk case, it must be emphasised that this claim is not covered by the legislative history of the Dutch exit charge. In the explanatory memorandum to the bill introducing the exit charge as of 1997, we read quite the opposite:

> The measure *aims* at *ending* tax-driven emigration through which the substantial interest taxation is *avoided* by means of an *establishment* [italics added] across the border, temporarily or otherwise.[47]

[46] See ECJ 11 March 2004, C-9/02 *de Lasteyrie du Saillant* [2004] ECR I-2409, paras 24-25 and 64.

[47] The text is an unofficial translation by the author. See *Memorie van toelichting* (explanatory memorandum), *Kamerstukken II* 1996/97, 24 761, no. 3, para 2.1.11. See also *Memorie*

Therefore, the aim of both the French and Dutch exit charges is prevention of tax avoidance. In other words, not only the technical mechanisms of the exit charges are comparable, also their aims. This means that with respect to the aim of preventing tax avoidance, the other tests of the rule of reason case law also need be applied: appropriateness and proportionality. It can hardly at all be questioned that the exit charges are effective to counter tax-driven emigration. Therefore, the test boils down to the question of whether the exit charge is proportionate to its aim. This will be discussed below. Firstly, other imperative reasons in the public interest will be analysed.

4.5.1.2 Ensuring fiscal coherence not accepted

In the De Lasteyrie du Saillant ruling, the Dutch government – and notably not the French government – put forward that the French exit charge could be justified by the fiscal coherence principle. The argument was made that the combined effect of taxation at the time of removal abroad and the requirement for guarantees to which the grant of suspension of actual payment of the tax is made subject, is necessary to ensure the coherence of the French tax system, since there is a direct link between, on the one hand, the postponement of the annual taxation of the growth in capital corresponding to the securities and, on the other, the actual collection of the tax at the time when the taxpayer moves his tax residence abroad.[48] However, this justification was not accepted because the objective of the French exit charge was not ensuring fiscal coherence, but it was designed to prevent temporary transfers of tax residence outside France exclusively for tax reasons. Furthermore, France allows imputation of tax levied upon alienation by the new state of residence with a possible result that France does not tax the increases in value acquired during the taxpayer's residence in France at all. In addition, France cancels the tax assessment imposed upon transfer of residence after five years from the date of departure, or at the date on which the taxpayer retransfers his place of residence for tax purposes to France, if earlier. Therefore, the French exit charge is not aimed at ensuring generally that increases in value are to be taxed, in the case where a taxpayer transfers his tax residence outside France, in so far

---

van toelichting (explanatory memorandum), Kamerstukken II 1996/97, 24 761, no. 3, explanatory notes to '*Artikel 49, vierde lid Wet op de inkomstenbelasting 1964*'.

48 See ECJ 11 March 2004, C-9/02 *de Lasteyrie du Saillant* [2004] ECR I-2409, paras 33 and 61.

as the increases in value in question are acquired during the taxpayer's stay in the French territory.[49] In the Van Dijk case, the tax inspector claimed that the Dutch 1997 exit charge can be justified by the fiscal coherence principle. This claim fuels the idea that position of the Netherlands taken in the De Lasteyrie du Saillant case has been taken only to try to save its own system, because the Netherlands expected that its exit charge would also be challenged under EC law. As analysed above, the Dutch 1997 exit charge does not have the objective of ensuring generally that increases in value are to be taxed either, in the case where a taxpayer transfers his tax residence outside the Netherlands, in so far as the increases in value in question are acquired during the taxpayer's stay in the Dutch territory.[50] The objective is tax avoidance comparable to the French exit charge. Furthermore, the Dutch exit tax charge is not coherent, since a non-resident substantial interest shareholder in a Dutch resident company continues to be liable to tax; the Netherlands allows imputation of tax levied upon alienation by the new state of residence; after a period of ten years the tax assessment imposed upon emigration is cancelled and unpaid taxes need not longer be paid; and finally, transients who reside in the Netherlands for a period not exceeding eight years are not taxed upon emigration out of the Netherlands. In substance, these measures underpin the anti-avoidance nature of the exit charge. As a result, the Netherlands cannot justify, in my opinion, the restriction on the fundamental freedom to freely move and reside in the territory of another Member State created by the Dutch exit charge with an appeal to the fiscal coherence principle.

4.5.1.3 Other imperative reasons in the public interest not accepted

Other imperative reasons in the public interest put forward, like allocation of tax jurisdiction, loss of tax receipts, and effectiveness of fiscal supervision were not accepted in the De Lasteyrie du Saillant ruling. This case does not concern the allocation of the right to tax between Member States, but the question of whether measures adopted to that end comply with the requirements of a fundamental freedom.[51] In addition, it is settled case

[49] See ECJ 11 March 2004, C-9/02 *de Lasteyrie du Saillant* [2004] ECR I-2409, paras 4 and 63-67.

[50] This objective has been expressed by the Dutch legislator in legislative history of the bill amending the Dutch statutory exit charge provisions because of ECJ 11 March 2004, C-9/02 *de Lasteyrie du Saillant* [2004] ECR I-2409. See *Memorie van toelichting* (explanatory memorandum), *Kamerstukken II* 2003/04, 29 758, nr. 3, para 15.

[51] See ECJ 11 March 2004, C-9/02 *de Lasteyrie du Saillant* [2004] ECR I-2409, para 68.

law that diminution of tax receipts cannot be regarded as a matter of overriding general interest which may be relied upon in order to justify a measure which is, in principle, contrary to a fundamental freedom. Therefore, a simple loss of receipts suffered by a Member State because a taxpayer has moved his tax residence to another Member State, where the tax system is different and may be more advantageous for him, cannot in itself justify a restriction on the right of establishment.[52] Furthermore, tax evasion or tax fraud cannot be inferred generally from the fact that the tax residence of a natural person has been transferred to another Member State and cannot justify a fiscal measure which compromises the exercise of a fundamental freedom guaranteed by the Treaty.[53] All of this is equally true for the Dutch 1997 exit charge. Therefore, the alleged imperative reasons in the public interest put forward in the De Lasteyrie du Saillant ruling cannot justify the restriction of Article 18 EC Treaty in the Van Dijk case, either.

4.5.2 Exit charge not proportionate to its aim

Whereas preventing tax avoidance by means of countermeasures to tackle-solely tax-driven temporary emigration has been accepted as an imperative reason in the public interest which may justify a tax measure, and countering effectively tax-driven emigration by means of an exit charge may be appropriate, the rule of reason test boils down to the question of whether the exit charge is proportionate to its aim. In the De Lasteyrie du Saillant ruling, the Court of Justice ruled that the French exit tax is not proportional, since it was not specifically designed to exclude from a tax advantage purely artificial arrangements aimed at circumventing French tax law, but that it was aimed generally at any situation in which a taxpayer with substantial shareholdings transfers his tax residence outside France for any reason whatever. However, the transfer of a natural person's tax residence outside the territory of a Member State does not, in itself, imply tax avoidance. Tax evasion or tax fraud cannot be inferred generally from the fact that the tax residence of a natural person has been transferred to another Member State and cannot justify a fiscal measure which compromises the exercise of a fundamental freedom guaranteed by the EC Treaty.[54]

[52] See ECJ 11 March 2004, C-9/02 *de Lasteyrie du Saillant* [2004] ECR I-2409, para 60.
[53] See ECJ 11 March 2004, C-9/02 *de Lasteyrie du Saillant* [2004] ECR I-2409, para 51.
[54] See ECJ 11 March 2004, C-9/02 *de Lasteyrie du Saillant* [2004] ECR I-2409, paras 50-51 and 57.

Therefore, the French exit charge taxing latent increases in value, where a taxpayer transfers his tax residence outside that state, is not proportional to its aim and cannot be justified.[55] Since the aim and mechanisms of the Dutch 1997 exit tax are comparable to the French exit tax, the Dutch exit tax is neither proportional nor can it be justified. The Dutch legislator has deliberately included a general rule and not a rule specially tailored rule to counter tax-driven emigration. This follows and clearly directly from legislative history:

> If the substantial interest regime is applicable and it is not a transient case, a frozen assessment will be imposed [ie, an assessment with deferment of payment; EK] on *every* emigration; *the motive on which the emigration is based upon, is not relevant* [italics added].[56]

Therefore, it is clear that the Dutch exit tax is also not specifically designed to exclude from a tax advantage purely artificial arrangements aimed at circumventing Dutch tax law, but that it is aimed generally at any situation in which a taxpayer with substantial shareholdings transfers his tax residence outside the Netherlands for any reason whatever. Based on the De Lasteyrie du Saillant ruling, the Arnhem Court of Appeals should have drawn the conclusion that the Dutch 1997 exit tax is not proportional and as a result, the fifth question should not have been asked, either.

Considering the aim of preventing a taxpayer from temporarily transferring his tax residence before selling securities with the sole aim of avoiding payment of the tax on increases in value due in France, the Court of Justice, in line with the Advocate General, put forward a less coercive or less restrictive alternative to the French exit charge. It suggested to provide for taxation of taxpayers returning to France after realising their increases in value during a relatively brief stay in another Member State. Such taxation would avoid affecting the position of taxpayers having no aim other than the bona fide exercise of their right of establishment in another Member State.[57] However, I believe that (the introduction of) this alternative taxation

55 See ECJ 11 March 2004, C-9/02 *de Lasteyrie du Saillant* [2004] ECR I-2409, paras 58 and 69.

56 The text is an unofficial translation by the author. See *Nota naar aanleiding van het verslag* (Memorandum in reply to the report), *Kamerstukken II*, vergaderjaar 1996/97, 24 761, no. 7 blz. 25.

57 See ECJ 11 March 2004, C-9/02 *de Lasteyrie du Saillant* [2004] ECR I-2409, para 54.

in domestic tax law is incompatible with tax treaties similar to the OECD Model Tax Convention. Without a special tax treaty provision, a substantial interest shareholder must be characterised as being a resident of his new state of residence and no longer of his state of departure, even if he has actually his residence in the new state of residence for a relatively brief period. By virtue of Article 13, paragraph 5 of the OECD Model, tax jurisdiction in the event of the alienation of shares is allocated exclusively to the new state of residence if its resident shareholders alienate their shares.[58] If the state of departure were to tax a re-emigrating substantial interest shareholder as suggested under its domestic tax laws, it would violate this allocation rule, if no specific tax treaty covered the suggested alternative. The state of departure would unilaterally change the tax jurisdiction allocation rules in its favour, because under the relevant tax treaty it would not have any tax jurisdiction on capital gains on substantial interest shares realised by residents of the other contracting state. Such a violation would be incompatible not only with the principle of good faith as included in Articles 26, 27, and 31 of the Vienna Convention on the Law of Treaties, but also with the OECD Model and its Commentary. A contracting state may not make a convention partially inoperative by amending its domestic law after signing the convention.[59] Furthermore, the alternative taxation may end in double taxation if both the new state of residence and the state of departure were to tax. Such a double taxation would not be in line with, inter alia, the Gilly ruling, in which the Court itself ruled that the abolition of double taxation within the Community is included among the objectives of the EC Treaty.[60] Consequently, the suggested alternative might not even be in line with the Court's own case law. Therefore, I believe that the suggested alternative should not be adopted by Member States. Below, I will give an outline of a proportional alternative system which not only covers the aim of preventing tax avoidance, but also of ensuring fiscal coherence. This system is a less coercive or less restrictive alternative to the exit charges discussed above and should be taken into account when assessing whether the aims of states could have been realised in a more proportional way than by virtue of their implemented exit charges.

---

58 Article 13, paragraph 4 OECD Model includes a specific provision for shares in a real estate company.

59 See Article 3, paragraph 2 OECD Model and its Commentary, para 13.

60 See ECJ 12 May 1998, C-336/96 *Gilly* [1998] ECR I-2793, paras 15 and 16.

5 Proportional alternative system: The residence-based compartimentalisation system

Considering that states want to claim tax jurisdiction in cases in which a substantial interest shareholder transfers (temporarily) his residence outside their territory exclusively for tax reasons and on the increase in value acquired during the taxpayer's residence on their territory, I will develop below a system which is, in my view, EU and tax treaty proof and which makes exit charges, as we know them now, superfluous. Furthermore, I believe that this system will enhance the level playing field, since nothing will fall between the cracks as may be true under the current systems. The alternative system is not only valid in respect of substantial interest shareholdings, but could be applied in any case in which nowadays an exit charge is applied. However, none of this implies that this system is my personal favourite. Based on the principle or origin, I believe that the state in which a company carries out or has carried out its substantial entrepreneurial activities should have tax jurisdiction on the capital gains realised upon alienation of the shares in that company, because the profits have been produced in that state. Under such a system, a transfer of residence of the company's shareholder would be irrelevant, because the allocation of tax jurisdiction on such capital gains does not link up the place of residence of the shareholder. Consequently, exit charges upon emigration of shareholder are not necessary under the origin-based system.[61] Therefore, the system developed below must only be considered as a technical contribution to a problem under the current system, but not as a matter of principle from my side.[62]

5.1 Appealable order to fix income on which state of departure wants to preserve tax jurisdiction

Upon emigration, an appealable order will fix the income, which concept includes capital gains on which the state of departure wants to preserve tax jurisdiction. I believe that such an order is a proportional measure, which is not only in the interest of the state of departure, but also of the departing resident. Legal security of both the departing resident and the

---

[61] See Kemmeren, *Principle of Origin in Tax Conventions, A Rethinking of Models*, diss. (2001), Katholieke Universiteit Brabant, Tilburg, pp 336-337 and 340-350.

[62] In substance, this system builds on an origin-based compartimentalisation system developed in my dissertation for tax treaties where assets or activities are transferred from one contracting state to another.

state of departure are enhanced. In this way, the possibility that after a number of years a dispute may arise on the amount of the income is prevented, which dispute may not be easy to settle as consequence of the lapse of time. Such difficulties will be avoided by means of such an order. The departing resident may appeal to this order based on the regular rules for objections and appeals if, for instance, he does not agree with the amount of income fixed by means of the order at issue. A substantial difference with an assessment, payment of which has been deferred, is that the order does not create a tax debt. In the De Lasteyrie du Saillant ruling, it was exactly the tax debt which constituted one of the unjustified restrictions. The fact that in respect of a pure internal transfer of residence such an order need not be issued does not amount to an unjustified restriction. Firstly, the order is also issued in the interest of the departing resident. Secondly, the order does justice to the difference in degree between purely domestic transfers of residence and transnational transfers, since in respect of purely domestic transfers the allocation of tax jurisdiction can never be an issue, whereas that will be an issue in the case of transnational transfers.

5.2 The compartimentalisation of tax jurisdiction

The tax jurisdiction on the amount of income fixed by the appealble order is allocated to the state of departure; the rest of the income to the new state of residence. In this way, each state may tax the increase in value acquired during the taxpayer's residence on its territory. An example may illustrate this mechanism. Assume X held a substantial interest in a company of which the acquisition price was 20. X emigrate from the Netherlands to another EU Member State, EFTA Member State or a state with which the Netherlands has concluded a tax treaty (heherafter: DTC state). Upon emigration, the fair market value of these shares was 100. An income order was issued for the amount of 100 -/- 20 = 80, to which the Netherlands was allotted tax jurisdiction. After that X became a resident of that EU Member State, EFTA Member State, or DTC state, the value of the shares increases and X alienates the shares for an amount of 150. The new state of residence may tax an amount of income of 150 -/- 100 = 50. In this way, the total amount of income of 150 -/- 20 = 130 is divided completely. It depends on the domestic tax systems of whether this amount of 130 will actually be taxed. Therefore, under this system, it is not necessary to harmonise the domestic tax systems of all states involved. The potential taxation takes place at the moment that the income is actually realised, so that the De Lasteyrie du Saillant ruling is satisfied in this sense as well. The moment of realisation should be determined per state involved and in the same manner as for persons who have not emigrated. In this way, persons who stay at home and departing/incoming residents will be taxed in the same manner.

The allocation of tax jurisdiction can be done by means of various legal instruments, for example: a bilateral tax treaty, a multilateral tax treaty, or a European regulation. Although this may be politically sensitive at this moment, I prefer the instrument of a regulation within the EU, because this instrument, unlike a directive, is binding in its entirety and directly applicable in all Member States.[63] Furthermore, if the political will is there, a regulation can be made quite quickly. The political crux also lies there. If politicians in Europe start to realise that enormous gaps in their budgets may arise as a consequence of the non-applicability of their current exit charges, a sense of urgency may hopefully be the result. A regulation may then appear to be a blessing in disguise.

5.3 The decrease of value after departure taken into account in state of departure if not included in taxable base in new state of residence

If the income, for example, capital gains, is not a part of the taxable base in the new state of residence and the income in the period after the departure turns out to be negative, the state of departure should take this negative item of income into account. In this way, the departing resident's personal ability to pay is satisfied. Furthermore, such a mechanism would be in line with the AMID, De Groot, and Wallentin rulings as well as with Advocate General Maduro's Opinion in the Marks & Spencer case: decrease of ability to pay (for example, as a consequence of losses incurred or personal and family circumstances) should be taken into account at least in one Member State, especially if the related increase of ability to pay is included in the taxable base of a Member State.[64] An example may

63 See Article 249 EC Treaty.

64 See ECJ 14 December 2000, C-141/99 *AMID* [2000] ECR I-11619; 12 December 2002, C-385/00 *de Groot* [2002] ECR I-11819; 1 July 2004, C-169/03 *Wallentin* [2004] ECR I-6443; and Advocate General Maduro in *Marks & Spencer* (ECJ C-446/03 *Marks & Spencer*, pending), 7 April 2005. This mechanism may go a step further than that which ECJ 5 July 2002, C-376/03 *D.*, not yet reported, strictly obliges. I would have preferred a pro rata parte application of the basic allowance of 10 %, because Mr D.'s capital was located for 10 % in the Netherlands. Thus, Mr D. did not get a basic allowance. Herewith, his personal ability to pay is not satisfied. It is a great pity that the Court did not take up the challenge to develop the *Schumacker* doctrine a step further and bring it really close to or even in line with the ability to pay principle.

illustrate this mechanism. Assume X held a substantial interest in a company which acquisition price was 20. X emigrated from the Netherlands to another EU Member State, EFTA Member State, or DTC state. Upon emigration, the fair market value of these shares was 100. An income order was issued for the amount of 100 -/- 20 = 80, over which the Netherlands was allotted tax jurisdiction. After that, X became a resident of that EU Member State, EFTA Member State, or DTC state, the value of the shares decreases and X alienated the shares for an amount of 80. The new state of residence did not include this item of income in its taxable base. As a result, the Netherlands might not ultimately tax an amount of 80, but an amount of 80 -/- 20 = 60.

5.4 Subsequent emigration may trigger taxable event

If the departing resident emigrates subsequently to a non-EU Member State, a non-EFTA Member State, or a state with whom the original state of departure has not concluded a tax treaty, then ultimately taxes must be paid in order to secure the state of departure's tax claim. In order to warrant the application of this final payment, it must be regulated separately in the relevant bilateral tax treaty, multilateral tax treaty, or European regulation. In substance, this means that a taxable event will be included in such an instrument. I believe that such a rule does not meet with constitutional problems, because democratic legitimacy is provided by virtue of vir the existing mechanisms: bilateral and multilateral tax treaties must be ratified according to the regular standards and procedures, and the European regulation is a legal instrument of which the scope has already been embedded in the EC Treaty. Essentially, the introduction of the final payment moves the fence, which is now around the individual Member States as a result of their individual exit charges, to the outside borders of the EU, EFTA, or the territories of the states which have concluded tax treaties with each other.

5.5 Mutual assistance in tax collection

To balance the residence-based compartimentalisation system, the relevant bilateral tax treaty, multilateral tax treaty, or European regulation must include an adequate mutual assistance in tax collection provision in order to guarantee that the taxes due are effectively and efficiently collected.

III Bujura (C-8/04): Most-favoured-nation Treatment Not Favoured

1 Facts, Circumstances and Assumptions

Mr Bujura had the German nationality and resided in Germany. As a consequence, he was liable to tax on his worldwide income in Germany. Together with his spouse, he owned a holiday home in Breskens, in the Netherlands. In 2001, he only received income from savings and investments in the Netherlands, because of this holiday home.[65] Mr and Mrs Bujura earned less than 90 % of their family income in the Netherlands. Mr Bujura did not opt to be treated as a resident taxpayer,[66] which option was introduced to meet with the Schumacker ruling but whose scope was and is much wider than the cases comparable to the Schumacker ruling.[67]

2 Domestic and Tax Treaty Law

Under Dutch domestic tax law, Mr Bujura could not claim the basic allowance and basic tax credits.[68] Based on the tax treaty Germany-the Netherlands (1959), he may not claim them either, because residents of Germany were entitled to the basic allowance and basic tax credits only if they earned more than 90 % of their family income in the Netherlands.[69] However, under the tax treaty between Belgium-the Netherlands (1970), a resident of Belgium was entitled to the basic allowance and basic tax credits based on Article 25, paragraph 3 of this treaty, which read as follows:

> Natural persons resident in one of the two Contracting States are entitled in the other State to the personal allowances, concessions and reductions which are granted by the latter to its own residents by reason of their civil status or dependants.[70]

---

[65] See Article 7.7, para 1, and para 2, under a. Personal Income Tax Act 2001 (*Wet inkomstenbelasting 2001*; PITA 2001).

[66] See Article 2.5 PITA 2001.

[67] See ECJ 14 February 1995, C-279/93 *Schumacker* [1995] ECR I-225.

[68] See Articles 5.5 and 8.10 PITA 2001.

[69] See Article 1, para 1 of the Supplementary protocol, also known as cross-border workers protocol (*Aanvullend protocol* or *grensarbeidersprotocol*), of 13 March 1980 of the tax treaty between Germany and the Netherlands concluded on 16 June 1959.

[70] This is an unofficial translation by the author. As of 2003, a new tax treaty is in force between Belgium and the Netherlands which does no longer includes this provision. The new tax treaty only includes a pro rata parte entitlement to the personal allowances, concessions

Bujura argued that he was also entitled to the relevant basic allowance and basic tax credits because of the most-favoured-nation (MFN) treatment doctrine. He argued that the fundamental freedoms should be interpreted in such a way that the MFN treatment was part of them. In the context of the EC Treaty and tax treaties, this doctrine means that Member States may not incorporate provisions in a tax treaty with a (non-) Member State which is more advantageous than a similar provision in a tax treaty with another Member State. As a result, Bujura believed that as he is a resident of Germany under the tax treaty Germany-the Netherlands (1959) he should also be entitled to the basic allowance and basic tax credits to which a resident of Belgium was entitled under Article 25, paragraph 3 of the tax treaty Belgium-the Netherlands (1970).

3 Preliminary Question

The Court of Appeal of 's-Hertogenbosch asked for a preliminary ruling in this case.[71] The Court asked the following question:

> Does a foreign taxpayer resident in a Member State, such as Germany, who is not entitled to the benefits afforded by the Netherlands-Germany Tax Convention because he does not satisfy the condition, laid down in that regard, that he receives at least 90 % of his income in the Netherlands, have the right, by virtue of EC law, to receive from the Netherlands the tax free allowance and tax credit for income tax in the calculation of his income from savings and investments if a foreign taxpayer who in resident in another Member State, in this case Belgium, has the right to such benefits in the calculation of his income from savings and investments by virtue of the Netherlands-Belgium Tax Convention (and the decision of the State Secretary for Finance of 21 February 2002, No CPP 2001/2745, BNB 2002/164) despite the fact that he does not receive at least 90 % of his income in the Netherlands?

Although the question does not refer explicitly to the MFN treatment, it is clear this is the real issue. The underlying ruling of the Court of Appeals described extensively the pro and con arguments for and against the application of the MFN doctrine.

and reductions which are granted by reason of civil status or dependants. See Article 26, paragraph 2 tax treaty Belgium-the Netherlands (2001).

71 See Hof 's-Hertogenbosch, MK IV, 8 January 2004, no. 03/00788, *V-N* 2004/18.9, and ECJ C-8/04 *Bujura*, pending, OJ C 59, 6 March 2004, p 17.

4 Possible Answer

Below I will make an analysis in order to give a possible answer to the question of the Dutch Court of Appeals, which, in my opinion, the European Court of Justice will likely give. The result of this analysis is that, in my opinion, based on the existing body of case law of the European Court of Justice, it is clear that the basic allowance and basic tax credit, to which residents of Belgium are entitled in the Netherlands by virtue of a specific provision under the tax treaty Belgium-the Netherlands (1970), may not be invoked by residents of other Member States, like Germany, because they may not rely on a MFN treatment under the fundamental freedoms. As a consequence, Mr Bujura will not be entitled to the basic allowance and basic tax credit, which he has claimed. In this respect, the D. ruling is, of course, the most relevant ruling.[72] Below, I will analyse not only the ruling itself, but also the Opinion of the Advocate General because the Bujura case illustrates perfectly that the reasoning of the Advocate General cannot be upheld. Therefore, I believe that the Court of Justice was right indeed in ignoring it when deciding the D. case. Although I feel that the decision is very sound,[73] it could and should have been motivated more solidly,[74] which would have enhanced its degree of appreciation.[75] However, I do not believe that the Court is on its way back and that its decision is politically driven. As I discuss below, I believe that the ruling fits within the body of the Court's case law. The Court has only made clear (again) that in creating a single market, its

---

72 See ECJ 5 July 2002, C-376/03 *D.*, not yet reported.

73 See also Kemmeren, The Termination of the 'Most Favoured Nation Clause' Dispute in Tax Treaty Law and the Necessity of a Euro Model Tax Convention, *EC Tax Review* 1997, pp 146-152, and Kemmeren, *Principle of Origin in Tax Conventions, A Rethinking of Models*, diss. (2001), Katholieke Universiteit Brabant, Tilburg, pp 127-131.

74 See also, e.g., Meussen, Exit Meestbegunstiging, *WFR* 2005, pp 1027-1028; and Pistone, National Treatment for All Non-resident EU Nationals: Looking Beyond the D Decision, *Intertax* 2005, pp 412.

75 See for criticism, eg, Thömmes, EG-Recht und Meistbegünstigung, *Internationale Wirtschafts-Briefe*, Fach 11a, pp 701-702; Meussen, Exit Meestbegunstiging, *WFR* 2005, pp 1027-1028; Lang, Das EuGH-Urteil in der Rechtssache D. – Gerät der Motor der Steuerharmonisierung ins Stottern?, *SWI* 2005, pp 365-375; Pistone, National Treatment for All Non-resident EU Nationals: Looking Beyond the D Decision, *Intertax* 2005, pp 412-413; Weber, Most-Favoured-Nation Treatment under Tax Treaties Rejected in the European Community: Background and Analysis of the *D.* Case, *Intertax* 2005, pp 429-445; van Thiel, A Slip of the European Court in the D Case (C-376/03): Denial of the Most-Favoured-Nation Treatment because of Absence of Similarity, *Intertax* 2005, pp 454-457.

competence was and is not unlimited. This is true as long as we accept within the EU that each Member State has its own tax system, including not only domestic tax laws, but also bilateral tax treaties. Those who expected the Court to rule otherwise ask too much from the Court. In the analysis below, I will only address the issue of MFN treatment and not the issue of national treatment, which was also under discussion in the D. case, since in the Bujura case, the MFN treatment is the only issue.

4.1 Untenable Opinion of Advocate General Colomer in the D. case

Before discussing the Opinion,[76] I will briefly highlight the facts, circumstances and assumptions of the case. Mr D., a married person, lived in Germany and held the German nationality. On 1 January 1998, 10 % of his assets consisted of immovable property in the Netherlands, whilst the remainder was located in his country of origin. Consequently, he was subject to the Net Wealth Tax Act in the Netherlands as a non-resident taxpayer. Germany did not impose a net wealth tax. Under Dutch domestic tax law, Mr D. could not claim a basic allowance.[77] He could not claim this allowance based on the tax treaty Germany-the Netherlands (1959), either. Referring to Article 25, paragraph 3 of the tax treaty between Belgium-the Netherlands (1970), he claimed to be entitled to the basic allowance, because of the MFN treatment doctrine. Belgium did not impose a net wealth tax in the taxable year at issue. The Advocate General pleaded in favour of the application of the MFN treatment.

4.1.1 The aim of bilateral tax treaties

The Advocate General rightly explained that avoidance of double taxation is an objective of the EC Treaty.[78] Subsequently, he pointed out that Member States shared out taxation powers through tax treaties. This is indeed true. They do this with the aim of facilitating the exchange of goods and services and movements of capital, technology and persons between the contracting states. In this way, the development of economic relations between the countries involved will be enhanced.[79] According to the Advocate General,

---

[76] See Opinion of Advocate General Colomer in *D.* (ECJ 5 July 2002, C-376/03 *D.*, not yet reported), 26 October 2004.

[77] See Article 14, para 2 Net Wealth Tax Act 1964 (*Wet op de vermogensbelasting 1964*; hence also NWTA 1964)

[78] See also, eg, ECJ 12 May 1998, C-336/96 *Gilly* [1998] ECR I-2793, paras 15 and 16.

[79] See OECD Model Tax Convention on Income and Capital, Introduction, para 1.

a tax treaty restricts fiscal sovereignty. It may be questioned whether this indeed the case. In my opinion, a bilateral tax treaty allocates tax jurisdiction to the contracting states involved. If such a state does not impose a tax on (certain items of) income or capital, the tax treaty does not restrict a state's fiscal sovereignty, because there is nothing to restrict. Therefore, the conclusion must be that a tax treaty is a means of allocating tax jurisdiction, not of restricting fiscal sovereignty.

Furthermore, the Advocate General acknowledged that disparities between tax treaties were possible in view of the fact that there is no harmonisation of national tax rules. Indeed, bilateral tax treaties build bridges between the tax systems of the contracting states and, as a result, differences between bilateral tax treaties are justified for that reason only. However, this is not the only reason why differences are justified, as I will discuss below.

4.1.2 Article 25 (3) NL-Belgium (1970) is a general rule not onlz applicable to Net Wealth Tax

It is settled case law that Member States remain competent to determine the criteria for taxation of income and wealth with a view to eliminating double taxation by means of, inter alia, tax treaties. In this context, the Member States are at liberty to determine the connecting factors for the purposes of allocating taxation rights between themselves. However, as far as the exercise of the right of taxation so allocated is concerned, the Member States nevertheless may not disregard Community rules.[80] The Advocate General advocated that the rights must be exercised within the limits of the object of allocating taxation. As a consequence, he argued that if nothing is to be divided, a tax treaty is meaningless. In this context he argued:

> In relation to the wealth tax, since at the material time there was no such tax in Belgium, Article 25(3) of the agreement with the Netherlands, (47) to the extent to which it extends to Belgian residents entitlement to the allowance it grants to Dutch residents, *becomes a mere privilege for which no consideration is given* and for which there is *no reciprocal basis* [italics added], and the test of its 'Community compatibility' must therefore be much more rigorous.

80 See, eg, ECJ 12 May 1998, C-336/96 *Gilly* [1998] ECR I-2793, paras 24 and 30; and ECJ 21 September 1999, C-307/97 *Saint-Gobain* [1999] ECR I-6161, paras 56-57.

In my view, the Advocate General's position is wrong and ill-motivated. First of all, Article 25, paragraph 3 of the tax treaty between Belgium-the Netherlands (1970) was a general rule which was not tailored only to the net wealth tax as the Advocate General suggested. In respect of all taxes covered by the treaty, personal allowances, concessions and reductions granted by reason of an individual's civil status or dependants must be given. The most obvious tax also covered by this provision was the personal income tax. It might even be true that it was predominantly this tax which underlay Article 25, paragraph 3. It was clear that both Belgium and the Netherlands imposed a personal income tax. Therefore, the Advocate General's reasoning could never be upheld in the Bujura case, which is a case under the personal income tax. This conclusion fuels the idea that the result desired by the Advocate General took him away from a sound and coherent legal reasoning.

4.1.3 Article 25 (3) NL-Belgium (1970) is based on reciprocity

Based on Article 25, paragraph 3 of the tax treaty between Belgium-the Netherlands (1970), residents of Belgium were entitled to claim personal allowances, concessions and reductions granted by reason of their civil status or dependants for personal income tax purposes in the Netherlands, and residents of the Netherlands were entitled to claim them in Belgium. Therefore, the provision laid down a reciprocal obligation for both contracting states. The Advocate General's opposite position was clearly inconsistent with the text and object and purpose of Article 25, paragraph 3. He did not test this provision against EC law, which should have been done, because tax treaty rules must also be compatible with EC law. In substance, he tested the individual case of Mr D. Article 234 EC Treaty was not written for such a test. For the reason that the provision included reciprocal obligations for both contracting states, the Advocate General's approach must be rejected. In any case, I feel that it is obvious that the personal allowances, concessions and reductions which the Netherlands must give to Belgian residents by virtue of Article 25, paragraph 3 cannot be characterised as "a mere privilege for which no consideration is given".

4.1.4 Personal allowances, concessions, and reductions are integral parts of ability to pay and not privileges

Furthermore, it is fundamentally consistent with the ability to pay principle to take personal and family circumstances into account. This is the basic approach under domestic tax law systems, especially as far as personal income and net wealth taxes are concerned.[81] Therefore, it is amazing that the Advocate General characterised a basic allowance, the aim of which is to take into account a person's ability to pay, as a 'privilege'. Under tax treaties, it is normally the state of residence which must take into account the taxpayer's personal circumstances. This rule is found in the OECD Model in Article 24, paragraph 3 which stipulates that the provision of non-discriminatory treatment of permanent establishments

> shall not be construed as obliging a Contracting State to grant to residents of the other Contracting State any personal allowances, reliefs, and reductions for taxation purposes on account of civil status or family responsibilities which it grants to its own residents.

We find confirmation of this rule not only in the Commentary to Article 24,[82] but also in the Commentary to the Articles 23A/23B. In the calculations, it is the state of residence which provides deductions for personal and family allowances.[83] In conclusion, tax treaties normally allocate personal allowances, reliefs and reductions on account of civil status or family responsibilities to the state of residence. Although Article 25, paragraph 3 of the tax treaty between Belgium and the Netherlands (1970) also allocates similar personal allowances, concessions and reductions to the state of source, I believe that this was a rule which allocated tax jurisdiction to contracting states as well. In line with settled case law, the Member States are at liberty to determine the connecting factors for the purposes of allocating taxation rights among themselves. Therefore, they are also at liberty to determine how personal and family circumstances are taken into account under tax treaties.

4.1.5 Residents of Belgium are not comparable to residents of Germany

Furthermore, the Advocate General believed that a resident of Germany, like Mr D., was factually comparable to a resident of Belgium. He felt that the relevant assessment of equality

> is a matter of identifying whether two individuals in comparable factual circumstances are subject without justification to disparate

81 See also, eg, 14 February 1995, C-279/93 *Schumacker* [1995] ECR I-225; 12 December 2002, C-385/00 *de Groot* [2002] ECR I-11819; 1 July 2004, C-169/03 *Wallentin* [2004] ECR I-6443; and ECJ 5 July 2002, C-376/03 *D.*, not yet reported.

82 See also Commentary to Articles 24, paras 4 and 22.

83 See Commentary to Articles 23A/23B, paras 41-42.

rules and, in comparing those rules, the sole pertinent inquiry is whether their application leads to differing effects to the detriment of either of them.

By allowing Mr D. to claim MFN treatment, he disconnected in substance Article 25, paragraph 3 of the tax treaty between Belgium-the Netherlands (1970) from this tax treaty and implemented it in the tax treaty Germany-the Netherlands (1959). It was only that provision which he disconnected and implemented. However, a bilateral tax treaty is the result of negotiation process between only the two states involved. As a rule, third states are not involved in this process. It is a matter of give and take only between the two contracting states. As a consequence, all provisions are connected with each other in a bilateral context. The Advocate General only took, without asking Germany to give something in return. He violated the principle of reciprocity on which every bilateral tax treaty is based. In respect to residents of Belgium, not only Article 25, paragraph 3 of the tax treaty between Belgium-the Netherlands (1970) was applicable, but the entire tax treaty. The ultimate tax position of residents of the contracting states is determined by the taxpayers' individual circumstances and the tax treaty as whole in conjunction with the domestic tax law systems of the contracting states. Some tax treaty provisions may be more beneficial than others. Whether that is the case, does not only depend on these rules, but also on the taxpayers' individual circumstances. If we want to compare tax treaties, we have to take into account the complete tax treaties and not only separate provisions. Otherwise, we compare situations which are by their nature non-comparable. Therefore, Mr D. was not comparable to a resident of Belgium. The same is true for Mr Bujura. Since they are not comparable with residents of Belgium, they may not claim a tax treatment equal to these residents.

4.1.6 Other observations

Without the intention of being exhaustive, the following additional observations can be made. The MFN treatment doctrine should not be applied because a tax treaty is also a reflection of a financial balance between contracting states.[84] Besides, the main concern of the European Court of Justice is that a tax treaty should eliminate or at least mitigate internatio-

[84] See also ECJ 21 September 1999, C-307/97 *Saint-Gobain* [1999] ECR I-6161, para 60; and 15 January 2002, C-55/00 *Gottardo* [2002] ECR I-413, para 36.

nal double taxation.[85] If this result is achieved, the Court is reluctant to interfere with tax treaties. Therefore, also from this perspective, there is no reason to apply the MFN treatment. This is also consistent with the subsidiarity principle included in Article 5 EC Treaty. I have even argued that the European Court had already rejected MFN treatment in the Bachmann ruling, more specifically in para 26.[86]

An unlimited application of the MFN treatment would have destroyed the system of tax treaties. It seems that such a consequence was even a bit too much for the Advocate General. At least, he did not advocate an automatic application of the MFN treatment. On the other hand, he was aware of the potentially far-reaching consequences of his position. He believed that the disruption of the equilibrium and reciprocity, which prevail in the system of tax treaties, was a possible implication, but acceptable when establishing the single market. I believe that the disruption of the equilibrium and reciprocity would not contribute to the establishment of the single market. On the contrary, MFN treatment would lead to cherry-picking taxpayers, likely both in the state of source and in the state of residence and, in circumstances, even simultaneously. This result would not enhance the level playing field that is one of the characteristics of the single market.

4.2 Sound decision of ECJ on 5 July 2005, Case 376/03 (D.)

Fortunately, the European Court did not follow the reasoning of the Advocate General. The Court repeats its settled case law that residents and non-residents are as a rule not comparable.[87] The Court rejected D.'s claim to MFN treatment without explicitly mentioning the term. The

[85] See, eg, ECJ 12 May 1998, C-336/96 *Gilly* [1998] ECR I-2793; 21 September 1999, C-307/97 *Saint-Gobain* [1999] ECR I-6161; and 12 December 2002, C-385/00 *de Groot* [2002] ECR I-11819.

[86] See Kemmeren, The Termination of the 'Most Favoured Nation Clause' Dispute in Tax Treaty Law and the Necessity of a Euro Model Tax Convention, *EC Tax Review*, 1997, pp 146-152; and Kemmeren, *Principle of Origin in Tax Conventions, A Rethinking of Models*, diss. (2001), Katholieke Universiteit Brabant, Tilburg, pp 127-131. ECJ 28 January 1992, C-204/90 *Bachmann* [1992] ECR I-249, para 26 reads as follows:

"It is true that bilateral conventions exist between certain Member States, allowing the deduction for tax purposes of contributions paid in a contracting State other than that in which the advantage is granted, and recognizing the power of a single State to tax sums payable by insurers under the contracts concluded with them. However, such a solution is possible *only* [italics added] by means of such conventions or by the adoption by the Council of the necessary coordination or harmonization measures."

[87] ECJ 5 July 2002, C-376/03 *D.*, not yet reported, para 34 and 52.

question was not framed in this terminology. The Court is very concise, I would say too concise, in turning down MFN treatment:

> 60 It is to be remembered that, in order to avoid the same income and assets being taxed in both the Netherlands and Belgium, Article 24 of the Belgium-Netherlands Convention *allocates powers of taxation between those two Member States* and *Article 25(3)* lays down a rule under which natural persons *resident in one of those two States* is entitled in the other to the personal allowances which are granted by it to its own residents.
>
> 61 The fact that those *reciprocal rights and obligations* apply *only to persons resident in one of the two Contracting Member States* is an *inherent consequence of bilateral double taxation conventions*. It follows that *a taxable person resident in Belgium* is not in the same situation as *a taxable person resident outside Belgium* so far as concerns wealth tax on real property situated in the Netherlands.
>
> 62 *A rule such as that laid down in Article 25(3)* of the Belgium-Netherlands Convention *cannot* be regarded as *a benefit separable from the remainder of the Convention*, but is *an integral part thereof* and *contributes to its overall balance*.
>
> 63 Having regard to the foregoing considerations, the answer to the second question asked must be that Articles 56 EC and 58 EC do *not preclude a rule laid down by a bilateral convention for the avoidance of double taxation* *such as the rule at issue* in the main proceedings from not being extended, *in a situation and in circumstances such as those in the main proceedings*, to nationals of a Member State which is not party to that convention [emphasis added].

Although I feel that the decision is very sound,[88] it could and should have been motivated more solidly. Considering the huge debate in tax Europe and the huge potential impact on the international tax practice, both for taxpayers and States, it would have been appropriate to discuss and weigh individually all arguments put forward in favour and against MFN treatment. In this way, the Court could have provided conclusive guidance for

88 Compare also Kemmeren, The Termination of the 'Most Favoured Nation Clause' Dispute in Tax Treaty Law and the Necessity of a Euro Model Tax Convention, *EC Tax Review* 1997, pp 146-152; and Kemmeren, *Principle of Origin in Tax Conventions, A Rethinking of Models*, diss. (2001), Katholieke Universiteit Brabant, Tilburg, pp 127-131.

the various claims of MFN treatment under tax treaties. I must admit the Advocate General's Opinion was not very helpful in this respect. He did not provide the Court with a balanced overview of all pros and cons.

4.2.1 Criticism

Reading especially the italicized and underlined parts of the Court's considerations above, it seems as if the Court wants to assess every individual MFN treatment claim itself. One may read them as follows. If the rule is not comparable to Article 25, paragraph 3 of the tax treaty between Belgium-the Netherlands (1970), eg, the double convention provision itself is not of a reciprocal nature, or if a situation or the circumstances are not comparable to Mr D's case, the Court did not turn down yet MFN treatment. The idea that the Court itself wants to assess every individual MFN treatment claim is not very attractive from a workload perspective. Furthermore, I do not believe that this is real intention of the Court. The text must be read in the light of the preliminary question.[89] Therefore, I do not believe that the ruling does not have a general impact. Furthermore, I believe that the Court's other arguments and the fact that a grand chamber ruled on the case prove that the Court's intention was indeed to give not only a decision for the D. case itself, but also to provide guidance for other MFN treatment claims.

Another criticism is that the Court characterised Article 24 of the tax treaty between Belgium-the Netherlands (1970) as a tax jurisdiction allocation rule. This rule stipulated the methods for elimination of double taxation comparable to the Articles 23A/23B OECD Model. In line with the Saint-Gobain, I would characterise this rule as post-allocation rule. After tax jurisdiction by virtue of other tax treaty provisions has been allocated to one or both contracting States, the method provision determines how the State of residence must eliminate or mitigate double taxation. From this perspective, the rule itself does not allocate any tax jurisdiction. On the other hand, it is clear that the method provision is closely linked with the tax jurisdiction allocation rules. However, the Court's confusing terminology gives rise to debate. It could have avoided this, because for its ultimate decision, I do not believe that it is really relevant. The Court's other argu-

89 The question reads as follows: "If not, does it make a difference in this case that the Netherlands has, under a bilateral treaty, granted to residents of Belgium, who in all other respects are in comparable circumstances, entitlement to the tax allowance (no wealth tax being levied in Belgium either)?"

ments are strong enough to mitigate this confusing terminology. Furthermore, as advocated above, I believe that Article 25, paragraph 3 of the tax treaty between Belgium-the Netherlands (1970) itself was a tax jurisdiction allocation rule. It was this provision and not Article 24 on which the claim of MFN treatment was based in the D. case. Therefore, Article 24 was not really relevant for that claim and could be left aside for answering the preliminary question.

4.2.2 Appreciation

The Court's observation that Article 25, paragraph 3 of the tax treaty between Belgium-the Netherlands (1970) confered rights on individuals who were residents of one the contracting States was completely right. They was entitled in the other contracting state to the personal allowances which that state granted to its own residents by reason of their civil status or dependants. Therefore, the Court's starting-point deviated completely from the Advocate General's opinion. As argued above, the Court was perfectly right in doing so.

I believe that the Court's analysis that Article 25, paragraph 3 of the tax treaty between Belgium-the Netherlands (1970) included reciprocal rights (for taxpayers in both Belgium and the Netherlands) and obligations (for both Belgium and the Netherlands) was right and convincing as well.

Furthermore, I feel that the Court's argument that the provision is part of the reciprocal rights and obligations of the tax treaty as whole was also very convincing. The provision was indeed an integral part of the bilateral tax treaty. In conjunction with this argument, the Courts drew the appropriate conclusion that the bilateral tax treaty provisions only applied to residents of one of the two the contracting states. As argued above, the ultimate tax position of residents of the contracting states is determined by the taxpayers' individual circumstances and the tax treaty as whole in conjunction with the domestic tax law systems of the contracting states. Some tax treaty provisions may be more beneficial than others. Whether that is the case not only depends on these rules, but also on the taxpayers' individual circumstances. If we want to compare tax treaties, we have to take into account the complete tax treaties and not only separate provisions. Otherwise, we are comparing situations that are by their nature non-comparable. Therefore, it is indeed an inherent consequence of a bilateral tax treaty that its provisions only apply to residents of one of the two the contracting states. The subsequent conclusion that a resident of a contracting state (in the D. case, a resident of Belgium) is not in a comparable situation to a non-resident of that contracting state (in the D. case Mr D. resident of Germany) is therefore persuasive as well.

The same is true for the argument that Article 25, paragraph 3 of the tax treaty between Belgium-the Netherlands (1970) could not be separated from the remainder of this treaty. It was part of bilateral tax treaty as whole which was the result of the negotiation (give and take) process between Belgium and the Netherlands in which, as a rule, Germany did not play any role. Therefore, the provision was indeed an integral part of this bilateral tax treaty and it contributed indeed to the overall balance of that treaty.

4.2.3 Member States do not have complete liberty to include any rule in a bilateral tax treaty

By no means should the Member States interpret the D. ruling as a licence to include in a bilateral tax treaty any rule which they like. I do not share the fear expressed in the tax literature that this would be a consequence of this ruling.[90] For instance, Van Thiel argued that, according to the logic of the D. decision, a Member State such as the Netherlands could in a first step set certain maximum CO_2 emission levels for imported cars or a minimum VAT rate of 18 % for intra-Community acquisitions, and subsequently in a second step agree bilaterally with one other Member State, for instance Belgium, to apply lower maximum CO_2 emission levels for cars imported from Belgium and to set a 16 % VAT rate for intra-Community acquisitions from Belgium. I do not believe that is consistent with the logic of the D. ruling.

First of all, although the Member States are at liberty to determine by means of bilateral tax treaties the connecting factors for the purposes of allocating taxation rights among themselves,[91] they nevertheless may not disregard Community rules as far as the exercise of the right of taxation so allocated is concerned.[92] The Court repeated this line of reasoning in

90 See, eg, Weber, Most-Favoured-Nation Treatment under Tax Treaties Rejected in the European Community: Background and Analysis of the *D.* Case, *Intertax* 2005, pp 440-441; and van Thiel, A Slip of the European Court in the D Case (C-376/03): Denial of the Most-Favoured-Nation Treatment because of Absence of Similarity, *Intertax* 2005, pp 454-457.

91 However, this must be seen in the context of determining the criteria for taxation of income and wealth with a view to eliminating double taxation.

92 See, eg, ECJ 12 May 1998, C-336/96 *Gilly* [1998] ECR I-2793, paras 24 and 30; and 21 September 1999, C-307/97 *Saint-Gobain* [1999] ECR I-6161, paras 56-57.

the D. ruling.[93] Secondly, a rule as suggested by Van Thiel is by no means an integral part of a bilateral tax treaty on income and capital since it has nothing to do with the allocation of tax jurisdiction on income or capital. Therefore, such a rule cannot contribute to the overall balance of the relevant tax treaty. As a result, such a rule is indeed separable from the remainder of the bilateral tax treaty in which it has been included. The same is true in respect of domestic tax law rules which are incompatible with EC law. Including them in a bilateral tax treaty will not make them unassailable. Furthermore, it is the Court itself that has to make the ultimate assessment. Therefore, the Court itself will be the watchdog to guarantee that Member States will not abuse tax treaties to frustrate the internal market or to make the Court's body of case law inoperative.

5 Future of Most-favoured-nation Treatment?

In any case, based on the D. ruling, it is clear that the basic allowance and basic tax credit to which residents of Belgium were entitled in the Netherlands by virtue of a specific provision under the tax treaty Belgium-the Netherlands (1970) may not be invoked by residents of other Member States, like Germany, because they cannot rely on an MFN treatment under the fundamental freedoms. As a consequence, Mr Bujura is not be entitled to the basic allowance and basic tax credit that he claimed.

Whether the MFN treatment still has a future after the D. ruling may be debated. As argued above, a more solid motivation of the D. case could have prevented that debate. In this respect, I would like to distinguish two groups of debaters: optimists versus realists. Optimists may believe that there is still life for MFN treatment after the D. ruling for bilateral tax treaties provisions which itself are not of reciprocal nature or which are not tax jurisdiction allocation rules. Striking examples may be: a tax sparing credit to be granted only by the state of residence or a tax credit for dividends to be granted only by the state of source.[94] Realists, in which group I include myself, believe that these provisions will not be susceptible to MFN treatment. Such provisions are also an integral part of the bilateral tax treaty involved and contribute also to the overall balance of that treaty. Therefore, they cannot be separated from the bilateral tax convention in which they have been included. For instance, a state may be willing to give a tax sparing credit because the other state accepts the inclusion of a

[93] See ECJ 5 July 2002, C-376/03 *D.*, not yet reported, para 56.

[94] See, eg, ECJ C-374/04 *Test Claimants in Class IV of the ACT Group Litigation.*

turn-key provision in respect of permanent establishments. Therefore, application of bilateral tax treaty provisions which itself are not of reciprocal nature or which are not tax jurisdiction allocation rules is also open only to residents of one of the two contracting states. That is an inherent consequence of a bilateral tax treaty, since a taxable resident of one of the contracting states is not in the same position as a taxable person resident outside that contracting state. This implies that the MFN treatment claimed in Test Claimants in Class IV of the ACT Group Litigation has to be turned down as well.

Furthermore, it has been suggested to supplement Article I-4 of the Treaty establishing the Constitution for Europe with an MFN clause (see italicised text):

1. The free movement of persons, services, goods and capital, and freedom of establishment shall be guaranteed within and by the Union, in accordance with the Constitution.
2. Within the scope of the Constitution, and without prejudice to any of its specific provisions, any discrimination on grounds of nationality shall be prohibited *and under the provisions on freedom of movement each situation shall be treated by a Member State in the same way.*
3. *The provision in paragraph 2 does not preclude measures in multilateral of bilateral agreements concluded between the Member States that make a distinction between Member States in the allocation of taxation rights for the avoidance of double taxation and the prevention of tax avoidance.*
4. *The measures in paragraph 3 shall not form a means of discrimination nor a disguised restriction of the freedom of movement.*[95]

If such a clause were to be included and the Treaty would be enacted in the end, it would be up to the European Court of Justice to interpret this provision. If, the Court's approach were similar to its approach in respect of the current Article 58 EC Treaty, the additional value of the MFN were clause would not be very high. As a consequence of the Verkooijen ruling, Article 58 EC Treaty does not contribute anything to the Court's rule of reason case law. The basis for the Court's decision was Article 58, paragraph 3 EC Treaty, which provision is quite comparable to the suggested Article I-4, paragraph 4. Therefore, Article I-4 offers the Court the opportunity to uphold its decisions such as the D. ruling.

95 See Weber, Most-Favoured-Nation Treatment under Tax Treaties Rejected in the European Community: Background and Analysis of the *D.* Case, Intertax 2005, pp 443-444.

IV Conclusions

In the Van Dijk case, the Dutch 1997 exit tax charge on substantial interest shareholdings was comparable to the French one, which was in dispute in the De Lasteyrie du Saillant ruling. The French exit charge was incompatible with thefundamental right of establishment. The Dutch exit tax charge was incompatible with the freedom to move and reside freely within the territories of Member States. The exit charge tax assessment itself triggered by the emigration of Van Dijk to the UK and the non-automatic and conditional deferment of payment of the tax owed did constitute two separate restrictions of freedom embedded in Article 18 EC Treaty. The release of the security in 2004 could not take away with retroactive effect a restriction of this freedom in 1997. The restrictions could not be justified. Like the French exit charge in the De Lasteyrie du Saillant ruling, the aim of the Dutch 1997 exit charge was to prevent tax avoidance and not to ensure fiscal coherence. Again like the French exit charge, the Dutch 1997 exit charge was not proportional to its aim. Therefore, the Dutch system was also inconsistent with the fundamental freedoms. The Arnhem Court should have drawn this conclusion from the existing body of case law. Therefore, it should not have asked preliminary questions. Considering that states want to claim tax jurisdiction in cases in which a substantial interest shareholder transfers (temporarily) his residence outside their territory exclusively for tax reasons and on the increased in value acquired during the taxpayer's residence on their territory, the residence-based compartimentalisation system has been developed, which is EU and DTCproof and which makes exit charges as we know them now superfluous.

The Bujura case is highly comparable to the D. ruling. Because of this ruling, it is clear that a basic allowance or a basic tax credit to which residents of Belgium were entitled in the Netherlands by virtue of a specific provision under the tax treaty Belgium-the Netherlands (1970) may not be invoked by residents of other Member States, like Germany, because they may not rely on an MFN treatment under the fundamental freedoms. As a consequence, Mr Bujura is not entitled to the basic allowance and basic tax credit that he claimed. As the Bujura case illustrates perfectly, the Advocate General's Opinion in the D. case was untenable. On the other hand, the D. ruling is very sound decision. However, it could and should have been motivated more solidly, which would have enhanced its degree of appreciation. By no means should the Member States interpret the D. ruling as a licence to include in a bilateral tax treaty any rule which they like. In the context of bilateral tax treaties, there will be no future for a claim to MFN treatment based on the fundamental freedoms. It is questionable whether an MFN clause in the Treaty establishing the Constitution for Europe will add much value.

Pending Cases Filed by Dutch Courts II: The Van Hilten-van der Heijden case

Pending Cases before Dutch Courts: "Bosal Holding" with third countries

Dennis Weber

1 Introduction

2 The facts in the pending cases

2.1 Van Hilten-van der Heijden

2.2 "Bosal Holding" with third countries

3 Van Hilten-Van der Heijden: Overt discrimination on grounds of nationality or restriction?

3.1 Introduction: the decision of the Court of Appeals of 's-Hertogenbosch

3.2 The nationality requirement: overt discrimination on grounds of nationality

3.3 Restriction of the freedom of movement?

4 Exercise of the free movement of capital between the Member States and third countries

5 Scope of the free movement of capital

6 Standstill clause of Article 57(1) EC

7 Conclusion

Free movement of capital between the Member States and third countries, nationality requirements, and the credit method

The Van Hilten-van der Heijden case and "Bosal Holding" with third countries

1 Introduction

Article 56 EC not only prohibits all restrictions of capital movements and payments between the Member States themselves but also all restrictions of such movements between the Member States and third countries.

The geographic scope of the free movement of capital and payments is thus broader than that of the other Treaty freedoms. The free movement of capital is also being exercised when a Spanish resident holds shares in a company established in, for example, the United States. The applicability of Article 56 EC to dealings with third countries has been described by Advocate General Geelhoed as "unique"[1].

The Community has unilaterally opened its capital market to the rest of the world. However, it is not clear whether the scope of the free movement of capital and payments with third countries is just as broad as it is within the EC. In addition, the scope of the standstill clause in Article 57(1) EC has to be clarified. The Van Hilten-van der Heijden case and in a case presently before the Netherlands Supreme Court (Hoge Raad) which is similar to the factual constellation in the Bosal Holding case deal with the scope of the free movement of capital and the standstill clause. This contribution discusses these issues[2].

2 The facts in the pending cases

2.1 Van Hilten-van der Heijden

In the Van Hilten-van der Heijden case (C-513/03) a woman with the Dutch nationality moved to Switzerland and in 1997, within ten years of

1 See opinion of AG Geelhoed in *Ospelt* (ECJ 23 September 2003, C-452/01 *Ospelt* [1993] ECR I-9743), 10 April 2003, para 33.

2 Other cases on the free movement of capital between the Member States and third countries are: ECJ C-492/04 *Lasertec*, pending; C-524/04 *Thin Cap Group Litigation*, pending; C-101/05 *Skatteverket v A*, pending; C-102/05 *Skatteverket v A and B*, pending; C-157/05 *Holböck*, pending; C-201/05 *Test Claimants in the CFC and Dividend Group Litigation*, pending.

her emigration, passed away there. Under the residence fiction in Article 3(1) of the Law on Succession 1956 (Sucessiewet 1956) she was deemed to be a resident of the Netherlands. Consequently, her entire estate (no matter where it was located worldwide) was taxed in the Netherlands. This fiction applies only if the testator has the Dutch nationality. Its aim is to combat tax avoidance that consists in a taxpayer who moves to another state of residence in order to avoid the levy of Netherlands inheritance tax.

The estate in Van Hilten-van der Heijden consisted of immovable property situated in the Netherlands, Belgium and Switzerland and further, apart from some personal effects, of stocks held as investment that were listed on the stock exchanges in the Netherlands, Germany, Switzerland and the United States, along with bank accounts held in and administered by Dutch and Belgian branches of various banks established in the European Community.

In its decision of 5 November 2003[3] the Court of Appeals of 's-Hertogenbosch held that the free movement of capital between a third country and the Member States is applicable, that there is overt discrimination on grounds of nationality and a restriction of the freedom of movement and finally that the standstill clause of Article 57(1) is not applicable. Since there is no European Court of Justice (ECJ) case law on this issue, the 's-Hertogenbosch Court decided to refer two preliminary questions to the ECJ:

1) Does Article 3(1) of the Netherlands Successiewet (Law on Succession) constitute a permitted restriction within the meaning of Article 57(1) EC?
2) Does Article 3(1) of the Successiewet constitute a prohibited means of arbitrary discrimination or a disguised restriction on the free movement of capital within the meaning of Article 58(3) EC where applicable to a capital movement between a Member State and a non-member country, having regard also to the Declaration on Article 73d of the Treaty establishing the European Community adopted on the occasion of the signature of the „Final Act and Declarations of the Intergovernmental Conferences on the European Union" of 7 February 1992?

[3] 's-Hertogenbosch 5 November 2003, no. 02/01531 FED 2004/427 (annotation by S.C.W. Douma).

Advocate General Léger published his Opinion in this case on 30 June 2005. Since he believes that there is no prohibited discrimination on grounds of nationality and no restriction of the freedom of movement, he did not go into a discussion of the scope of the free movement of capital with third countries. Neither did he examine the standstill provision of Article 57(1) EC.

2.2 "Bosal Holding" with third countries

A case is pending before the Netherlands Supreme Court in which the issues are similar to those in the Bosal Holding decision[4]. At issue is a Netherlands regulation which allows participation costs[5] of the parent company to be deducted only if the profits of the subsidiary were derived in the Netherlands. The regulation is applicable to participations of 5 % or more in the capital of the subsidiary. In the Bosal Holding decision the ECJ had held that the regulation was not compatible with the freedom of establishment.

In the case presently before the Supreme Court a parent company resident in the Netherlands had majority participations in subsidiaries in various non-EC countries in the years 2000 and 2001. In its decision of 2 March 2005[6] the Court of Appeals of Amsterdam ruled that the free movement of capital with third countries had been exercised and that there was a restriction of the freedom of movement. However, the restriction in the case at hand was permitted under the standstill clause of Article 57(1) EC. An appeal (cassation) has been brought before the Supreme Court.

3 Van Hilten-van der Heijden: Overt discrimination on grounds of nationality or restriction?

3.1 Introduction: the decision of the Court of Appeals of 's-Hertogenbosch

Mrs Van Hilten-van der Heijden was deemed to be a resident of the Netherlands under the residence fiction of Article 3(1) of the Law on Succession 1956. As a consequence, her entire estate was taxed in the

---

4 ECJ 18 September 2003, C-168/01 *Bosal* [2003] ECR I-9409.

5 To be specific, interest expenses paid on a loan taken out to acquire a participation are involved.

6 Hof Amsterdam 2 March 2005, No. 04/2310, FED 2005/81, with annotation by E. Thomas. See also Smits, Deductibility of costs in connection with a participation in the capital of a subsidiary, *European Taxation* 2005, p 359.

Netherlands. This fiction applies only if the testator dies within ten years of emigrating from the Netherlands and has the Dutch nationality. If Mrs Van Hilten had been in exactly the same circumstances but she had had the French nationality, her worldwide assets would not have been taxed. In the instant case the Court of Appeals of 's-Hertogenbosch was of the opinion that on the grounds of the D'Hoop decision[7] there was discrimination of citizens of the Union, since if a testator has the Dutch nationality more inheritance tax is levied than if the testator has another nationality: in short, because the Netherlands structurally only levies compensatory tax but never refunds it. The national court held that i) there was overt discrimination on grounds of nationality and ii) that the credit method used by the Netherlands for the avoidance of double taxation was a restriction of the freedom of movement because the Netherlands levies compensatory tax if less inheritance tax is levied abroad than in the Netherlands but it does not refund or credit tax if more inheritance tax is levied abroad than in the Netherlands. Since in the view of the national court it was not clear whether the free movement of capital between the Member States and a third country was also being restricted, it referred a preliminary question on this matter to the ECJ (the second preliminary question).

3.2 The nationality requirement: overt discrimination on grounds of nationality

Unlike the Court of Appeals of 's-Hertogenbosch, Advocate General Léger is of the opinion that the nationality requirement is not prohibited discrimination on grounds of nationality. This is because i) this is not a situation in which a national of a Member State who has availed himself of the freedom of movement is treated worse than a national who did not avail himself of the freedoms; ii) the Member States retain the competence to determine the criteria for the allocation of taxation rights for the avoidance of double taxation (the Gilly decision[8]) and iii) it is not unreasonable for the Member States to follow international practice and the Model Estate Tax Convention drafted by the OECD when exercising their sovereignty in the area of taxation. According to Léger, the Netherlands regulation is compatible with the system the Fiscal Committee describes in the Commentaries on the OECD Model Convention. It is striking that Advocate General Wattel (of the Netherlands Supreme Court) came to the

7 ECJ 11 July 2002, C-224/98 *D'Hoop* [2002] ECR I-6191.
8 ECJ 12 May 1998, C-336/96 *Gilly* [1998] ECR I-2793.

opposite conclusion in a similar case that is before the Supreme Court[9]. Wattel argues that the Gilly decision clearly differs from the problem in the Dutch case. In the case at hand there is no allocation of jurisdiction (un-doubling) on the basis of nationality (as in Gilly), but rather of an establishment of jurisdiction on the basis of nationality. In the case at hand making a link to nationality creates double taxation. According to Wattel, what the Court permitted in Gilly is an un-doubling of source state taxation and residence state taxation on the basis of nationality as the allocation criterion and not its opposite: discriminatory doubling of taxation on grounds of nationality. One could add that in the case at hand it is an anti-avoidance measure that is at stake (to combat tax flight). I do not see why such an anti-avoidance measure should only cover persons having the Dutch nationality. Aren't persons having the French nationality likely to exhibit the same tendency to flee from taxation? I believe that the ten-year term should consequently be applied to all nationalities and not just to those having the Dutch nationality.

3.3 Restriction of the freedom of movement?

The Court of Appeals of 's-Hertogenbosch was of the opinion that the credit method used by the Netherlands for the avoidance of double taxation is, in principle, a restriction of the freedom of movement. This is because the Netherlands does levy compensatory tax if less inheritance tax is levied abroad than in the Netherlands, but does not give a refund or a credit if more inheritance tax is levied abroad.

Advocate General Léger observed with respect to this point that, in his opinion, the credit method is not a restriction of the freedom of movement because there is no restriction on leaving the country, since the only capital movement that is affected is the passing by inheritance of the testator's estate. In addition, according to the Advocate General, the fact that there is no refund of tax if the inheritance tax levied abroad is higher is not a restriction either. In his view, this can be ascribed to the fact that the national provisions on inheritance tax have not been harmonized. According to the Advocate General, because of this lack of harmonization the Treaty is not able to guarantee a citizen of the Union that moving his activities or simply moving his residence from his former residence state to another state will be completely fiscally neutral. He refers in this regard to the Gilly decision and to the Lindfors decision[10].

---

9 Opinion of Advocate General Wattel of 7 July 2004, No. 39.261.

10 ECJ 15 July 2004, C-365/02 *Lindfors* [2004] ECR I-7183.

In the above-mentioned Opinion, Advocate General Wattel also discussed whether the credit method is a restriction of the freedom of movement. In his opinion, the heirs of Dutch emigrants face a possible disadvantage that heirs of residents and beneficiaries of non-Dutch emigrants do not. Since the new state of residence also has a claim to taxation (in the instant case not only on grounds of residence but the situs or source principle as well) double taxation arises, which has to be avoided, and which is avoided inconsistently in the credit method used by the Netherlands (asymmetrical effect of the ordinary credit method): The Netherlands levies compensatory tax if the foreign rate is lower but does not give a refund if it is higher. The Netherlands also levies compensatory tax if the rates are reasonable by Dutch standards. According to Wattel, one may not draw the conclusion from the Gilly decision that the ECJ has held that such an asymmetrical effect (compensatory tax levied but no refund if the foreign tax is higher than the domestic tax) is compatible with the free movement of persons. The French method that was being examined in Gilly was called a "credit" but what was being credited was not the German tax, but rather the French tax that would be levied on the Gillys' German income. It is thus clear that the Gilly decision was not about credit, but instead about exemption. The ECJ did not give any holding whatsoever – it was also not at issue - on the permissibility of compensatory taxation by the residence state if the work state taxation is lower than the residence state taxation. According to Advocate General Wattel, the ECJ made neither a positive nor a negative statement in the Gilly decision about the "possibility of a disadvantage" that the Court of Appeals of 's-Hertogenbosch had considered to be a restriction of the movement of capital.

According to Wattel, the Netherlands extraterritorial taxation of ex-residents on grounds of their nationality by the granting a credit for inheritance taxes levied abroad may be a restriction of the movement of capital that needs to be justified: after all, residents of the Netherlands may, as was held in the Sandóz decision[11], be discouraged from moving to another EC Member State because they (their heirs) do not have "the possibility of benefiting from the absence of taxation" abroad, viz. the lower inheritance tax rate in the new residence state of the testator. After all, the Netherlands is levying – as worded in Eurowings[12] - a "compensatory tax levy" that "prejudice[s] the very foundations of the single market". And,

[11] ECJ 14 October 1999, C-439/97 *Sandoz* [1999] ECR I-7041.

[12] ECJ 26 October 1999, C-294/97 *Eurowings* [1999] ECR I-7447.

according to the Advocate General, the Netherlands levies compensatory tax even though – in the wording of ICI[13] and Lankhorst[14] – receiving the inheritance "will in any event be subject to the tax legislation of the State of establishment" of the testator. In Wattel's view, the credit system is indeed inconsistent, protectionist, and restrictive and hence incompatible with an internal market if the taxable item in the other Member State is taxed there at the normal rate. However, he is not certain that in cases not involving the avoidance of double taxation the ECJ has casually blown up the credit system. He thinks that preliminary questions on this general issue should be put to the ECJ. In the instant case, however, this is unnecessary, because the national regulation in itself is discriminatory on grounds of nationality. For this reason alone, in the Advocate General's view, it is incompatible with Community law (for more details, see above). Moreover, Advocate General Wattel thinks that there is a restriction because the heirs face an administrative burden (double assessments, requests to avoid double taxation and so on) and that they possibly face a cash-flow disadvantage that they would not have in a domestic context and that non-Dutch citizens do not have to cope with.

I myself wonder whether the credit method in itself is incompatible with the EC Treaty freedoms. It may be in conflict with the objective of the internal market, as Wattel argues, but whether it is a restriction of the freedom of movement is debatable. When you use the credit method, you are actually simply applying your own tax system and granting a credit for foreign tax. It is measure without distinction. If no credit were given, the residence state would levy compensatory tax under its own tax system and there would be double taxation. By crediting the foreign tax the real double taxation is removed. In my view, one cannot say that under the credit method compensatory tax is levied in the event the residence state has a higher rate than the source state. The residence state does not levy compensatory tax but is simply applying its own tax system with its own tax bases and tax rates. Hence, in my opinion, the credit system is not asymmetrical: you tax on the basis of the rules of your own tax system and grant relief for double taxation only to the extent there is double taxation. This means that where taxation in the residence state is higher than in the source state you do not have to give more relief than for the tax that was levied abroad and where taxation in the residence state is lower than in the

13 ECJ 16 July 1998, C-264/96 *ICI* [1998] ECR I-4695.

14 ECJ 12 December 2002, C-324/00 *Lankhorst-Hohorst* [2002] ECR I-11779.

source state you do not have to refund the foreign tax. If you were to do so, you would be doing a lot more than granting relief for double taxation: as residence state, you would actually be giving up all of your taxation rights. A credit method is instead really an example of the application of mutual recognition: you recognize the taxation of the other state by giving a credit for it, but you may still levy your own tax. I believe that the credit method for the avoidance of double taxation meets the EC standard. In this regard one could draw a parallel with the VAT case Gaston Schul[15].

4 Exercise of the free movement of capital between the Member States and third countries

In the Van Hilten-van der Heijden case an inheritance passed from the testators to the heirs. According to the national court, this is a capital movement between a third state and the Member States since the nomenclature contained in Annex 1 of Directive 88/361/EEC lists (under point XI, personal capital movements) "(…) inheritances and legacies (…)" as a capital movement.

In the Supreme Court case on the EC law compatibility of the deduction of costs that is similar to Bosal Holding, there is a more extensive discussion of the exercise of the free movement of capital and third countries. According to the tax inspector, the free movement of capital was not exercised in this case because majority interests in subsidiaries established in third countries are involved. On the grounds of the Baars decision[16] when there is a majority interest only the right of establishment is applicable, but, according to the tax inspector, this right is not applicable to establishment in a third country. The taxpayer countered this with the argument that the right of establishment as laid down in the EC Treaty is not applicable where a participation is held in a company established in a third country (see para. 31 to 33, inclusive of the ICI decision). Therefore, in the instant case, the right of establishment as laid down in the EC Treaty may not be invoked. The limitation on the deduction of costs hence cannot impede the right of establishment, since in the instant case the right of establishment may not be exercised. Consequently, in the instant case we do not have to look at whether the right of establishment takes precedence over one of the other Treaty freedoms (for example, the free movement of

15 ECJ 5 May 1982, 15/81, *Gaston Schul* [1982] ECR 1409. For a more in-depth discussion of this point-of-view, see Weber, Tax Avoidance and the EC Treaty Freedoms (2005) p 153.

16 ECJ 13 April 2000, C-251/98 *Baars* [2000] ECR I-2787.

capital – see below), since the right of establishment is not applicable whatsoever and thus, in the taxpayer's view, cannot take precedence. The taxpayer's position that the free movement of capital between a Member State and a third country is applicable was followed by the Court of Appeals of Amsterdam and is presently before the Supreme Court.

5 Scope of the free movement of capital

The text of Article 56 EC does not give grounds to assume that there is a difference between the ECJ's interpretation of the free movement of capital between the Member States themselves and between the Member States and third countries. Nevertheless, in the literature the observation has been rightly made that, given the more limited objective of the free movement of capital between the Member States and third countries compared to the free movement of capital within the EC, the former should actually be interpreted more narrowly[17]. The objective within the EC is, in fact, an internal market based on solidarity, while the free movement of capital between the Member States and third countries does not have this aim. Furthermore, the free movement of capital with third countries is unilateral and since there is a lack of reciprocity it is not based on solidarity. What the precise objective of the free movement of capital between the Member States is remains vague. In the proceedings before the Supreme Court on the limitation of the deduction of costs the Netherlands Under-Minister of Finance argued that the free movement of capital with third countries was introduced in response to the desire to ensure the importance and the credibility of the single currency (the Euro) in the financial markets and to keep international financial centers within the EU[18].

Since it is not unlikely that the free movement of capital with third countries has a more limited objective than within the EC, I can imagine that in certain situations there may be an objective difference between the free movement of capital within the EC and with third countries. Advocate General Kokott also pointed out in her Opinion in Manninen that there may be an objective difference[19]. It is therefore, in my opinion, not the case that principles that are the foundation of the internal market, such as

---

17 See, for example, Ståhl, Free movement of capital between member States and third countries, *EC Tax Review* 2004, p 47.

18 Reference is made to Hebing/Lichtenhahn in Léger (ed) *Commentaire article par article des traités UE et CE* (2000), p 485.

19 Opinion of AG Kokott in *Manninen* (ECJ 7 September 2004, C-319/02 *Manninen* [2004] ECR I-74771), 18 March 2004, para 79.

the principle of the mutual recognition of national rules, which are based on the mutual solidarity of the Member States, are applicable to the free movement of capital and payments with third countries. It is very much an open question whether the ECJ's case law that is based on or inspired by the principle of mutual recognition may be extended to the freedom of movement with third countries. The Eurowings decision[20] can serve as an example. In this decision lease payments were only deductible if the lessor was subject to the German Gewerbesteuer. As a result, Eurowings could not deduct all of its lease payments because the lessor was resident in Ireland (and was taxed there at a rate of only 10 %). The ECJ held that "such compensatory tax arrangements prejudice the very foundations of the single market". In the framework of the principle of mutual recognition, this means that Germany must "recognize" the lower taxation in Ireland and that this unpleasant disparity may not be removed by levying compensatory tax (in the case at hand, by refusing the deduction of lease payments). The Eurowings decision is consequently understandable since within the internal market the level of another state's tax rates must be recognized. Nevertheless, it does not appear that such a duty of mutual recognition exists with regard to third countries. In concrete terms, this means that a compensatory tax test might very well be allowed in relations with a third country. It should be noted, however, that the compensatory tax test in Eurowings was a very strict one. There had to be a compensatory tax in Germany. It would seem to me to be correcter to argue that the requirements of compensatory taxation (for example, in the case of the deduction of rental payments) call for a tax that is comparable to a domestic tax. This would make compensatory taxes more neutral and would also subsume taxes in third countries.

In the case currently before the Supreme Court, the Court of Appeals of Amsterdam, just as in Bosal Holding, held that the limitation of the deduction of costs was a restriction of the freedom of movement. In doing so, it did not pay any attention to whether the scope of the free movement of capital is broad enough to include non-EC countries. As mentioned above, this issue has been discussed during the appeal proceedings, so that it is to be expected that the Supreme Court will give a holding on this and most likely will make a reference for a preliminary ruling.

20 ECJ 16 October 1999, C-294/97 *Eurowings* [1999] ECR I-7447.

6 Standstill clause of Article 57(1) EC

The movement of capital with third countries is limited by the standstill clause of Article 57(1) EC according to which "the provisions of Article 56 shall be without prejudice to the application to third countries of any restrictions which exist on 31 December 1993 under national or Community law adopted in respect of the movement of capital to or from third countries involving

- direct investment – including in real estate –
- establishment,
- the provision of financial services or
  - the admission of securities to capital markets".

"Restrictions under Community law" refers to the exceptions that were allowed under Article 6 of Directive 88/361/EEC on the liberalisation of capital movements. It should be observed that on the grounds of Article 73E EC Treaty the Member States were permitted to maintain the exceptions that were allowed under Community law until 31 December 1995, at the latest. This article was cancelled by the Treaty of Amsterdam.

In the Sanz de Lera decision[21] the ECJ held that "the exception provided for in Article [57(1)] of the Treaty concerning the application to non-member countries of the restrictions existing on 31 December 1993 under national law or Community law regarding the capital movements listed in it to or from non-member countries is precisely worded, with the result that no latitude is granted to the Member States or the Community legislature regarding either the date of applicability of the restrictions or the categories of capital movements which may be subject to restrictions". The exception must be interpreted strictly. The tax measures must be a restriction in respect of the movement of capital to or from third countries involving the categories of capital movements mentioned in Article 57(1) EC. According to the Court of Appeals of 's-Hertogenbosch in the Van Hilten-van der Heijden case, the restrictive provision in the Law on Succession 1956 (the ten-year fiction in Article 3(1)) does not fall under the standstill clause because it has to do with the passing of an "inheritance" to the heirs and not to one of the categories of capital movement mentioned in Article 57(1) EC. The Court has referred a preliminary question to the ECJ on this interpretation. In his Opinion of 30 June 2005,

[21] ECJ 14 December 1995, C-163/94, 165/94, and 250/94 *Sanz de Lera* [1995] ECR I-4821.

Advocate General Léger did not discuss the issues with respect to Article 57(1) EC because in his view there was no discrimination (and he thus did not get to an analysis of the application of the standstill provision in Article 57(1) EC).

What is meant by "direct investment" in the sense of Article 57(1) EC is unclear. In the nomenclature to Directive 88/361[22] direct investments are defined as "I-1. Establishment and extension of branches or new undertakings belonging solely to the person providing the capital, and the acquisition in full of existing undertakings". The explanatory notes to the nomenclature add that "the undertakings mentioned under I-1 of the Nomenclature include legally independent undertakings (wholly-owned subsidiaries) and branches". In addition, direct investments are defined in the nomenclature as "I-2. Participation in new or existing undertakings with a view to establishing or maintaining lasting economic links". In the explanatory notes to Directive 88/361 on the liberalisation of capital movements the observation is made that "direct investments" means: "Investments of all kinds by natural persons or commercial, industrial or financial undertakings, and which serve to establish or to maintain lasting and direct links between the person providing the capital and the entrepreneur to whom or the undertaking to which the capital is made available in order to carry on an economic activity. This concept must therefore be understood in its widest sense" and "As regards those undertakings mentioned under I-2 of the Nomenclature which have the status of companies limited by shares, there is participation in the nature of direct investment where the block of shares held by a natural person of another undertaking or any other holder enables the shareholder, either pursuant to the provisions of national laws relating to companies limited by shares or otherwise, to participate effectively in the management of the company or in its control". In Case C-174/04 Commission v Italy[23], among other cases, the ECJ held, with a reference to the nomenclature in the Annex to Directive 88/361 and the explanatory notes, that "a direct investment, in particular, is characterised by the possibility of participating effectively in the management and control of a company" (see paras 28 and 30 of the decision). This means that direct investments clearly means majority interests.

[22] See the nomenclature in Annex I of Council Directive 88/361/EEC of 24 June 1988 for the implementation of Article 67 of the Treaty, OJ L 178 , 08/07/1988, p 5. Compare also the observation of AG Tesauro in *Sanz de Lera* (ECJ 14 December 1995, C-163/94, 165/94, and 250/94 *Sanz de Lera* [1995] ECR I-4821), para 14.

[23] ECJ 2 June 2005, C-174/04 *Commission v Italy*, not yet reported.

It would therefore seem that the standstill clause may only be invoked if there is the possibility of actually participating in the management and control of a company (in other words: when there is a majority interest). The issue is whether a measure that covers both minority and majority interests is protected by the standstill clause. In the case before the Supreme Court on the EC-compatibility of the Netherlands limitation of the deduction of costs, the issue has been raised whether this measure is connected to capital movements that involve direct investment. The limitation on the deduction of costs is applicable to participations of 5 % and more in the capital of the subsidiary, in other words both minority and majority participations. The Court of Appeals of Amsterdam held in the decision that is being appealed that in this specific factual constellation there can be said to be a measure connected to a direct investment since in the instant case there is a majority participation and thus a direct investment. The Court of Appeals of Amsterdam hence does not consider it relevant that the national measure itself includes situations in which there is no direct investment (viz. minority interests) but considers it decisive that the participation is a direct investment on factual grounds. The Supreme Court will in all probability refer a preliminary question to the ECJ on these issues. This preliminary question will have to deal with whether under Article 57(1) EC there must be a direct investment on factual grounds or whether the national measure in itself has cover direct investment.

Another question that may come up is whether the measures that were enacted in the legislation after 31 December 1993 can still fall under the standstill clause. The Konle decision could be applied by analogy[24]. In that decision the ECJ observed with regard to Article 70 of the Act of Accession of Austria[25]: "Thus, if [a measure] is, in substance, identical to the previous legislation or if it is limited to reducing or eliminating an obstacle to the exercise of Community rights and freedoms in the earlier legislation, it will be covered by the derogation [the standstill provision of Article 57(1) EC]".

---

24 ECJ 1 June 1999, C-302/97 *Konle* [1999] ECR I-3099. This decision was analogously applied to Art 57(1) EC by AG Geelhoed in his Opinion 5on ECJ 23 September 2003, C-452/01 *Ospelt* [1993] ECR I-9743 and by Hof Amsterdam 2 March 2005, No. 04/02310, V-N 2005/16.9.

25 Article 70 of the Act of Accession provides: "Notwithstanding the obligations under the Treaties on which the European Union is founded, the Republic of Austria may maintain its existing legislation regarding secondary residences for five years from the date of accession." OJ 1994, C 241, p 21 and OJ 1995, L 1, p 1.

In the Lasertec case (C-492/04) the issue is whether the German thin capitalization rules are incompatible with the free movement of capital and third countries. Such thin capitalization rules are discriminatory and within the EC infringe the right of establishment (compare Lankhort-Hohorst[26]). In Lasertec an interest payment was made from Germany to Switzerland (a third country). The deduction of the interest paid was disallowed in Germany under the thin capitalization rules. The issue is whether the Lankhorst-Hohorst decision can be extended to the free movement of capital and third countries. At stake here are the conditions that had to be met on 31 December 1993 in order for a rule to fall under the standstill provision. The German thin capitalization rules were in force on 1 January 1994 but had been enacted by the German parliament and published at an earlier date. At issue is whether there may be said to a measure that existed on 31 December 1993 under national law[27].

6 Conclusion

In Van Hilten-van der Heijden the extent to which making a link to nationality in order to extend a state's tax jurisdiction is at issue, along with the important issue of whether the credit method for the avoidance of double taxation is incompatible with the freedom of movement. The Van Hilten-van der Heijden case and the "Bosal Holding with third countries" case deal with the scope of the free movement of capital between Member States and third countries and the standstill provision of Article 57(1) EC. All of which are significant issues with respect to the relationship between Community law and provisions in the direct tax law of the Member States. We eagerly await the final decisions in these cases.

[26] ECJ 12 December 2002, C-324/00 *Lankhorst-Hohorst* [2002] ECR I-11779.

[27] Other cases in which Art. 57(1) EC is at issue are ECJ C-157/05 *Holböck*, pending; C-524/04 *Thin Cap Group Litigation*, pending; and C-201/05 *Test Claimants in the CFC and Dividend Group Litigation*, pending.

Pending Cases involving Spain: Commission v Spain

Francisco Alfredo García Prats

1 Introduction

2 Pending case

3 Analysis of the facts and law of the case

4 Analysis of the EC Law infringement

4.1 Violation of EC fundamental freedoms

4.2 Grounds for justification of the restrictive and discriminatory effects

5 The real problem of the case: the amendment of Spanish legislation in conformity with EC Law

Commission v Spain (C-47/05)

1 Introduction

Spain is one of the Member States of the European Union less directly affected by the case law of the ECJ on direct tax matters. Up to now, just a few cases have been issued by the European Court of Justice on direct taxation. Most of them concern the application of the State aid rules on direct taxation. One of the reasons for this is the decentralised structure of the tax power in Spain, which allows the possibility of regions and nationalities to establish and modify taxes and tax benefits, thus leading to state aid measures of a regional character.

In the area of fiscal State aids, the Commission has been very active in modulating the scope of fiscal regional benefits, especially those established by the Foral Historic Territories of the Basc Country and Navarre. Since the Decision of 11 July 2001 of the Commission relative to the State aid in favour of Alava enterprises establishing a tax credit of 45 % of investments (C(2001) 1759)[1], other cases followed. For instance, the Decision of 20 December 2001 of the Commission on a State aid regime in favour of certain enterprises recently created in Alava (2003/28/EC)[2], the Decision of 20 December 2001 of the Commission on a State aid regime in favour of certain enterprises exempted in Guipúzcoa, the Decision of the Commission of 11 July 2001, on a regime of State aid executed by Spain in favour of Guipúzcoa enterprises through a tax credit of 45 % of investments (C(2001) 1764)[3].

This activity of the Commission in the field of State aid has led to some jurisprudence of the ECJ referred to Spanish direct tax rules. For instance, as regards the specific Basque Country benefits: the Decision of the Court of First Instance of 6 March 2002, Territorio Histórico de Alava/ Diputación Foral de Alava, RAmondín SA y Ramondín Cápsulas SA v Commission[4], the Decision of the Court of First Instance of 6 March

1 DOCE L296 of 30 October 2002, pp 1-19.

2 DOCE L17 of 22 January 2001, pp 20-39.

3 DOCE L314 of 18 November 2002, pp 26-44; the Decision of the Commission of 11 July 2001 on a regime of state aid applied by Spain to certain enterprises recently established in Navarre (C(2001)1762), DOCE L314 of 18 November 2002, pp 17-25; or the Decision of the Commission of 22 August 2002 on the aid scheme implemented by Spain in favour of coordination centres in Vizcaya (C(2002) 3141) C 48/2001, ex NN 43/2000, OJEU L31 of 6 February 2003, p 26-31.

4 Court of First Instance 6 March 2002, T-92/00 and 103/00.

2002, Territorio Histórico de Alava/Diputación Foral de Alava, Comunidad Autónoma del País Vasco y Gasteizko Industria Lura, SA, and Daewoo Electronics Manufacturing España, SA, v Commission[5], the Decision of the ECJ (Second Chamber) of 11 November 2004, Daewoo Electronics Manufacturing España SA (Demesa)[6] and Territorio Histórico de Álava – Diputación Foral de Álava v Commission of the European Communities.[7]

Some other cases referred to the specifics of the Basque Country tax regimes, on the contrary, ended with the Order of the President of the ECJ of 16 February, removing from the register the reference for a preliminary ruling posed by the Tribunal Superior de Justicia del País Vasco, after the Opinion of Advocate General Saggio of 1 July 1999, Administration of the State v Juntas Generales de Guipúzcoa and others[8] and the "tax truce" between the Central Government and the Basque Government.

The Decisions of the Commission in the field of State aid have lead to other ECJ rulings. For example, the original Decision of the Commission of 31 October 2000, relative to the Spanish rules of the Corporate Tax (C(2000) 3269)[9], considered that Article 34 of Law 53/1995 on the Corporate Income Tax constituted a State aid within the meaning of the EC. However, after appeal of the Spanish government, the ECJ considered in its judgment of 15 July 2004[10], that the measure had to be considered as an existing State aid on the grounds of the EC Treaty.

In the field of State aid, the ECJ has recently given some other decisions affecting Spanish direct tax rules, provisions or administrative actions.

In the judgment of the ECJ (Second Chamber) of 14 September 2004, Spain v Commission[11], the ECJ annulled the Commission Decision 2002/935/EC of 14 May 2002 on the State aid granted to Grupo de Empresas Álvarez, holding that Spain had made all efforts possible to take

5 Court of First Instance 6 March 2002, T-127/99, 129/99, 148/99, DEMESA.

6 ECJ, C-183/02 *Daewoo Electronics Manufacturing España SA* [2004] ECR I-10609.

7 ECJ C-187/02 P and 183/02; 11 November 2004 *Daewoo Electronics Manufacturing España SA* [2004] ECR I-10609.

8 ECJ 16 February 2000, C-400/97, (C-401/97, and 402/97) *Juntas Generales de Guipúzcoa* [2000] ECR I-1073.

9 DOCE L060 de 01/03/2001 pp 57-61.

10 ECJ 15 July 2004, C-501/00 *Spain v Commission* [2004] ECR I-6717.

11 ECJ 14 September 2004, C-276/02 *Spain v Commission* [2004] ECR I-8091.

measures under Spanish law (separately enforced collection procedures) to prevent firms from continuing to operate without fulfilling their tax and social security obligations. Therefore, Spain did not concede a procedural fiscal State aid.

The Decision of 11 November of 2004, Spain v Commission[12], considered, however, that certain capital gains tax relief for agricultural land was State Aid incompatible with the common market.

Just a few cases on direct taxation have been the result of areferral by a national court, which contrasts with the situation of indirect tax measures: For example, the Decision of the ECJ of 15 March 1994, Banco Exterior de España v Ayuntamiento de Valencia[13], in which the national court asked whether certain exemptions of local taxes could be considered State aid measures. More recently, the Decision of 9 December 2004, Commission v Spain[14], considered that a certain regulation of the capital gains tax applicable to non-residents constituted a restriction to the freedom of capital movements and, therefore, was considered contrary to EC law.

There are many reasons for this result. First, the reaction of the Spanish legislator to ECJ case law on direct tax matters. With some relevant exceptions[15], the Spanish legislation has introduced changes in order to accommodate the Schumacker[16] doctrine, to end certain discriminatory and/or restrictive measures affecting permanent establishments, or to eliminate the application of thincapitalisation rules and CFC rules for companies and entities resident in other EU Member States, thus opening a line of reaction clearly different to the one followed by other EU Member States and, certainly, more respectful of the elimination of barriers to the free movements of economic factors in the single market.

12 ECJ 11 November 2004, C-73/03 *Spain v Commission*, unpublished.

13 ECJ 15 March 1994, C-387/92 *Banco Exterior de España* [1994] ECR I-877.

14 ECJ 9 December 2004, C-219/03 *Commission v Spain*, unpublished.

15 For example, the discrimination suffered by the taxation of foreign-source dividends in the hands of individual resident taxpayers, contrary to the requirements set in *Verkooijen* (6 June 2000, C-35/98 *Verkooijen* [2000] ECR I-4071), *Manninen* (7 September 2004, C-319/02 *Manninen* [2004] ECR I-7477), or *Lenz* (15 July 2004, C-315/02 *Lenz* [2004] ECR I-7063). See, in that respect, García Prats, La corrección de la doble imposición económica internacional en el IRPF, *Tribuna Fiscal 175* 2005, pp 8-15.

16 ECJ 14 February 1995, C-279/93 *Schumacker* [1995] ECR I-225.

Some other decisions of the ECJ, such as Bosal[17], have not affected the Spanish system, as the solution formulated by the ECJ was clearly anticipated by the Spanish legislator.

Second, the situation may be a consequence of a certain reluctance of Spanish courts to request preliminary rulings from the ECJ in order to obtain the proper interpretation and requirements derived from EC law on a particular and specific situation. Until now, just two cases on direct taxation have been referred to the ECJ by domestic courts, the rest being the consequences of actions of infringement against Spain or the result of the appeal of previous decisions of the Commission or the Court of the First Instance.

Nevertheless, it is certainly difficult to establish the final effect of EC law as interpreted by the ECJ to domestic and international direct taxation. In the present situation, in which limited action to the justificative criteria mechanisms is accepted by the ECJ, it is relatively easy to find -several – points of conflict between direct tax rules and EC law. taking into account the interpretative approach taken by the ECJ on the content of the last and the very few space and scope rendered to the first, and the incoherent development of national tax systems on income tax, especially from an international perspective.

2 Pending Case

At present, there is only one pending case on Spanish direct taxation before the ECJ: Commission v Spain[18]. The pending case is the result of the action brought on 7 February 2005 by the Commission of the European Communities against the Kingdom of Spain. It is the result of the infringement proceeding against Spain as a consequence of the failure of Spain to properly accommodate its legislation on the tax treatment of contributions to occupational pension schemes to the requirements of the single market as interpreted by the ECJ.

The case has to be seen, therefore, in the common framework of action of the Commission on the elimination of tax obstacles to the cross-border provision of occupational pensions. For the first time, the Commission decided to take positive action to support the elimination of fiscal barriers derived from the application of direct tax provisions in a certain field: that of

17 ECJ 18 September 2003, C-168/01 *Bosal* [2003] ECR I-9409.

18 ECJ C-47/05 *Commission v Spain*, pending.

the provision of cross-border services consisting of occupational pension schemes.

On 19 April 2001, the Commission submitted a Communication on the elimination of tax obstacles to the cross-border provision of occupational pensions[19]. In that Communication the Commission stated its intention to support the action taken by the ECJ on the elimination of fiscal obstacles to the cross-border provision of occupational pensions. As a result, the Commission started infringement procedures under Article 226 of the EC Treaty against Belgium, Spain, France, Ireland, Italy, Portugal and the United Kingdom. Of all these infringement procedures, Belgium, Spain and Denmark were referred to the ECJ. Pending is the reaction of Sweden to amend its legislation as a result of the Skandia[20] case.

The main issue of the case is the denial of tax deductibility of contributions to foreign pension funds. According to Article 48 of Law 40/1998 on the Personal Income Tax[21], the deduction is only allowable for contributions made to domestic occupational pensions and pension schemes, and, therefore, this territorially restricted approach may violate the exercise of rights derived from EC fundamental freedoms. Moreover, the action of the Commission considers that the requirement of establishment for foreign pension managers also violates EC law.

In brief, the Commission considers that the denial of tax deductions to contributions paid under contracts concluded with undertakings formed in other Member States, but allowing them to contributions paid under contracts concluded with undertakings established in Spain, constitutes a violation of Articles 39, 43, 49 and 56 of the Treaty establishing the European Community and Articles 28, 31, 36 and 40 of the EEA Agreement. The requirement of establishment for foreign pension managers constitutes, separately, a restriction contrary to the free provision of services. Therefore, according to the Commission, the four basic freedoms of the EC Treaty are violated (labour, establishment, services and capital). And

[19] For an in-depth analysis of that Communication, its origin and its consequences, see García Prats, The Tax Treatment of Cross-Border Pensions from an EC Law Perspective, *ET* 2001, December Special Issue, pp 12-27. Schonewille, Safeguarding pension taxation rights in cross-border situations, *EC Tax Review* 2005, pp 78-82.

[20] ECJ 26 June 2003, C-422/01 *Skandia and Ramstedt* [2003] ECR I-6817.

[21] Now Article 60 of the RDL 3/2004, of 5 March, Texto Refundido de la Ley del Impuesto sobre la Renta de las Personas Físicas.

what is more important, as we will see in subsequent paragraphs, the freedoms enshrined in the EEA Agreement are also violated as the result of the application of the Spanish tax provision.

3 Analysis of the Facts and Law of the Case

The action of the Commission aims to eliminate the fiscal obstacles that exist in Spanish law for the contributions made to foreign pension schemes in favour of resident taxpayers.

However, the drafting of the action in the OJ does not appear to me to technically correct, and it appears that the objective is twofold. On the one hand, the Commission asks the ECJ to declare contrary to EC law the tax concessions given, in the matter of life insurance and pensions, by Article 48 of Law 40/1998. On the other, the arguments supporting the plea the Commission refer only to the different tax treatment given to pension plans taken out with undertakings established in Spain, or with undertakings formed in other Member States. The clarification would be important and necessary as there are, according to Article 48 of Law 40/1998, different mechanisms that benefit from the application of a tax deduction to the amount of the contribution. In other words, not only pension plans taken out with undertakings established in Spain deserve the tax concession, but other alternative instruments as well.

To proceed in a structured way, according to Article 48 of the Law 40/1998[22], there are three possibilities/mechanisms that enjoy a beneficial and special tax treatment as regards the payments and contributions to a social prevision system (alternative scheme):

1. In the first place, payments and contributions made to 'pension plans', including the contributions of the promoter of the plan attributed to the participant as income from labour. According to a strict literal interpretation of Law 40/1998, nothing allows one to conclude that the Law is contrary to the EC law requirements, to the extent that the provision simply mentions the 'pension plans' as addressees of the contributions, but not the pension plans promoted by pension funds established or located in Spain. Therefore, it could be stated that the Income Tax Law would allow, the same tax treatment foreseen in the law for foreign EU non-established pension plans.

---

22 Article 60 of the RDL 3/2004.

However, this is not the case in Spain. When interpreting the meaning of 'pension plans', both administrative bodies and courts have had recourse to a literal interpretation. . It is only the pension plans recognised as such by Spanish law, in the Texto Refundido de la Ley de Reguladora de los Planes y Fondos de Pensiones[23] that may benefit from the tax treatment foreseen in Article 48 of the Law 40/1998[24]. Therefore, payments to foreign pension plans are excluded from the application of the tax benefits enshrined in Article 48 of Law 40/1998, suffer a worse tax treatment in Spain, and thus restrict foreign other EU members pension plans. The reference to the deductibility of amounts to a pension plan is made with regard to the pension plans that meet the criteria and requirements, and are recognised, by the TRLRPFP (Texto Refundido de la Ley Reguladora de los Planes y Fondos de Pensiones).

The binding answer of 2 July 1998 of the Tax General Directorate (DGT, Dirección General de Tributos) can be mentioned here. In that situation, a Dutch national working and residing in Spain made contributions to a Dutch pension plan established according to the Dutch legislation. These payments were deductible according to the Dutch legislation on the Dutch income tax. Nevertheless, the Spanish Tax Administration considered that the reference of the LIRPF to the pension plans corresponds exclusively to those set up according to the Law 8/1987, regulating the Spanish pension plans and funds. Therefore, the tax reduction is not applicable to amounts invested in other entities with similar content but set up according to a different legislation.

The same line of reasoning is maintained by the Superior Court of Justice of Madrid (TSJ Madrid) in the decision of 4 October 2000. The Court gives a literal interpretation of the domestic income tax legislation (the one applicable to the case is Article 71.1 of Law 18/1991), considering that the concept of a 'pension plan' is not a factual concept but a legal one, and therefore that it has to be determined according to the Spanish legislation, that is to say, Law 8/1987. It is not possible, according to the Court, based on the General Tax Law, to interpret analogously the rules defining tax benefits. Therefore, the amounts paid to a British pension fund are not deductible from the tax base under the Spanish Income Tax.

---

23 RDL 1/2002 of 29 November 2002.

24 See, in that respect, Marcos Cardona, *Tributación de los planes y fondos de pensiones* (2003) Universidad de Murcia, Murcia.

From this analysis it could be concluded that it is the excessively literal interpretation of the Spanish tax law by these bodies, which refer to the Spanish law regulating the complementary pension mechanisms and not to the mandatory EC Law on pensions and alternative mechanisms, that leads to the result contrary to the EC Law requirements.

2. The second possibility for obtaining the treatment foreseen in Article 48 Lay 40/1998, refers to the income and contributions made to the so-called mutualidades de prevision social (social prevision mutualities), which are bodies, normally of a professional character, devoted to raising funds for the prevention of certain contingencies. The contributions to such bodies are made through the implementation of certain types of insurance contracts. Nevertheless, the Law 40/1998, and the Law of the Pension Plans and Funds establish certain additional requirements (both of a subjective and objective character) to make sure that the requirements for enjoying the fiscal benefits apply in the same way as those applicable to pension funds.

However, this does not mean that the pension funds and the Social Prevision Mutualities receive the same tax treatment. On the contrary, the pension funds are taxed at 0 % rate for corporate income tax purposes; the Social Prevision Mutualities are taxed at 25 %, thus leading to a different tax treatment.

Therefore, insurance contracts that formalise pensions between workers and enterprises do not receive the same treatment that the ones foreseen for pension plan contributions. Only those insurance contracts falling within the scope of Article 48 Lay 40/1998 will benefit from the deduction from the taxable base. That is to say, insurance contracts entered into with mutualidades de prevision social are subject to the following conditions:

In the case of professionals not incorporated in Social Security systems, or professionals that enter the contract as a complement to the Social Security system, they may obtain the benefit of Article 48

- only for the part of the contribution that corresponds to the contingencies covered by the Pensions Plans and Funds Spanish Law;
- provided it has not been considered an economic income deductible expense expense that is deductible for income tax purposes.

In the case of dependent workers, or worker-shareholders, the benefit of Article 48 is available for contributions, whether individual contributions or entrepreneur contributions, made to an insurance contract entered with a social prevision mutuality, provided

- the contributions are made in accordance with the requirements of Disposición Adicional Primera of the Law of the Pensions Plans and Funds.

In both cases, consolidated rights can only be made effective on the same conditions than those applicable to Pension Plans and Funds, thus leading to cash-flow problems until the contingency occurs. Previous disposal determines the corresponding regularisation of the personal income tax for all years that the deduction has been applied.

3. The third possibility for obtaining the tax benefits of Article 48 Lay 40/1998 is to enter an insurance contract under the form of 'plan de prevision asegurado'. This type of insurance contract must meet the conditions established in Article 48.3 Law 40/1998, and only insurance contracts that meet the specific requirements of this article may receive the name 'plan de prevision asegurado'. Apparently, there is no impediment for foreign insurance companies to provide that service in Spain and receive the same tax treatment.

4 Analysis of the EC Law Infringement

The infringement of EC law by the Spanish tax law provision previously considered is quite clear, if one takes into account the interpretation by the ECJ in similar cases and the content given to the fundamental freedoms and the rights arising from them. Settled case law is, therefore, directly applicable and few points of controversy arise. This may explain why one of the main arguments of the Spanish government simply consisted in a major delay of the time to amend the Spanish tax rule in conformity with EC law.

In my view, the provision at stake is clearly incompatible with the case law of the ECJ in decisions such as Safir[25], Skandia[26], or Danner[27], which are directly applicable to the Spanish provision.

However, the Commission argued that there is a broader infringement of EC law, and also an infringement of the EEA Agreement.

25 ECJ 28 April 1998, C-118/96 *Safir* [1998] ECR I-1897.

26 ECJ 26 June 2003, C-422/01 *Skandia and Ramstedt* [2003] ECR I-6817.

27 ECJ 3 October 2002, C-136/00 *Danner* [2002] ECR I-8147.

4.1 Violation of EC fundamental freedoms

The Spanish provision mainly infringes the freedom to provide services on the basis of the Skandia and Danner cases. Taking into consideration the arguments posed in Danner, the Spanish provision also constitutes a restriction and for foreign workers to perform their activities in Spain and indirect discrimination. As the foreign workers coming to Spain cannot continue to make the contributions and payments to their original occupational schemes under the same conditions that domestic workers enjoy under Article 48 Law 40/1998, the Spanish legislation restricts the movement of workers.

Article 48 Law 40/1998 can also be considered indirect discrimination of establishment, taking into account the Lankhorst-Hohorst[28] doctrine. The indirect different treatment of establishments located in Spain and outside of Spain, suffered by the contributor of the pension schemes, could be considered a restrictive measure under EC law. As for the movement of capital, the concept of restriction of the movement elaborated under the doctrine of the cases Verkooijen[29] and Baars[30], among others, is directly applicable to the payments/contributions made to a foreign pension scheme in comparison with the payments made to a domestic pension scheme, and therefore, a restriction exists.

The most clear infringement, however, appears to be the one of the freedom to provide services. As foreign pension schemes do not receive the same treatment as domestic pension schemes, there is a violation of the freedom to provide services enshrined in Article 49 EC Treaty. Restrictions on freedom to provide services within the Community are prohibited in respect of nationals of Member States. The original formulation of the existence of a restriction by a tax provision dates back to the Safir case[31]. In that case the Court stated "in those circumstances, legislation such as that in question in the main proceedings contains a number of elements liable to dissuade individuals from taking out capital life assurance with companies not established in Sweden and liable to dissuade insurance companies from offering their services on the Swedish market".

[28] ECJ 12 December 2002, C-324/00 *Lankhorst-Hohorst* [2002] ECR I-11779.

[29] ECJ 6 June 2000, C-35/98 *Verkooijen* [2000] ECR I-4071.

[30] ECJ 13 April 2000, C-251/98 *Baars* [2000] ECR I-2787.

[31] ECJ 28 April 1998, C-118/96 *Safir* [1998] ECR I-1897, para 30

According to the Danner arguments "in view of the important role played, at the time when a pension insurance contract is taken out, by the possibility of obtaining tax relief under that head, such legislation is liable to dissuade individuals from taking out voluntary pension insurance with institutions established in a Member State other than Finland and to dissuade those institutions from offering their services on the Finnish market".[32] The same position is maintained in the Skandia case[33]. In that last case, it was also made clear that "it is irrelevant that Mr Ramstedt does not pay the premium itself, as Article 50 does not require that the service be paid for by those for whom it is performed. Moreover, the premiums unquestionably represent remuneration for the insurance companies which receive them"[34].

If one considers the different indirect tax treatment received by foreign services providers and domestic services providers to be a restrictive measure – by its dissuasive measures – one has to consider, then, whether there is a justification of such a restrictive treatment. Established case law, however, as it stands at present does not accept grounds for justification.

4.2 Grounds for justification of the restrictive and discriminatory effects

The need to maintain the fiscal cohesion of the system and/or the tax provision has been one of the most often invoked reasons for keeping a restrictive or discriminatory tax measure despite EC law incompatibility. After the ECJ permitted this justification in the Bachmann[35] case, the Member States have made such abundant use of it that the ECJ was forced to re-define the limits and scope of the criteria – same tax, same subject, direct link between charge and benefit – for deciding what 'coherence' of the tax system should mean.

However, it is very difficult to accept the fiscal coherence of the measure of the Spanish tax provision at stake. According to the argument in Bachmann, "there exists under the Belgian rules a connection between the deductibility of contributions and the liability to tax of sums payable by the insurers under pension and life assurance contracts. According to Article 32a of the CIR, cited above, pensions, annuities, capital sums or

32 ECJ 3 October 2002, C-136/00 *Danner* [2002] ECR I-8147, para 31.

33 ECJ 26 June 2003, C-422/01 *Skandia and Ramstedt* [2003] ECR I-6817, para 28.

34 ECJ 26 June 2003, C-422/01 *Skandia and Ramstedt* [2003] ECR I-6817, para 24.

35 ECJ 28 January 1992, C-204/90 *Bachmann* [1992] ECR I-249.

surrender values under life assurance contracts are exempt from tax where there has been no deduction of contributions under Article 54"[36].

Despite the original formulation of the fiscal cohesion argument in Bachmann, the ECJ reformulated the concept as regards the correlation between tax benefits and tax charges referred to in supplementary pension schemes. The connexion between tax deductibility and tax charge cannot be assumed, and may not even exist, as it depends on the residence situation at the moment of receiving the income from the pension scheme.

In Danner, we read: "In fact, under the Finnish tax system, pensions payable by foreign institutions to Finnish residents are taxed, irrespective of whether the insurance contributions paid to build up such pensions were or were not deducted from the taxable income of their recipients. If Mr Danner continues to live in Finland, the pensions which he will receive from the BfA and the Berliner Ärzteversorgung will be subject to income tax in that Member State, despite the fact that he has not been entitled to deduct the contributions paid to those schemes"[37].

In fact, the ECJ already considered in Bachmann the temporal aspect of the cohesion in that case: "It follows that, as Community law stands at present, it is not possible to ensure the cohesion of such a tax system by means of measures which are less restrictive than those at issue in the main proceedings"[38] which determined that the Belgian provision was justified by the need to ensure the cohesion of the tax system of which they form part[39].

Therefore, as the concept of fiscal cohesion stands at present, it is not possible to justify the Spanish measure by reason of the fiscal cohesion, either national or international.

Other possible grounds of justification of the restrictive measure are not acceptable either. In order to ensure the effectiveness of fiscal controls, the application of the Mutual Assistance Directive and the exchange of information mechanisms foreseen in tax treaty may be considered as a barrier, as they represent a less restrictive measure. As for the loss of

36 ECJ 28 January 1992, C-204/90 *Bachmann* [1992] ECR I-249, para 21.

37 ECJ 3 October 2002, C-136/00 *Danner* [2002] ECR I-8147, para 38.

38 ECJ 28 January 1992, C-204/90 *Bachmann* [1992] ECR I-249, para 27

39 ECJ 28 January 1992, C-204/90 *Bachmann* [1992] ECR I-249, para 28.

public revenue, there is consistent ECJ case law that does not consider this a valid mandatory reason of general public interest,, due to its economic nature.

As a result, it is difficult to justify, under present circumstances, the proportionality and acceptability of the different treatment resulting from Article 48 Law 40/1998, and, therefore, it may be considered contrary to EC law.

5 The Real Problem of the Case: the Amendment of Spanish Legislation in Conformity with EC Law

In our view, however, the main importance of the case is not the determination of the points of failure or infringement of EC Law by the Spanish domestic tax provision being examined. More interesting, in our view, seems to be the determination of the amendments needed to be made in Spanish tax law (or in the Law of the Pensions Plans and Funds) in order to comply with EC Law.

The evolution of the ECJ case law on direct taxation and fundamental freedoms and the far- reaching consequences of that case law pose the question of the need to establish a certain safe harbour legislation which accommodates EC law with no possible or potential infringements. The many possibilities and perspectives opened to analyse a case/law provision (direct, indirect, inbound, outbound), the different possibilities to determine the infringement (restriction or discrimination), the different levels and uncertainties in establishing the comparison, the material scope of the requirements derived from each particular fundamental freedom, the absolute absence of real criteria and positive elements in primary and secondary EC law to determine the acceptance of direct taxation action in such areas, and the relative application of the principle of proportionality by the ECJ lead to many difficulties for the national legislator in trying to comply with EC Law. In other words, and to express it in a simple form, at present it seems to be easier to find points of incompatibility between direct tax rules of EU Member States and EC law than to find points of certain compatibility between them, while maintaining the tax coherence needed for tax systems. Total elimination of tax barriers and restrictions seems, therefore, a difficult task in view of the present case law of the ECJ.

This general concern is clearly transposable to the area of access to foreign pension funds with a national tax treatment. The first response would be that foreign pension funds – or better, payments to them[40] – deserve the same national tax treatment that that applicable to payments made to domestic pension funds. Nevertheless, it should be borne in mind, as regards the Spanish tax case cited above that:

- Even for contributions to foreign pension funds, there are some requirements that must be governed by the law of the country from which the contribution is made, or when equality of tax treatment is invoked. Therefore, acceptance of the mutual recognition principle, as we will examine, cannot be total or cannot lead to the application of the tax rules of the State of the pension fund rendering the service.
- The solution will, nevertheless, depend on the extent of the infringement cited by the Commission and examined by the ECJ as regards Article 48 EC. If just pension plans and funds are covered, the comparison to be made appears easier than if all contracts and entities of Article 48 Law 40/1998 are involved.

In other words, the analysis of the scope of the discriminatory or restrictive treatment needs, at a certain level, to determine who are the parties and entities interested in the decision; that is to say, to establish what entities will be allowed to exercise the freedom to provide services on equal grounds with national entities.

At a time when relationships with third states are important for the development of ECJ case law, taking into account the pending cases in that respect, making the terms of the comparison specific is crucial. [I still don't know what he is trying to say, but at least it is English] That is to say, there is a need to specify the persons and entities that may invoke the protection of EC law in the host Member State. But apart from the question of third country entitlement, there is a need to establish the specific entities that, in a specific field, may be entitled to the same tax treatment guaranteed by EC law.

The question is specifically relevant in the field of occupational pension schemes, and that of the entities providing services in that sector. Each Member State has different regulations for the sector, and of the condi-

[40] In fact, the tax treatment of national and foreign pension funds gives rise to other restrictions than those the Commission seems to attempt to eliminate through the recourse of infringement procedures. For instance, withholding taxes applicable to foreign pension funds income may violate fundamental freedoms when domestic foreign pension fund income is exempt.

tions for providing the services involved, not to mention the tax treatment of the contributions, the income of the schemes or the distributions. Therefore, when designing the tax system in line with EC law requirements, the EU Member States should consider which companies, entities and types of services should be the addressees of the tax rules in order to maintain cohesion and compatibility with fundamental freedoms.

Apparently, some Member States are waiting to enact rules in conformity with EC law standards, and accept the extension of national tax treatment to transnational payments and contributions. Nevertheless, in order to determine the beneficial foreign institutions, plans and schemes, there is a need to establish, in domestic tax or commercial rules, the comparable transnational contributions that are entitled to similar national or domestic tax treatment. This is not to say, as the ECJ reasoning, what is the comparable national tax treatment or national entity to the one that is protected by ECJ, but the opposite. Once the national entity and the tax treatment to be extended has been identified, there is a need to specify the conditions and the entities that deserve such a treatment as a consequence of the protection of the free provision of services inside the EU.

The different approaches for determining the conditions of the entities providing occupational pension schemes and the different content of schemes may be resolved by taking into account the general principles derived from EC law. In that respect, the final approval of the Pensions Funds Directive, Directive 2003/41/EC, by the European Parliament and by the Council of 3 June 2003 on the activities and supervision of institutions for occupational retirement provision may serve as a starting point in order to determine the entities qualifying for equal treatment for the provision of similar services of occupational pensions.

In this sense, the acceptance of the principle of mutual recognition of those institutions and entities could determine the entities that should benefit from equal treatment. Article 20 of the Directive provides that an institution wishing to accept sponsorship from a sponsoring undertaking located within the territory of another Member State must be subject to a prior authorisation by the competent authorities of its home Member State, as referred to in Article 9(5). It must notify its intention to accept sponsorship from a sponsoring undertaking located within the territory of another Member State to the competent authorities of the home Member State where it is authorised. Therefore, there is sufficient ground to say that, under Article 20 of the Directive, the principle of mutual recognition could determine the beneficiaries of the equal tax treatment requirement under Article 49 EC Treaty. Another possibility could be that entities affected by Directive 2003/41/EC would be entitled to the same treatment.

Member States could thus avoid the problems of incompatibility with EC law of certain tax law provisions and, at the same time, prevent, as a consequence of the ECJ case law and the primacy of EC law, foreign institutions from benefitting from a better treatment than national institutions. At the same time, there would be a secondary law reference to counteract the vagueness of the requirements of primary EC law for domestic direct tax rules, as interpreted by the ECJ.

Nevertheless, the solution still poses some problems for the correct amendment of Spanish domestic tax legislation in view of the arguments put forward by the Commission. As stated previously, the Spanish tax legislation is considered to violate not only the EC Treaty but also the EEA Agreement, and therefore, entities from EEA countries should also be able to invoke the right to provide services in Spain in favour of the extension of the tax treatment.

However, it is not possible to achiebe the same result as in the previous case. As Directive 2003/41/EC does not directly apply to EEA Member States, it is not possible to rely on the same concepts or the mutual recognition principle in order to determine the beneficiary entities located in such countries. The same would apply in the opposite situation.

The considerations made serve to point out the need to find alternative solutions for amending the tax law provisions of Member States in line with EC law. Up to now, the Member States have not considered it necessary to establish measures of coordination for bringing their respective tax legislation into EC conformity. The right to unilaterally confront that compatibility has been accepted as the normal way of achieving that conformity. However, the complexity of the cases and the broader approach the ECJ is taking to direct taxation nowadays, would favour taking a more coordinated approach, especially since the reaction to some leading cases may lead to a greater restriction than that pursued by the establishment of a European single market. The reaction to the Lankhorst-Hohorst case[41] may serve as a good example, and the reaction against the extension of tax incentives to foreign pension schemes may follow the same path. To change

[41] ECJ December 2002, C-324/00 *Lankhorst-Hohorst* [2002] ECR I-11779.

an EET system into a TEE system may provide a Member State more certainty that its approach is non-discriminatory and, in a parallel way, a bigger result in terms of collection of taxes, but it seems quite a negative approach to the single market in view of the restriction of access to that market.

In order to avoid such results, which may theoretically be in line with EC law concerns but teleologically are contrary to its goals, there should be a greater effort by Member States – both EU and parties to the EEA Agreement – to seek more coordinated solutions. Many possibilities arise, depending on the institutions taking care of the coordination. The Commission could play a role monitoring the coordination among Member States, in order not to exercise influence on the ECJ decisions, but to concentrate efforts to find common solutions to overcome problems arising from ECJ case law for existing domestic and international tax provisions in conflict with it. And, obviously, the Council may also play a role in defining a common understanding of the measures to be followed after ECJ cases in tax matters. In any case, the soft law created as a result of that coordinated approach would be subject to the control and the correct interpretation by the ECJ of primary law, but could also establish a common understanding of the Treaty and its influence over direct tax matters.

Pending Cases Filed by Swedish Courts: The Skatteverket v A, Skatteverket v A and B, and Bouanich Cases

Bertil Wiman

I Introduction

II Skatteverket v A (C-101/05)

III Skatteverket v A and B (C-102/05)

IV Bouanich v Skatteverket (C-265/04)

V Conclusions

I Introduction

Sweden has three pending cases for me to describe and discuss. They all concern the free movement of capital under Articles 56 and 58. Two of the cases, C-101/05 Skatteverket v A, and C-102/05 Skatteverket v A and B, involve capital movements with third countries.[1] No Opinions by the Advocate General have yet been delivered. C-101/05 involved dividend exemption when a Swedish individual received shares from a Swiss corporation as a dividend. In C-102/05 the question was whether one must take into account circumstances in a Russian branch of a Swedish company when the amount of dividend exempted from taxation at the level of the shareholder is computed. Both case C-101/05 and case C-102/05 are rulings from the Revenue Law Commission (RLC), appealed to the Supreme Administrative Court (SAC). The Supreme Administrative Court subsequently asked the European Court of Justice for a preliminary ruling.

In the third case, C-265/04 M. Bouanich v Skatteverket, Advocate General Juliane Kokott delivered an Opinion on 14 July 2005. This case involved repurchases of shares by a Swedish company from a resident of France. It stems from regular tax litigation, and the request for a preliminary ruling came from the Court of Appeals in Sundsvall.

The Swedish revenue rulings procedure is normally a fast way for taxpayers to get certainty as to matters of law. Matters of fact may not be tested. One applies to the Revenue Law Commission (RLC) , an independent authority consisting of members from different sectors, both private and public. The decisions by the Revenne Law Commission may be appealed directly to the Supreme Administrative Court, who takes the case without having to grant a certiorari.

Even if it appears as if the facts presented are purely hypothetical, this is not the case. An application always concerns a taxpayer with a concrete and actual tax issue based on true facts. However, as revelation of the name of the taxpayer and of the facts may be sensitive from for instance a business point of view, the taxpayer is often concealed. This is achieved by masking the taxpayer as A, B, X, Y or other letters.

I have had access to or made use of the following materials. In C-101/05 and C-102/05, the ruling from the RLC, the Supreme Administrative

---

1 Mattias Dahlberg has briefly commented on both decisions by the Revenue Law Commission in Dahlberg, *Direct Taxation in Relation to the Freedom of Establishment and the Free Movement of Capital* (2005) pp 325-326.

Courts request for a preliminary ruling from the European Court of Justice (ECJ) and finally, the opinion of the Swedish government in the proceedings before the ECJ. I did have not had access to the original applications for a ruling by the taxpayer. This is unfortunate as these sometimes contain useful information. In C-265/04, I have had the Opinion of the Advocate General, the request from the Court of Appealss in Sundsvall and the Swedish government's opinion. All materials are in Swedish.

II Skatteverket v A (C-101/05)

In this case, a Swiss listed company wished to distribute shares in a Swiss subsidiary to its shareholders. One of the shareholders, individual A resident in Sweden, asked for a preliminary ruling on whether he (or she) is taxable on the dividend distribution. The tax issue concerns the application of the provisions on divisions or spin-offs. These provisions exist because divisions at the shareholder level may be difficult to achieve without severe tax effects when the taxpayer is an individual. Normally, a division whereby shares in a subsidiary are distributed will be taxed to the shareholders. In the process of merging the Swedish company ASEA and the Swiss company Brown Boveri in the early 90's, it was thought desirable to divide ASEA before the merger. However, because of the tax consequences, special legislation was introduced to facilitate that division, the "lex Asea".

The rules are primarily found in Chapter 22 of the Income Tax Act (ITA), and in Chapter 42, sections 16 and 16a ITA. Lex Asea deals with the tax effects at both the corporate level and at the shareholder level. At the corporate level, the distributing company is not taxed on any difference between tax basis and the market value on distributed shares. For the shareholder the main effect is that the dividend is not taxed. Instead, the tax basis of the received shares will be computed by comparing the market value of the shares held in the parent company before and after the distribution. The difference will be attributed to the received shares, and the same amount will lower the tax basis in the shares of the distributing parent company.

Lex Asea applies, and consequently shareholders are not taxed on a dividend distribution, if certain requirements are met. One important requirement is that the distributed shares must be of a Swedish or foreign company. A foreign company is in Swedish tax law a technical term (utländskt bolag) excluding legal entities where they are not sufficiently taxed in the other jurisdiction. Although this was not the issue in this case, it is conceivable that someone would raise the issue, especially within the European Economic Area (EEA) area, whether this requirement conforms to the EC Treaty.

The distributing parent company must be listed on a stock exchange. It is not stated that it has to be a Swedish stock exchange so also foreign market places qualify. Furthermore, the parent company must be either a Swedish limited liability company (aktiebolag, AB) or a foreign company resident in a state within the EEA. Also foreign companies outside the EEA qualify, provided Sweden has concluded a tax treaty with that state containing an exchange of information article.

In this case the problem was that the treaty between Sweden and Switzerland does not contain an exchange of information article. There were loose statements in a protocol to the treaty, in which the parties indicated that they would assist each other in carrying out the provisions of the treaty.

Individual A asked for a ruling from the Revenue Law Commission on the issue whether A was exempt from dividend taxation under lex Asea on shares received from a Swiss company. The issue to be tested by the Revenue Law Commission was the requirement that the parent company be a foreign company resident in a state with which Sweden has entered a tax treaty containing an exchange of information article. The Revenue Law Commission concluded that the statements in the protocol did not oblige Switzerland to render Sweden such information as may be necessary to carry out domestic Swedish legislation. I think this is correct. Thus, even if the parties would have been bound by the statements in the protocol, they might not be applicable in this particular case.

The non-existence of an exchange of information clause with this third country rendered lex Asea non-applicable, and thus the dividend would be taxable to A. Under Article 56.1 EC restrictions on the capital movements between a Member State and a third country are prohibited. According to the Revenue Law Commission, the exchange of information requirement constituted a restriction. From the preparatory works it could be concluded that the requirement was motivated by control reasons. After having described the content of Article 58.1-3 EC, it tested whether the restriction could be justified. It noted that the ECJ normally rejects such arguments, and refers in particular to the Mutual Assistance Directive (1977).

That Directive is not applicable with respect to third countries, so it might appear as if the control argument could be accepted. But was it proportionate? The Revenue Law Commission thought it was not, and for two reasons. First, after all, the protocol appears to give Sweden some possibilities to obtain information. Second, the taxpayer himself can be given opportunity to show that all requirements under lex Asea are fulfilled. I think the first argument is open to some discussion, as I indicated above. However, the Revenue Law Commission decided that one of the conditions for the ruling was that all requirements were met. Having this in mind, the Revenue Law Commission found that the fiscal control argument was not strong enough to justify the requirement that with respect to third countries there must be a tax treaty containing an exchange of information clause. Thus, the dividend was tax exempt. One may here note that since the ruling is written, no information at all is required from Switzerland, as the condition for the positive ruling was that they are fulfilled. One must therefore not take the decision too far. The taxpayer has the burden to prove that the conditions are met.

The National Tax Agency (the revenue service) appealed the ruling to the Supreme Administrative Court. The Court asked the ECJ for a preliminary ruling on the issue whether the provisions on free movement between Member States and third countries prevented Sweden from taxing A on the grounds that the distributing company X is not resident in an EEA state or in a country with which Sweden has a tax treaty containing an exchange of information clause. In its opinion the Swedish government argued, inter alia, that Article 56 EC must be interpreted more restrictively on third-country movements than with respect to movements between Member States. I am not convinced this follows from the text of Article 56 EC. The government also stated that in relation to third countries the free movement of capital is a unilateral liberalisation. If one treats also third-country movements in the same way as intra-EU movements, the outcome may be random. The Swedish government also questioned whether dividend distributions of shares should at all be treated as a capital movement, as compared to a normal cash distribution. I have sympathy for this idea. It also stated that the room for asserting fiscal control as justification for a restriction should be greater in relation to third countries compared to between Member States. I agree that one should consider the different possibilities in obtaining information in the two situations.

III Skatteverket v A and B (C-102/05)

Third-country transactions and the free movement of capital are also at issue in this case. As with C-101/05, this case emanates from the Revenue Law Commission. It involves the provisions for determining the amount of tax-exempt dividends under the provisions in Chapter 43 ITA. Sweden employs a classical system for taxing corporations, with only a very limited relief at the shareholder level in the case of dividends distributions from non-listed companies. Furthermore, this relief is proposed to be abolished as of 31 December 2005. However, the underlying issue is also relevant in determining the amount of dividends from closely held corporations that under the Swedish dual income tax system are taxed as capital income at 30 % tax rate, and not at progressive tax rates as earned income. The computation in both cases has the same starting point in Chapter 43 ITA for determining the basis for the calculation.

Under Chapter 43 Sections 3-4 ITA, dividends are exempt if they do not exceed 70 % of the government lending rate, which for 2005 boils down to roughly 2.8 %, applied to the sum of the shareholder's cost basis, unused exemption from previous years and paid out salaries in the distributing company or its subsidiaries. It is the latter amount that is at issue here. The higher salary payments, the higher the basis for determining tax-free amount of distributed dividends. To the taxpayer, it is therefore important to include all salaries paid out within the group of companies. However, the salaries covered by the statute are only those on which Swedish social security fees are levied, Ch. 43 Sec. 12 ITA. Normally, salaries paid to non-resident employees are not subject to social security fees, and consequently, salaries to those employed in a foreign branch or in a foreign subsidiary are not included, while if they were resident in Sweden, they would be.

The taxpayers, individuals A and B, asked whether salaries paid out through a branch located in another Member State, or through a branch in Russia, may be included in the basis for determining the dividend exemption on dividends distributed from company X. X was an unlisted company that was a consulting firm having around 70 shareholders (consultants). X started its business in 1991, and most likely, previously conducted business pursued by the then active consultants was transferred to X. It contained activities both in Sweden and in a Russian branch. Later that branch was transferred to a Swedish subsidiary Y, and some years down the road that branch was dissolved. However, in 1997 X or its Swedish subsidiary Y started a new branch in another Russian city than the first-mentioned branch.

Referring to an earlier Supreme Administrative Court decision, RÅ 2000 ref 47 I and II, in which salaries paid out by subsidiaries in another Member State were included with reference to Article 43 EC, the Revenue Law Commission decided that the same conclusion could be drawn with respect to branches in other Member States.

This part of the ruling was not appealed, and is not before the ECJ. With respect to salaries paid through the Russian branch, the Revenue Law Commission examined Article 56 EC. It discussed at some length why this article should be applicable in the same manner with respect to third countries as with respect to Member States, and concluded that it should. It was clear to the Revenue Law Commission that the provision at stake constituted a restriction under Article 56 EC. The next issue was then whether it can be justified. It continued by expressing that even if it was not explicitly stated in the preparatory works, it could be concluded that the limitation to Swedish salaries was dictated by fiscal supervision and control. As the ECJ normally refers to the possibility to exchange information, the Revenue Law Commission stated that an exchange of information clause in the treaty between Sweden and Russia would suffice for fiscal control purposes. Here, the Revenue Law Commission referred to the legislative history of lex Asea (see case C-101/05 above) in which it was stated that the requirements of fiscal control were satisfied if a tax treaty with an exchange of information clause existed. As the treaty with Russia contained such a clause, there were no grounds for justification under Article 58 EC. Thus, salaries paid by the Russian branch should be included.

The National Tax Agency appealed the ruling to the Supreme Administrative Court. Some of the arguments put forward by the National Tax Agency and the taxpayers are worth mentioning. The National Tax Agency argued that if A and B did not own shares in X at the point in time when X established its business in Russia, and it X does not have any plans of extending its business in Russia, then it is not a capital movement in connection with an establishment. Rather, it is a continuous economic activity in a branch that is already established. A and B rejected any fiscal control justification. Their point was that under Swedish accounting rules all bookkeeping with respect to the branch must be kept in Sweden. Even if in practice I am not sure it is possible to follow that rule, it highlights that the burden is on the taxpayer to prove that the conditions are met, in this case, to prove that there have been salary payments. Thus, it may not even be necessary with an exchange of information clause.

In a request for a preliminary ruling by the ECJ, the Supreme Administrative Court asked two questions. First, do the provisions on free movement of capital between a Member State and a third country prevent Sweden from taxing A and B less favorably on dividends from X because

Y, a subsidiary of X, conducts business activities in Russia instead of in Sweden? Second, does it have any relevance whether A and B acquired the shares in X before or after the activities in Russia started or changed direction? This second question was probably prompted by the arguments put forward by the National Tax Agency.

IV Bouanich v Skatteverket (C-265/04)

The Swedish Withholding Tax Act provides for a 30 % withholding tax on the gross amount of dividends to non-resident individuals (and companies). The same applies to amounts distributed in connection with repurchases of shares, payments to shareholders on liquidation of Swedish companies and similar situations. That means that a 30 % withholding tax is levied on the gross payment in the case of a repurchase of shares by the company. No consideration is taken as to the cost basis of the shares. By comparison, a resident Swedish shareholder is not subject to the Withholding Tax Act. Instead, a repurchase is treated as capital gain, subject to 30 % tax rate on the net gain.

Under the tax treaty between Sweden and France, the withholding tax rate is lowered to 15 % in the case of an individual shareholder. According to Article 10.5 of the tax treaty, income from shares and income that in the source state is also treated as a dividend is covered by Article 10. The Commentary to Article 10 of the OECD Model Treaty states that bonus shares, constructive dividends, liquidation proceeds etc. also constitute dividends for the purposes of Article 10. Capital gains are taxed in the residence state according to Article 13, and the Commentary (p 31) here states that the difference between sales price and nominal value may be treated as distribution of accumulated profit, ie dividend, and not as capital gain.

Margaretha Bouanich, a resident of France, held shares in Ratos, a Swedish investment company listed on the stock exchange. Ratos repurchased her shares and distributed 8,639,402 SEK, just under 1 million euro. Under the combined effects of the Withholding Tax Act and the tax treaty with France, her tax liability was set at 15 %, i.e. 1,295,910 SEK. Had she been a Swedish resident, she would have been taxed on a net capital gain at a 30 % tax rate. From what I been able to see, her acquisition cost is not stated, so it is not clear to me what her real gain was. I assume that it would have caused a lower tax liability than the withholding tax actually levied. The Administrative Court of Appeals in Sundsvall asked the

ECJ to answer three questions. First, do Articles 56 and 58 EC permit Sweden to tax Bouanich without permitting her a deduction of the acquisition cost, when a Swedish resident is taxed on the net capital gain? Second, if the first question is answered in the negative, is it still contrary to the free movement of capital if the tax treaty allows for a lower tax rate and also allows for a deduction of the nominal share value? And finally, do Articles 43 and 48 EC permit the Swedish legislation?

On 14 July 2005, Advocate General Juliane Kokott delivered her opinion. She stated that any transfers of monetary or other values, crossing a border between two Member States, not related to goods or services, constitute a capital movement. A reference to Annex 1 of Directive 88/361/EC was made, which could be used as guidance in defining capital movement. The free movement of capital also covers liquidation or disposal of shares, and repatriation of liquidation payments. Her conclusion was that it is a capital movement.

She also seemed to conclude that there was a both discrimination and a restriction under Article 56.1 EC. Swedish law distinguishes those acting on financial markets depending on where they are resident, since in a repurchase Swedish residents are allowed to deduct the acquisition cost, while non-residents are not. There is also a restriction. The reasoning here started with the obvious assumption that the goal of an investment is to obtain a net profit. If at the time of the investment it is clear that the net profit will be lower for the non-resident than for a resident individual, this fact will affect the attractiveness of investing in Swedish shares. It also constitutes a restriction on Swedish companies as it will prevent them from attracting foreign capital, given the higher tax liability on distributions.

Here I may add a few observations. To me, it is not that obvious that a foreign investor would anticipate being subject to a higher tax burden. The reason is that normally the foreign investor would sell the shares. In such a case, there is no Swedish tax liability, as Sweden does not normally tax non-residents on capital gains on shares. As a matter of fact, it appears as Bouanich should have availed herself of some tax advice, since the prudent behavior for a well-informed non-resident in a case like this is to sell the shares before the repurchase.

Having determined that a breach of the treaty exists, the Advocate General continued by performing the usual test whether a justification existed. Referring to C-319/02 Manninen, she concluded that Article 58.1

EC should be interpreted strictly. Any different treatment is only acceptable if there is an objective difference, and here a non-resident and a resident were in a comparable situation. Regardless of residence, there is a direct link between the cost for acquiring the shares and the payment when the shares are repurchased. There was no objective ground for denying non-resident shareholders a deduction for the acquisition cost. It was therefore a breach of the free movement of capital.

The second question asked was whether the answer on the first question will be different if one takes into account the tax treaty between Sweden and France. Replying to statements from the EC Commission and from Bouanich that the tax treaty cannot be considered at all, the Advocate General stated that it can. Her starting point was that one of the objectives of the EC Treaty is to remove double taxation within the Community (Article 293 EC) and that the Member States have the authority to achieve this by concluding tax treaties. Member States must, when exercising this right, also consider Community law. From this follow two things, none of which are present in this case. First, a Member State may not subject its obligations under the Treaty to a condition of reciprocity in a tax treaty with another Member State. Second, a Member State may not justify a tax disadvantage that constitutes a breach of the EC Treaty by referring to a tax advantage conferred in a tax treaty that is not relevant in the specific case.

Consequently, the provisions in the tax treaty should be considered in determining whether national law conforms to the basic freedoms. As I interpret the Opinion by the Advocate General, one should compare the tax liability that would be the result if Bouanich were a resident of Sweden with the result that occurs when she is a non-resident applying the tax treaty. If the tax liability as a non-resident under the tax treaty is higher than if she would be a resident, then it should be lowered to the latter amount. According to the Opinion, the tax treaty can improve the situation either by allowing a deduction of the nominal value or by applying the 15 % tax rate on the repurchase price. The Advocate General seems to be of the opinion that if one allows a deduction of the nominal value, then a 30 % tax rate should be applied on the remainder, see the example given in the Opinion, paragraph 58. However, it can be argued, as paragraph 31 in the OECD Commentary on Article 13 seems to suggest, that one should apply 15 % on the net distribution. Assume that the repurchase price is 100, the acquisition cost is 80 and the nominal value is 40. A resident shareholder would pay 30 % tax on 20 (100-80) which amounts to 6. With no tax treaty, a non-resident would pay 30. Under the tax treaty between Sweden and France, and following the interpretation by the Advocate General, either one should apply 15 % tax rate on the gross payment, which results in a tax liability of 15, or 30 % tax rate on 60 (100 minus the nominal value 40), which is 18. The alternative interpretation indicated above would instead lead to a tax rate of 15 % applied to 60 (100-40), in other words 9. Regardless of interpretation, under the numbers assumed in the example, the tax liability when applying the tax treaty exceeds what a Swedish resident would suffer and should therefore be lowered to 6.

The Advocate General suggests that the referring court should make this comparison and refrain from applying the Withholding Tax Act and the provisions in the tax treaty, if this is necessary in order to achieve an equal treatment of resident and non-resident shareholders.

One can play around with the numbers in many ways. It then becomes clear that a non-resident taxpayer may actually be in a better position than a resident, e.g. if the nominal value equals the repurchase price, in which case there is no room to levy a withholding tax, while the acquisition cost is lower than the nominal value. However, the Advocate General pointed to the fact that the shareholder will normally also be taxed in its residence state, so even in cases like this it was not certain that the non-resident actually will be in a better position.

She did not answer the third question as it was not clear from the file whether Bouanich had a definitive influence over Ratos, and that therefore the right of establishment should be tested. In my opinion, it is highly unlikely that she has such an influence as Ratos is a company listed on the stock exchange, and her holding probably was a relatively small amount.

The Swedish government conceded in its intervention that the Withholding Tax Act is not in line with Community law and stated that it intends to change the Act so that withholding tax is levied on the difference between repurchase price and acquisition cost. However, there are some apparent difficulties in applying such a rule. For instance, at the time of the distribution, the acquisition cost must be known to the entity responsible for withholding the tax in order for that entity to withhold the correct amount. It will not be an easy task to obtain that information. Furthermore, the question of losses arises. If the acquisition cost exceeds the repurchase price, then a Swedish resident would wholly or partly (depending on whether the shares are held in a listed company, and whether any corresponding gains are on shares in a listed company) be able to deduct the loss towards other capital income. Assuming there is no other capital income, a resident may even be entitled to a tax credit amounting to 30 % based on 70 % of the loss. This raises the issue for the legislator how to deal with the loss situation for a non-resident.

An alternative approach when the law is changed is to compare the non-resident having its shares repurchased with another non-resident selling its shares. In the latter case, Sweden would not tax the non-resident unless he falls under the ten-year trailing tax rule (provided a tax treaty provision to the contrary does not apply). It therefore appears a logical solution simply to abstain from taxing the non-resident on repurchases. Furthermore, from a practical viewpoint, two categories of non-resident shareholders would be treated equally. As indicated above, given the different tax effects a well-advised non-resident individual would rather sell the shares then have them repurchased. That option may only be available if the shares are listed on a stock exchange. If not, the shareholder may not be able to sell the shares.

V Conclusions

There are many interesting issues raised in these cases. One is what constitutes a capital movement under Article 56. It may be time for the ECJ to further develop its views in this respect. I have sympathy for those arguing that a strict interpretation of Article 56 may lead to some movements being covered where they should not be. It will also be a good opportunity for the Court to take a stand on the issue of third-country transactions. Even if Article 56 does not make any difference between intra-EU and third-country movements, there may be a possibility for the ECJ to make a distinction under Article 58. The issue of fiscal control is raised here. To the extent the burden may be put on the taxpayer to provide reliable information, as in the Russian branch case, it may not even be necessary to require an exchange of information clause.

Pending Cases Filed by UK Courts I: The Cadbury Schweppes Case, the CFC and Dividend GLO and the Vodafone 2 Case

Philip Baker

1 Introduction

2 Cadbury Schweppes

2.1 Discrimination or restriction?
2.2 Can one abuse a treaty freedom?
2.3 Justification – combating tax avoidance

3 The CFC and Dividends GLO and Vodafone

4 Concluding comments

The Three CFC References

1 Introduction

There are seven cases currently pending before the Court from the United Kingdom and no recently-decided UK cases. This paper discusses three of the pending cases that have a common theme to them; they are concerned with controlled foreign company – "CFC" – legislation. These cases are: Cadbury Schweppes[1], the CFC and Dividend GLO[2] and Vodafone 2[3].

All three of these cases concern a common issue, which is the UK controlled foreign company legislation. Like some eleven other Member States, the UK has CFC legislation. The operation of the legislation is relatively straightforward. If you have a UK parent company with a controlled foreign subsidiary, and the subsidiary is in a country with a lower level of tax (a lower level of tax is defined as 75 % of the UK tax liability or lower), then the CFC legislation operates by taking the profits of the subsidiary, attributing them up to the parent, and the parent is immediately taxed on those profits. So the legislation counters the possibility of tax avoidance by deferring profits, keeping them in a low-tax subsidiary. Double taxation, is avoided in two ways: first of all, when the profits are attributed up, if there is tax in the subsidiary that is immediately credited; and, secondly, if the profits are later paid up as a dividend, then any further tax on the dividend is credited against the tax already paid in the UK. So it should not result in any double taxation.

2 Cadbury Schweppes

The facts in Cadbury Schweppes illustrate this. (This article focuses on Cadbury Schweppes and then adds further points on the other cases.) The case relates to the year 1996 – not that long ago. Cadbury Schweppes plc is a UK-resident company with a number of subsidiaries. In that year Cadbury Schweppes had two wholly-owned subsidiaries, both of which were resident in Ireland in the Dublin International Financial Services sector where they were subject to a 10 % tax rate. This resulted in a tax charge less than 75 % of that in the UK, so they were subject to a lower level of tax. After investigation, the then Inland Revenue issued a direc-

1 ECJ C-196/04 *Cadbury Schweppes*, pending.
2 ECJ C-201/05 *Test Claimants in the CFC and Dividend Group Litigation*, pending.
3 ECJ C-203/05 *Vodafone 2*, pending.

tion that the profits of these subsidiaries should be attributed to the UK parent and taxed in the UK. The result was a tax bill of roughly € 12m. Cadbury Schweppes appealed the assessment to the Special Commissioners – who are the first instance tax tribunal in the UK. Cadbury Schweppes accepted that they had controlled foreign companies and the legislation applied to them but argued, quite simply, that the legislation was contrary to Community Law. The Special Commissioners decided that they needed the guidance from the European Court of Justice to decide the issue and so they made the reference in April 2005.

The schedule to the reference by the Special Commissioners is a model of clarity (unlike some of the other references from the UK which are perhaps not models of clarity).

The question is very simply put in the reference, which asks a single question. It refers to three of the freedoms: freedom of establishment, freedom to provide services, and free movement of capital and asks very simply: is the UK CFC legislation compatible with Community Law?

Before looking further at the reference, one should explain the relationship between Cadbury Schweppes and the other two cases. You can regard Cadbury Schweppes as the "plain vanilla" case – the case that asks the straightforward question – is the CFC legislation compatible?

The other two cases add the extra topping. They raise further issues in addition to the basic question. It might have been good if the cases had been heard together. Sadly that will not happen. Cadbury Schweppes is now fixed for a hearing on 13 December 2005. In the CFC and Dividends GLO, the written procedure has only just closed, so there will not be a hearing until next year; the reference in Vodafone is subject to an appeal in the UK. HM Revenue and Customs (which have now replaced the Inland Revenue and Customs & Excise) are appealing against the making of the reference and it is quite probable that Vodafone will never actually be heard by the ECJ.

Turning then to the key issue in Cadbury Schweppes. One can look at it with the same structured approach that is used for many of the direct tax cases. The first question is: Is there a breach of the freedoms by a discriminatory or a restrictive measure? Secondly, can it be justified? Thirdly, if so, is the measure proportionate?

2.1 Discrimination or restriction?

Taking the first question – is there a discrimination or a restriction? You could start with a quite simplistic approach to this by saying that the CFC legislation only applies to non-resident subsidiaries; it does not apply to UK subsidiaries. So, looking at it very simplistically, you can say that it is very obviously on its face discriminatory. But that is probably rather too simplistic an approach. If you ask whether it is discriminatory, then discrimination involves a comparison with a comparator. If you take a UK parent with a controlled foreign subsidiary, and you compare that with a UK parent with a UK subsidiary, of course if you have a UK subsidiary it is going to be paying taxes in the UK on its profits as they arise. That is exactly the same as the effect of the CFC legislation. So if the comparison is with a UK parent-UK subsidiary, you can come to the conclusion that there is no discrimination. In fact you could say the legislation is anti-discriminatory: it removes a positive discrimination against subsidiaries in low-tax jurisdictions. So, on that approach, you would conclude that there is no discrimination whatsoever.

The Special Commissioners, in their schedule to the reference, introduced a very interesting discussion of the correct comparator. Is the comparison to be made with a UK parent-UK subsidiary, or a UK parent with a foreign subsidiary in another Member State that does not have a lower level of tax? In other words, in Cadbury Schweppes, should you be comparing a UK parent with its Irish subsidiary against a UK parent with a French, German or Italian subsidiary? In the latter situation, France, Germany or Italy would tax the subsidiary; the UK would not tax the subsidiary until its profits are distributed by way of a dividend. What is the correct comparator when you look at the discriminatory approach?

One answer to that question is to recall that we are looking here at the freedom of establishment – freedom to establish yourself elsewhere in the Community. If you take that as the issue, then it seems that the logical comparator is the UK parent-UK subsidiary (ie investing at home – no exercise of the freedom of establishment) versus UK parent-Irish subsidiary. It will be interesting to see what the ECJ says in terms of the correct comparator.

The alternative approach to a discriminatory analysis is to ask whether the CFC legislation is restrictive or not. Does it make it less attractive to exercise your freedom and establish yourself elsewhere, as opposed to remaining at home? Yet arguably, a restriction approach also requires a comparison. Is it less restrictive than ... what? The measure must be deterring you from an alternative course, so again you could say this is a question which involves a comparison. Again, is one comparing a subsidiary at home versus a subsidiary in a low-tax jurisdiction?

The author's expectation is that the Court will say the CFC legislation is restrictive, in that it makes it less attractive to establish oneself, for example, in Ireland, but hopefully on the way the Court may consider more fully the whole process of analysing a discrimination and analysing a restriction.

2.2 Can one abuse a treaty freedom?

Before moving on to the second question – that of justification – there is also a completely different way of looking at the case. It is this way: what you can say is that in the Single Market, the freedoms are the freedom to take advantage of what the Market offers, and the Market offers you the freedom of low-tax jurisdictions. It is an invitation to use the Irish, low-tax jurisdiction or the other low-tax jurisdictions. It is part of the basis of the Single Market and so, looking at the line of cases that include Centros[4] and Inspire Art[5], you can say that the Single Market permitted Cadbury Schweppes to do what they were doing and they can only be stopped – or the advantage can only be taken away from them – if they are abusing the freedom they are given. So you could look at this by asking, "Is there a freedom to use a low-tax jurisdiction, and, if so, what should be regarded as an abuse of that freedom?"

This is not saying anything particularly new here. The Special Commissioners predicted that question, and in the first issue that they highlighted in the schedule to the reference, they asked particularly whether Cadbury Schweppes were acting abusively when they established their Irish subsidiaries. I shall come back to these questions of the scope of the freedom and what is abuse in a moment.

2.3 Justification – combating tax avoidance

Turning then to the second element of the analysis and that is the question of justification. One suspects that the Court will conclude at the first stage that there is a restriction and so they will look at the issue of justification.

4 ECJ 9 March 1999, C-212/97 *Centros* [1999] ECR I-1459.

5 ECJ 30 September 2003, C-167/01 *Inspire Art* [2003] ECR I-10155.

The only justification that seems to be put forward is that of combating tax avoidance, though again, one can pose the question: if you have a freedom to use low-tax jurisdictions, can you ever abuse that freedom truly and can there ever be tax avoidance in this way? In other words, if you are combating tax avoidance, you have to define what the avoidance is. If the avoidance is doing exactly what you are allowed to do, it is hard to see how governments can be permitted to justify legislation on the grounds of combating tax avoidance unless it is very clear that it is an abusive exercise of the freedom.

To understand the approach of justification one needs to explain a bit more about the CFC legislation in the UK. The legislation does not just apply to all foreign subsidiaries. That would be obviously disproportionate. There are six exceptions and the legislation only applies if you do not fall into any of those six exceptions. First of all, there is an exempt activities exception. If you are carrying out active trading activities in the low-tax jurisdiction, you are fine. Secondly, there is a public quotation exception. If the subsidiary is quoted on a recognised stock exchange, you are fine. Thirdly, there is a de minimis exception. If the profits of the subsidiary are less than £ 50,000, then you are fine. Fourthly, there is a White List exception. The UK Government has a list of countries that are okay, and setting up a subsidiary there will not bring you within the legislation. Fifthly, there is an acceptable distribution exception. If the subsidiary is distributing 90 % or more of its profits and they are being taxed in the UK, then clearly it has not been set up to defer tax to a low-tax jurisdiction. Finally, if you cannot get through any of those, there is a "facts and circumstances" motive test. The onus is then on the UK company to show that there is no tax avoidance motive. More specifically, it has to show that it was not one of the main purposes of the controlled foreign company to reduce the UK tax, and it was not one of the main reasons to reduce tax by diverting profits out of the UK. This is a very-targeted motive test, which would exclude any company that is not set up for the purpose of reducing UK tax by diversion of profits.

One can look at those exceptions in the light of the line of cases that was mentioned yesterday, running from ICI[6] to De Lasteyrie[7]. Those cases say that it is a justification to have measures that combat tax avoidance provided it is considered on a case-by-case basis, and targets artificial struc-

6 ECJ 16 July 1998, C-264/96 *ICI* [1998] ECR I-4695.
7 ECJ 11 March 2004, C-9/02 *de Lasteyrie du Saillant* [2004] ECR I-2409.

tures that have been designed to circumvent the tax legislation. Does the CFC legislation, in the light of those six exceptions, satisfy the ICI etc test? Arguably, the answer is yes.

One can put this the other way round. The motive test is clearly a case-by-case examination. But if you had to go case-by-case, and examine every subsidiary of every UK company, we would be here for a very long time. Instead, we obviously need to have some safe harbours – some companies that are clearly excluded, and arguably, that is what the other five exceptions are. If you have exempt activities, you are clearly not avoiding tax. If you have a publicly quoted company, that ought to be a safe harbour company. If it is de minimis, you should be outside the legislation. White list companies take you outside. The final safe harbour is an acceptable distribution policy. So the argument is that, what you come down to with the CFC legislation, at the end of the day, is a targeted anti-avoidance measure, on a case-by-case basis, recognising the difficulties of applying that to all companies by having a number of safe harbours.

It will be interesting to see whether the Court accepts that, and gives more guidance on what really is the scope of the justification of combating tax avoidance in the ICI line of cases.

Putting all of that together, it will be interesting to see what happens with this reference. One suspects that the Court may say that the CFC legislation is restrictive and then go on to consider whether it can be justified as a targeted anti-avoidance measure. Two years or so ago, the author would probably have put his money on the UK Government losing the case. Now this is not so certain, and now the odds are much more balanced as to whether, at the end of the day, the UK Government will win or the taxpayer will win.

3 The CFC and Dividends GLO and Vodafone

Turning quite briefly to the other two cases. The second of the three cases is the CFC and Dividend Group Litigation Order[8]. It is helpful to explain first what is a "Group Litigation Order". They are a form of class action where a number of claims which all raise the same basic issue are handled together as if they were a single case: they are similar claims based upon the same issues even if the facts vary, obviously, from one claim to another. It is a relatively new procedure in the UK, only five or six years old,

[8] ECJ C-201/05 *Test Claimants in the CFC and Dividend Group litigation*, pending.

and it is ideally suited to multiple tax claims which raise the same issue. The Group Litigation Order is an Order made by the Court. The Order identities the common issue, it identifies a managing judge who manages all the cases, it appoints one firm of lawyers to handle the claim as the lead lawyers, and the costs are shared between all the claimants. The Order opens a register and any claimant can add themselves to the register if they have the same issue. A few of the claims are then selected as the test cases. So, for example, in the CFC and Dividends GLO case, three claimants are the test cases: Anglo-American, Cadbury Schweppes and the Prudential Insurance Company are the three nominated claimants.

In the CFC and Dividends GLO, the Order was made in July 2003, the managing judge is my former colleague, Mr Justice Andrew Park. The leading firm of solicitors are Dorsey & Whitney who are involved in many of these cases and counsel for the taxpayers involves Graham Aaronson QC and Paul Farmer. They are involved in many of the other UK cases which is one of the reasons why there is some similarity in the questions raised in this case and the questions raised in some of the other cases as well.

The questions were referred by Mr Justice Park. They raise a large number of issues and a number of them overlap with some of the other GLO issues. It is probable that, by the time this case comes to the ECJ, many of the questions will already have been resolved. Cadbury Schweppes[9] will have resolved the fundamental question of compatibility. There may be only some of the questions left for discussion.

Let me just identify what some of those additional questions are. Question 2 on the reference raises a special point concerning insurance companies. Up to July 1997, UK insurance companies had a choice with regard to the taxation of dividends received from UK companies. If they received a dividend from a UK company they could choose: they could either have it treated like normal dividends and not have it taxable, or they could choose to have it taxed (in which case the tax credit was repayable). That election was not available when dividends came from non-resident companies; non-resident companies' dividends were always taxed. That particular issue for insurance companies is a separate specific issue.

Another part of the question is more relevant to the CFC legislation, and it is one that does not arise directly in Cadbury Schweppes. That is the

9 ECJ C-196/04 *Cadbury Schweppes*, pending.

question of whether, leaving everything else aside, CFC legislation imposes additional compliance obligations on the UK company with foreign subsidiaries. That partly relates to a change in UK law. Up until 1999, the UK CFC legislation only operated if the Inland Revenue made a direction that the taxpayer had to apply the legislation. We then moved over to a self-assessment system and now any UK parent with foreign subsidiaries has to ask itself each year: "Do we have any CFCs"? That involves an almost continuous process of reviewing the activities of subsidiaries to see whether they fall within the legislation. That is a substantial compliance obligation. Take, for example, the Anglo-American company. That company had 1,271 subsidiaries, and every year it had to ask itself, of all those 1,271 subsidiaries, were they caught by the legislation? You could see that as a challenge on proportionality. Even if the legislation is justifiable, does it, in practice, put a disproportionate burden on the taxpayer?

The third question asks, what about the CFC in a third country? What is the position if you have a subsidiary in a third, non-Member State. Does the freedom extend to that? The fourth question is, if it does, what about Article 57? The CFC legislation pre-dates 1994. Is its operation with regard to third countries preserved by Article 57, or have the amendments to the legislation since 1993 meant that, effectively, in practice there is new legislation that Article 57 does not protect. So there are still those additional issues that arise in that GLO that do not arise in Cadbury Schweppes.

Finally, Vodafone[10]. It is the third CFC reference, and one might be thinking – one reference on CFCs is sensible, two references are cautious, three looks like panic! In fact, HM Revenue and Customs have appealed this reference and it may well be that the High Court will strike out the reference. It arose from an investigation by the Inland Revenue of Vodafone, who have a Luxembourg subsidiary with a Swiss branch. The Inland Revenue wrote and said: "We think this might be a CFC. Can you please send us some documents?" Vodafone refused to do so, saying that CFC legislation is contrary to Community Law and they would not give them the documents. That was appealed to the Special Commissioners and they said that it raised the compatibility of CFC legislation with Community Law so it should be referred to the Court, even though they had not found

[10] ECJ C-203/05 *Vodafone 2*, pending.

any facts. But they could prepare a "working hypothesis" as to the facts. They could set out what they thought the facts would likely be, and agree those and refer it over to the Court. So the question has been referred. It does raise certain issues that are not expressly set out in the other two cases, but one suspects the other two cases are likely to determine all those issues and there will be nothing left. The reference has been made, the Revenue and Customs have appealed the making of the reference, and one would not be at all surprised if the reference were withdrawn and Vodafone is never finally heard.

4 Concluding comments

One suspects that many of the issues relating to CFC legislation will be resolved in the Cadbury Schweppes case, leaving some further details – especially relating to the third country issue – to be resolved in the CFC and Dividend GLO case. While two years ago one might have been quite confident of victory for the taxpayer, the position is now far more open. Hopefully, the decision in Cadbury Schweppes will provide some clarification of the process of deciding if a restriction exists, and, in particular, some explanation of the scope of the defence of combating tax avoidance.

Pending Cases Filed by UK Courts II: The ACT, FII, and Thin Cap Group Litigations and the Marks & Spencer Case

Malcolm Gammie

I Introduction

1 The UK cases covered in this paper
2 The applicable Community law principles
3 Host and origin State perspectives
4 Justification and cohesion

II The ACT Group Litigation (C-374/04)

1 The UK ACT and tax credit system
2 The questions referred to the ECJ
3 Observations on the questions

III The FII Group Litigation (C-446/04)

1 Intra-corporate dividends under the imputations system
2 The UK taxation of foreign dividends
3 The questions referred to the ECJ
4 Observations on the questions

IV The Thin Capitalisation Group Litigation (C-524/04)

1 The UK background
2 The questions referred to the ECJ
3 Observations on the questions

V The Marks & Spencer Case (C-446/03)

1 The UK background
2 The grounds for M&S' claim and the Commissioners' decision
3 Advocate General Maduro's Opinion

I Introduction

1 The UK Cases covered in this paper

This paper covers the following pending UK cases:

- C-374/04 Test Claimants in Class IV of the ACT Group Litigation
- C-446/04 Test Claimants in the FII Group Litigation
- C-524/04 Test Claimants in the Thin Capitalisation Group Litigation
- C-446/03 Marks & Spencer plc v David Halsey

The remaining pending UK cases are covered by Philip Baker. Among the issues referred to the European Court of Justice in the Group Litigation cases are issues relating to the appropriate remedy if the UK tax legislation in question breaches Community Law. In this paper I deal solely with the issue of breach.

The Group Litigation Orders are a form of class action that is now available in the United Kingdom. It enables a large number of litigants to bring a single action, the outcome of which binds them all. While facilitating one action rather than many, with whatever benefits that brings in terms of sharing legal costs, from a European perspective it has proved somewhat cumbersome in formulating the questions for the European Court.

This is because the questions are designed to cover each and every issue that arises for the parties to the litigation, as well as seeking to illustrate a number of complex issues. As a result each of the GLO Test Cases comprises a multiplicity of lengthy questions that can be difficult to comprehend.

It seems quite unlikely that the European Court will attempt to answer each and every question. It is more likely to seek to cut through the questions to the essential issues that underlie them. In this paper I will endeavour to adopt this approach to make sense of the questions that have been referred and the issues they raise.

2 The applicable Community law principles

Before considering my selection of UK Cases I should say something about the principles that in my view guide their answer and that I seek to apply in commenting on the issues.[1]

[1] For a more detailed analysis see Gammie, *The compatibility of "national tax principles of the Member States" with a fully integrated market*, European Association of Tax Law Professors, Paris, June 2004.

It is trite law to say that while direct taxation remains a matter of member State competence, the member States must nevertheless exercise their direct taxing powers in a manner consistent with the fundamental freedoms enshrined in the EC Treaty.

In this respect, Community law enshrines two basic principles of particular relevance to the direct taxation measures implemented by member States –

(1) The market access principle, under which a measure (in this case a tax rule) may not impede or restrict the cross-border movement of goods, services, capital or persons (whether employed or self-employed), and

(2) Nationality non-discrimination, under which a national measure (ie the rules (in this case the tax rules) governing a member State's domestic market may not treat one person less favourably than another on grounds of nationality (or, in this context, tax residence).

Discrimination is not a necessary feature of a market access breach of the EC Treaty. What matters is that the effect of the particular rule impedes or restricts market access. This may be because the rule creates a difference in treatment between a domestic and cross-border situation but it is the effect of the rule in impeding or restricting the exercise by Community nationals of the fundamental freedoms that the EC Treaty enshrines that matters. Thus a non-discriminatory rule or a rule that does not involve any difference in treatment between a domestic and a cross-border situation may still be capable of impeding market access.

On the other hand, an impediment to intra-Community trade or investment that arises from the different choices that member States makes as to what to tax or not, and how to tax, is not a market access breach. This is just the natural outcome of leaving member States with competence in the direct taxation field rather than it being a matter of Community competence. In other words, the issue of market access breach is one that has to be examined in the context of the direct taxation system of a particular member State and not by comparison with the direct taxation systems of other member States.

The market access principle applies to the rules (in this case the tax rules) of a member State that have a cross-border application. Thus if the issue is really how a Member State regulates its domestic market, ie how its rules (in this case tax rules) operate to regulate its domestic market rather than how those rules affect cross-border situations, the relevant principle is nationality non-discrimination. This always requires discrimination to be shown ie that two persons in comparable positions are treated differently on grounds of nationality. Identifying the correct comparator is fundamental to this principle.

3 Host and origin State perspectives

In applying the Community law principles it is important to consider whether the State occupies the position of host or origin State in relation to the tax rule in dispute. Nationality discrimination generally involves a member State in its capacity as host State; ie as the State into whose domestic market a non-national has entered and about which the non-national complains of discrimination vis-à-vis host State nationals in a comparable position.

In the tax field, the factor that usually underlies the comparison is whether the member State is exercising a comparable taxing jurisdiction for the purposes of the particular tax rule. In other words are nationals and non-nationals subject to the same taxation in the context of the particular tax rule. For example, nationals and non-nationals will generally be in the same position in respect of a rule for computing host State profits for tax purposes even if nationals are subject to unlimited (worldwide) taxation and non-nationals are subject to limited (source) State taxation only. In the context of a general allowance against total income, nationals and non-nationals will only be in a comparable position if they are each in fact subject to host State taxation on their total income.

The market access principle may affect a member State in both its capacity as host State (eg banning imports) and as origin State (eg banning exports). In the direct tax field, however, the market access principle is particularly important because, at an international level, all tax systems necessarily distinguish domestic and international situations. Inevitably, therefore, origin State nationals may be subject to different tax rules according to whether they operate or invest in the domestic or foreign markets.

The essential issue raised by many of the cases being referred to the European Court is whether it is in fact possible for an origin State to draw any lines in its tax system between the treatment of taxpayers and their transactions in its domestic market as compared to the treatment that it accords to its taxpayers and their transactions in other member States' markets.

4 Justification and cohesion

One major reason why member States need to draw these lines is to protect domestic tax revenues. However, because the protection of domestic tax revenues does not afford any justification for tax rules that otherwise breach Community law by impeding access to other markets, the outlook for the continued application in the single market of many ordinary rules of international taxation is potentially bleak.

In practical terms member States may have to adopt one of two choices:

(1) either to extend a particular international tax rule to its taxpayers and their transactions in its domestic market, or

(2) to extend domestic tax treatment to its taxpayers and their transactions within the single European market and, possibly, by reason of bilateral treaty non-discrimination principles, to third countries.

In this respect, however, the Manninen decision[2] may represent an important watershed in the development of Community law principles in the tax field.

In Manninen, the European Court had little difficulty in concluding that the Finnish dividend imputation system breached Community law given the function of the imputation system in a domestic context. The issue that then arose was to identify the appropriate treatment in a cross border context to the treatment that had been extended to a Finnish national in a domestic context.

When nationality discrimination is involved, the solution will usually be to allow the same tax treatment for nationals and non-nationals because nationals and non-nationals have, by definition, been found to be in an objectively comparable position.

By contrast, when the issue is one of market access, the solution is not necessarily to extend the domestic rule to the cross-border situation. This is because domestic and international situations are not usually the same. It is just that the effect of the particular cross-border rule (ie the difference in treatment that it produces between domestic and cross-border situations) impedes or restricts market access.

The solution in that case is not necessarily to impose the same rule in both situations when they are in fact different, but to eliminate the market

---

[2] ECJ 7 September 2004, C-319/02 *Manninen* [2004] ECR I-7477.

access effect of the difference in treatment; in other words to secure equal treatment of the two situations after allowing for the fact that domestic and cross-border situations are different.

It is on this basis that the Bachmann[3] coherence or cohesion justification has new life. Against that understanding of Community law I shall now consider my selection of UK pending cases.

[3] ECJ 28 January 1992, C-204/90 *Bachmann* [1992] ECR I-249.

II The ACT Group Litigation (C-374/04)

1 The UK ACT and tax credit system

The UK introduced its imputation system of corporation tax in 1973. It replaced the classical system of corporation tax that had been in place since 1965, when corporation tax itself was first introduced. Before 1965 companies had paid two taxes on their profits – income tax and profits tax – and the income tax element discharged the shareholders' income tax liability on their dividends.[4]

The 1973 system, while not replicating the pre-1965 system, was similar because it was a partial imputation system. Prior to 1965 profits tax was not credited or refunded to shareholders. From 1973 ACT discharged only part of the company's final corporation tax liability. In other respects, notably the way in which it dealt with company distributions of foreign earnings, the 1973 and pre-1965 systems differed.[5]

There were many changes of detail in the imputation system between its introduction in 1973 and its effective abolition in 1999. A general description will suffice, however, to illustrate the issues that have now been referred to the European Court of Justice.

Under the 1973 system, a UK resident company on paying a dividend[6] had to account to the Inland Revenue for advance corporation tax ("ACT"). At the time of its abolition in 1999, the rate of ACT was equal to one quarter of the dividend paid. Thus, on a dividend of 80, a company would have to account for ACT of 20. The company could offset the 20 of ACT against its final corporation tax bill. The company, however, remained subject to a minimum corporation tax liability, equal to the difference between the ACT rate and the full corporation tax rate.

For their part, shareholders would generally receive a tax credit equal to the basic income tax liability on their dividends.[7] Thus a recipient of

---

[4] And would be repaid if the shareholder had no liability to tax. Higher income shareholders might have additional tax (surtax) to pay on their dividends.

[5] Before 1965 there was a system known as the "net UK rate" of income on dividends. From 1973 distributions of foreign earnings could give rise to "surplus ACT", a phenomenon that underlies some of the questions referred to the ECJ.

[6] I shall refer only to dividends but the ACT system applied equally to most other forms of company distributions.

[7] Higher income shareholders might have to pay income tax at the higher rates by reference to the aggregate of dividend and tax credit.

the 80 dividend would be treated as having income of 100 and the tax credit of 20 would discharge the basic 20 % income tax liability on the dividends. The tax credit on dividends was available to UK resident shareholders, to EEA Nationals and to non-resident shareholders who benefited from a bilateral treaty that conferred an entitlement to the tax credit.

Until 1997, the tax credit was repaid in full to tax exempt and non-taxable UK shareholders and (subject to a withholding tax) to treaty-entitled shareholders. Since 1997 the tax credit has no longer been repaid to most tax exempt shareholders and from 1999 repayment of the tax credit ceased for virtually all shareholders.

The repayment of the tax credit up to 1997, however, had particular significance for the UK imputation system. This was because by the 1980s and beyond over 50 % of quoted equity on the London Stock Exchange was held by tax exempt pension funds or by insurance companies in respect of their tax exempt pension business. The fundamental policy underlying the imputation system, therefore, was to ensure that there should be no repayment of a dividend tax credit unless there had been a corresponding payment of ACT.

The corresponding ACT payment would usually be made by the dividend-paying company or by members of its group. As we shall see in Chapter III, however, the ACT might also have been paid by another, unrelated company on an inter-corporate dividend giving rise to franked investment income ("FII").

The basic UK rule was that non-resident shareholders were not entitled to any tax credit on their dividends. On the other hand, a non-resident shareholder had no basic income tax liability on the dividend and there was no UK withholding tax on dividends. In effect, the UK as the source state gave no credit for the underlying corporation tax but exempted dividends paid to non-resident shareholders.[8]

The UK was, however, prepared to offer the benefit of the tax credit on UK dividends to non-resident shareholders where that was agreed with another contracting State under a bilateral tax treaty. The basic treaty provision extended a full tax credit to portfolio investors, subject to a 15 % withholding on the aggregate of the dividend and tax credit. Direct

[8] Technically a non-resident individual shareholder might still have a higher rate income tax liability on the dividend but I doubt whether the UK ever sought to collect such tax.

investors (normally, those holding 10 % or more of a UK company) were entitled to a half tax credit less a withholding of 5 % on the aggregate of the dividend and half tax credit.

Thus, the basic position for shareholders in respect of (a) dividends received, (b) tax credit, (c) gross UK taxable income, (d) UK basic income tax liability and (e) post-UK tax outcome was as follows –

UK resident individual	UK tax exempt	Non-resident	Treaty Portfolio investor	Treaty direct investor
(a) 80	80	80	80	80.0
(b) 20	20	0	20	10.0
(c) 100	100	80	100	90.0
(d) 20	0	0	15	4.5
(e) 80	100	80	85	85.5

2 The questions referred to the ECJ

The question that have been referred to the European Court all relate to the application of the imputation system to dividends paid by a UK resident subsidiary of a parent company based in a member State (assumed to be Germany) that does not have the benefit of a bilateral treaty conferring any tax credit; in other words, dividends that occupy the centre column of the above table.

The questions are essentially as follows –

(1) Should a German parent company be entitled to a tax credit given that the UK extends a tax credit to all other investors illustrated in the above table?

(2) Should a German parent company be entitled to a half tax credit given that the UK extends a half tax credit to parent companies resident in other member States with the benefit of a bilateral treaty, such as The Netherlands (ie column 5 in the above table)?

(3) Is the UK entitled to deny the half tax credit to a Dutch company if it is controlled by a German parent company when the half tax credit is not denied if the parent company is Dutch or resident in another member State with the benefit of a treaty, such as Italy?

(4) Is the UK entitled to deny the half tax credit to a Dutch company if it is controlled by a German parent company when the half tax credit is not denied to an Italian company irrespective of who controls it?

(5) Are the answers to (3) and (4) different if a company resident in a third country controls the Dutch company?

It is impossible to provide a detailed analysis of the issues within the short compass of this paper. At the risk of doing less than justice to the respective arguments that will be presented by the parties to the GLO, the following represents some brief observations on the questions.

3 Observations on the questions

The essential complaint in question (1) is that a German parent company is discriminated against under the domestic UK rules for taxing dividends on the basis of its German nationality (no tax credit) as compared to British nationals (tax credit). In other words, the complaint is one of nationality non-discrimination.

Such discriminatory treatment may obviously affect cross-border investment, ie the absence of a tax credit may discourage a German parent company from investing in the UK (although it would be surprising for the UK to discourage inward capital investment). Nevertheless, this does not mean that the issue can be reformulated as a market access issue. In this respect, the UK situation differs to that in the Fokus Bank case,[9] where Norway appears to have been seeking to impose an additional withholding tax on non-resident shareholders and to justify it by reference to their origin State tax liability. In the UK the issue is essentially a nationality discrimination issue under which the source state taxes once but in certain cases allows tax to be repaid through the tax credit mechanism. The question then is whether a non-resident shareholder is in a comparable position to those resident or treaty shareholders to whom the tax is repaid.

In this respect I would not regard a German parent company as being in a comparable position and able to claim the tax credit by reference to the credit extended UK resident shareholders. I do not think that Community law goes so far in these situations as to deprive a source state of its taxing rights even in a case in which the tax credit is potentially repayable to domestic shareholders who prove not to have any liability to domestic taxation.

Question (1) in part and Question (2) more directly raise the issue of most favoured nation (MFN) treatment under bilateral tax treaties. The issue

---

9 EFTA-Court 23 November 2004, E-1/04 *Fokus Bank ASA*.

was raised with the European Court but not answered by it in Metallgesellschaft and Hoechst cases.[10] The MFN issue, however, appears to have been settled in favour of the member States by the D case.[11]

In my view the D case was correctly decided,[12] essentially for these reasons –

(1) The fact that The Netherlands imposed a wealth tax and that Germany did not, may impede or restrict the supply of capital from Germany into The Netherlands. A German investor has an incentive to invest in Germany or elsewhere (without wealth tax) than to invest in The Netherlands (and suffer wealth tax). This is not a breach of Community law. It is a difference in tax systems that arises from the fact that there is no harmonised or Community system of direct taxation and each State is free to chose what to tax and what not to tax.

(2) The Dutch domestic rule, under which it levied wealth tax, gave an annual allowance to a Dutch national (and non-national who hold more than 90 % of their wealth in The Netherlands) but denied the allowance to a German national. This is a matter of nationality non-discrimination (the application of a particular rule to different taxpayers each of whom is subject to tax in Holland). It is not a matter of market access (a cross-border rule). Thus it is not a question of whether the rule impedes or restricts investment from Germany but whether it discriminates against a German national on the basis of his nationality (indirectly through tax residence).

(3) There was no nationality discrimination for the reason that a German national is subject to limited wealth taxation only and is not in a comparable position to a Dutch national subject to worldwide wealth taxation.[13] This is in relation to a rule that offers an allowance based on the person's taxable capacity (ie his total wealth or income) rather than a rule relating to the computation of the wealth tax base. The European

[10] ECJ 8 March 2001, C-397/98 and C-410/98 *Metallgesellschaft/Hoechst* [2001] ECR I-1727.

[11] ECJ 5 July 2002, C-376/03 *D.*, not yet reported.

[12] See Gammie, Double Taxation, bilateral treaties and the fundamental freedoms of the EC Treaty, in *A Tax Globalist* (2004).

[13] In this respect the Advocate General confused the tax base (wealth) with the scope of the exercise by The Netherlands of taxing rights over the tax base. As the ECJ correctly decided, D did not have 100% of his wealth in the Netherlands just because Germany did not tax his wealth outside the Netherlands.

Court correctly distinguished its previous decision in Wallentin,[14] where the student was being supported by his parents and received a German State bursary precisely because he had no taxable capacity of his own (ie he had no recognised income tax base outside Sweden).

(4) The fact that there was no wealth tax in Germany was therefore irrelevant because what was in issue was the application of a domestic Dutch tax rule. What mattered was how The Netherlands defined its wealth tax base not the extent of the taxing rights that The Netherlands exercised over that tax base.

(5) Does it make any difference that The Netherlands had concluded a bilateral treaty with Belgium extending a personal wealth tax allowance to Belgian nationals even though Belgium did not impose a wealth tax? In my view it does not. First, a nationality non-discrimination issue does not become a market access issue just because The Netherlands agrees a bilateral treaty with Belgium. The issue therefore remains one of whether a German national is in an objectively comparable position to a Belgian national in the context of the Dutch domestic wealth tax rule.

(6) This represents an attempt to use the nationality non-discrimination by reference not to the host State's nationals but another State's nationals. Even though Belgium has chosen (for the time being) not to impose a wealth tax, its nationals remain subject to its taxing jurisdiction so that there is no like-for-like comparison between German and Belgian nationals in the context of a Dutch domestic tax rule.

By similar analysis, therefore, I would expect the European Court to decide that a German parent company is not in the same position as a Dutch parent company and that the UK did not discriminate against German parent companies by denying them the half tax credit while allowing Dutch parent companies to benefit.

Question (3) raises a slightly different issue, however; namely, whether a limitation of benefit (LOB) article in a tax treaty breaches Community law. From a UK host State perspective, the issue now is whether the UK is entitled to treat two Dutch nationals differently depending upon who controls the Dutch national. Questions (4) and (5) provide variations on this theme, combining both LOB and MFN issues.

---

[14] ECJ 1 July 2004, C-169/03 *Wallentin* [2004] ECR I-6443.

In so far as the LOB provision in the UK/Dutch treaty is of general application unrelated to any specific treaty abuse, the UK is unlikely to be able to justify the restriction (if it is a restriction) on anti-abuse grounds. Can one Dutch company, however, complain that it is treated differently from another Dutch company in the context of the UK domestic rules for dividend taxation or is this merely permissible terms upon which the UK has legitimately agreed with The Netherlands to extend the tax credit to Dutch investors?

The comparison sought to be drawn, as in MFN, is between nationals of another member State in the context of a UK domestic tax rule rather than directly between a national of the host State and a national of another member State. In this case, however, the nationals are in a directly comparable position, both being Dutch and subject to Dutch taxing jurisdiction. On the other hand, should the real complaint be against The Netherlands for agreeing to this restriction in its treaty with the UK rather than against the UK which has only been prepared to concede the tax credit to Dutch nationals on these terms? Furthermore, the effect of the UK/Dutch treaty might now be said to have market access overtones in restricting German establishment in The Netherlands.

The Metallgesellschaft[15] and Open Skies[16] decisions[17] may offer taxpayers the prospect of a better outcome but the real vice involved in Questions (3) to (5) remains elusive and the outcome therefore seems less predictable.

---

[15] ECJ 8 March 2001, C-397/98 and C-410/98 *Metallgesellschaft/Hoechst* [2001] ECR I-1727.

[16] ECJ 5 November 2002, C-466/98 *Commission v United Kingdom* (Open Skies) [2002] ECR I-9427.

[17] See Kofler, European Taxation under an 'Open Sky': LoB Clauses in Tax Treaties Between the US and EU Member States, *Tax Notes International* 2004, p 45 and the articles and cases cited there.

III The FII Group Litigation (C-446/04)

1 Intra-corporate dividends under the imputation system

The 1973 imputation system was designed to ensure that ACT only had to be paid once so long as the dividend remained within the UK corporate sector. A UK corporate shareholder was entitled to a tax credit on any dividends that it received from other UK resident companies and the dividend and tax credit was known as "franked investment income" (FII).

On paying its own dividends, a UK resident company was not required to account for ACT to the extent that its own dividends were covered by FII. Thus, assume that company A pays a dividend of 80 to company B and accounts for 20 ACT. This represents FII of 100 for company B. The FII is exempt from corporation tax and company B may now pay a dividend of 80 to its shareholders without accounting for ACT. Company B's shareholders take their 80 dividend with the usual tax credit (as described in Chapter II above) even though it is company A rather than company B that accounted for the 20 ACT.

Company A did not have to account for ACT if it paid its dividends under a group income election with company B. A group income election was possible where company A was a 51 % subsidiary of company B or both were 51 % subsidiaries of a third company. In that case company A could pay a gross dividend of 100 to company B. Company B would then pay a dividend of 80 to its shareholders and account for 20 ACT. A group election was restricted to UK resident companies but this was ruled contrary to Community law in the Metallgesellschaft case[18].

A company that paid ACT was entitled to deduct the ACT against its corporation tax liabilities for the period (up to specific limits). Within a group of companies ACT could also be surrendered from one company to another to offset against the other's current corporation tax liabilities. To the extent that the ACT could not be used currently it could be carried back to a limited extent or carried forward indefinitely.

ACT that a company was unable to deduct immediately, because its current or past UK tax liabilities were insufficient, was known as "surplus ACT". The most prevalent cause of surplus ACT in the 1980s and 1990s was the availability of foreign tax credits which eliminated the company's

---

[18] ECJ 8 March 2001, C-397/98 and C-410/98 *Metallgesellschaft/Hoechst* [2001] ECR I-1727.

UK tax liability on foreign profits. To deal with surplus ACT, the UK introduced in July 1994 a system of paying dividends as foreign income dividends ("FIDs").

A company still had to account for ACT on its FIDs, unless it qualified as an international headquarters company ("IHC"). However, it could reclaim the ACT on its FIDs provided it could match its FID with foreign profits that had borne foreign tax at the UK rate. The counterpart to the company's ability to recover the ACT on FIDs, however, was that no repayable tax credit attached to a FID. Corporate recipients of FIDs could pay on the dividends as FIDs at no additional ACT cost in the same way as FII.

In summary, therefore, a UK company that received a FID of 80 could pay 80 as a FID with no additional liability to pay ACT but without conferring any entitlement to a repayable tax credit. A company that received an ordinary dividend of 80 was treated as receiving FII of 100, including the tax credit of 20. It could pay on 80 as an ordinary dividend without accounting for ACT and deliver to its shareholders a dividend and tax credit of 100 in aggregate. A parent company that received from its subsidiary a gross dividend of 100 as group income could pay a dividend of 80 and account for ACT of 20.

2 UK Taxation of foreign dividends

The imputation system only applied to dividends paid by UK resident companies. Dividends paid by companies resident outside the UK were (and remain) subject to income tax or corporation tax in full with credit for any foreign tax suffered. In the case of portfolio foreign dividends, the credit for foreign tax extends to tax directly charged on the dividend only, ie the withholding tax. In the case of direct foreign investment, where there is a minimum 10 percent holding in the foreign company, the credit extends to the underlying tax on the profits from which the dividend is paid.

3 The questions referred to the ECJ

In view of the relative complexity of the interaction of ACT, FII and the UK's foreign tax credit system and of the detail of the questions that have been referred, I shall paraphrase the questions to some extent. In essence the issues they raise are as follows –

(1) Is it permissible for the UK to exempt domestic dividends but to tax foreign dividends subject to foreign tax credit?

(2) Was it permissible for the UK to remit the obligation to account for ACT on dividends when the dividends were funded by FII but not when they were funded by foreign dividends?

(3) Was it permissible for the UK to allow a company to set ACT against its liability to UK corporation tax but not to allow corporation tax or ACT to be repaid by reference to foreign tax liabilities and to allow foreign tax credits to restrict the relief for ACT?

(4) In relation to FIDs, was it permissible for the UK to require companies to account for ACT and only recover it later and to deny a repayable tax credit on FIDs?

The focus of the questions posed in the ACT Group Litigation is on out-bound dividends on inward investment; essentially host State issues. The questions under the FII GLO concentrate on the taxation of in-bound dividends on outward investment by UK companies and the effects of the UK foreign tax credit system on the payment of ACT and relief for surplus ACT. These are origin State issues of market access. In other words, the issue is whether the UK FII and FIDs rules were liable to impede or restrict a UK company's choice to establish or invest in another member State.

4 Observations on the questions

In relation to each of the questions put it is relatively easy to conclude that the difference in treatment accorded to domestic and foreign dividends is likely to have impeded or restricted establishment or investment abroad as compared to domestic establishment or investment. Indeed, the introduction of the FIDs system was to some extent an admission that the earlier UK regime was more restrictive than it might have been. Whether the FIDs regime went far enough in seeking to alleviate surplus ACT and establish a more equal treatment between UK and foreign dividends is among the questions to be answered.

In many respects it seems that the UK government is likely to have an uphill task in justifying the operation of this element of the UK imputation system. To the extent that the claims arise under Article 56 of the Treaty it may be able to rely on the saving in Article 57 for measures in force at the end of 1993. A separate question raises the issue of whether the introduction of the FIDS regime in 1994 affects Article 57.

On the basis that the regime did involve a restriction on market access, however, the most interesting aspect of any justification argument seems to me to relate to the repayment of the tax credit to many UK resident and treaty-entitled shareholders. As previously noted, this was predicated on the basis that what was repaid always represented tax that had previously been paid to the UK Treasury. Did the UK's obligation to repay extend to foreign tax that the UK Treasury had never received or was this a factor to which the UK could legitimately have regard in designing its regime?

The logic of an imputation system suggests that corporate profits should only be taxed once in the hands of the company and its shareholders. In this respect the logic of Community law would suggest that it does not matter whether the corporate tax is imposed in the UK or another member State, although the taxation of corporate profits by another member State would not by itself preclude additional UK tax with a foreign tax credit system.

The imposition of an additional ACT liability over and above the foreign tax liability and any additional UK tax on foreign dividends, however, departs from the underlying principle of the imputation system unless it can be justified from the perspective of the tax credit. What is interesting to contemplate in relation to this is whether the UK could more easily have justified a system based on the pre-1965 net UK rate system, under which in effect the credit that shareholders obtained on dividends paid out of foreign profits was restricted rather than the company incurring additional liabilities to ensure that shareholders always received the full tax credit.

IV The Thin Capitalisation Group Litigation (C-524/04)

1 The UK background

I shall deal only briefly with the thin capitalization GLO. Since 1965 the UK has dealt with thin capitalization issues as part of its distribution rules. In essence interest paid on securities issued to non-resident related companies was treated as a dividend and non-deductible rather than as interest and deductible. The treatment of related party interest in this way under domestic law was frequently modified under a bilateral treaty so that, subject to the treaty article terms, interest was treated as interest rather than as a dividend.

These thin capitalization rules were substantially modified in 1995 but remained largely embedded within the distribution regime. In nominal terms the revised distribution rules were applicable to any related party interest but through a separate provision of the Act, interest paid between UK related parties was effectively taken out of the distribution rules so that the distribution rules continued to apply (subject to limited exceptions) to cross-border related party interest payments. It was pointed out to the Inland Revenue at the time that the revised rules probably remained in breach of Community law. The GLO will now test whether that is the case.

2 The questions referred to the ECJ

I shall again paraphrase the questions to identify the essential issues they raise –

(1) Is it contrary to Community law for the UK to restrict the deduction of interest when a UK subsidiary borrows from a parent company in another member State when it does not restrict the deduction on a borrowing from a UK parent company?

(2) Is it the same answer if the lending company is a fellow subsidiary and both the lender and the parent company are resident in member States other than the UK?

(3) Is it the same answer if the parent is resident in a third country?

(4) Is it the same answer if the parent is resident in a third country and the lender lends through a third country establishment?

(5) Is it the same answer if both parent and lender are resident in a third country?

(6) In what circumstances could the lending arrangements amount to an abuse of the EC Treaty freedoms?

(7) To what extent is the Article 57 provision affected by the 1995 re-writing of the thin capitalisation rules?

3 Observations on the questions

Question (1) offers a re-run of the Lankhorst decision[19] and, as such, seems likely to produce a similar outcome. In some respects, however, Lankhorst is an unsatisfactory decision because the European Court apparently did not recognise that within a single market member States still require rules to allocate the tax base to different States. This does not arise in a purely domestic situation where the whole of the tax base is under a single taxing jurisdiction and, in that respect, the domestic situation differs from the cross-border situation.

Nevertheless, this argument was put to the Court in Lankhorst and was rejected. It therefore seems rather unlikely that the Court will be persuaded to reach a different conclusion in relation to the UK rules, which are hardly a sophisticated attempt to arrive at the correct allocation of the tax base. Furthermore, if the issue is viewed entirely as a nationality discrimination issue rather than as a market access issue, it is by no means easy to see why the UK subsidiary of a foreign parent should be subject to a different rule.

It is difficult to envisage why the Court would arrive at a different answer for question (2) where the lending company is a fellow subsidiary rather than the parent company, given that there was no restriction on interest deductibility in a purely UK context.

The subsequent questions focus largely on what impact a third country has on the analysis and in this respect raise the issue of whether Article 56 has equivalent scope in its application to third countries as for member States or whether its application is limited and in what way.

Overall the immediate relevance of the Court's decision on this GLO is reduced given the reforms introduced by the UK government in 2004. These repealed the old distribution rules for thin capitalisation and placed

[19] ECJ 12 December 2002, C-324/00 *Lankhorst-Hohorst* [2002] ECR I-11779.

the UK thin capitalisation rules within the mainstream of the UK's transfer pricing rules. Both transfer pricing rules and thin capitalisation rules were then extended to the domestic and well as the cross-border context to protect them against further challenge.

The immediate impact of the Court's decision in this GLO is therefore likely to be its financial impact on the government rather than in terms of what changes it induces to UK tax legislation.

V The Marks & Spencer Case (C-446/03)

1 The UK background

The facts of the Marks & Spencer case ("M&S") hardly require repeating. M&S, a UK-based retailer, expanded its operations into Continental Europe. It chose to operate through locally-incorporated subsidiaries and over a number of years those subsidiaries made substantial losses. Eventually, M&S closed down its subsidiaries in Germany, Belgium and France and claimed relief for their accumulated losses against its own UK taxable profits.

The UK allows a loss-making group company ("the surrendering company") to surrender current losses to another group company ("the claimant company") which can then use those losses to reduce its taxable profits for the period. Group relief is only allowed on a current period basis. The claimant company must be able to use the losses against its current profits and cannot, for example, carry them forward to back to other periods. Once it has used the losses against current period, the losses are "spent". In other words, there can be no reversal of the loss offset process in later periods.

There are strict rules that are designed to prevent losses being used twice. Thus, once it has surrendered its losses, the surrendering company loses all entitlement to use the losses itself in another period. It cannot, for example, "recover" those losses in a later period to use against its own profits. Having surrendered its losses, a surrendering company may therefore have to pay tax at an earlier time than if it had just retained and carried forward those losses. For this reason, a claimant company usually 'buys' the losses by paying for them. Payments for group relief are neither deductible nor taxable in the hands of the claimant and surrendering companies.

This group relief system only operates between UK resident companies and the UK branches of non-resident group companies. The fundamental reason for this is that it is only such companies that have UK taxable profits. It is only such companies, therefore, that can incur losses that correspond to taxable profits and that can reduce such profits. The obvious objection to M&S' claim from a UK Revenue perspective is that its German, Belgian and French subsidiaries in fact had no UK losses for which to claim relief.

M&S' claim for group relief came first before the Special Commissioners, the first instance tax appeals tribunal in the UK. I heard the case with my fellow Commissioner, John Avery Jones. We rejected M&S' claim and declined to refer the case to the ECJ. M&S appealed our decision to the High Court, which referred the case to the ECJ without expressing any view on the correctness or otherwise of our decision.

2 The grounds for M&S' claim and the Commissioners' decision

Before the Special Commissioners and subsequently M&S has made its claim for loss relief on the ground that the restriction of group relief to UK resident group companies and UK branches of non-resident group companies represents a restriction on its freedom to establish elsewhere in the EU.

In support of that it seeks to compare a foreign subsidiary of a UK parent company with a foreign branch of that company. As a credit country the UK taxes the foreign branch profits of a UK resident company and accordingly gives relief for branch losses. Thus, M&S claims that the absence of relief for foreign subsidiaries' losses inhibits a UK company's freedom of choice as to whether to establish abroad as a branch or as a subsidiary.

Alternatively, M&S seeks to compare the situation of a UK subsidiary and a foreign subsidiary. By extending group relief to the former but not to the latter, M&S claims that the UK group relief rules are liable to inhibit the choice of establishing outside the UK through a foreign subsidiary.

It is true that the EC Treaty guarantees nationals of any member State the freedom to establish elsewhere within the European Union through either a branch or a subsidiary. But does the freedom of establishment require that the tax rules of a member State as an origin State do not influence the choice between branch or subsidiary, as compared with ensuring that its tax rules do not influence the choice between a domestic establishment and a foreign establishment?

It is clear that the domestic tax rules of a member State as a host State may not discriminate in favour of its nationals (ie domestic companies) as compared with branches of foreign companies when they are both within the charge to the same tax. But the reverse is not the case.

An origin State's tax rules must not impede the right of its nationals to establish elsewhere in the Union, whether through a branch or a subsidiary, but this does not imply an equivalent unimpeded freedom to choose between a branch or a subsidiary. They are different legal persons and, apart from anything else, different Community nationals. Thus, the Special Commissioners decided that there was no breach of Community Law on this ground, and their decision on this is now supported by Advocate General Maduro.

What of M&S' second ground, that the limitation of the UK group relief rules to group companies within the UK charge to tax impeded M&S' choice to establish abroad through a foreign subsidiary? There is undoubtedly a difference in treatment between a UK resident and a foreign subsidiary, but is it one that matters in a relevant sense, ie in a sense that implies a restriction on or an impediment to the exercise of the freedom of establishment guaranteed by the EC Treaty?

The Special Commissioners thought not. Based on the case law up to the time of their decision, the Commissioners reasoned that M&S had a choice when it came to expand its operations: it could establish in the UK, pay UK tax and get relief in the UK for its losses; or it could establish abroad through a foreign subsidiary, in which case it would pay foreign tax and get relief for its losses under the foreign tax system. The UK had not sought to exercise any taxing rights over the foreign operations of these foreign subsidiaries. They were subject to tax solely in the State in which they were incorporated and operating, and the UK was therefore under no obligation as a matter of Community Law to give relief for their losses.

The Special Commissioners, however, also considered the outcome if they were wrong in their primary conclusion and the limitation of the scope of UK group relief was in fact a breach of the EC Treaty. In that case they concluded that the UK could justify its group relief rules on fiscal cohesion grounds because, whether the matter was considered from M&S' or its foreign subsidiaries' perspective, the rules satisfied the fiscal cohesion test laid down by the ECJ in Bachmann.

3 Advocate General Maduro's Opinion

Advocate General Maduro's Opinion does not fully support the Special Commissioners' decision on this second ground. In part I would say that this reflects the way in which the ECJ's case law has moved on since the Commissioners heard the M&S case and gave their decision. In part I would say that it reflects a more positive integrationist view of the Court's competence in the direct tax area.

The mantra of the ECJ since Schumaker has been that, "although direct taxation does not as such fall within the purview of the Community, the powers retained by the Member States must nevertheless *be exercised* consistently with Community law." But the UK has never sought to exercise any direct taxing powers over M&S' foreign subsidiaries.

If the UK is to be required to give relief for the losses of those subsidiaries, however, the Court will be requiring the UK to extend its taxing jurisdiction to those subsidiaries. Apart from anything else, it will be necessary to undertake a UK tax computation to see whether any losses do arise for which group relief may be claimed.

Thus, until now, the Court has limited its action in the direct tax field to striking down tax rules in situations in which a member State has exercised its taxing powers but in a way that has impeded or restricted the fundamental freedoms of the EC Treaty. In this case, however, the Court would be requiring the UK to exercise a tax jurisdiction where previously it had refrained from doing so.

Nevertheless, most rules are concerned with the positive aspects of exercising taxing jurisdiction, namely the charging and collection of tax. A State must exercise taxing rights to recover tax but can decline to do so to deny relief for losses. Advocate General Maduro may not have thought it a major departure from previous case law to require an origin State to give relief for losses when it has exercised its power to tax a parent company but then declined to exercise its taxing rights in respect of the source of the losses sought to be relieved. It remains the case, however, if relief is to be given for losses, that a State's taxing competence will only be engaged at the point at which the negative amounts in a computation (deductions) exceed positive amounts (receipts) in the particular period.

The other aspect of the Advocate General's Opinion lies in the development of the ECJ's market access analysis in direct tax cases, notably in Manninen, which indicates that little is required to establish a prima facie breach of the market access principle in the tax field. In essence it indicates a shift in the analysis of cross-border tax rules away from the question of whether the rules are likely to impede market access – they usually will – to the stage of justification.

It is clear, however, that the justification analysis has to be conducted at a Community level and not at the domestic or national level. Thus, it may be appropriate at the national level to have a no tax/no loss rule but from a Community perspective, this cannot be framed as no national tax/no loss relief. The need to preserve national tax revenues or national tax interests is not a legitimate public interest justification in Community terms. It is not the case that there is no tax outside the national jurisdiction; it is just that another member State has the right to tax. Thus, cohesion must be understood in its Community context rather than a national context and must also, of course, be proportionate to the issue in question.

It is this analysis that the AG has adopted in his Opinion in the M&S case. Thus the UK cannot justify its group relief rules solely on the basis that the UK has chosen not to tax the foreign profits of foreign subsidiaries. Those profits are being taxed by another member State. At the same time, however, the possibility that another State is taxing and relieving the losses would permit a UK rule that denies double relief for the losses when the domestic application of its group relief rules similarly deny the possibility of double relief.

Member States tax rules will have to be designed for Community-wide application without the opportunity to justify them in terms of their domestic context. In their Community-wide application the issue will be whether particular rules achieve equivalence between the domestic and cross-border treatment of a particular situation.

In the absence of common direct tax rules, this will not be an easy issue to resolve. It is easy to refer, for example, to cross-border relief for losses not offering the prospect for double relief for losses. It becomes more complicated to see how that principle should be applied when you consider that each State's definition and quantification of tax losses are different, quite apart from the differences that exist in the rules for carry forward, carry back and consolidation of losses.

For a UK perspective, if the European Court eventually follows the Advocate General's opinion, the most likely outcome is that the UK rules prohibiting double relief for foreign branch losses will be extended to the losses of foreign subsidiaries to limit the impact of the decision. That apart I imagine that the litigation to resolve past claims for loss relief will continue for some years to come.

Annex

List of Authors

Prof. Philip Baker QC

Philip Baker is a Visiting Professorial Fellow and co-director of the School of Tax at Queen Mary University London. He is a barrister specialising in international taxation in Gray's Inn Tax Chambers and a Fellow of the Chartered Institute of Taxation. Philip Baker is also honorary Senior Research Associate at the School of Oriental and African Studies, University of London.

Prof. Malcolm Gammie CBE QC

Malcolm Gammie is in practice at 1 Essex Court, Temple and was previously a tax partner at Linklaters; a Research Fellow at the Institute for Fiscal Studies and Research Director for the IFS' Tax Law Review Committee; a past Chairman and Secretary of the IFS' Executive Committee; Chairman from 1999 to 2005 of working parties on EC Taxation at the Centre for European Policy Studies, Brussels; Member of the Permanent Scientific Committee of the International Fiscal Association and Vice-Chairman of the IFA's British Branch; Visiting Professor of Tax Law at the London School of Economics; visiting Professorial Fellow, Queen Mary College, London; Visiting Professor of International Taxation, Sydney University Law Faculty, Australia; Member of the Inland Revenue's Tax Law Rewrite Consultative Committee; Past President of the Chartered Institute of Taxation; Past Chairman of the Law Society's Revenue Law Committee; 1998 Unilever Professor of International Business Law at Leiden University, the Netherlands; Consultant Editor of Butterworths Tax Handbooks (1994–2004); Founding Editor of British Tax Library's Land Taxation.

Malcolm Gammie sits as a Deputy Special Commissioner and as VAT and Duties Tribunal Chairman.

Prof. Francisco Alfredo García Prats

Francisco Alfredo García Prats is Profesor Titular de Derecho Financiero y Tributario at the University of Valencia (Spain). He has been visiting professor at the Universities of London, Harvard, Leiden, Bergamo, Luigi Bocconi and Leuven. His research mainly focuses on international and EC tax law. Since 1995 he is observer/adviser of the Ad Hoc Group of Experts on International Cooperation in Tax Matters of the United Nations.

Prof. Marjaana Helminen

Professor Marjaana Helminen (Doctor of Laws, University of Helsinki; Master of Arts, economics, Turku School of Economics) works as a professor of international and comparative tax law in the University of Helsinki. She specializes on international and EC tax law. She has worked as a professor of international tax law also in the Helsinki School of Economics and has lectured in other Finnish and foreign universities. Marjaana Helminen has worked also as a tax-adviser in Loyens&Loeff in Amsterdam and as a referendary in the Supreme Administrative Court of Finland. Her doctoral thesis "The Dividend Concept in International Tax Law" (Kluwer), was awarded with the Mitchell B. Carrol Price of the International Fiscal Association. Marjaana Helminen has published also several other books and articles on international and EC tax law among which a comprehensive work on international taxation. A condensed version of the Finnish language work is published in English ("Finnish International Taxation").

Prof. Dr. Eric C.C.M. Kemmeren

Professor of international tax law at the Fiscal Institute Tilburg of Tilburg University. He is also a member of the board of the European Tax College and of counsel to Ernst & Young, Tax Advisers in Rotterdam, the Netherlands.

Prof. Dr. Jürgen Lüdicke

Jürgen Lüdicke is tax partner at PricewaterhouseCoopers in Hamburg and holds a chair at the International Tax Institute of the Hamburg University.

His main areas of work include international tax planning, restructuring, M&A consulting and tax litigation. He leads PwC's German Tax Technical Group and the EU Direct Tax Group. His numerous publications on international and domestic tax law deal, in particular, with EU and treaty aspects. Also, he is a frequent speaker at tax conferences and leads the annual Hamburg Tax Conference on International Taxation (Hamburger Tagung zur Internationalen Besteuerung).

Jürgen Lüdicke is a member of numerous professional bodies, eg of the International Tax Committee of the Federal Chamber of Tax Consultants, of the Corporation Tax Committee of the Institute of Chartered Accountants and of the "Kommission Steuergesetzbuch". He is one of the editors of "Internationales Steuerrecht", a leading German tax journal.

Prof. Dr. Jacques Malherbe

Is partner at Liedekerke, Wolters, Waelbroeck and Kirkpatrick in Brussels and Professor at the Ecole Supérieure des Sciences Fiscales (Brussels) as well as Professor of Law emeritus at the Catholic University of Louvain.

Prof. Dr. Pasquale Pistone

Pasquale Pistone is associate professor at the University of Salerno and also researches – as winner of the 2005 ESF-EURYI award and guest professor – at the Vienna University of Economics Business Administration on the impact of European law on the relations with third countries in the field of direct taxes.

Author of two books (one of which in English on the impact of European law on tax treaties, including the text of a full draft for an EU Model Tax Convention) and almost 60 articles on issues of European and international tax law, written in various languages. Fluent in seven EU languages, he regularly participates at international conferences and has been extensively lecturing in Europe and South America. He is member of the editorial board of Intertax.

Alexander Rust

Alexander Rust was born on 17 February 1973 in Hannover (Germany). He studied law in Freiburg, Geneva and Munich. After his second state examination he actually works as an assistant professor at the University of Munich, where he teaches constitutional law and tax law.

Prof. Dr. Claus Staringer

Professor Claus Staringer (Doctor of Laws, University of Vienna) is professor for tax law at the Institute for Austrian and International Tax Law at the Vienna University of Economics and Business Administration where he is the head of the Institute's Corporate Tax Group.

Claus Staringer is also a tax partner in the Vienna office of the international law firm Freshfields Bruckhaus Deringer.

Prof. Melchior Wathelet

Professor Melchior Wathelet is Professor of European Law at the Universities of Louvain and Liege (Belgium). He is also Of-Counsel at the CMS-Bureau Francis Lefebvre (Paris) and an Honorary Judge at the ECJ.

Melchior Wathelet was a former Deputy Prime Minister and Minister of Justice of Belgium.

Dr. Dennis Weber

Dr. Dennis Weber (1970), (Master of laws; University of Tilburg), has taught European indirect and direct tax law at the Universiteit van Amsterdam (the Netherlands) since 1997 and is the academic co-ordinator of the European and International Tax Law specialisation module of the LL.M. Postgraduate Programme European Business Law of the Amsterdam Law School. He also works as a tax lawyer at Loyens & Loeff and is the head of the Loyens & Loeff EC tax desk. In addition, he is a deputy judge at the Court of Appeals of s'Hertogenbosch.

From 1996 to 1997 he was a lecturer in tax law at the University of Tilburg and from 1996 to 1998 he worked as a tax lawyer at PriceWaterhouseCoopers. His publications are mostly on European tax law. He has published numerous articles in the leading international tax law journals (Intertax, European Taxation, EC Tax Review and Weekblad voor Fiscaal Recht). In 2005 his book 'Tax avoidance and the EC Treaty Freedoms' was published in the EUCOTAX-series on European Taxation (Kluwer Law International). He is the Dutch correspondent of EC Tax Review, editor of Tijdschrift voor Formeel Belastingrecht and managing editor of the e-mail newsletter EU Tax Alert (see: www.eutaxalert.com). He has written over 150 articles on tax law for various newspapers. He is a visiting lecturer at the International Tax Center Leiden (LL.M Program in International Taxation) and at the Erasmus University Rotterdam.

Prof. Dr. Bertil Wiman

Bertil Wiman is since 1996 a Professor of Tax Law, Center for Tax Law, Stockholm School of Economics, Sweden. His research and teaching is primarily on Swedish and international business taxation and on EC tax law. He is the Chairman of the Swedish IFA Branch. He was a visiting professor at Georgetown University Law Center, 2001–2002 and 2004–2005, and in addition, he has lectured at a number of foreign universities, including the Wirtschaftsuniversität in Vienna. The Center for Tax Law is supported by Skeppsbron Skatt AB, a member of the international network of independent tax Consultants Taxand.

Prof. Niels Winther-Sørensen

Since 2000, Niels Winther-Sørensen is professor in Tax law at the Law Department, Copenhagen Business School. His field of research and teaching is Danish and internatinal tax law, including European tax law. From 2001 to 2005 he was Chairman of the Danish National Tax Assessment Board.

Schriftenreihe zum Internationalen Steuerrecht

Band 1
Die Weiterentwicklung des OECD-Musterabkommens
Lang/Loukota/Lüthi
Wien 1996, 80 Seiten
ISBN 3-85122-537-6

Band 2
Die unbeschränkte Steuerpflicht natürlicher Personen
Innerstaatliches Recht und Doppelbesteuerungsabkommen
Edgar Huemer
Wien 1996, 200 Seiten
ISBN 3-85122-538-4

Band 3
Die Wegzugsbesteuerung
§ 31 Abs. 2 Z 2 EStG
Gerald Toifl
Wien 1996, 184 Seiten
ISBN 3-85122-545-7

Band 4
Die neuen Verrechnungspreisrichtlinien der OECD
Mit dem Text der Richtlinien im Anhang
Lahodny-Karner/Schuch/Toifl/Urtz/Vetter
Wien 1996, 272 Seiten
ISBN 3-85122-610-0

Band 5
Kurzkommentar zum neuen Doppelbesteuerungsabkommen Österreich-USA
Gröhs/Jirousek/Lang/Loukota
Wien 1997, 246 Seiten
ISBN 3-85122-648-8

Band 6
Die Auslegung von Doppelbesteuerungsabkommen in der Rechtsprechung der Höchstgerichte Deutschlands, der Schweiz und Österreichs
Lang/Mössner/Waldburger
Wien 1998, 136 Seiten
ISBN 3-85122-651-8

Band 7
Multilateral Tax Treaties
New Developments in International Tax Law
Lang/Loukota/Rädler/Schuch/Toifl/Urtz/Wassermeyer/Züger
Wien 1997, 264 Seiten
ISBN 3-85122-727-1

Band 8
Verluste im Recht der Doppelbesteuerungsabkommen
Josef Schuch
Wien 1998, 224 Seiten
ISBN 3-85122-812-X

Band 9
Das österreichische Steuerrecht im Lichte der Freiheit des Kapitalverkehrs
Bettina Matzka
Wien 1998, 180 Seiten
ISBN 3-85122-838-3

Band 10
Die Zukunft des Internationalen Steuerrechts
Gassner/Hemetsberger-Koller/Lang/Sasseville/Vogel
Wien 1999, 134 Seiten
ISBN 3-85122-885-5

Band 11
The Application of the OECD Model Tax Convention to Partnerships
A Critical Analysis of the Report Prepared by the OECD Committee on Fiscal Affairs
Michael Lang
Wien 2000, 102 Seiten
ISBN 3-85122-989-4

Band 12
Besteuerung von E-Commerce
Toifl/Züger
Wien 2000, 472 Seiten
ISBN 3-7073-0020-X

Band 13
Tax Treaty Interpretation
Michael Lang
Wien 2001, 398 Seiten
ISBN 3-7073-0204-0

Band 14
Personengesellschaften im Internationalen Steuerrecht
Urtz/Züger
Wien 2001, 456 Seiten
ISBN 3-7073-0170-2

Band 15
Kapitalanlagefonds im Recht der Doppelbesteuerungsabkommen
Dietmar Johannes Aigner
Wien 2001, 160 Seiten
ISBN 3-7073-0211-3

Band 16
Schiedsverfahren für Doppelbesteuerungsabkommen
Mario Züger
Wien 2001, 264 Seiten
ISBN 3-7073-0249-0

Band 17
Verrechnungspreisgestaltung im Internationalen Steuerrecht
Schuch/Zehetner
Wien 2001, 496 Seiten
ISBN 3-7073-0263-6

Band 18
Kapitalertragsteuer im Internationalen Steuerrecht
Steuerabzug und Rückerstattung der KESt aus innerstaatlicher, abkommensrechtlicher und europarechtlicher Sicht
Ulf Zehetner
Wien 2001, 264 Seiten
ISBN 3-7073-0288-1

Band 19
Die Zeit im Recht der Doppelbesteuerungsabkommen
Josef Schuch
Wien 2001, 304 Seiten
ISBN 3-7073-0315-2

Band 20
Settlement of Disputes in Tax Treaty Law
Lang/Züger
Wien 2002, 596 Seiten
ISBN 3-7073-0265-2

Band 21
Erbschaftssteuern und Doppelbesteuerungsabkommen
D. J. Aigner/H. J. Aigner/Fellner/Fraberger/Heinrich/Konezny/Loukota/Sutter/Zehetner/Züger
Wien 2002, 280 Seiten
ISBN 3-7073-0313-6

Band 22
Personengesellschaften im Recht der Doppelbesteuerungsabkommen
Gerald Toifl
Wien 2003, 406 Seiten
ISBN 3-7073-0527-9

Band 23
Die steuerliche Abschirmwirkung ausländischer Finanzierungsgesellschaften
und ihre Durchbrechung aus österreichischer Sicht
Georg W. Kofler
Wien 2002, 522 Seiten
ISBN 3-7073-0394-2

Band 24
Freistellungs- und Anrechnungsmethode in den Doppelbesteuerungsabkommen
Sutter/Wimpissinger
Wien 2002, 380 Seiten
ISBN 3-7073-0407-8

Band 25
Direct Taxation: Recent ECJ Developments
Michael Lang
Wien 2003, 208 Seiten
ISBN 3-7073-0436-1

Band 26
Avoidance of Double Non-Taxation
Michael Lang
Wien 2003, 504 Seiten
ISBN 3-7073-0489-2

Band 27
Unilaterale Maßnahmen zur Vermeidung der Doppelbesteuerung
Die Verordnung zu § 48 BAO
Bauer/Burgstaller/Haslinger/Herdin/Hofbauer/Lang/Loukota H./Loukota W./Schilcher/Schuch/Stefaner/Strasser/Sutter/Zieseritsch
Wien 2004, 288 Seiten
ISBN 3-7073-0536-8

Band 28
Die Auswirkungen der Diskriminierungsverbote in der Praxis
Konezny/Zehetner
Wien 2003, 312 Seiten
ISBN 3-7073-0566-X

Band 29
Permanent Establishment in International Tax Law
Aigner/Züger
Wien 2003, 560 Seiten
ISBN 3-7073-0553-8

Band 30
CFC Legislation
Lang/Aigner/Scheuerle/Stefaner
Wien 2004, 654 Seiten
ISBN 3-7073-0589-9

Band 31
Betriebstättengewinnermittlung
Clemens Nowotny
Wien 2004, 204 Seiten
ISBN 3-7073-0603-8

Band 32
Hinzurechnungsbesteuerung und DBA-Recht
Hans-Jörgen Aigner
Wien 2004, 168 Seiten
ISBN 3-7073-0622-4

Band 33
Subject-to-tax-Klauseln in der österreichischen Abkommenspraxis
Michael Schilcher
Wien 2004, 158 Seiten
ISBN 3-7073-0697-6

Band 34
Triangular Tax Cases
Sutter/Zehetner
Wien 2004, 450 Seiten
ISBN 3-7073-0704-2

Band 35
WTO and Direct Taxation
Lang/Herdin/Hofbauer
Wien 2005, 772 Seiten
ISBN 3-7073-0710-7

Band 36
Das EG-Beihilfenverbot und sein Durchführungsverbot in Steuersachen
Franz Philipp Sutter
Wien 2005, 414 Seiten
ISBN 3-7073-0762-X

Band 37
Die Auslegung von Quellenstaatsregelungen in Doppelbesteuerungsabkommen
Christof Strasser
Wien 2005, 220 Seiten
ISBN 3-7073-0763-8

Band 38
Source versus Residence in International Tax Law
Aigner/Loukota
Wien 2005, 630 Seiten
ISBN 3-7073-0764-6

Band 39
Tax Treaty Policy and Development
Stefaner/Züger
Wien 2005, 536 Seiten
ISBN 3-7073-0765-4

Band 40
Das Prinzip der Meistbegünstigung im grenzüberschreitenden Ertragsteuerrecht
Ines Hofbauer
Wien 2005, 244 Seiten
ISBN3-7073-0880-4